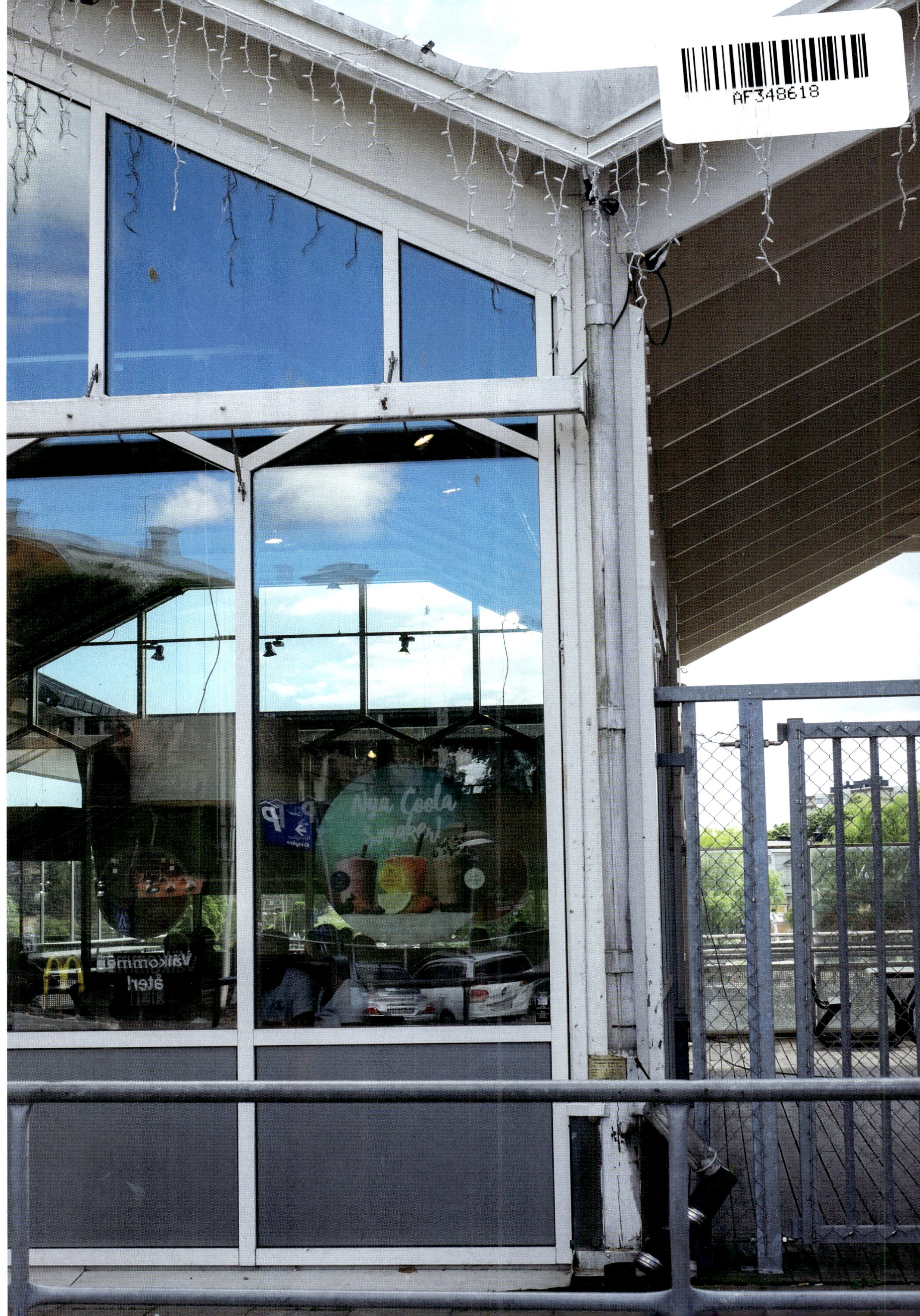

Nya Coola
smaker!
Välkommen
åter!

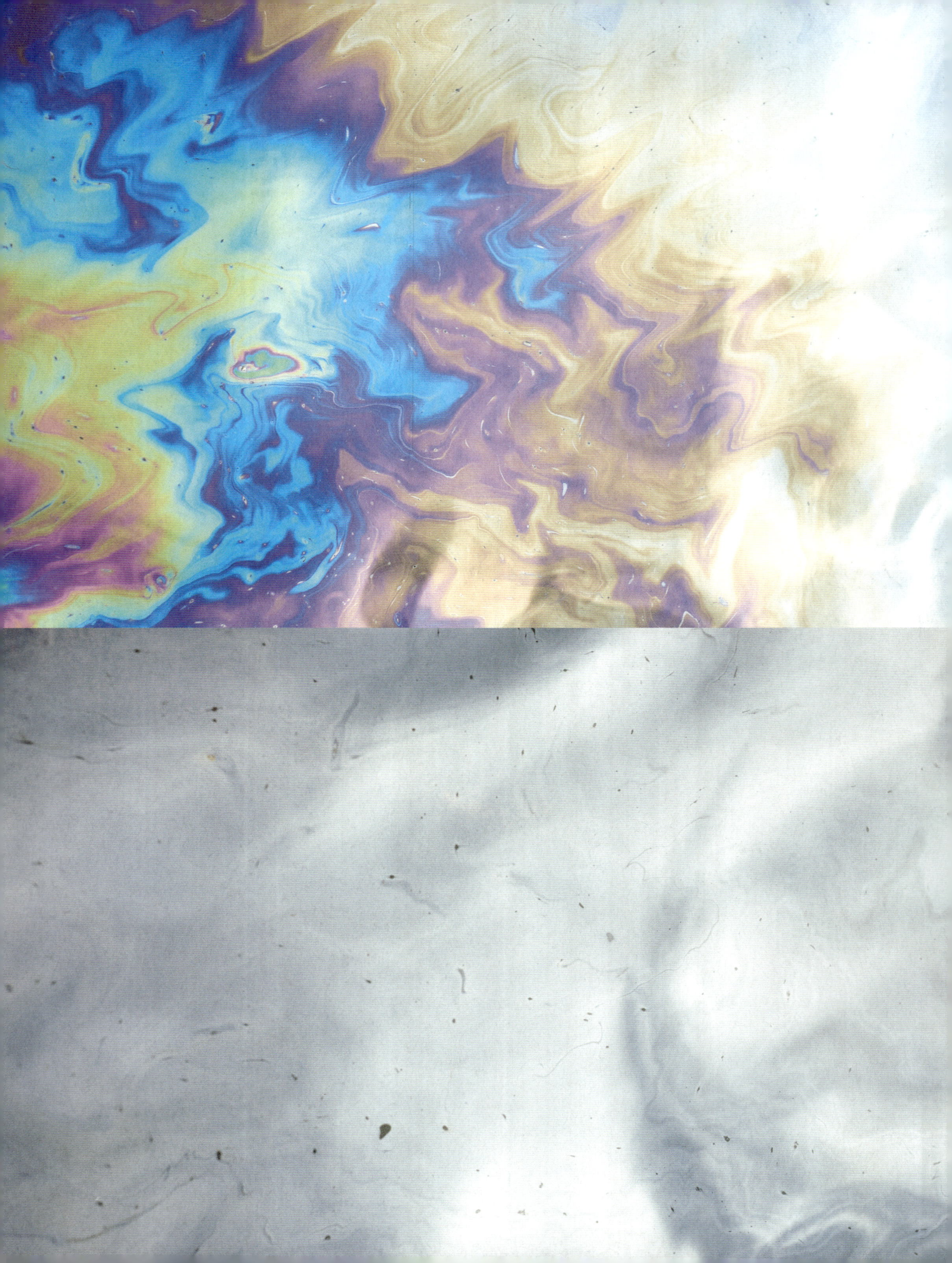

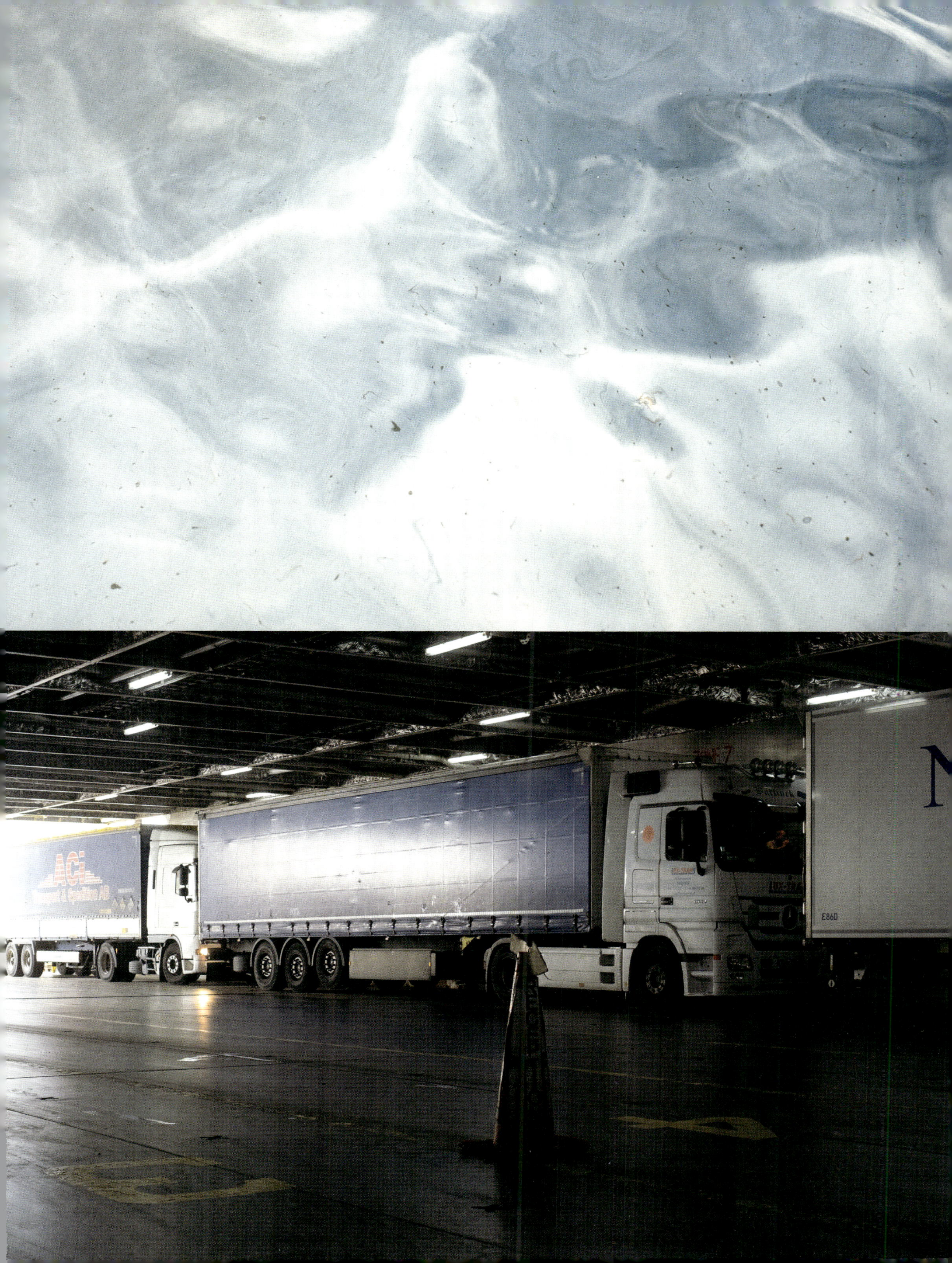

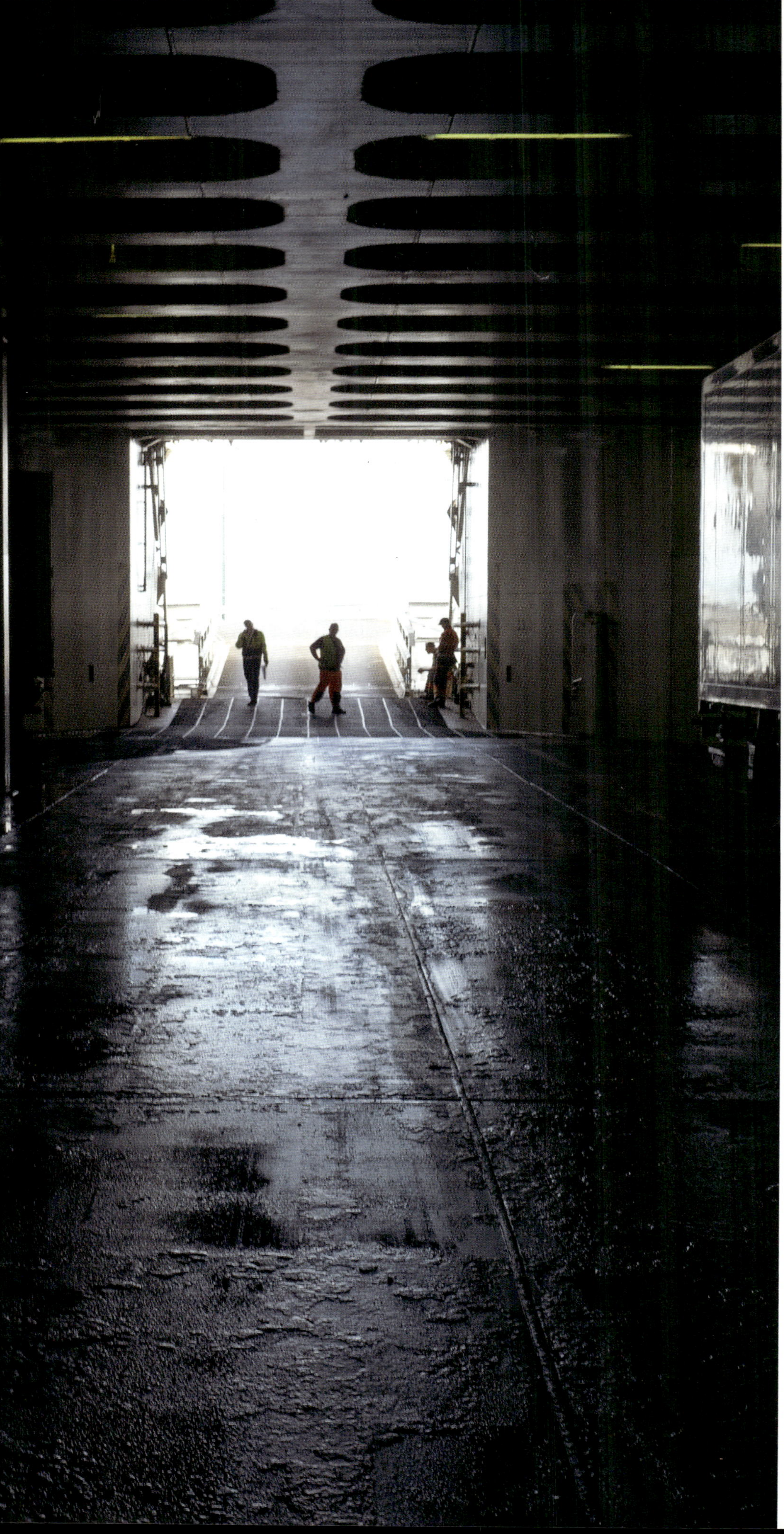

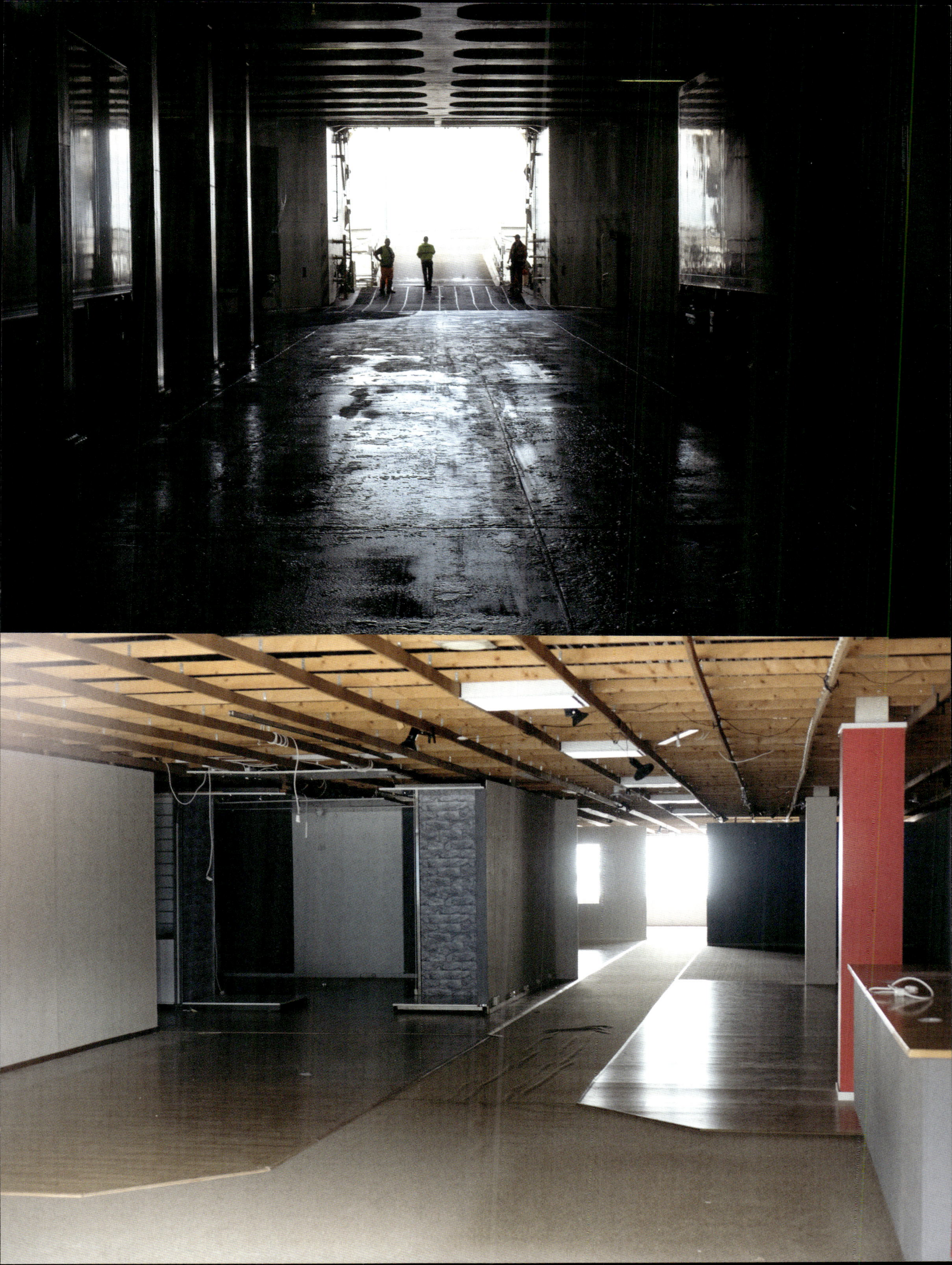

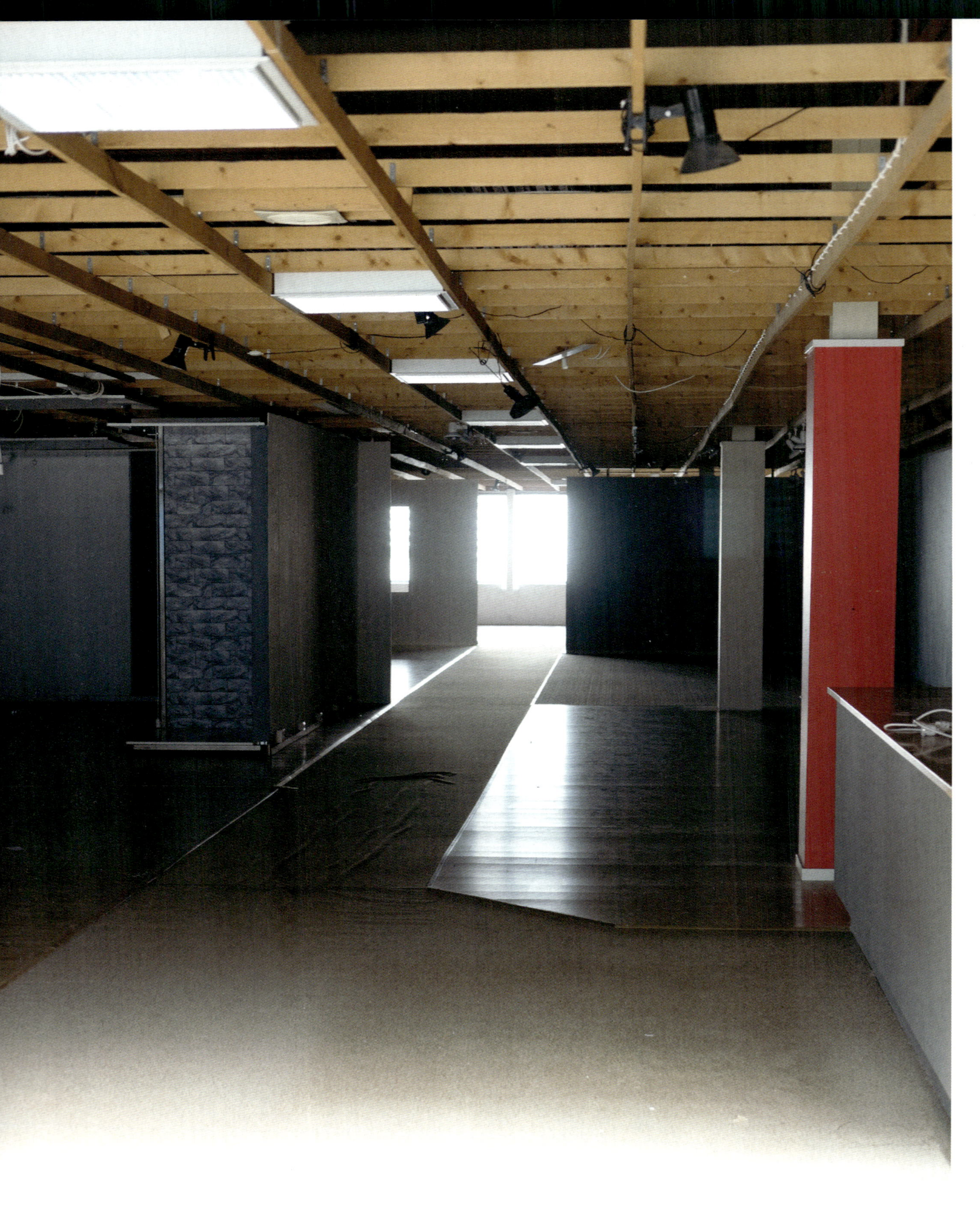

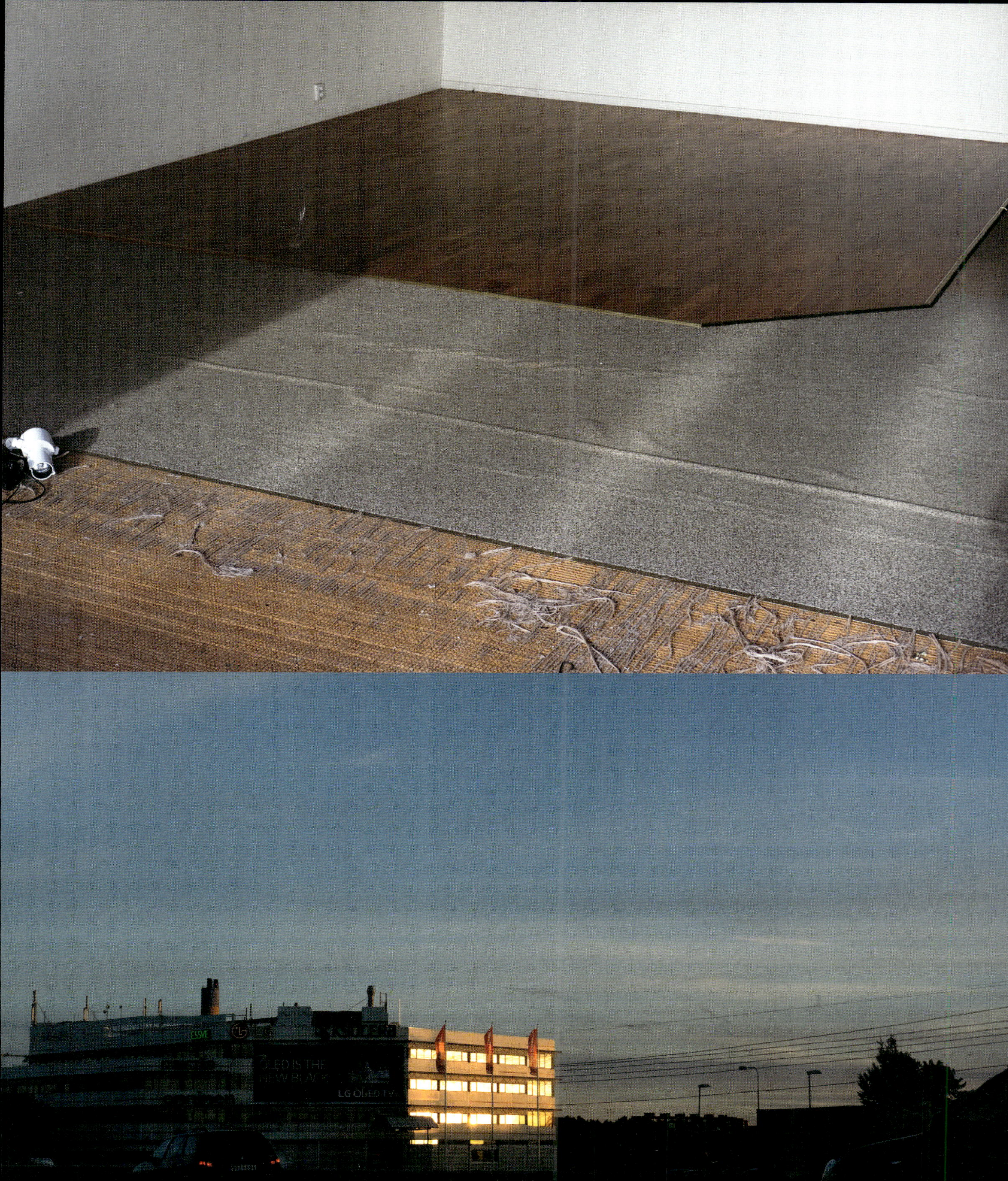

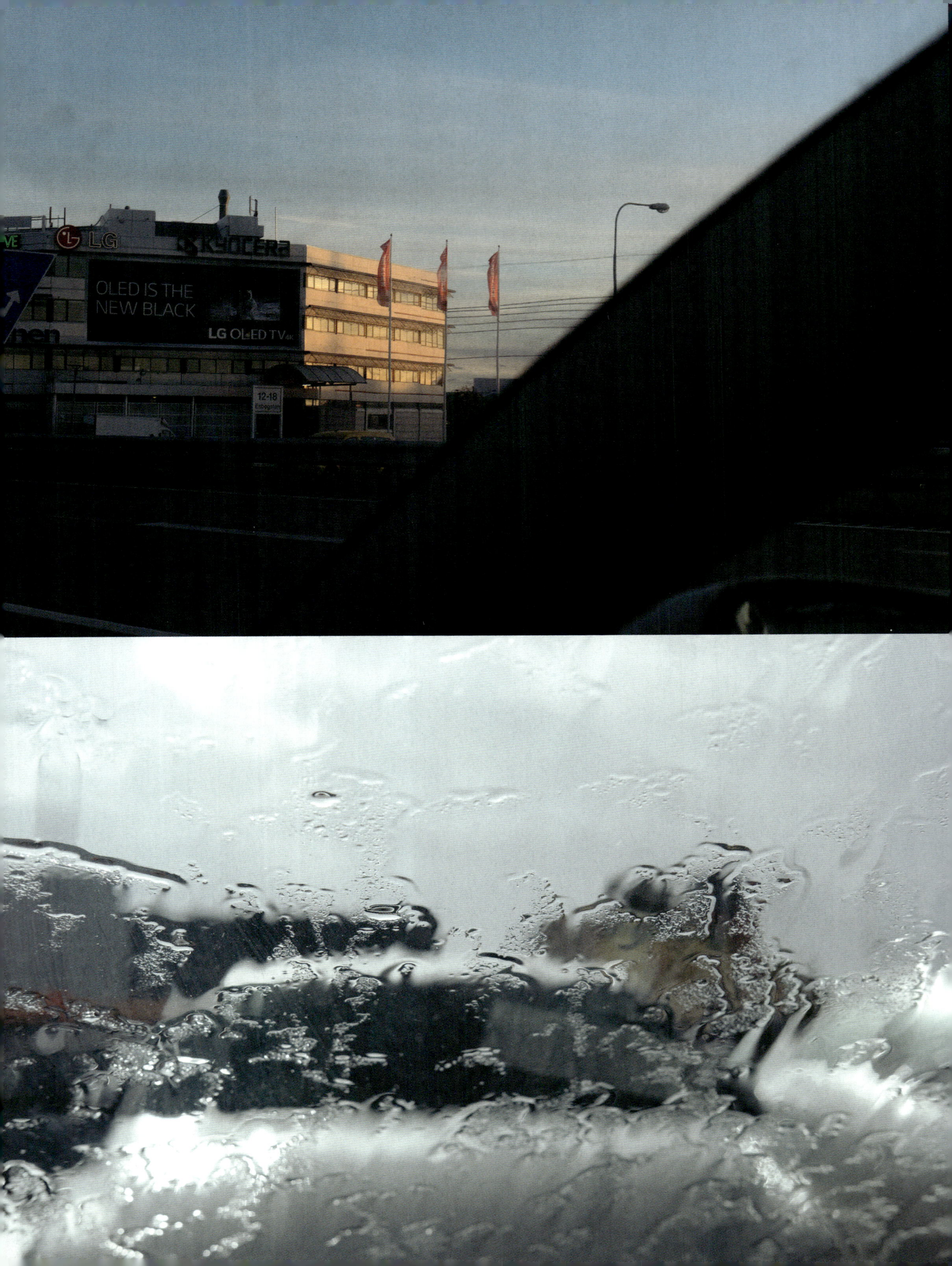
LG
KYOCERA
OLED IS THE
NEW BLACK
LG OLED TV 4K
12-18
Esbogtan

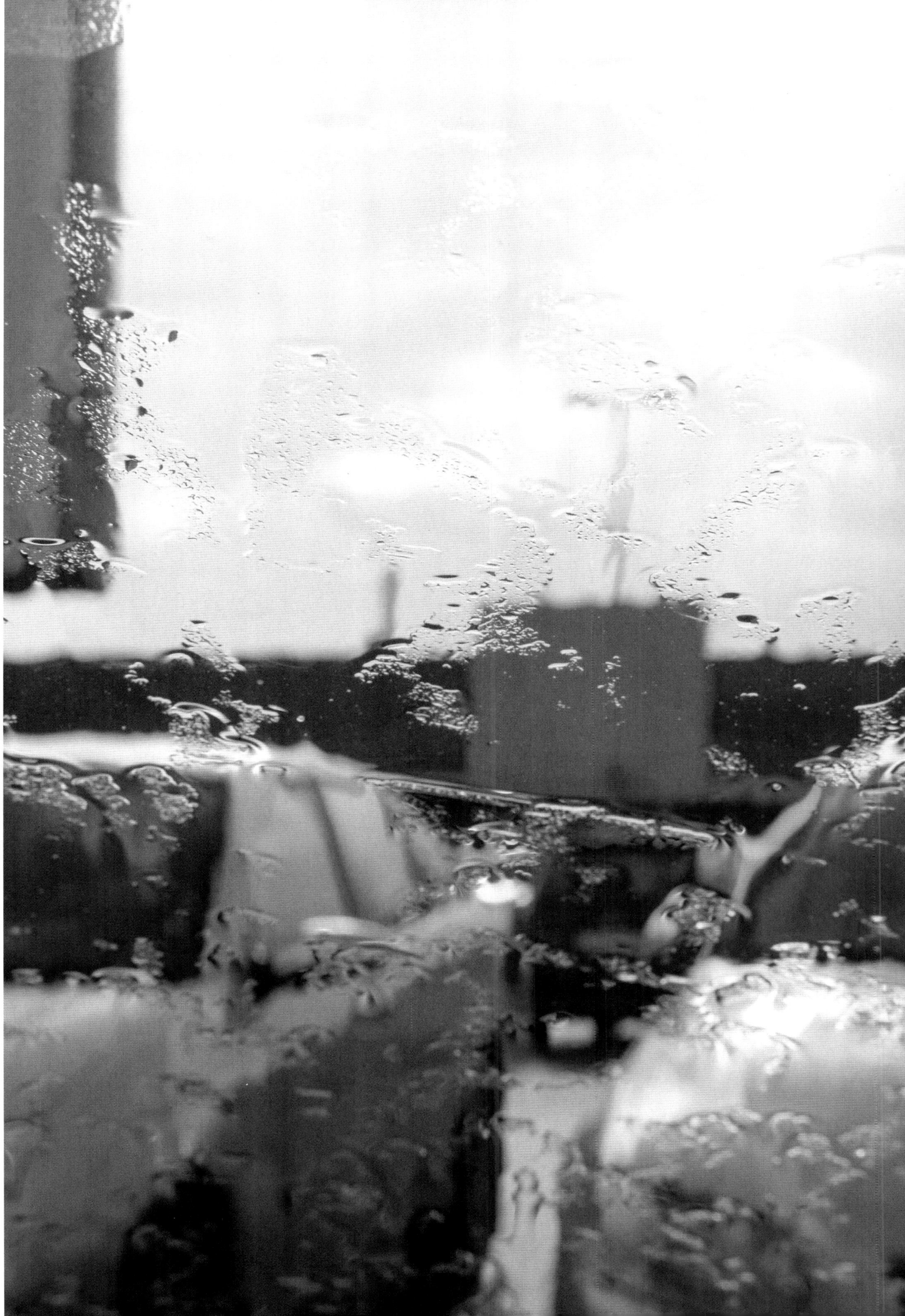

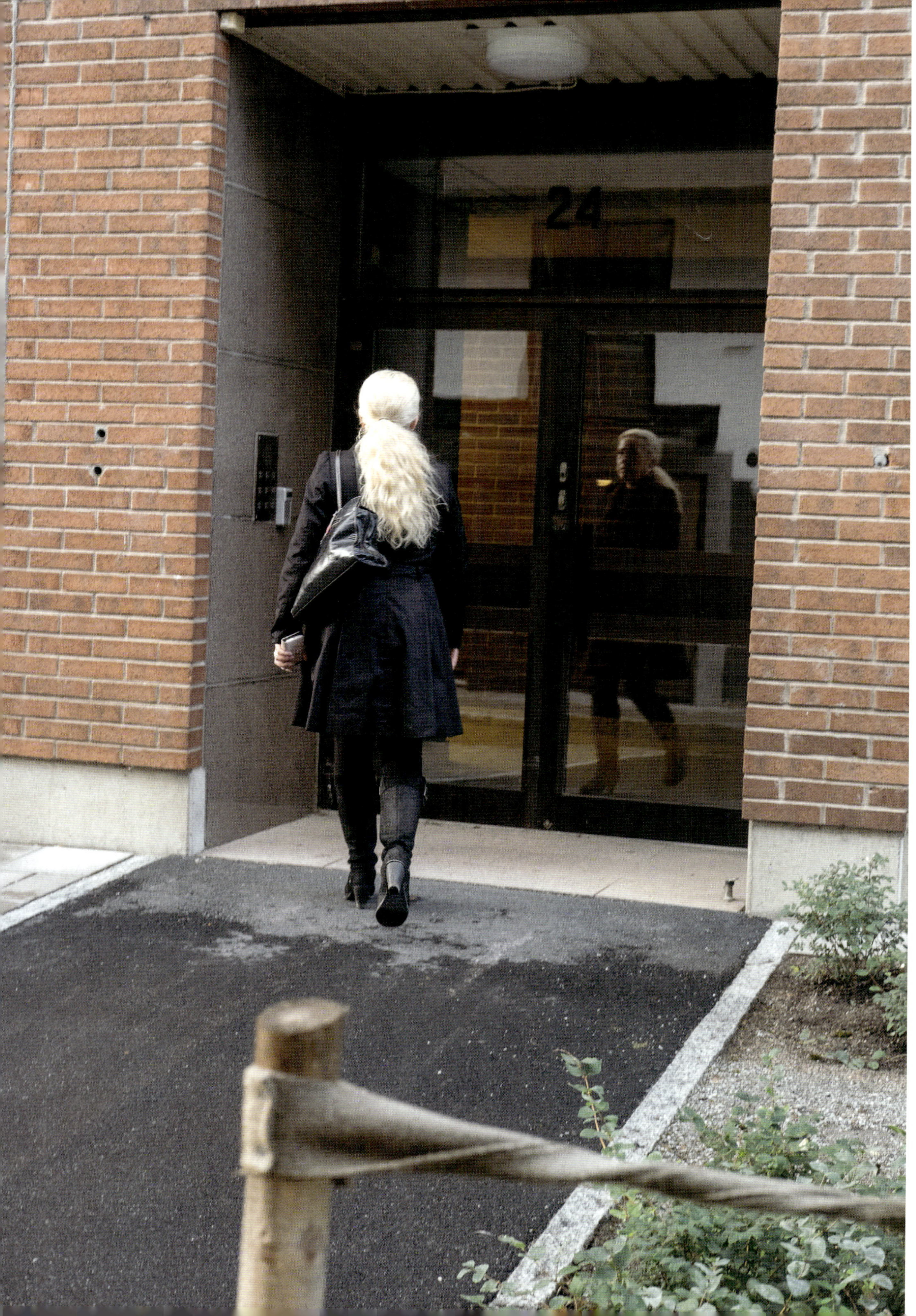

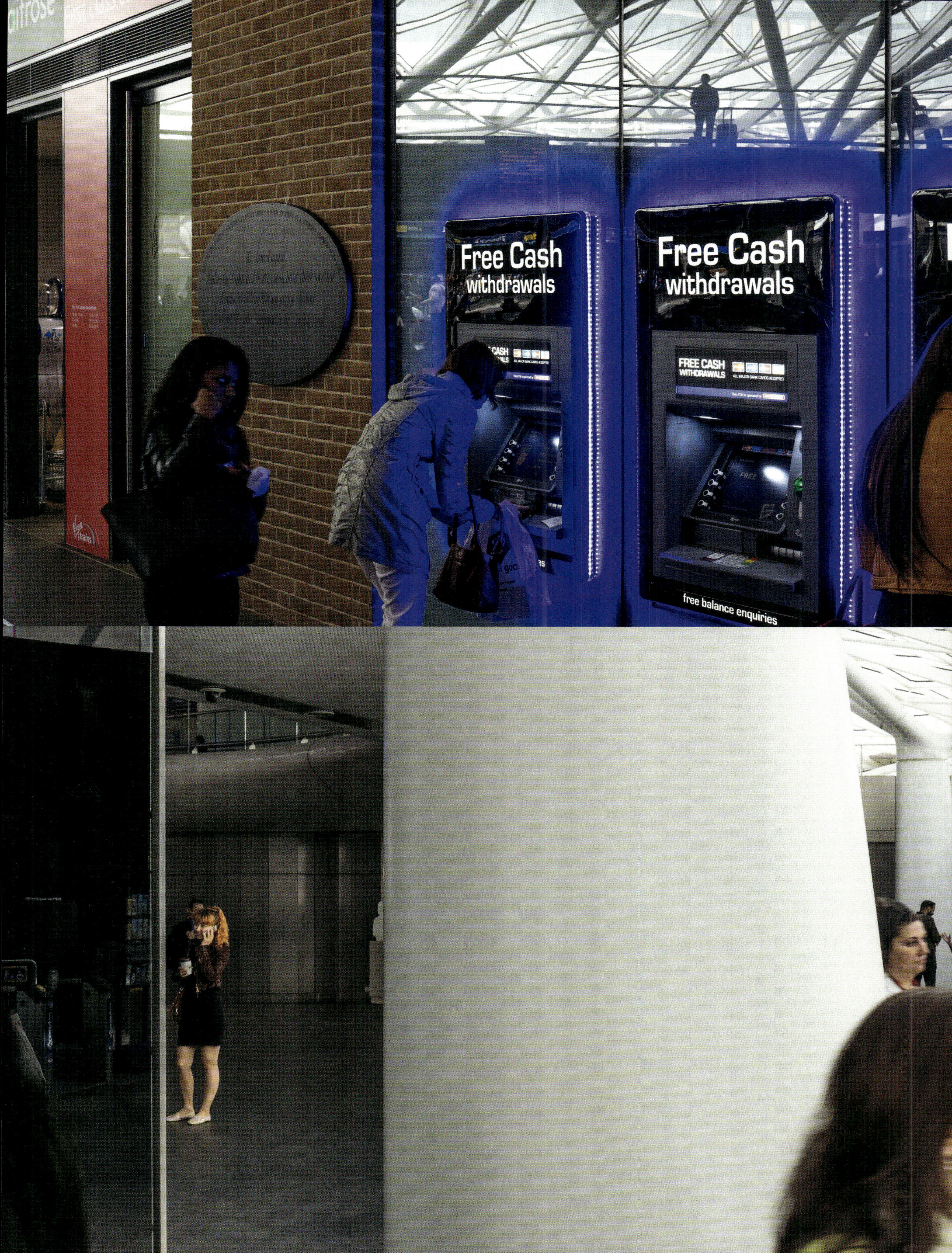
Free Cash
withdrawals
Free Cash
withdrawals
FREE CASH
WITHDRAWALS
ALL MAJOR BANK CARDS ACCEPTED
FREE CASH
WITHDRAWALS
ALL MAJOR BANK CARDS ACCEPTED
free balance enquiries

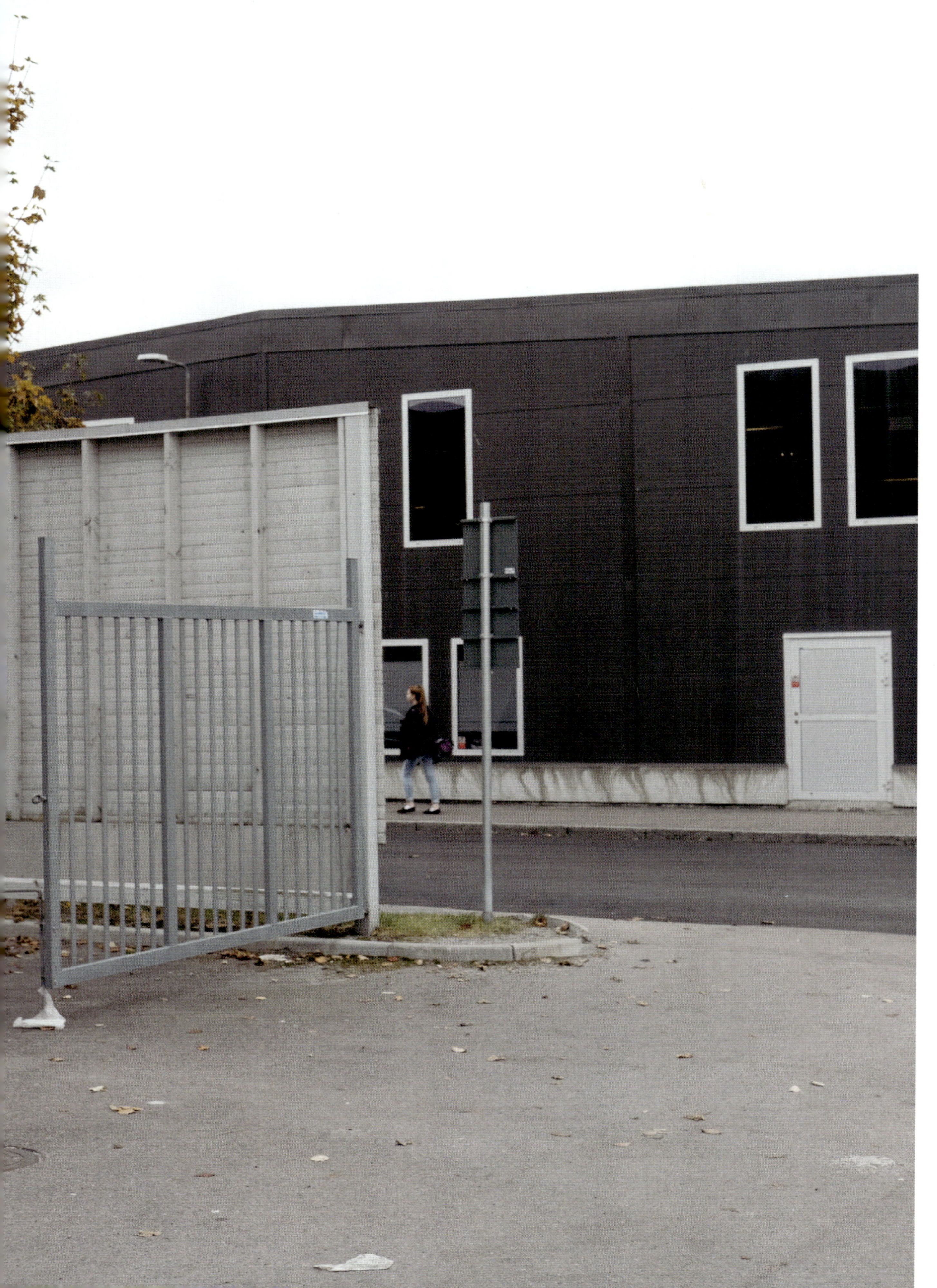

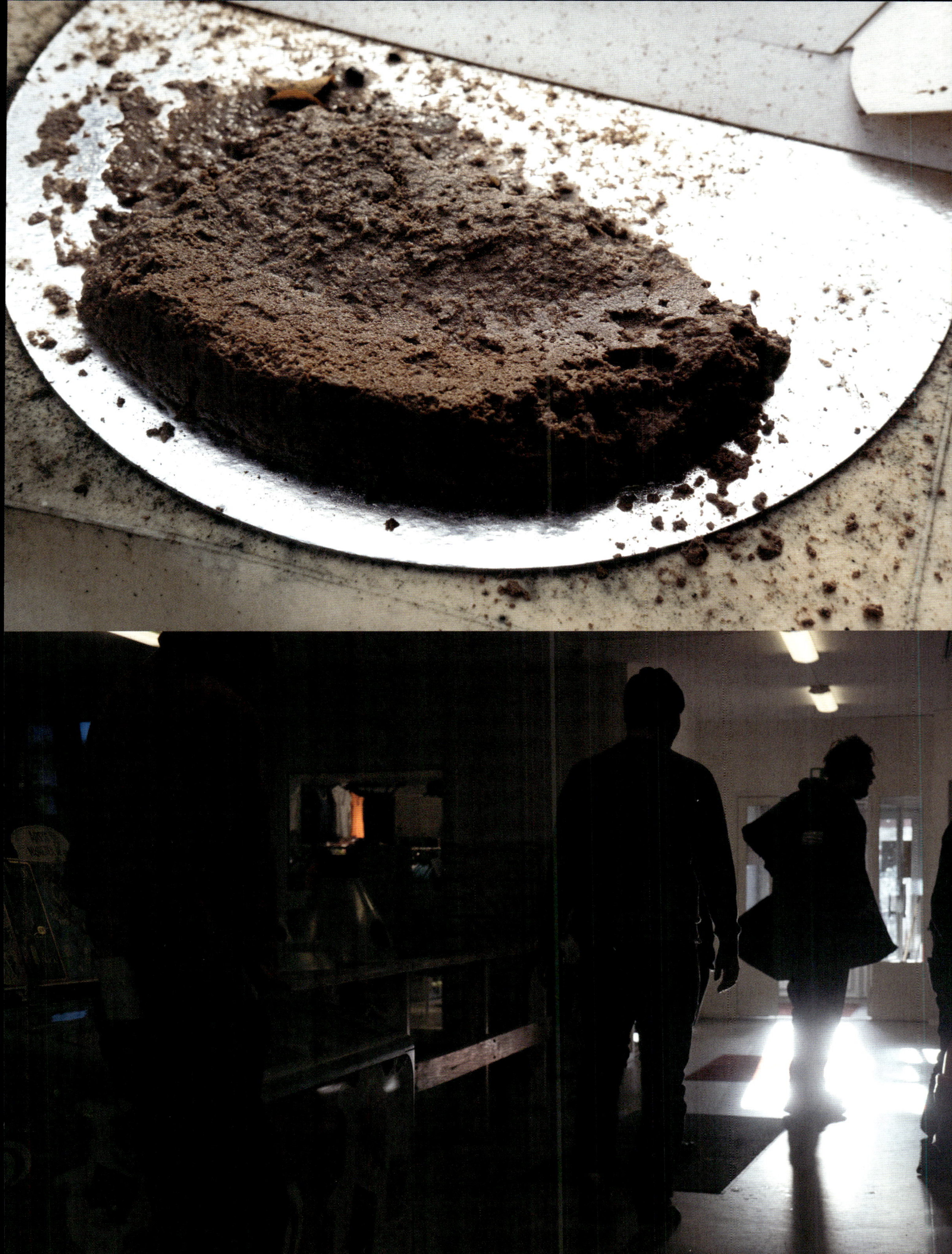

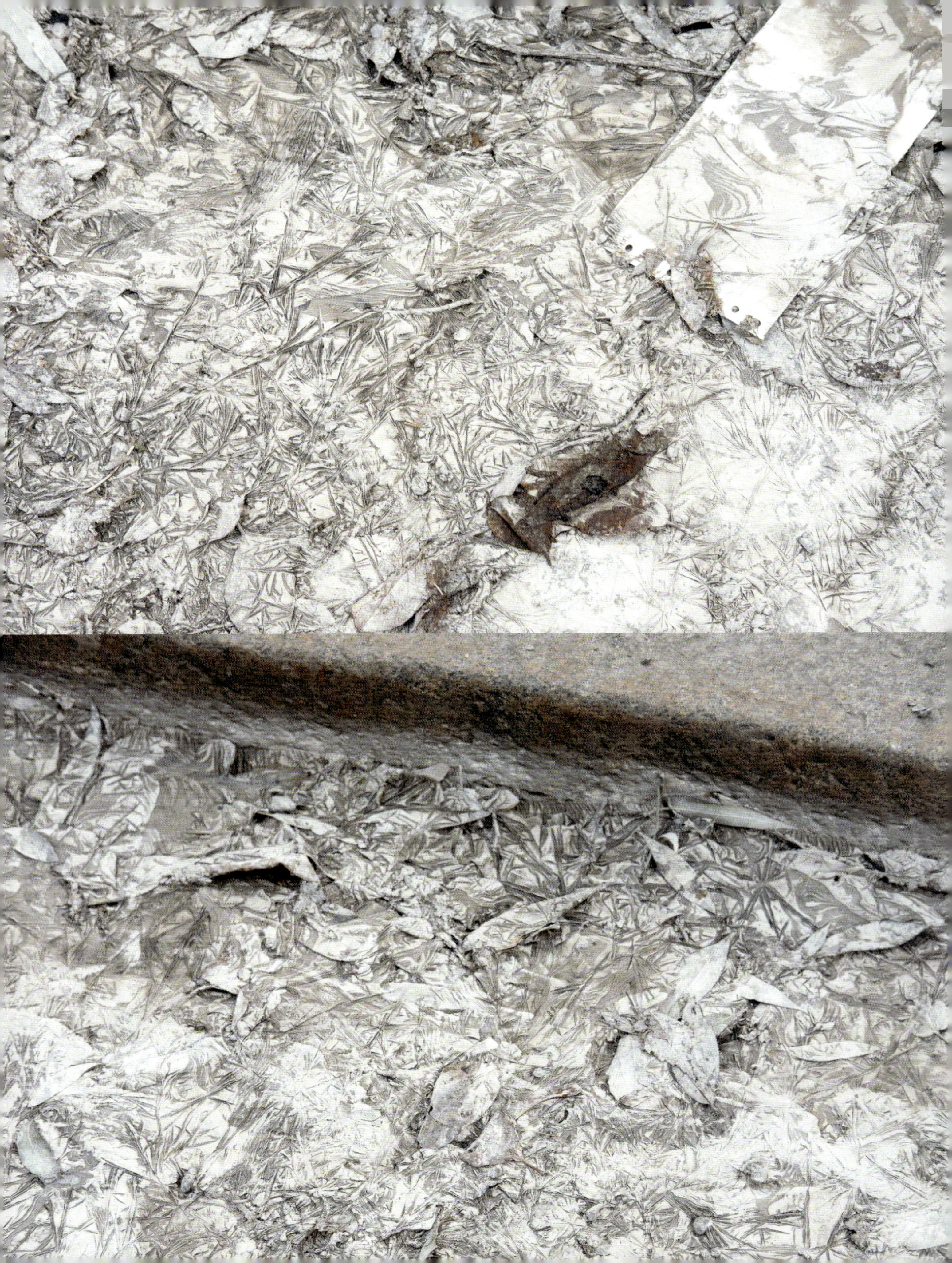

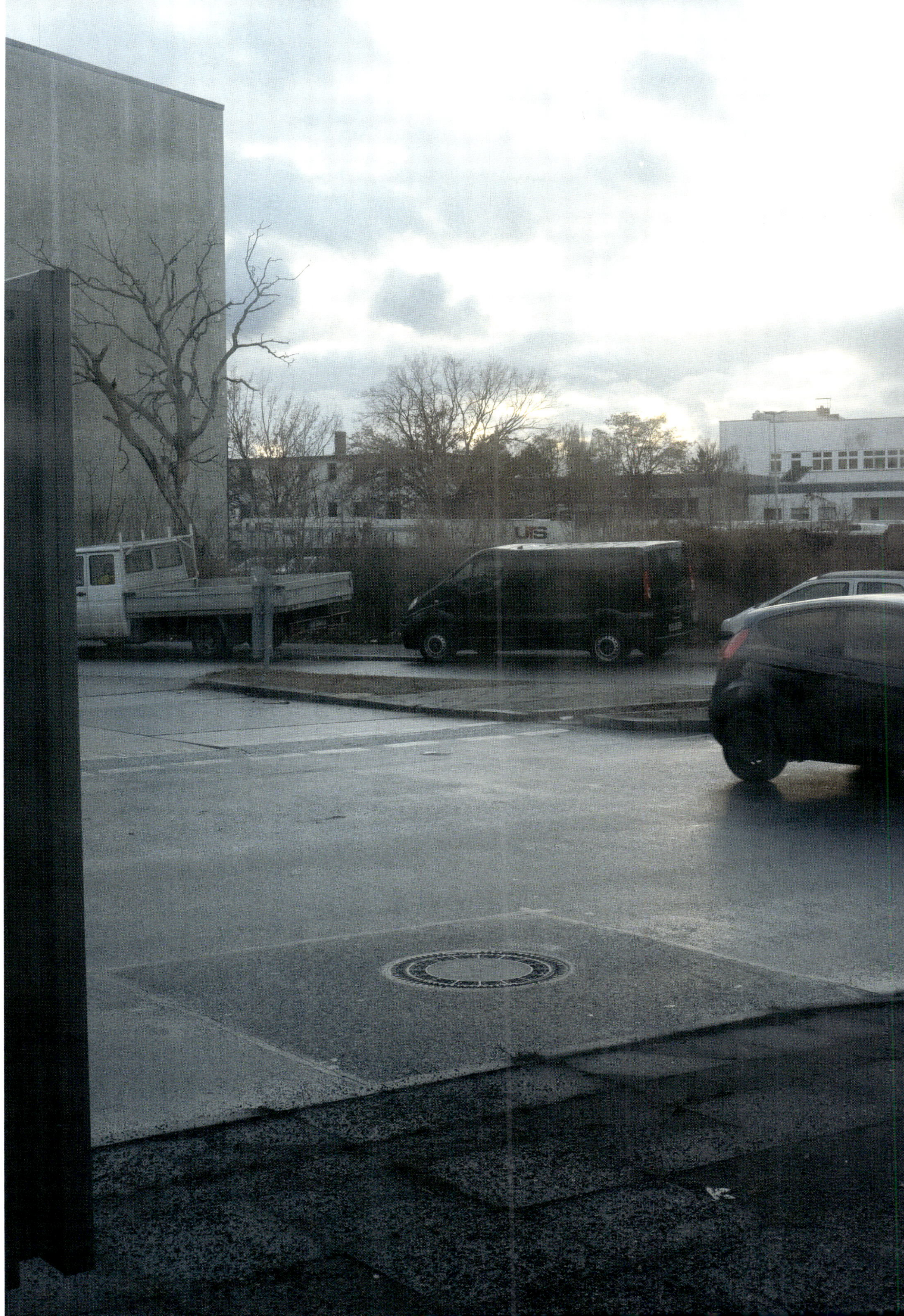

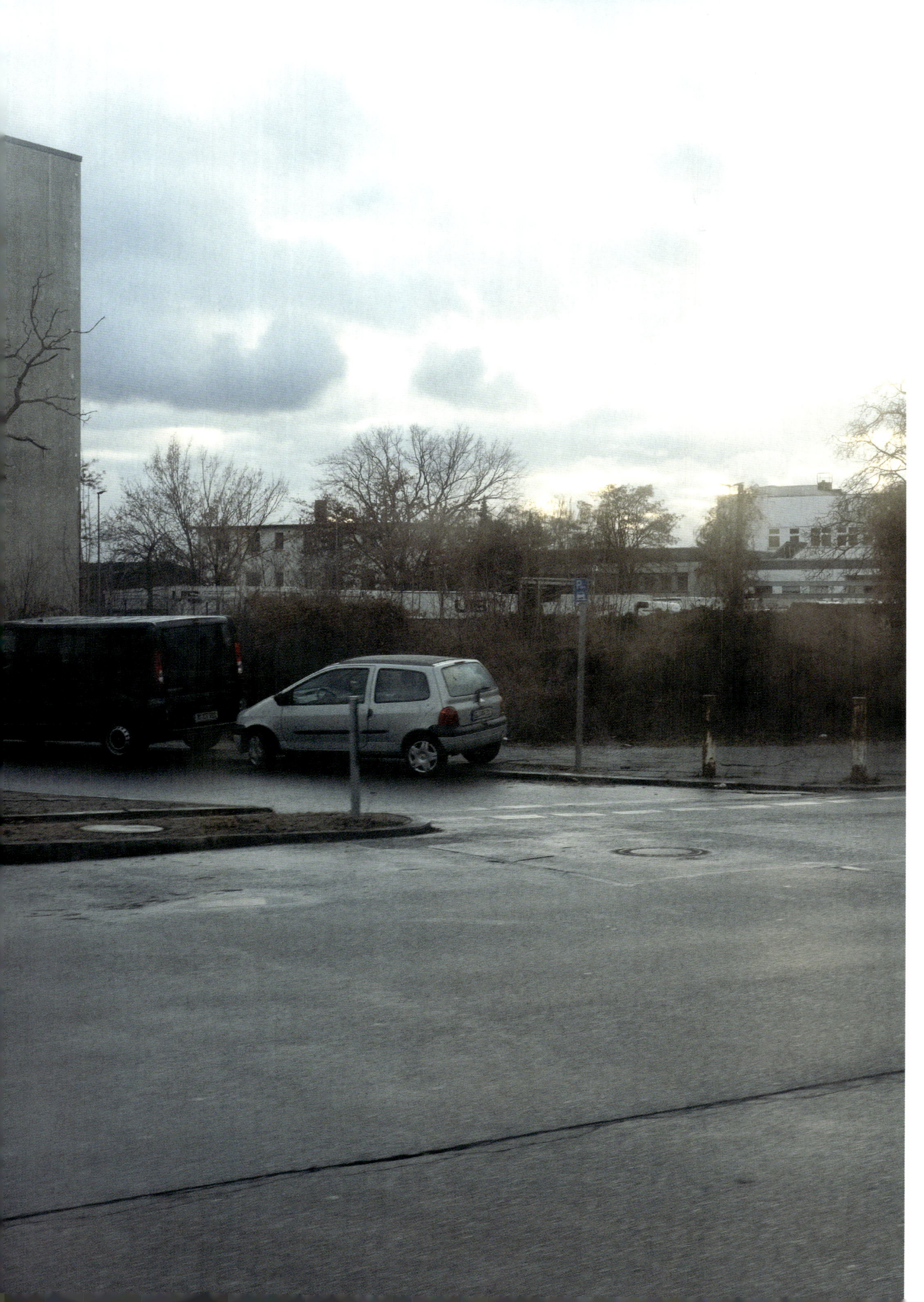

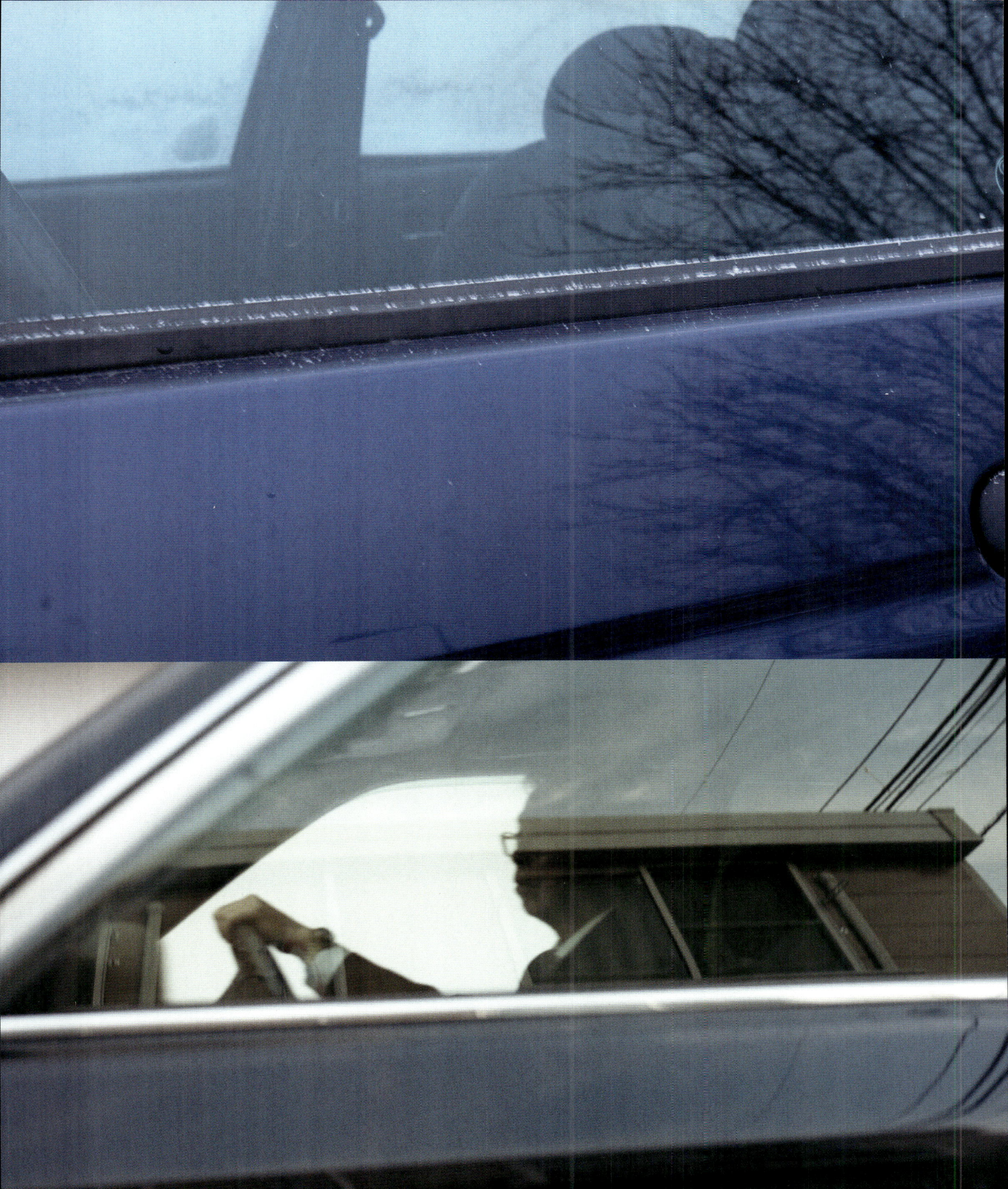

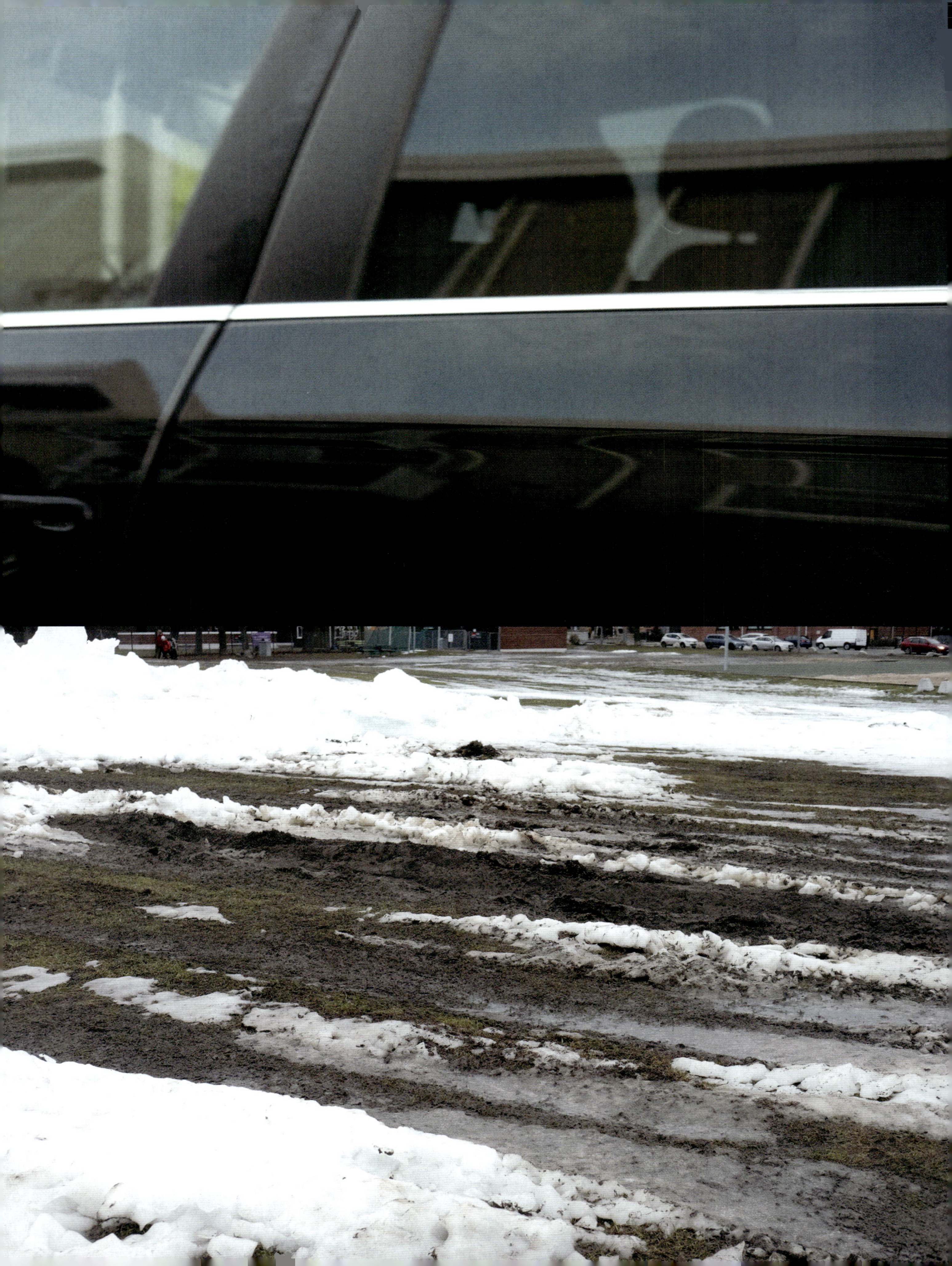

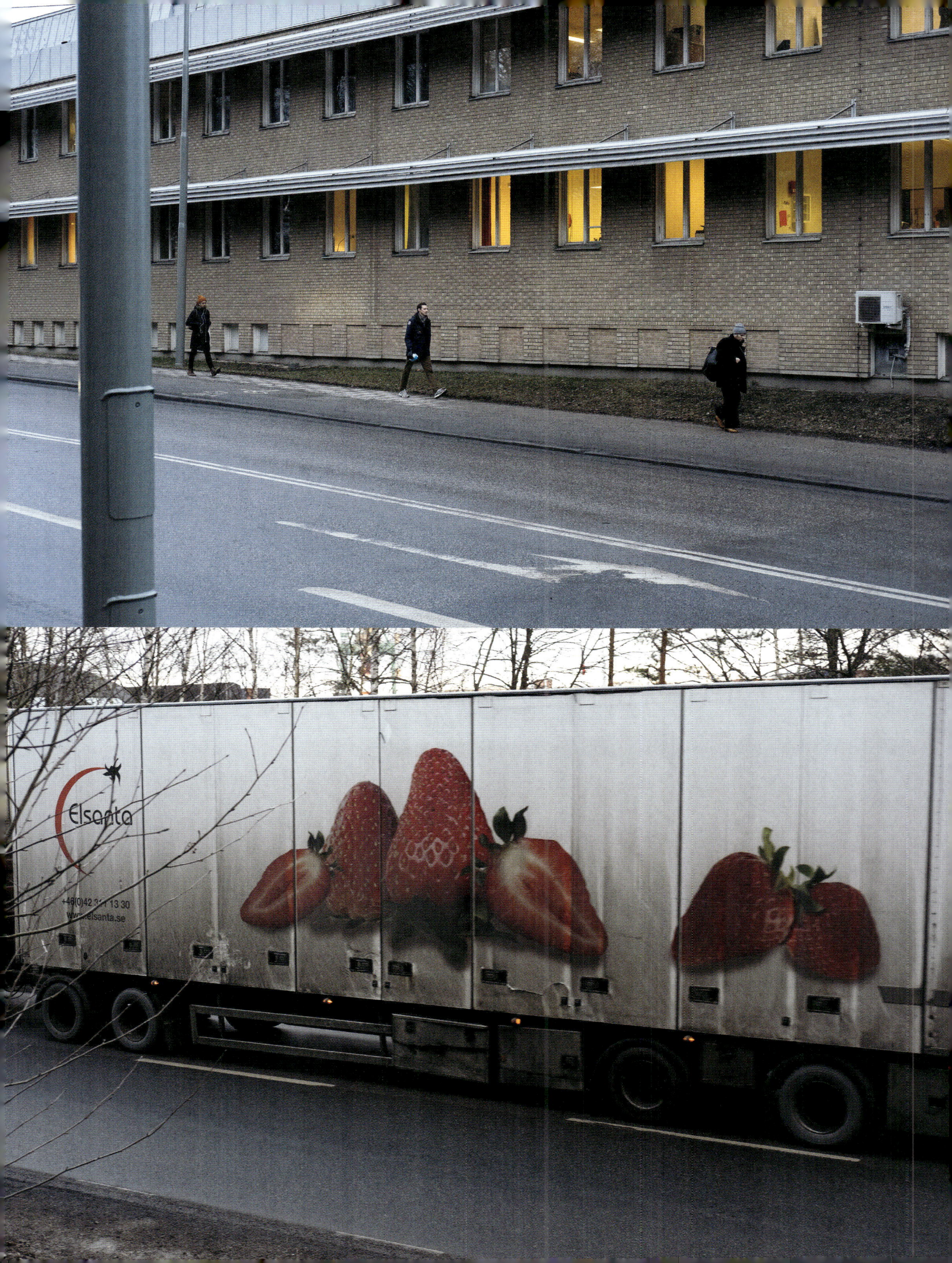

Elsanta
+46(0)42 3 1 13 30
www.elsanta.se

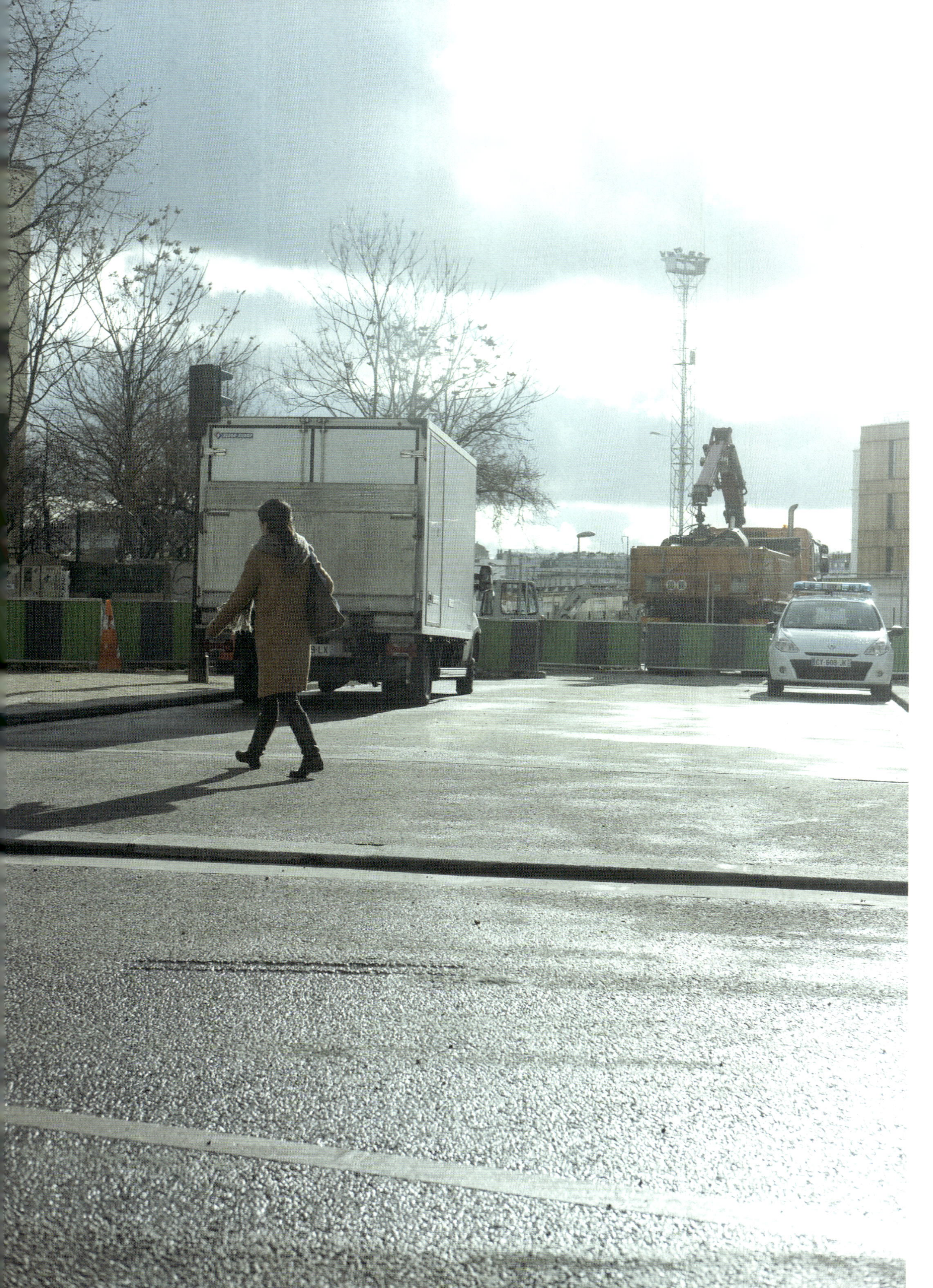

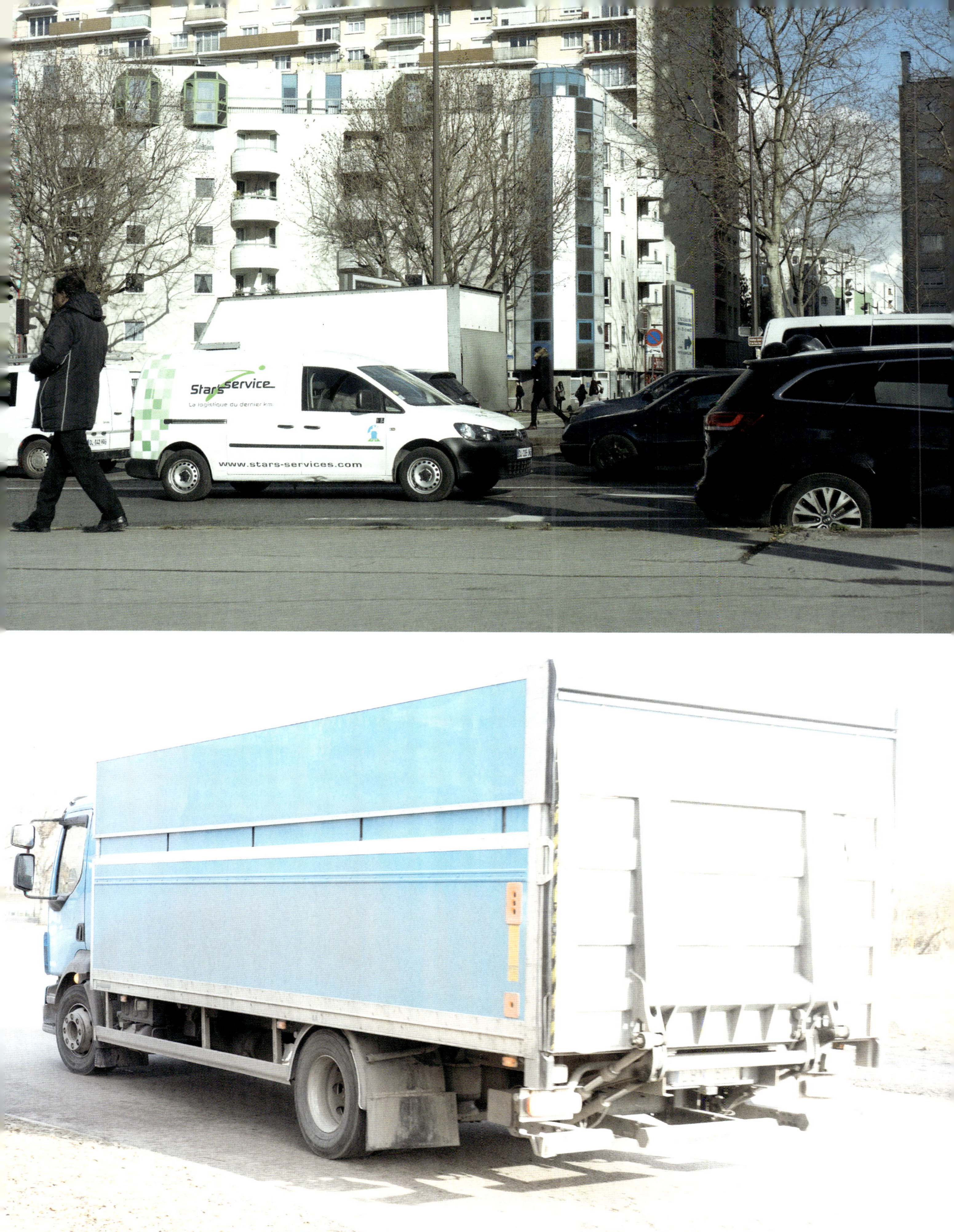

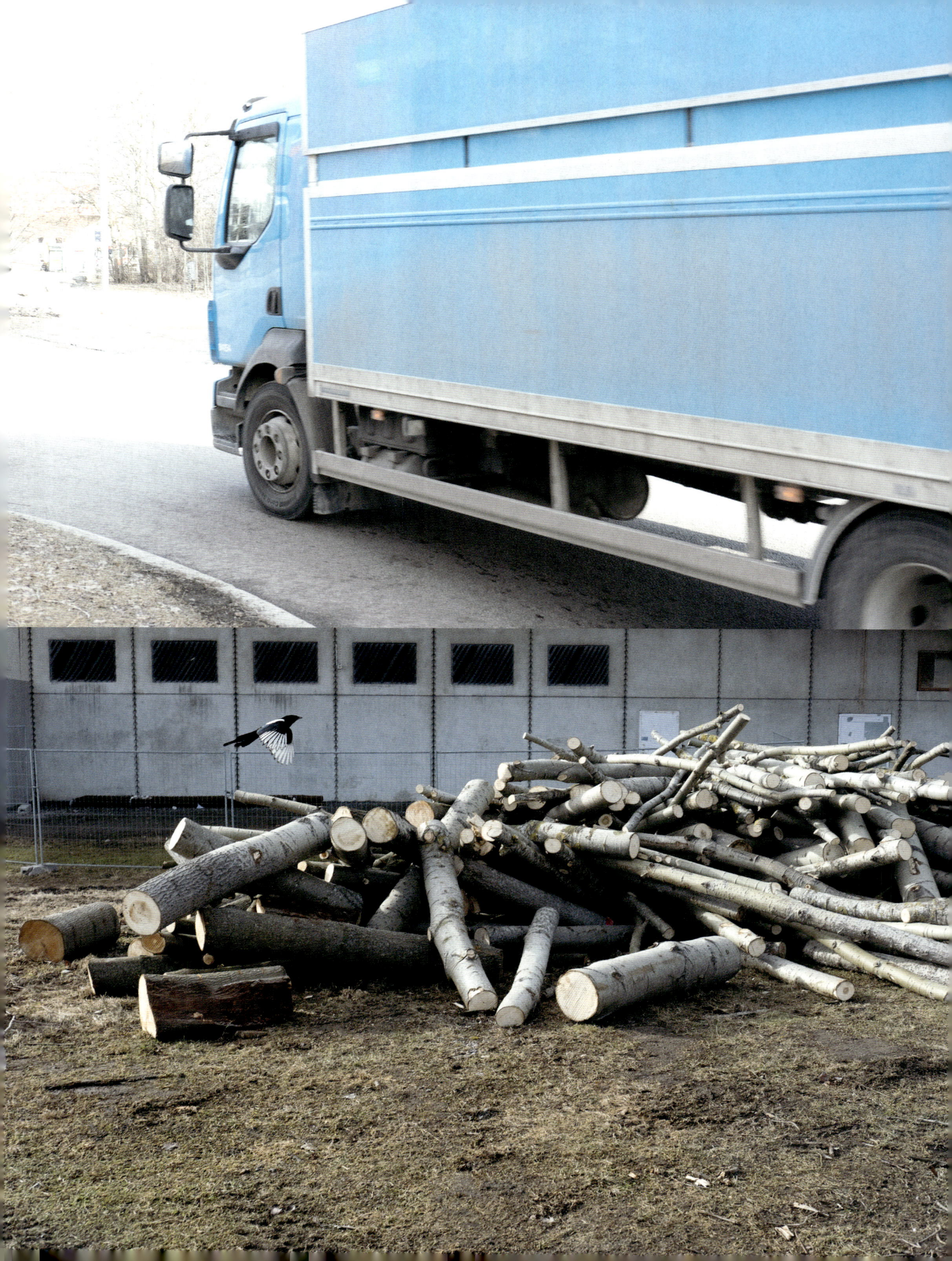

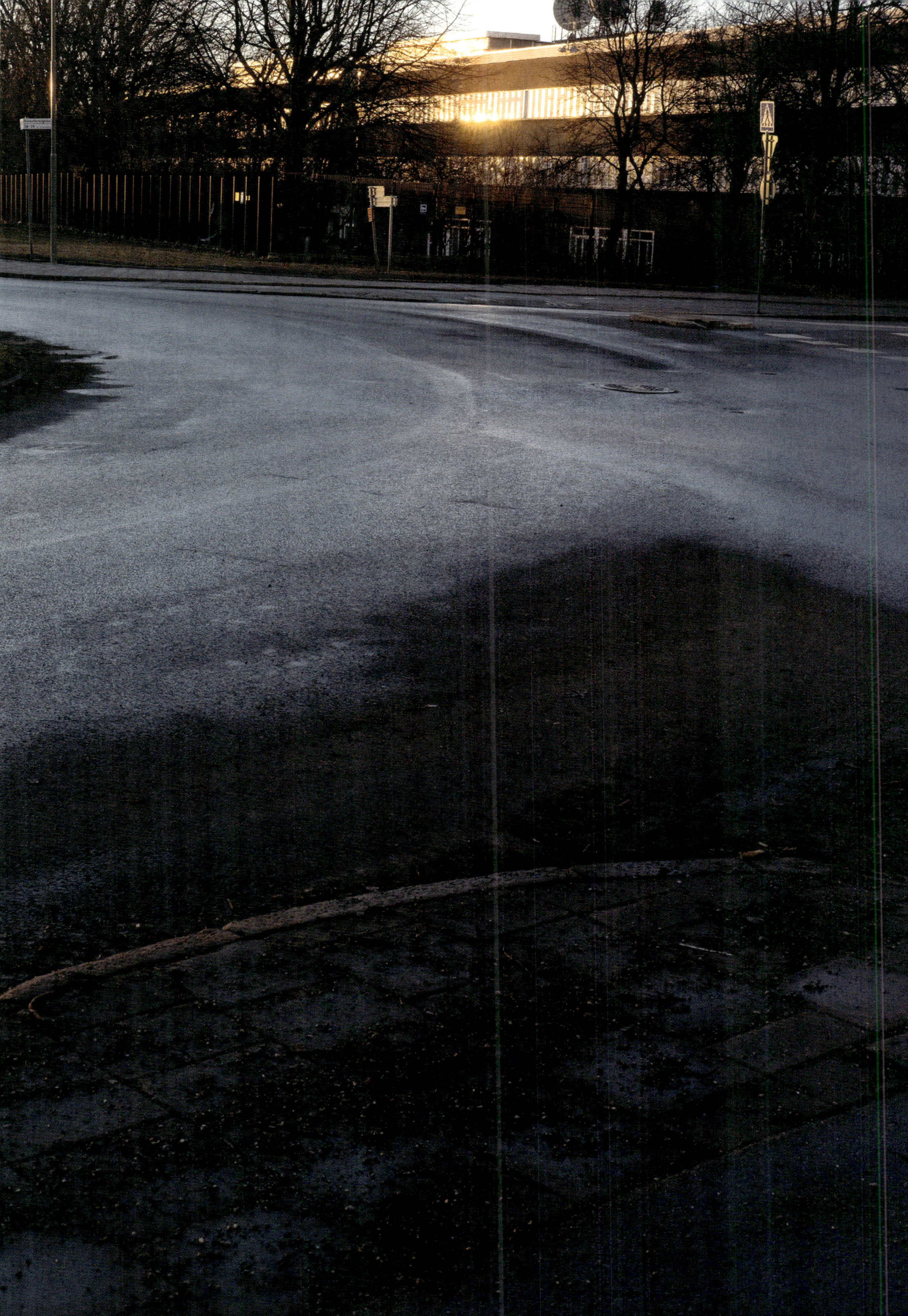

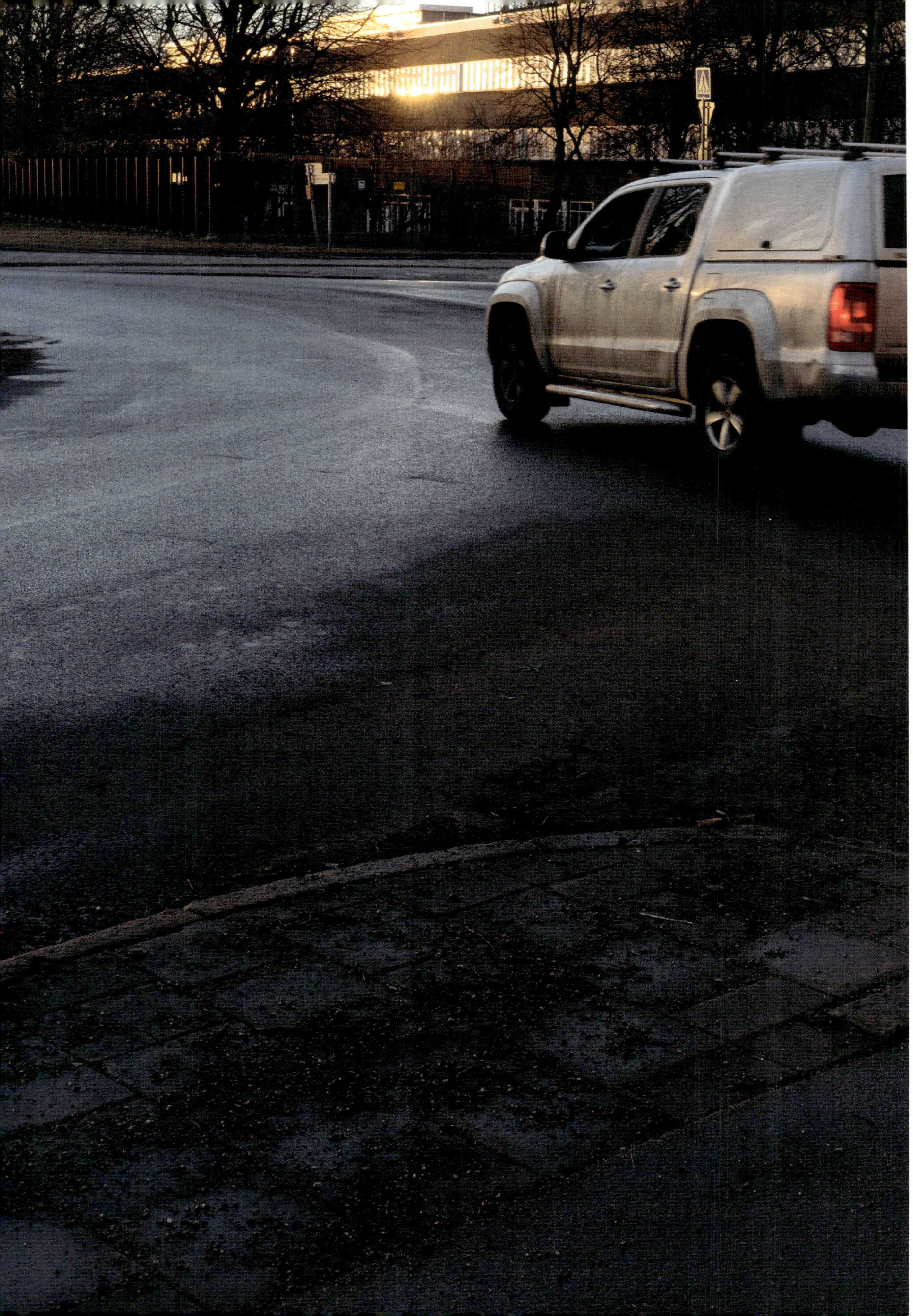

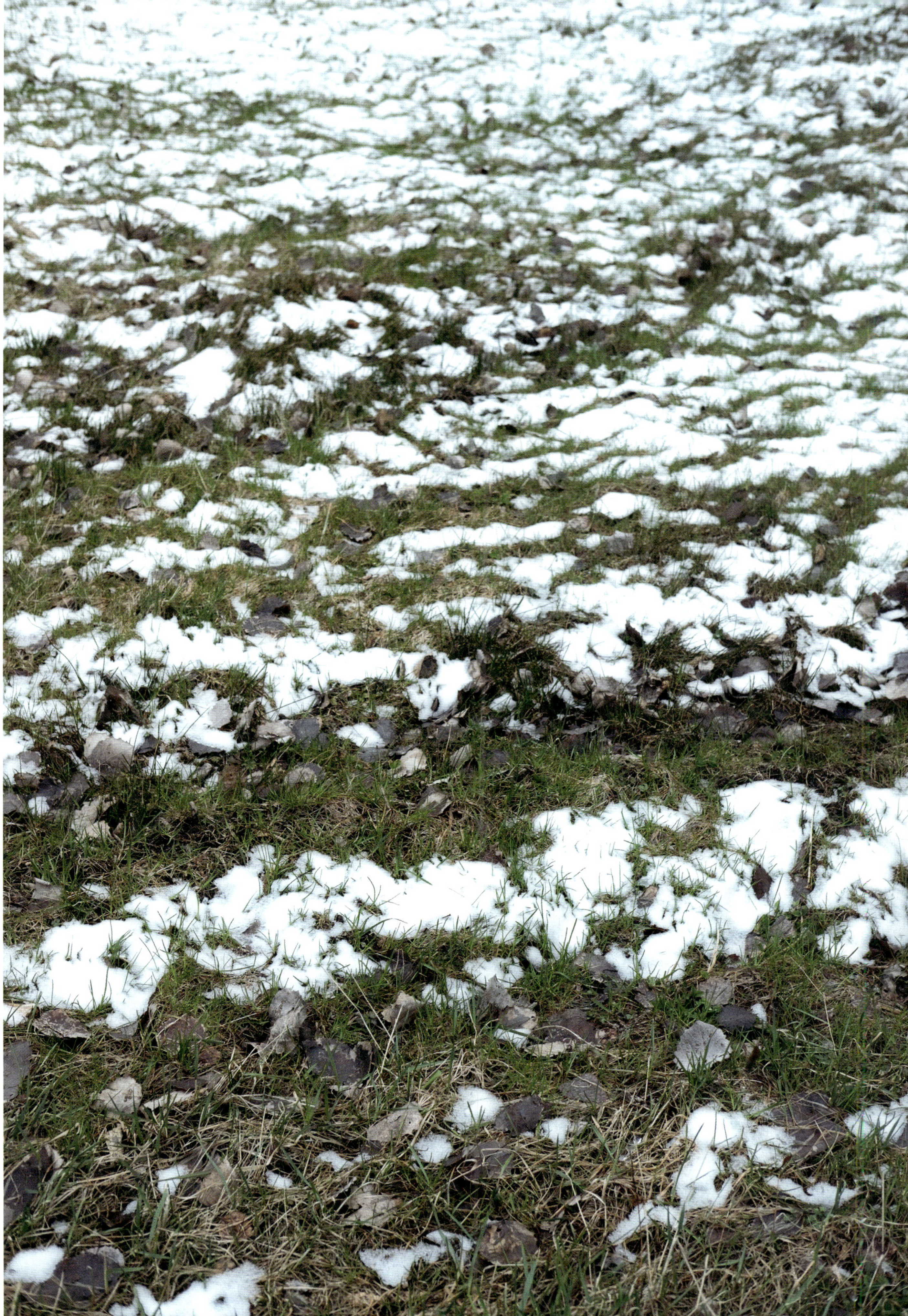

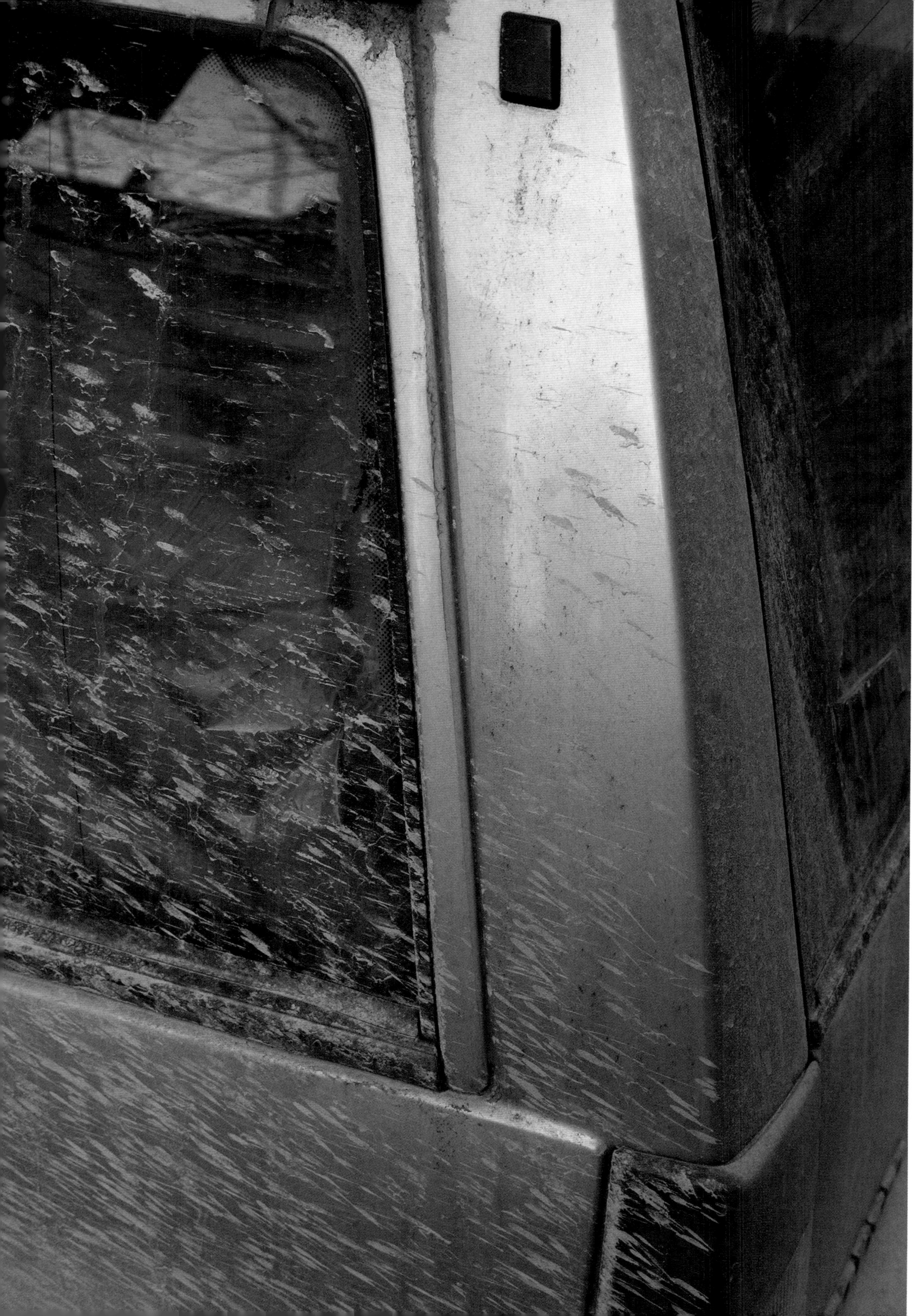

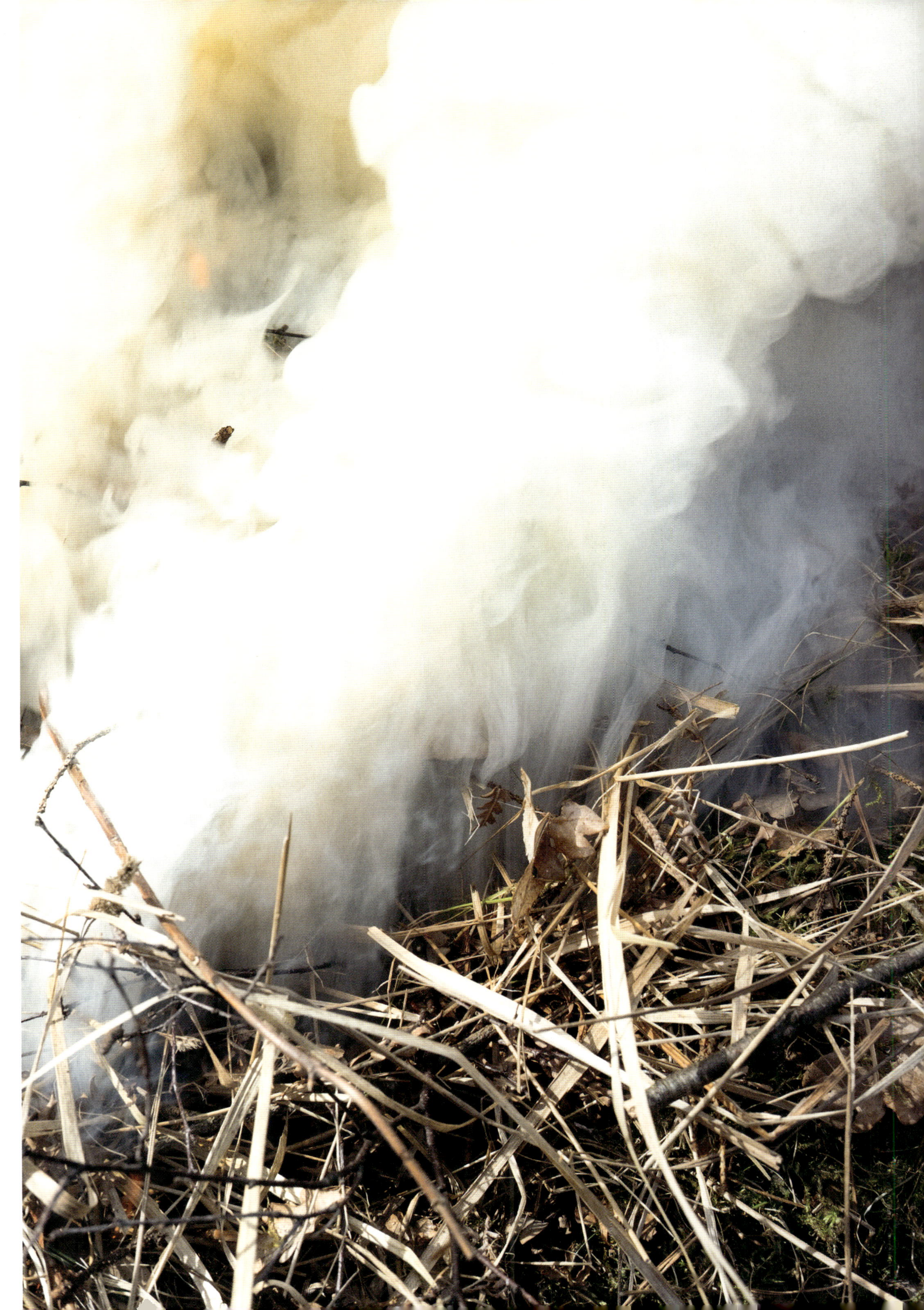

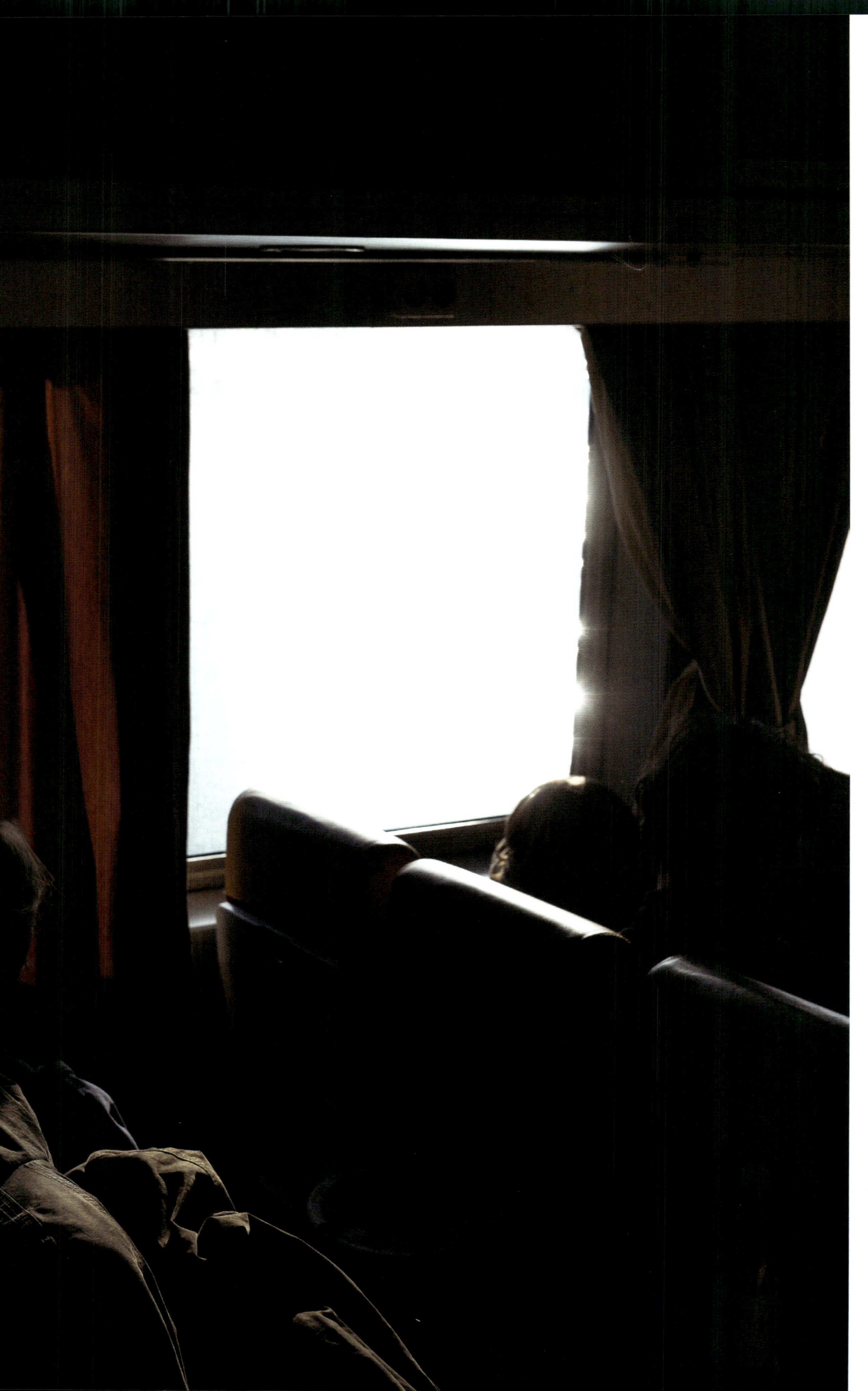

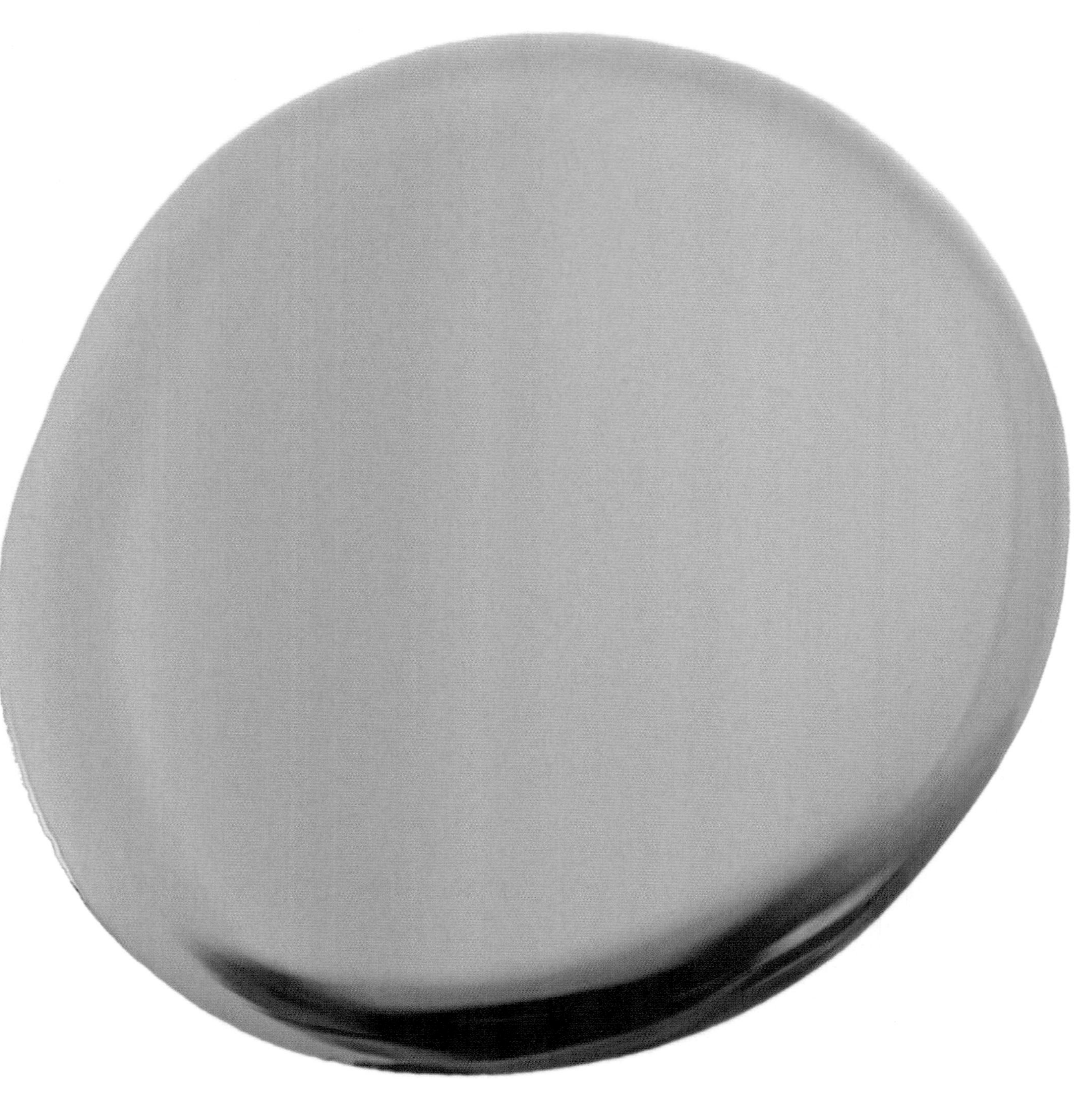

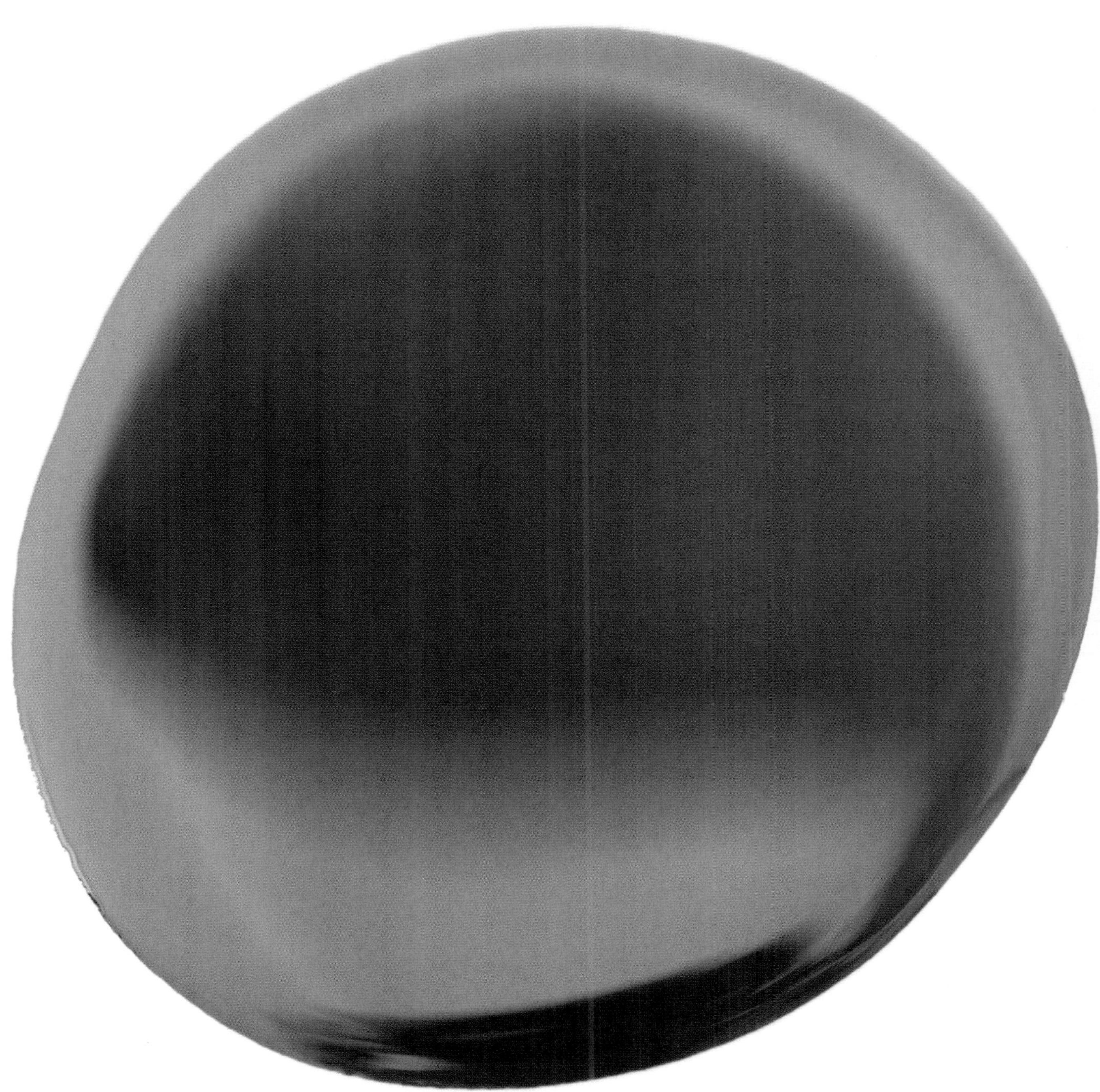

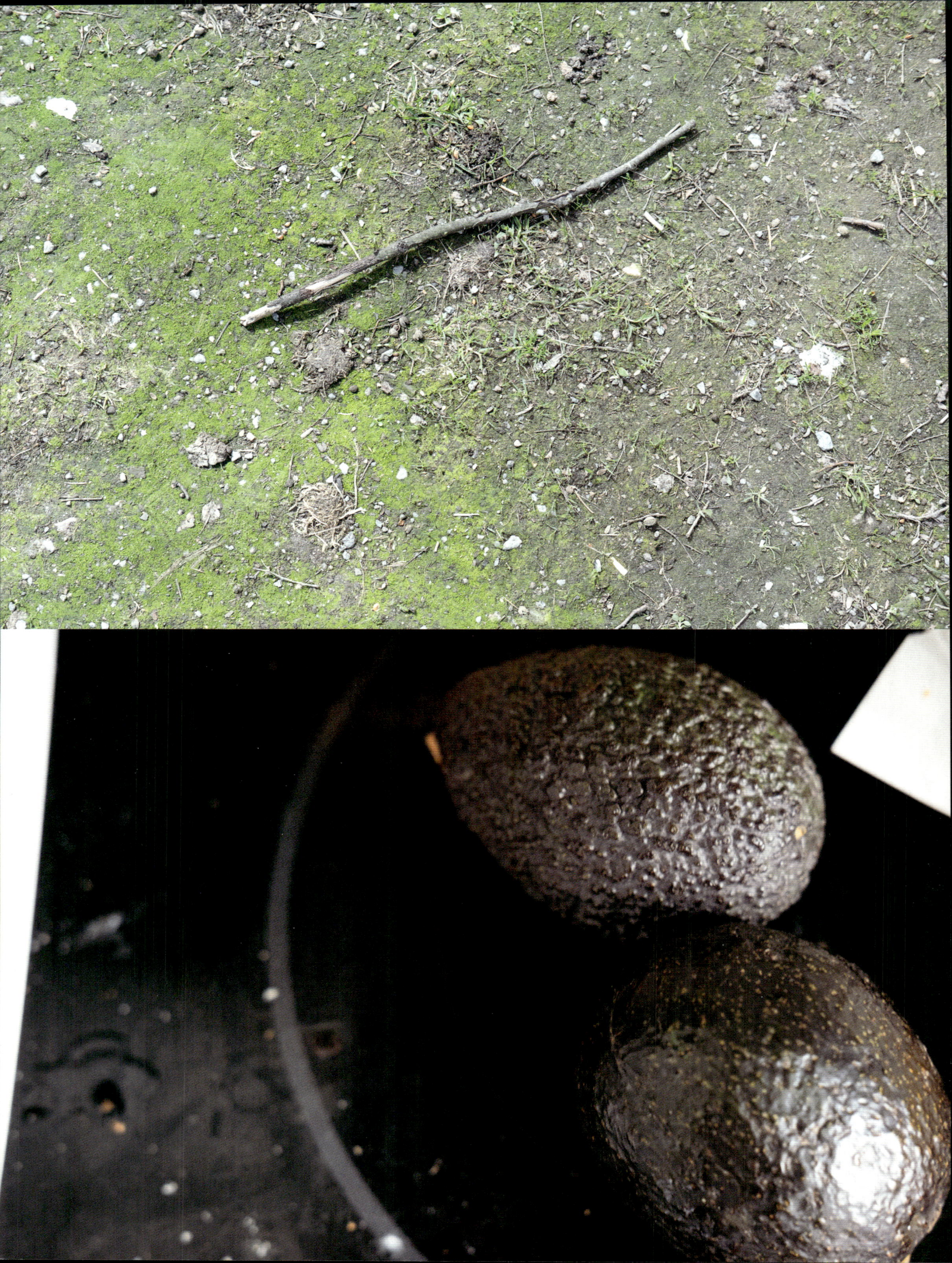

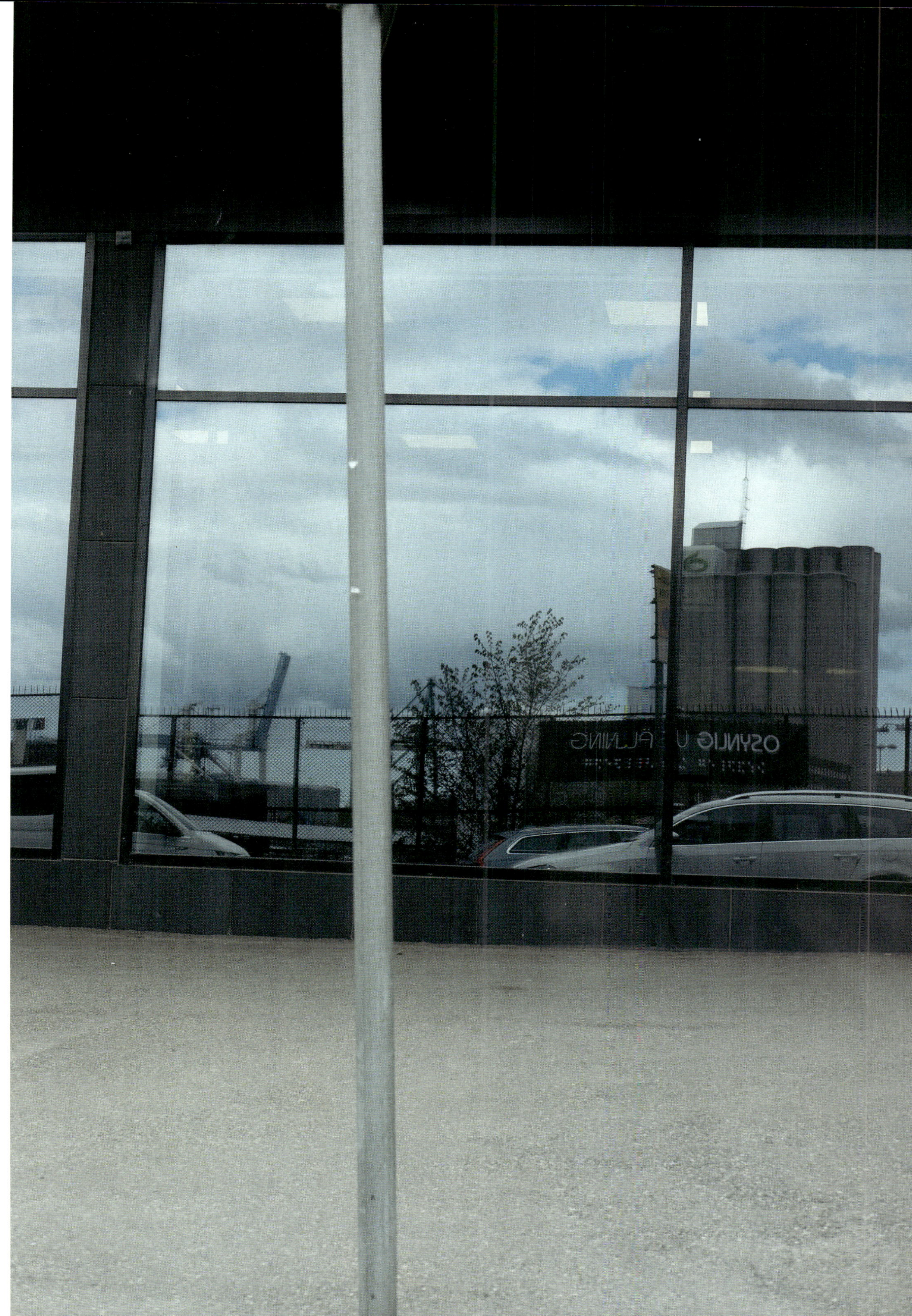

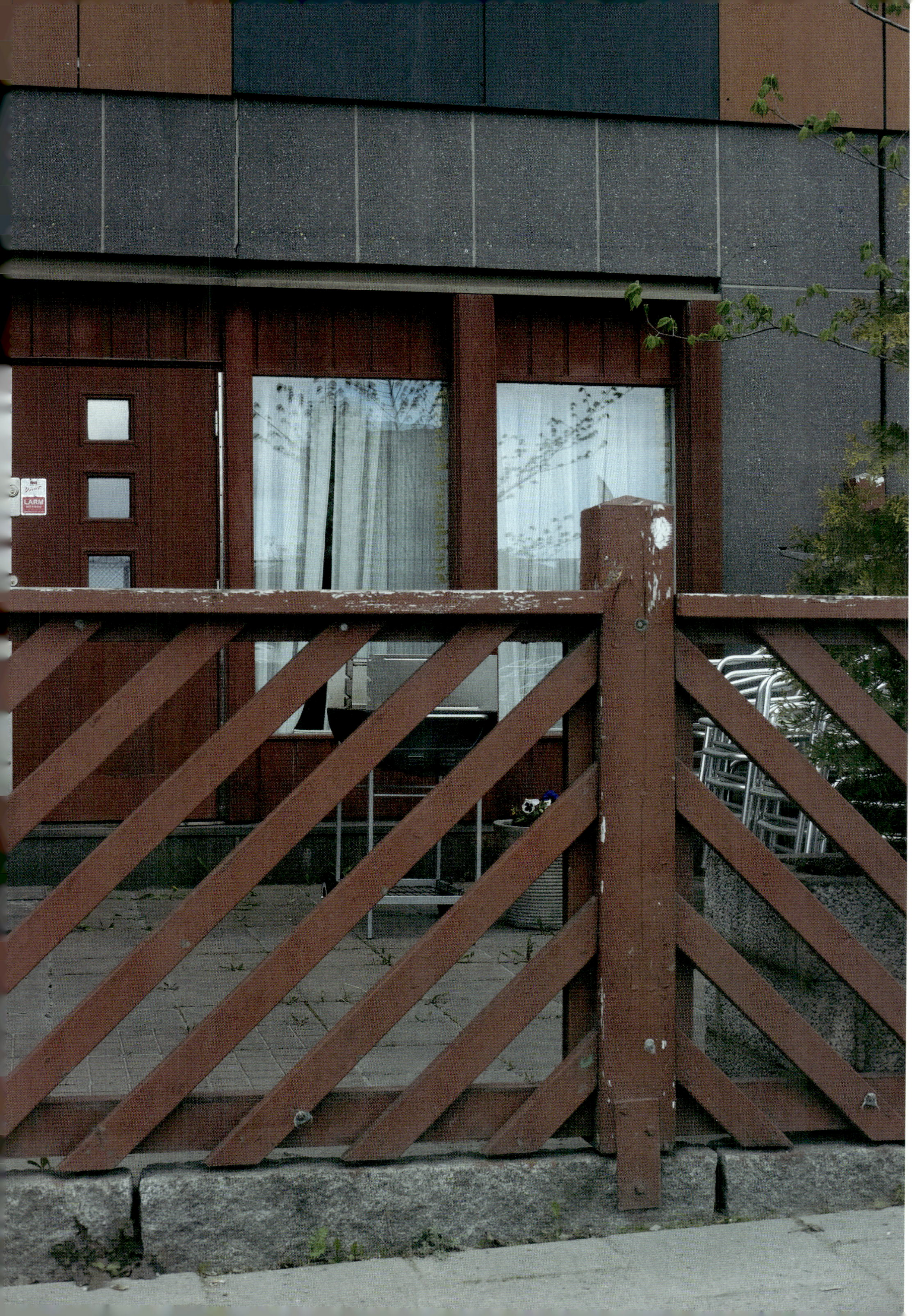

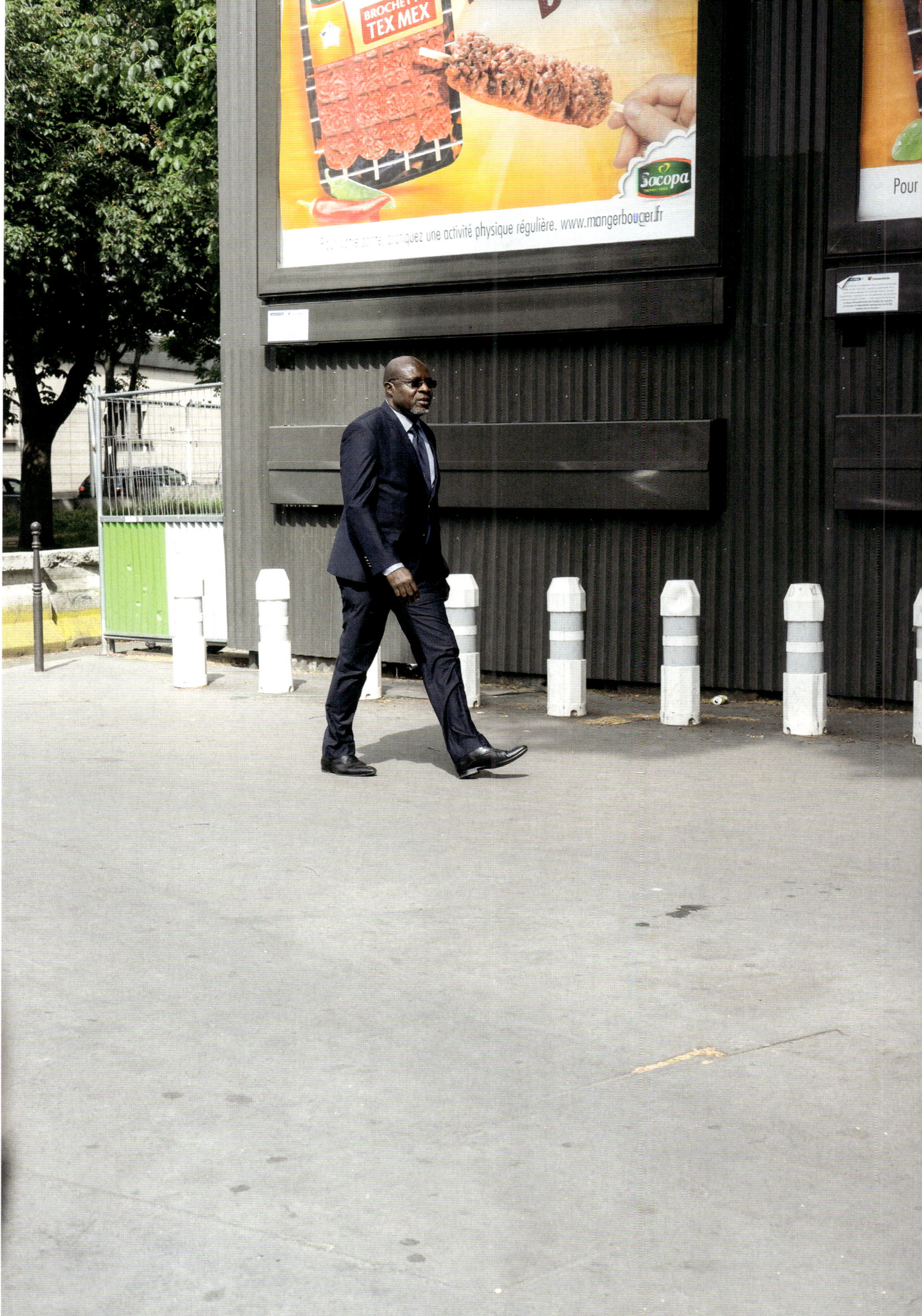
BROCHET
TEX MEX
Sacopa
Pour votre santé, pratiquez une activité physique régulière. www.mangerbouger.fr
Pour

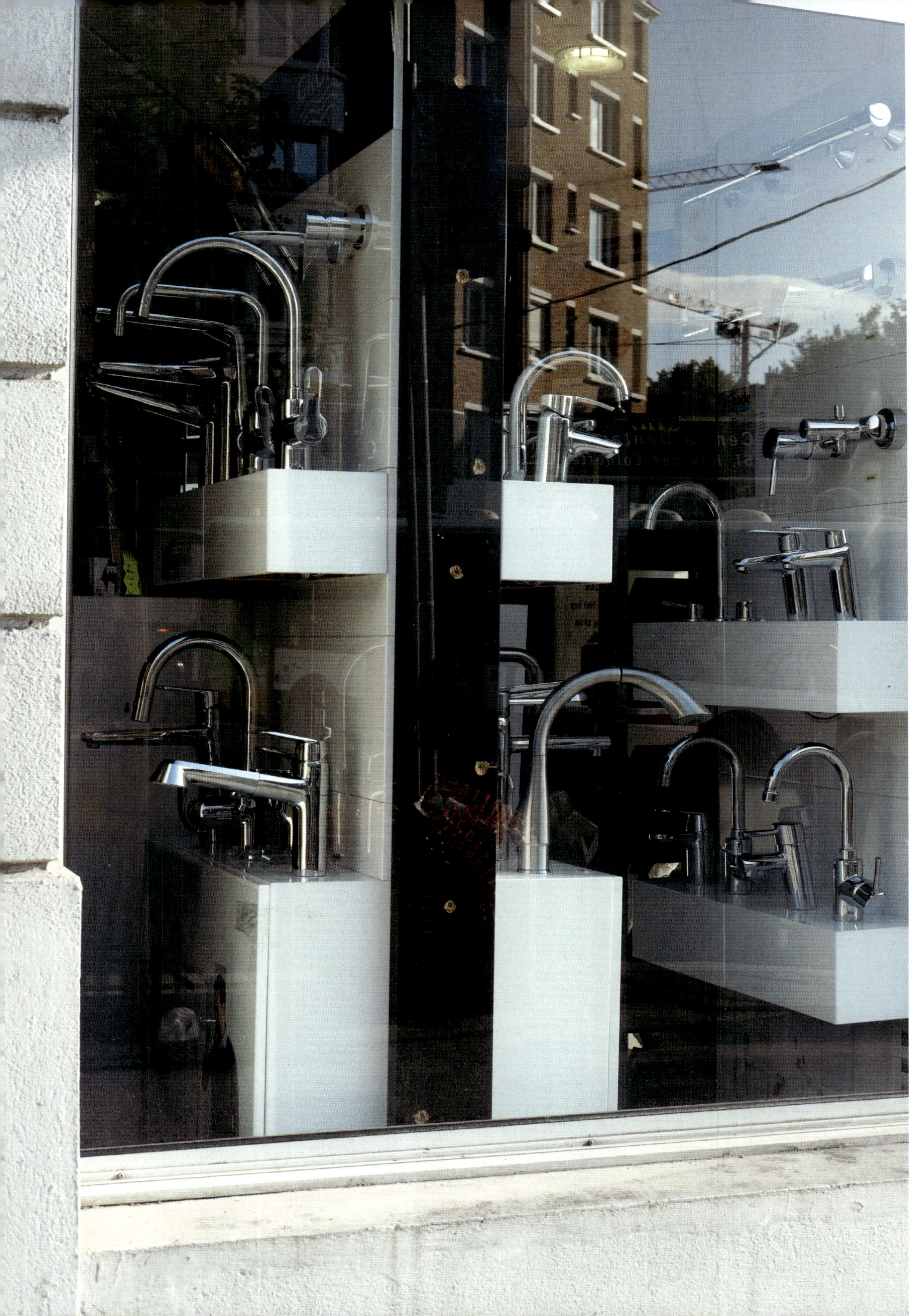

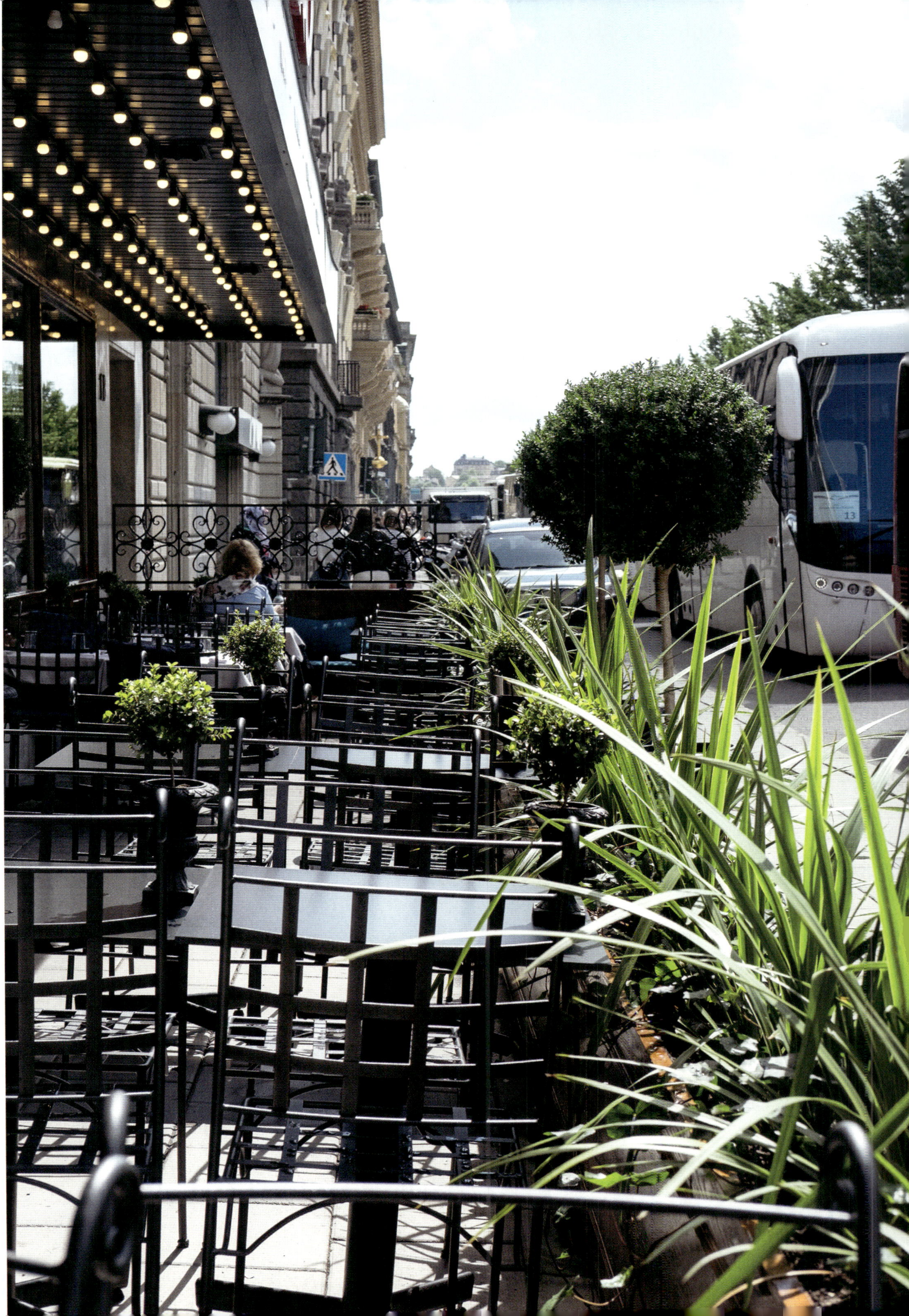

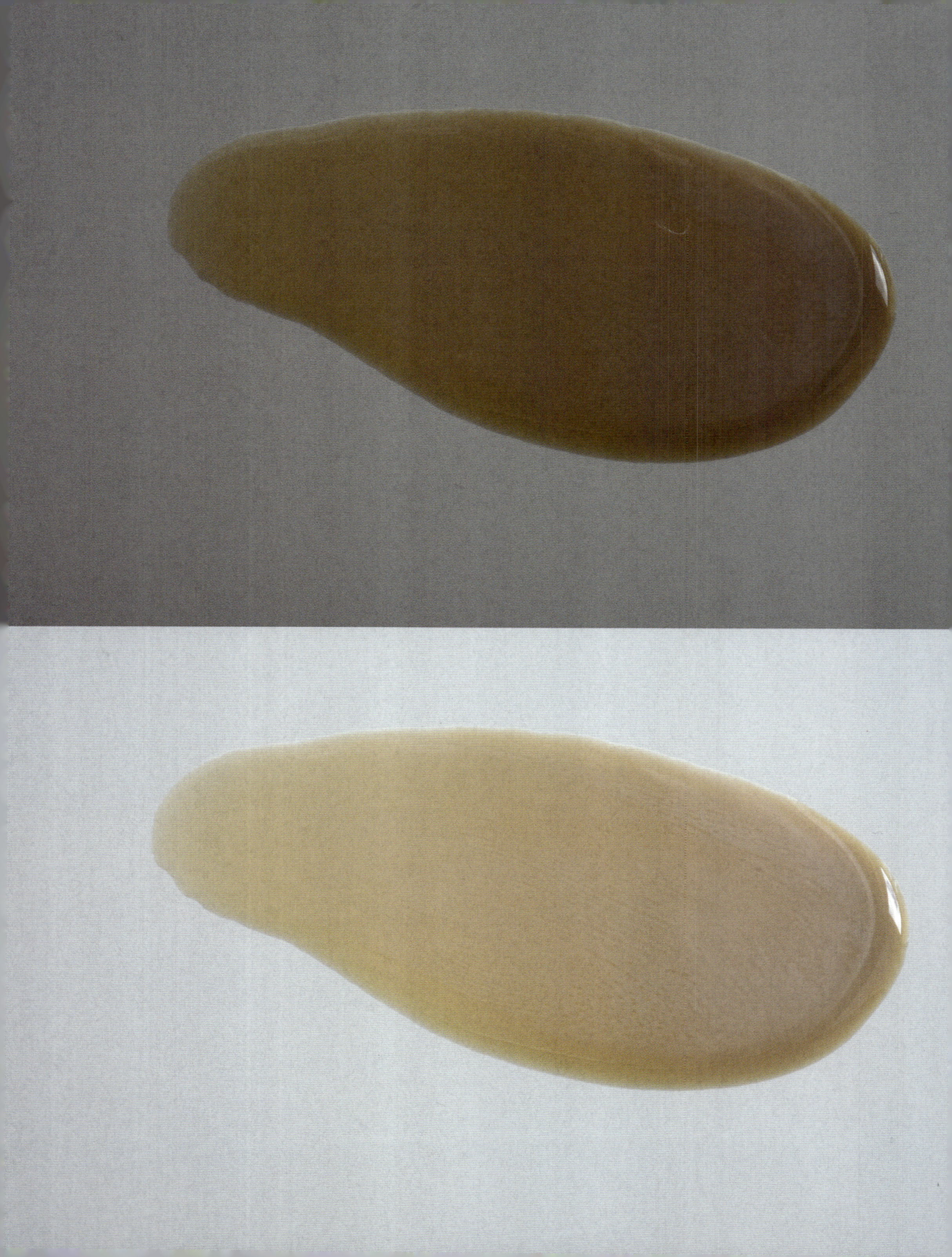

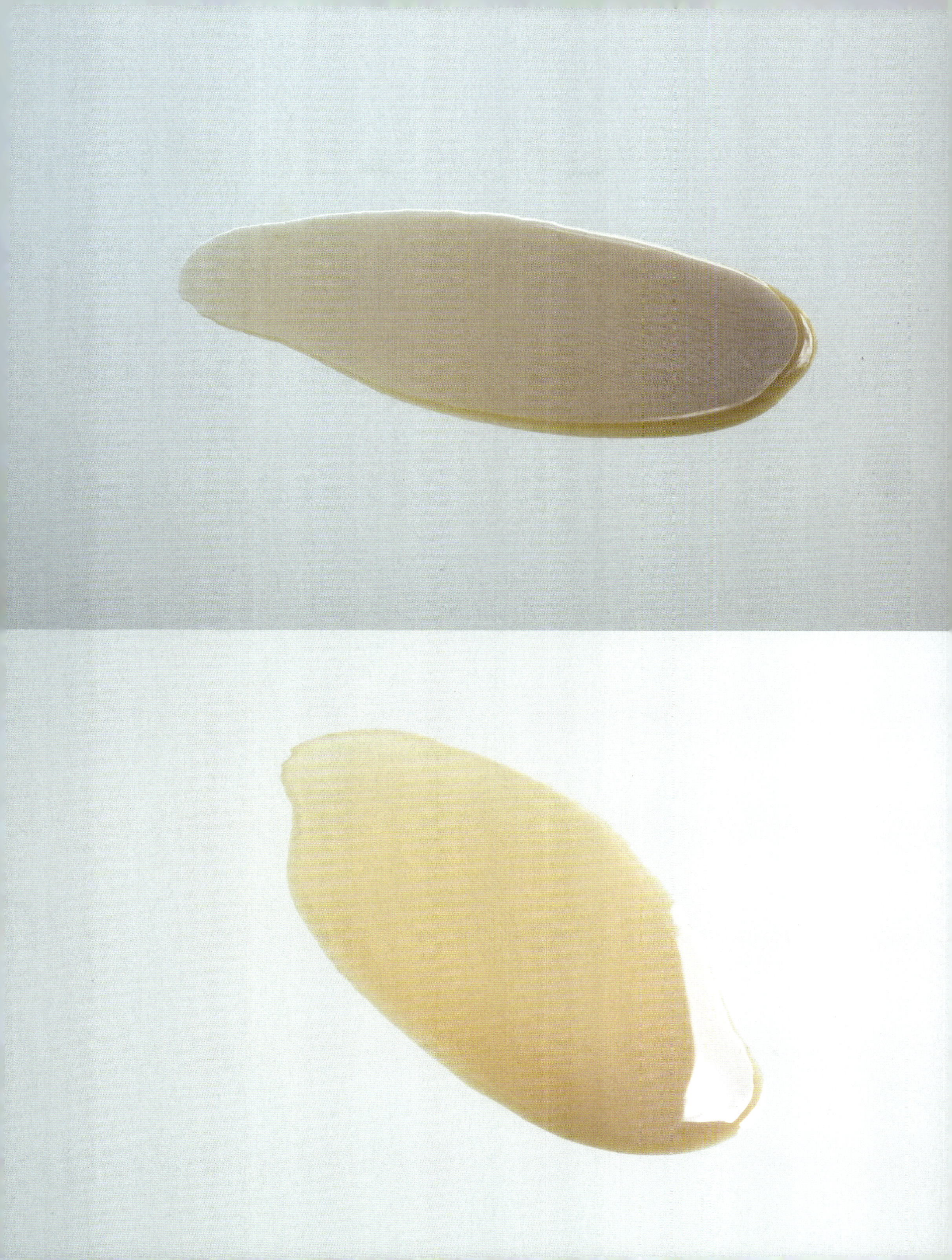

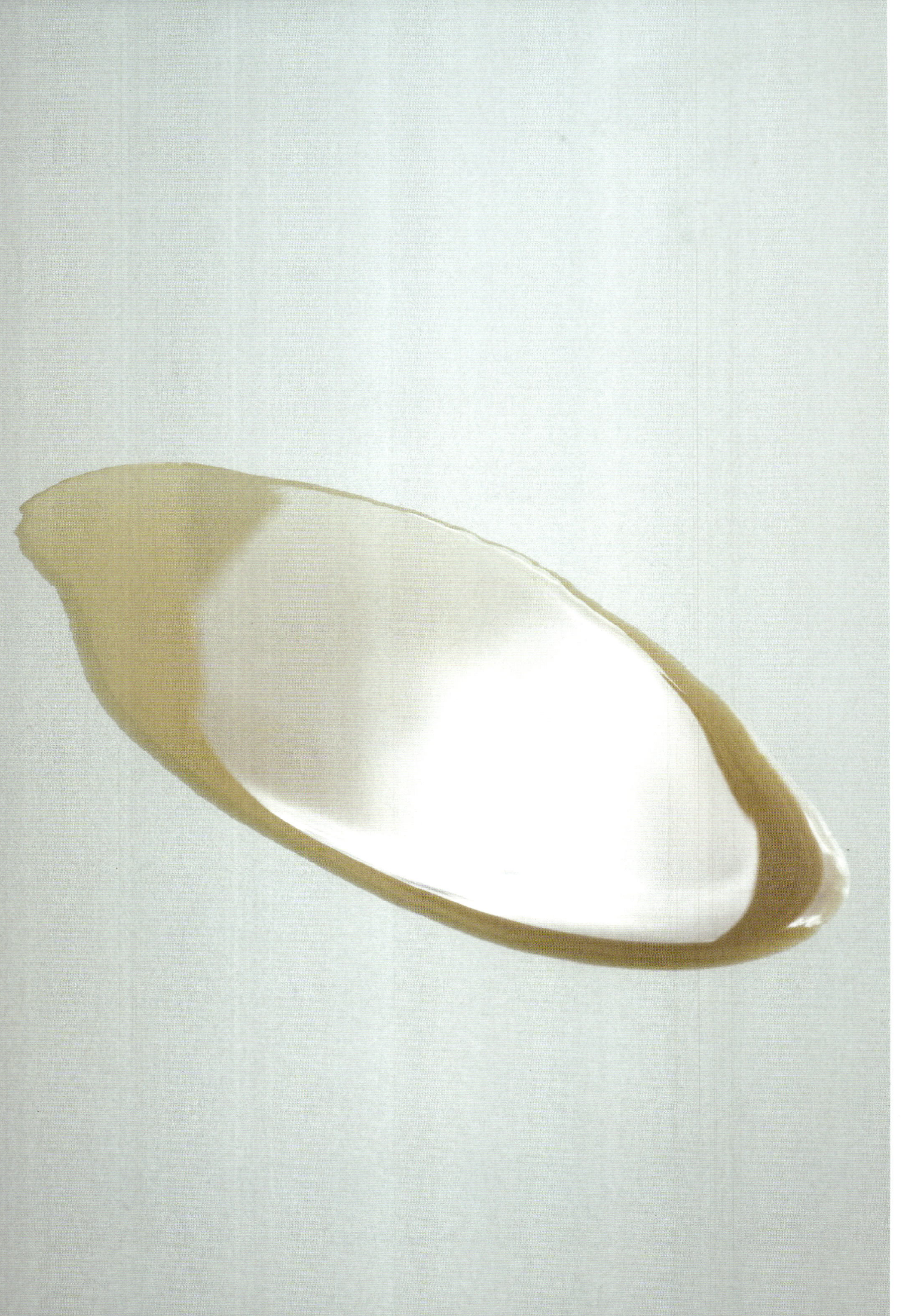

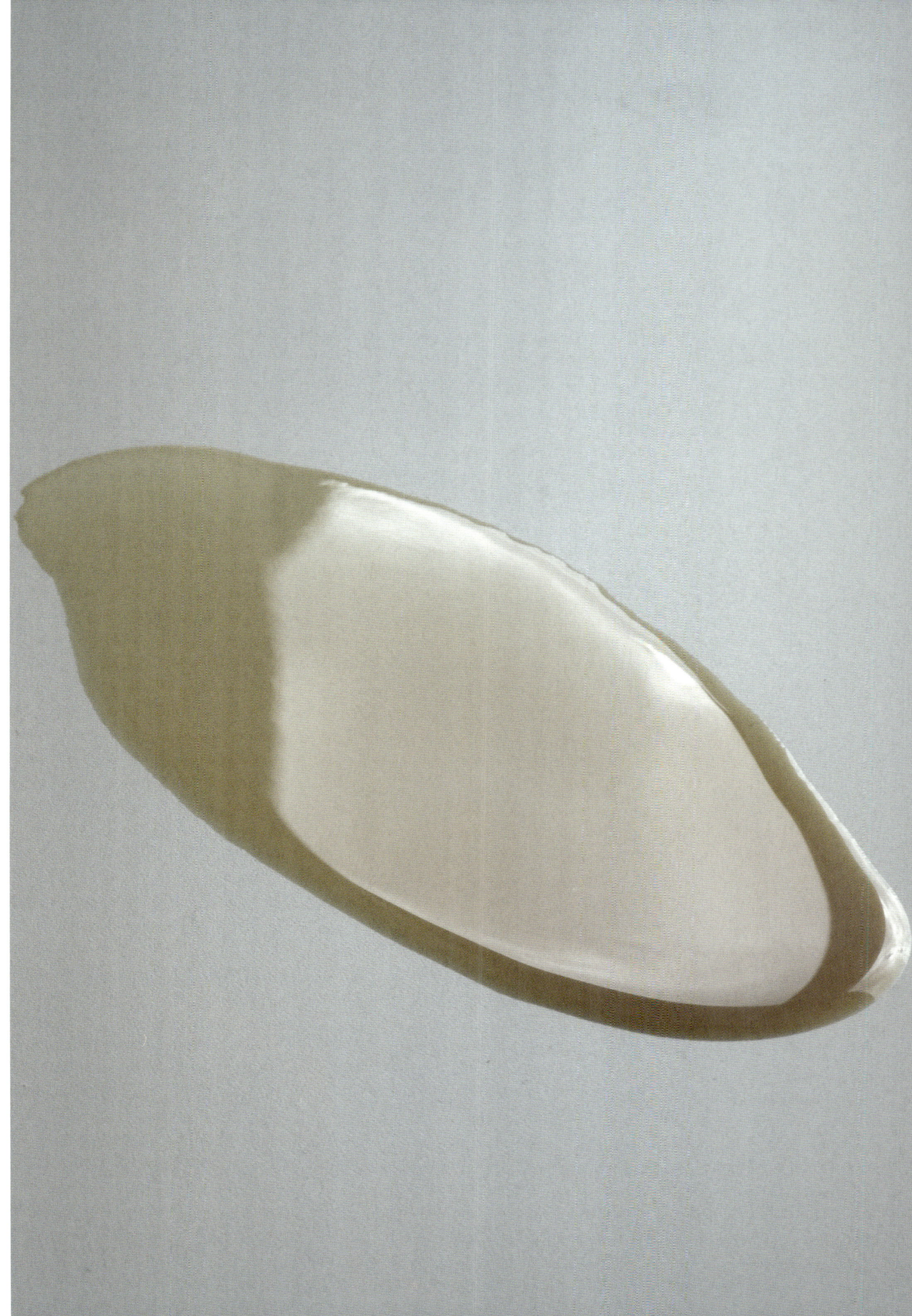

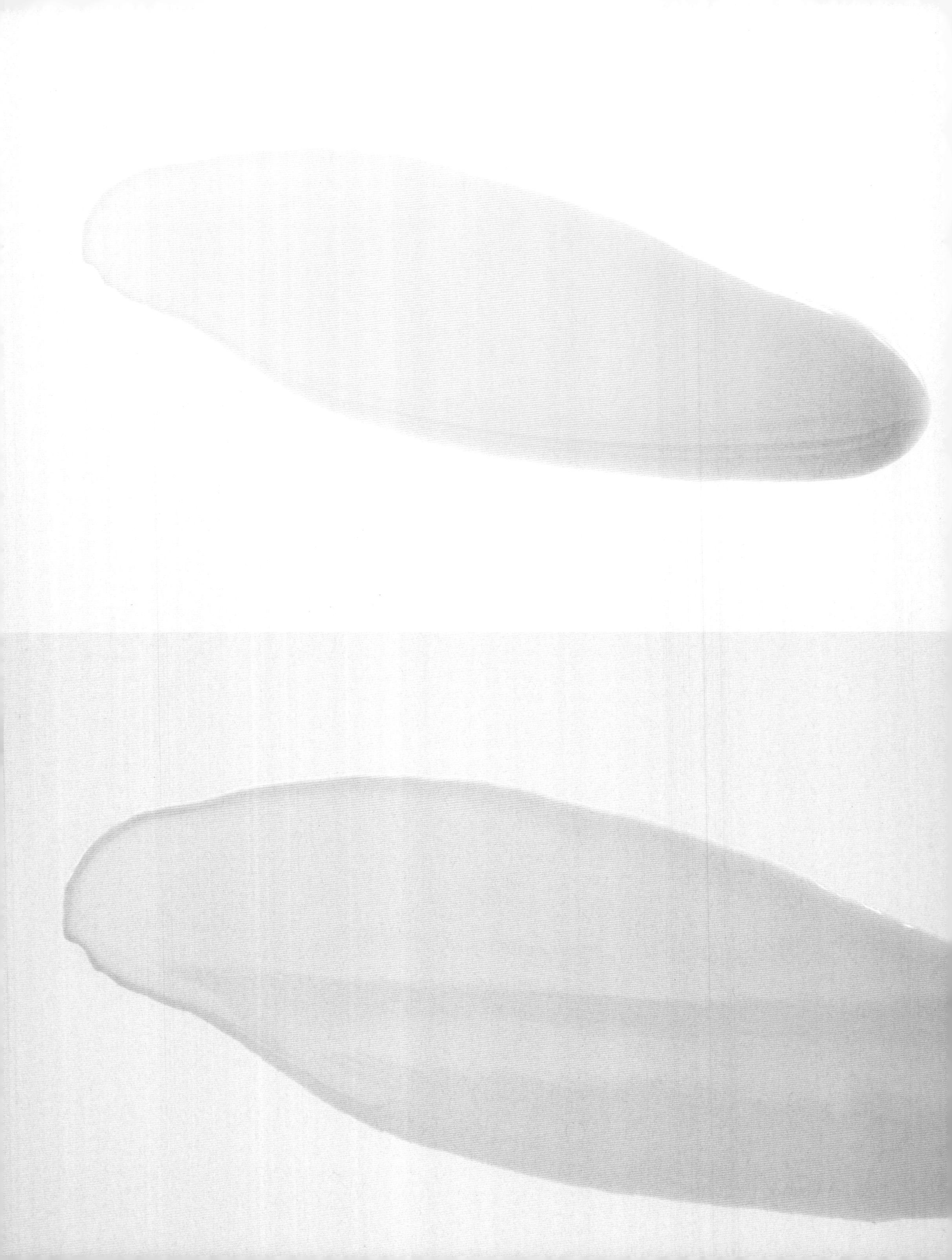

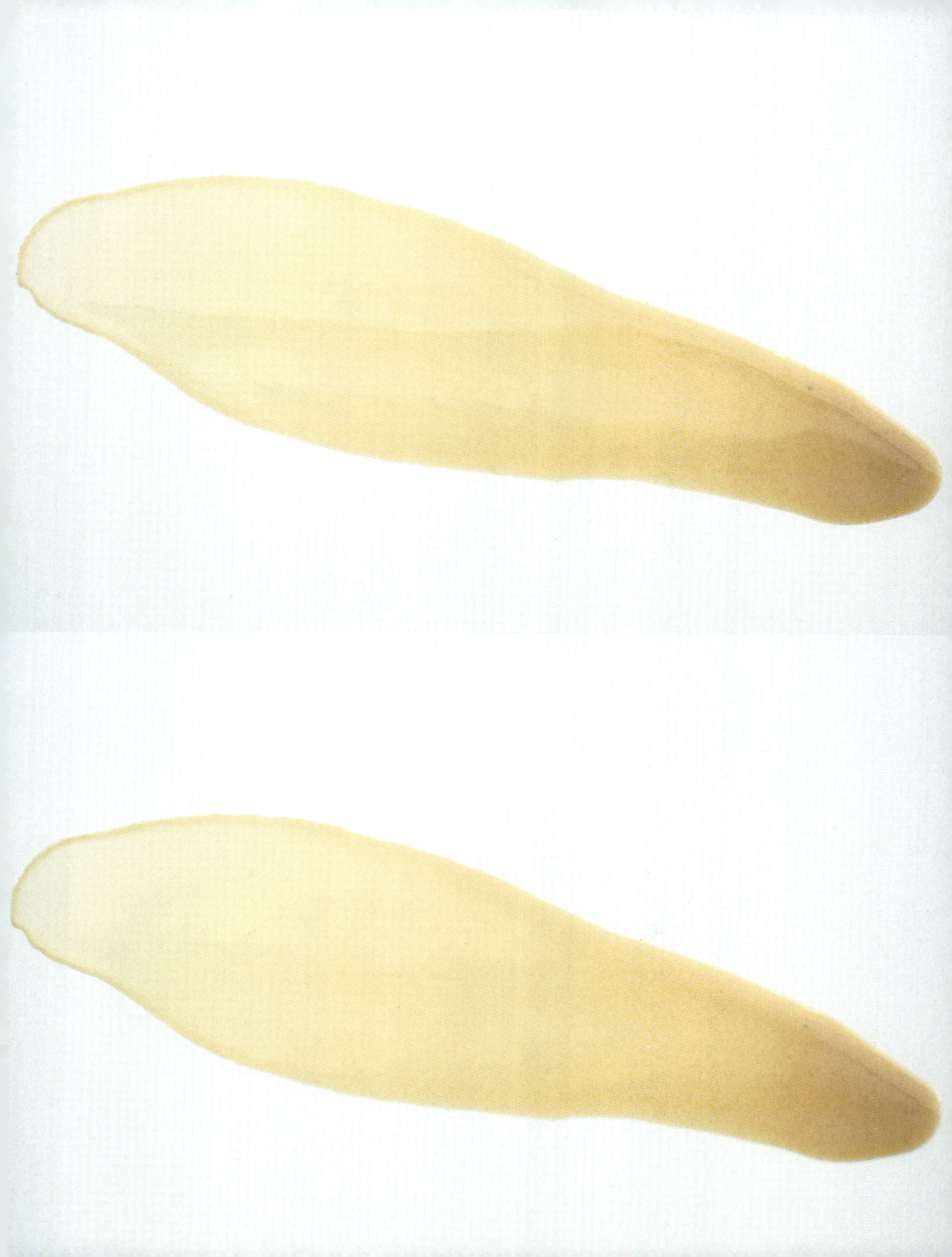

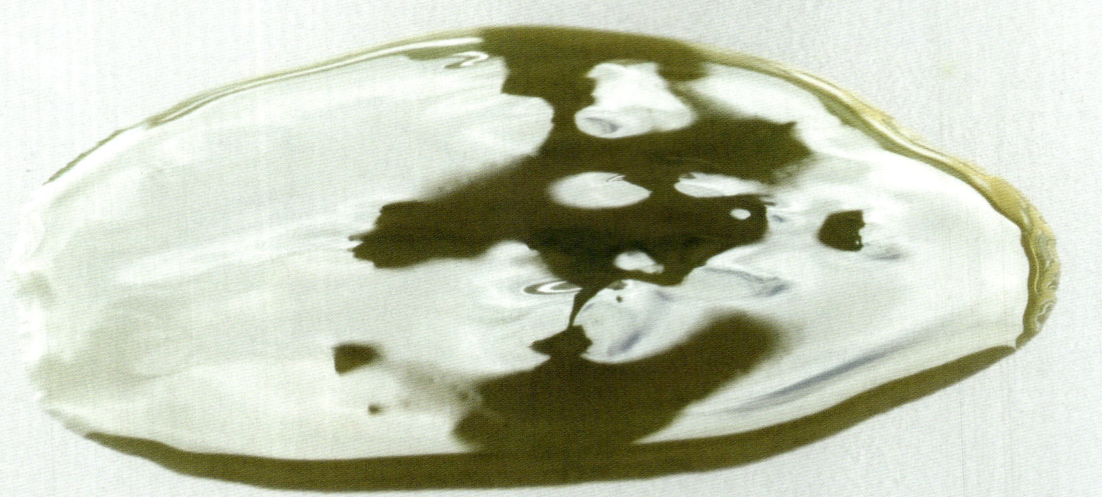
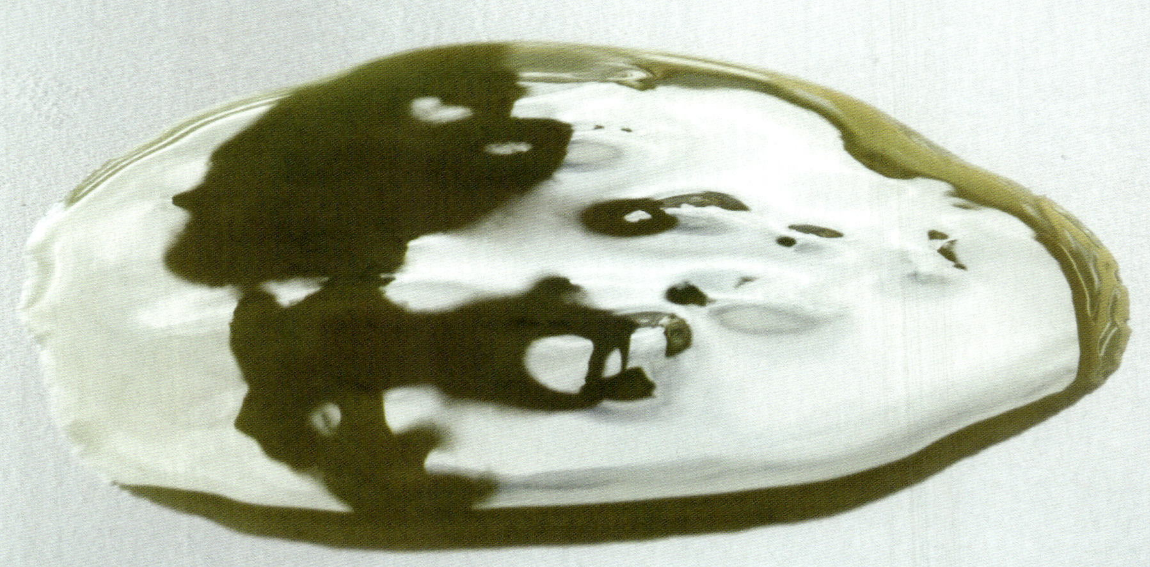

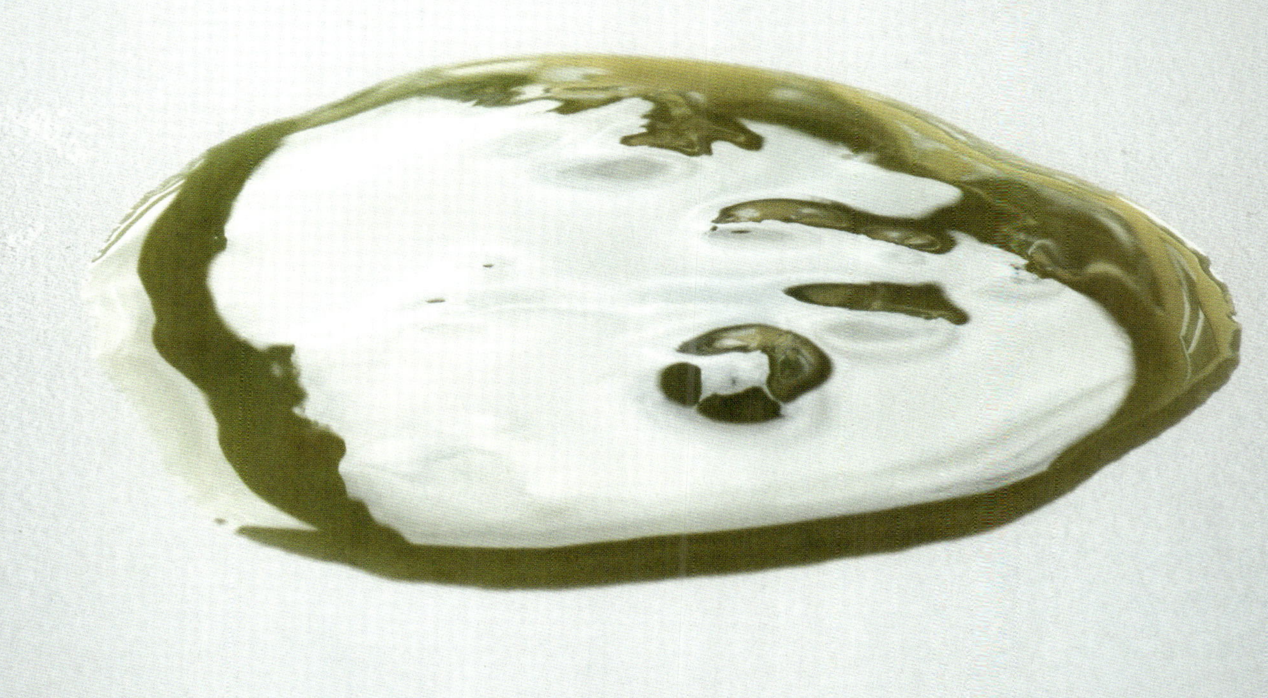
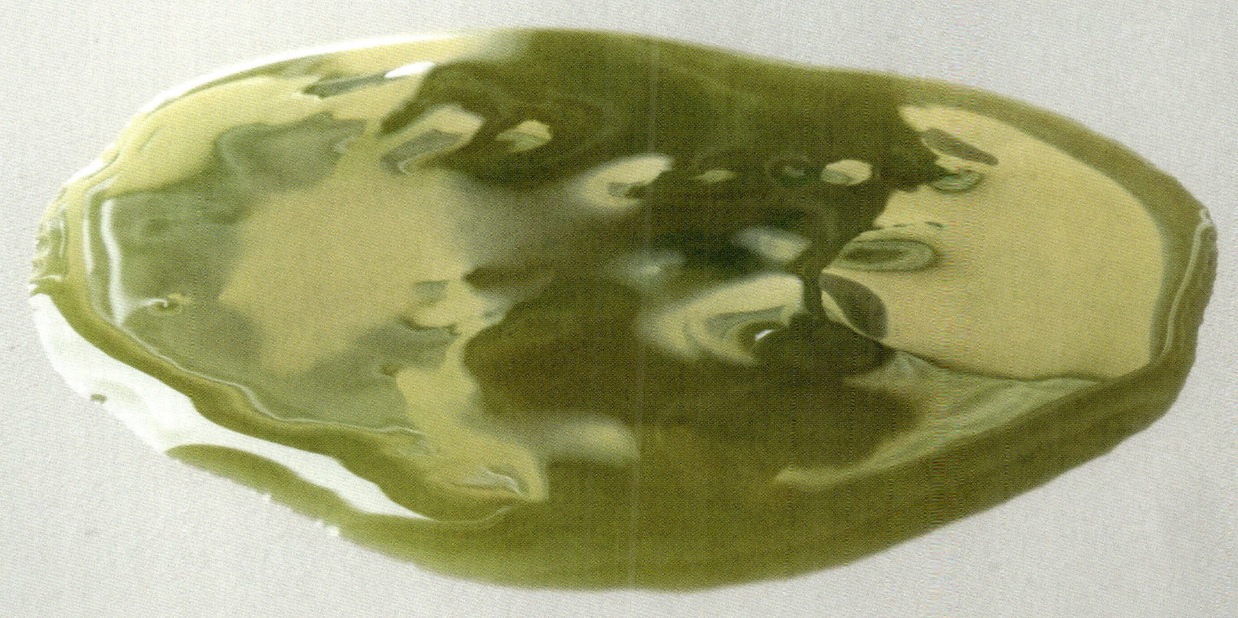

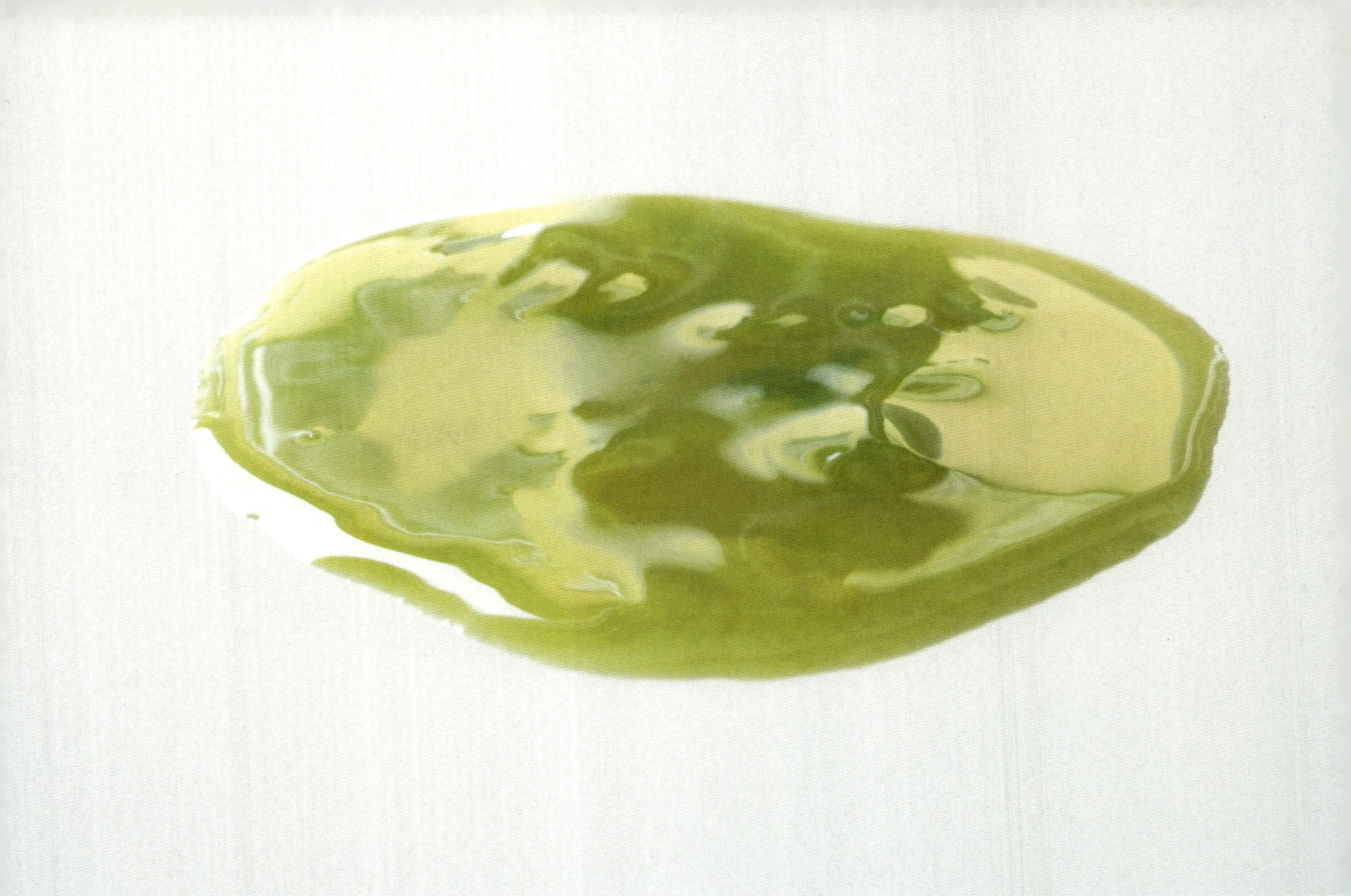

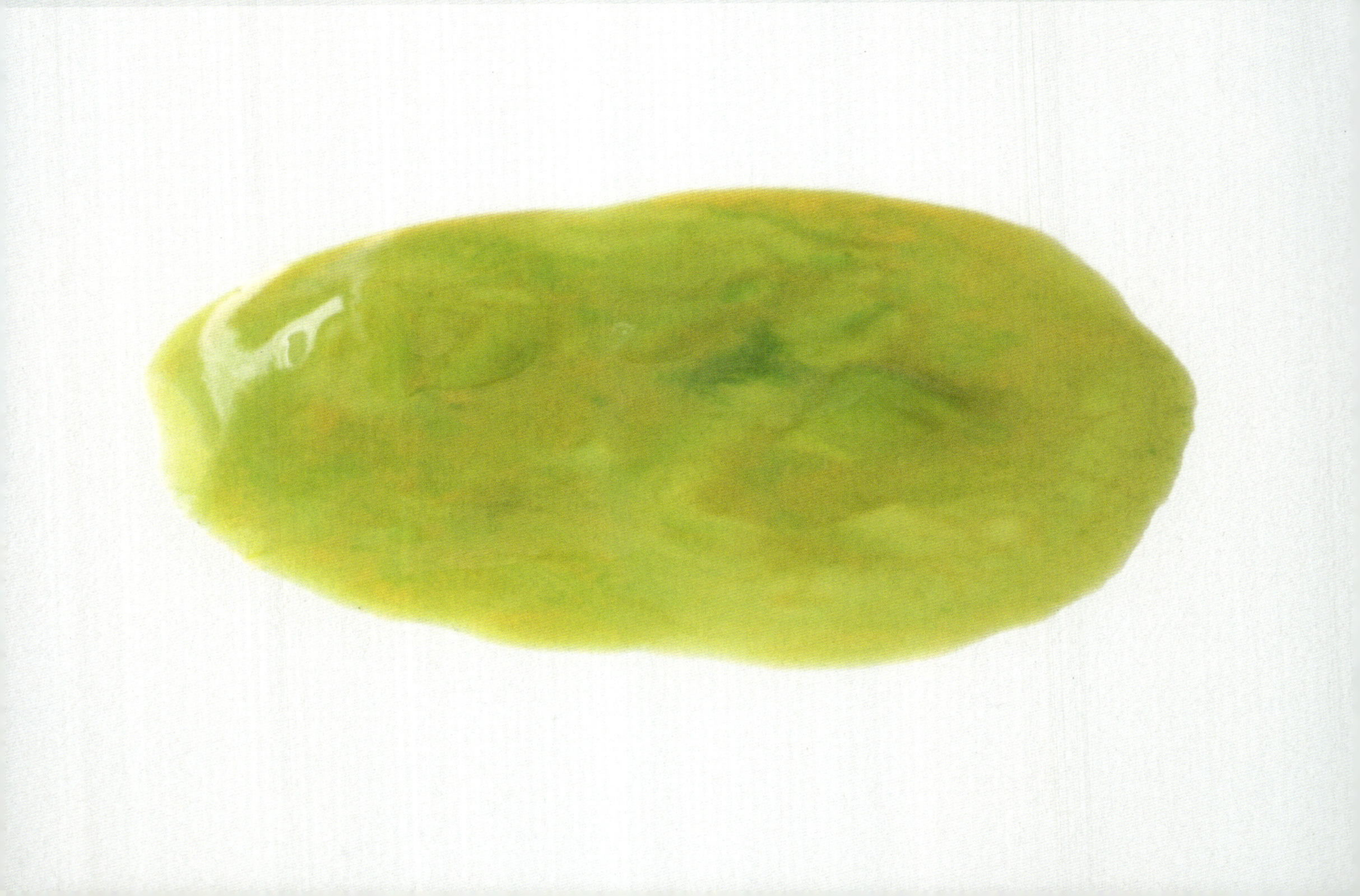

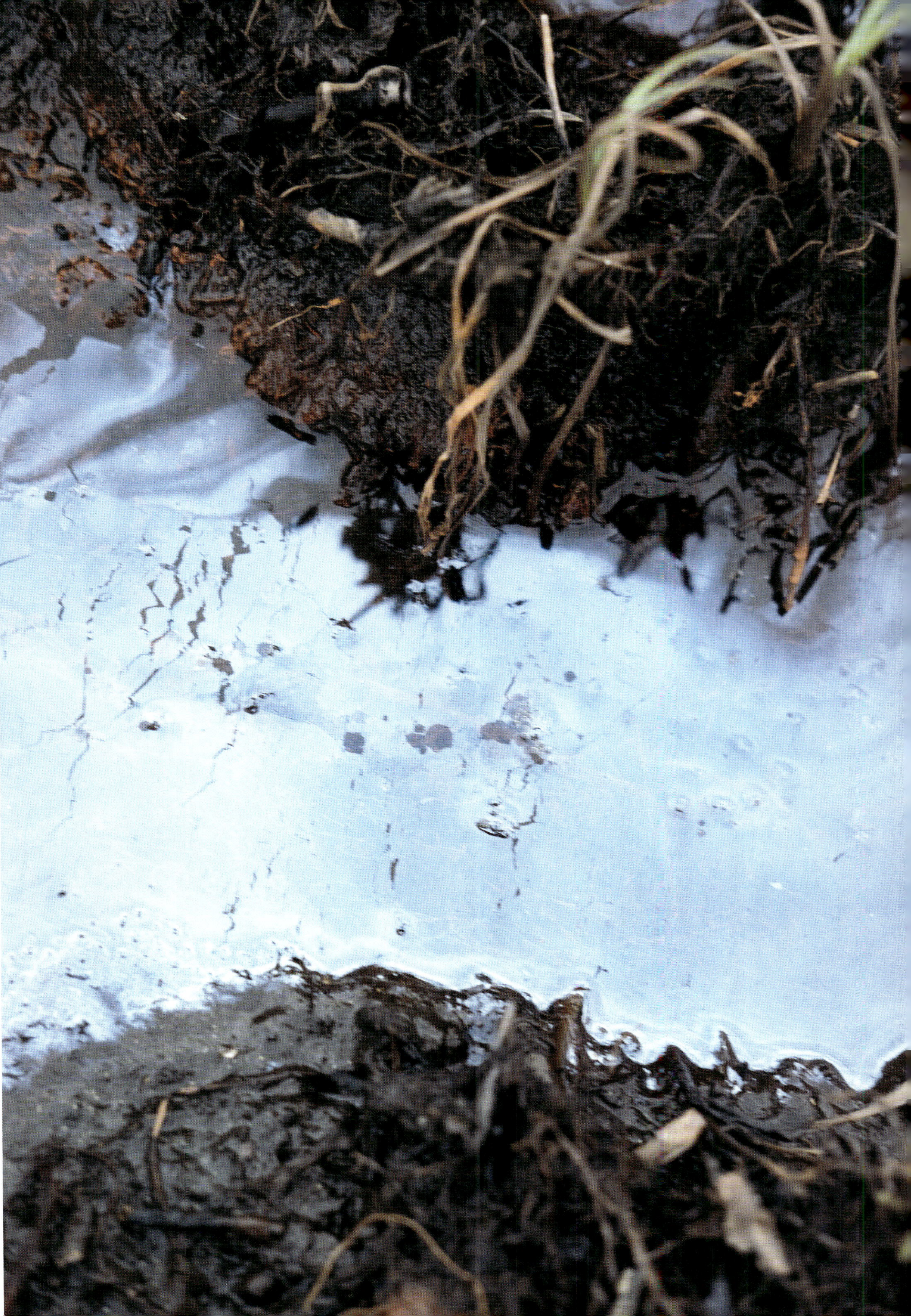

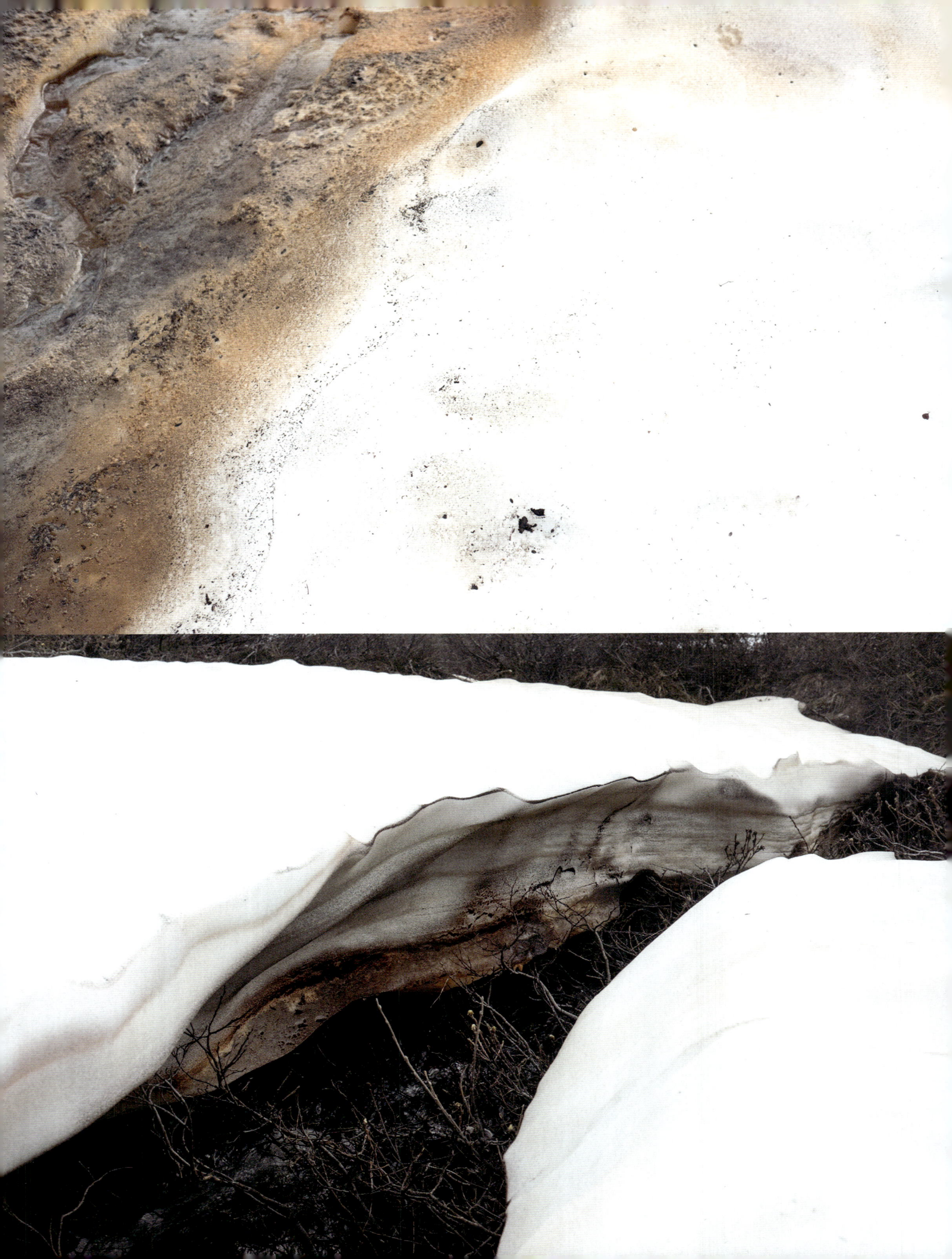

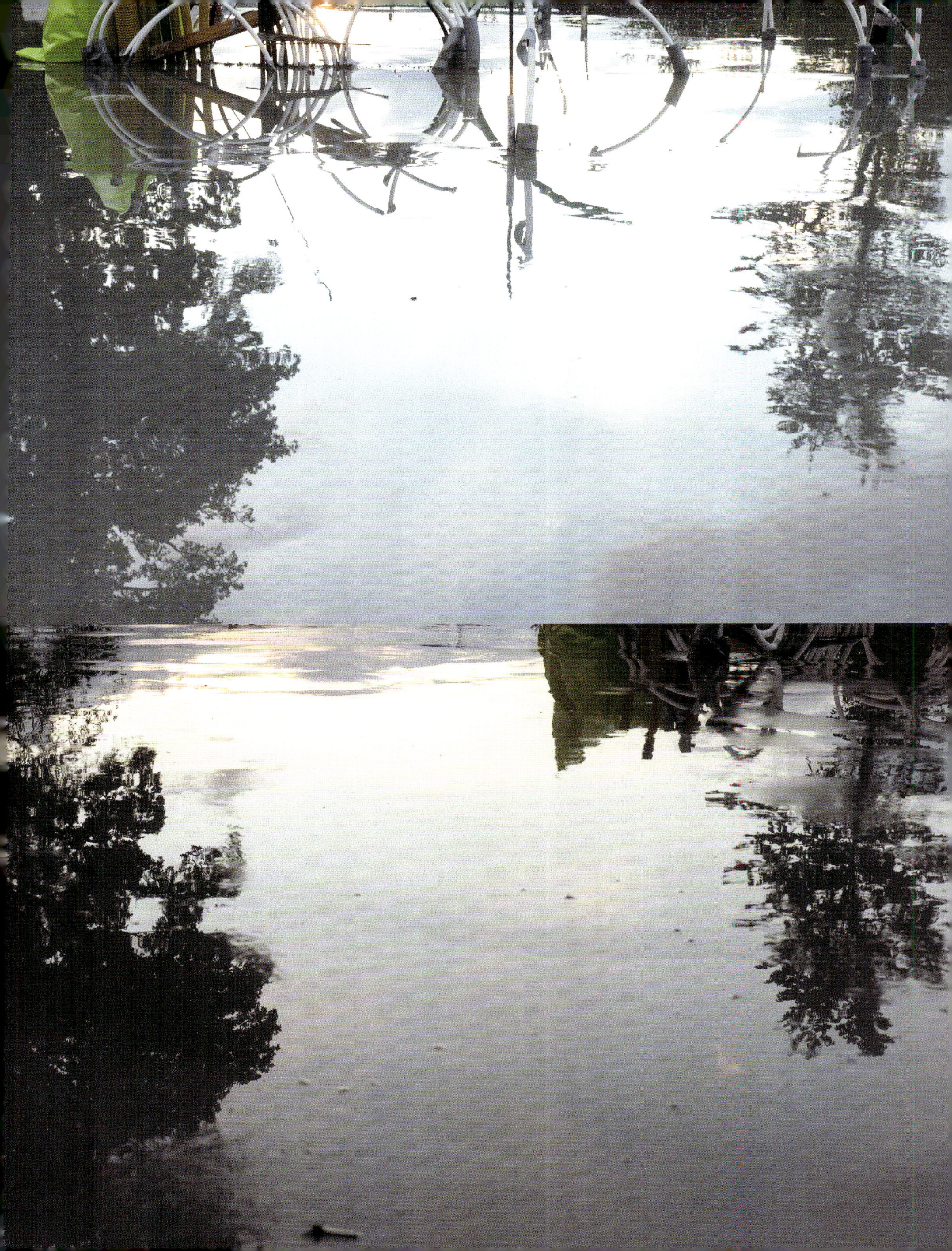

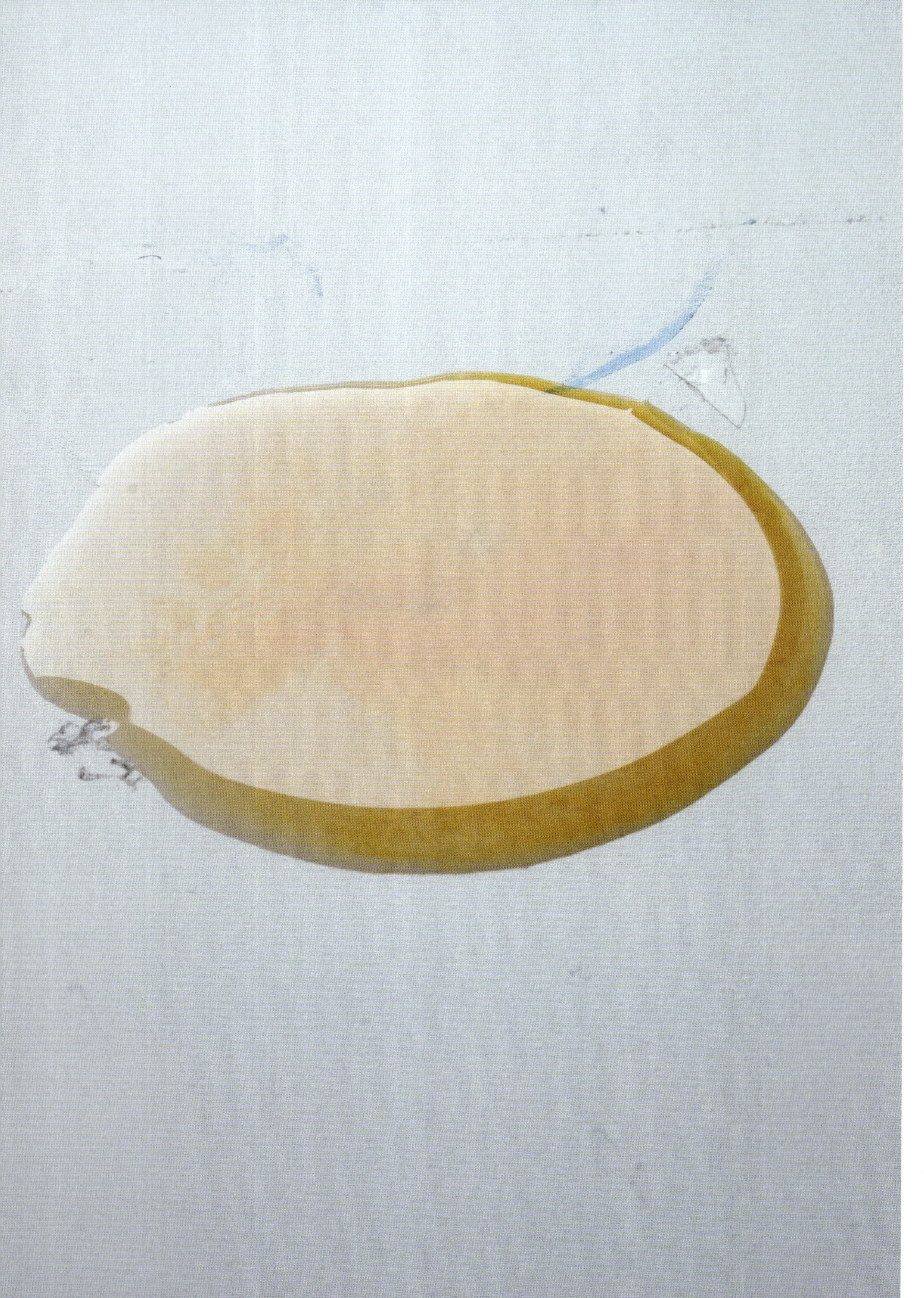

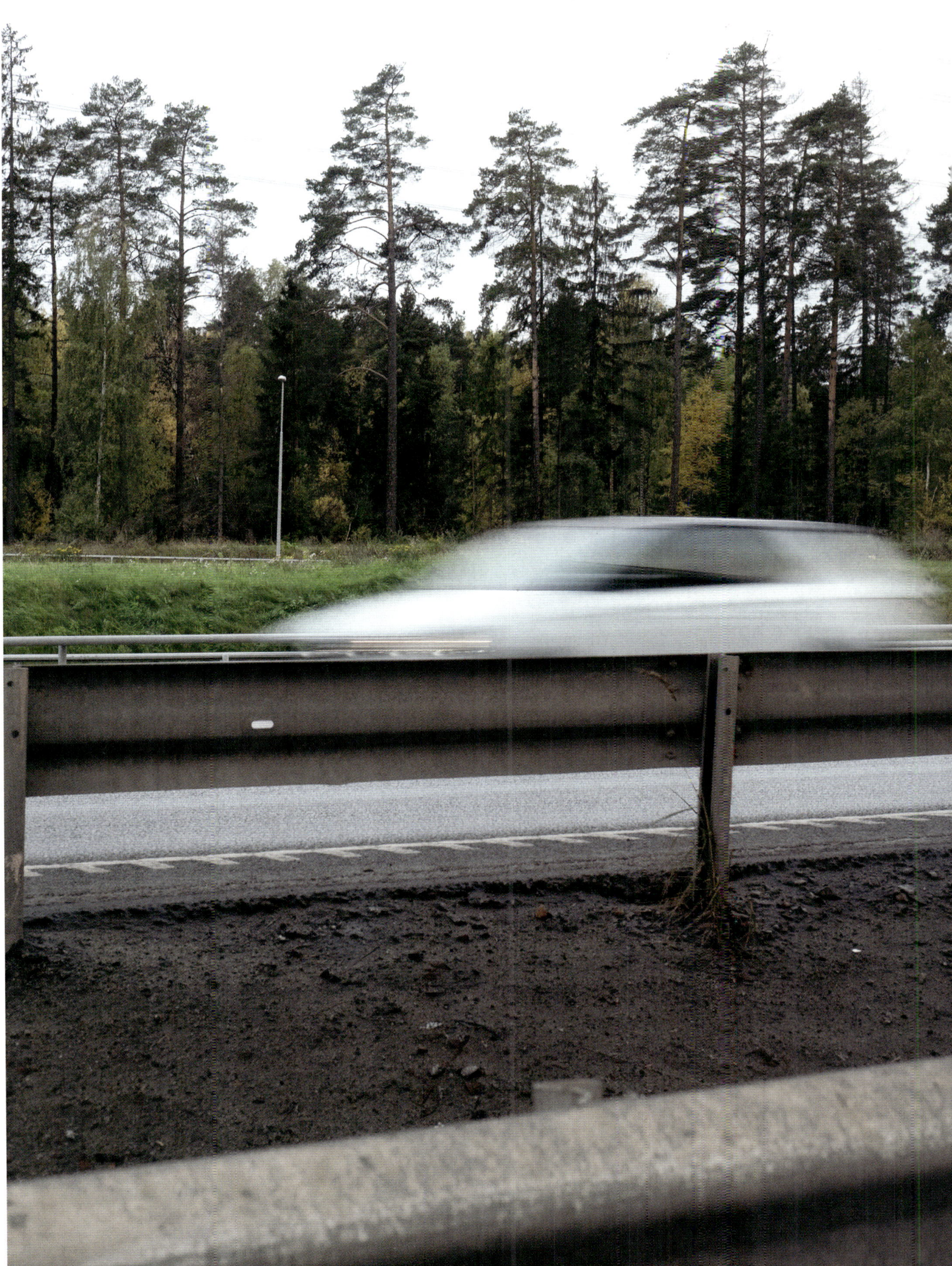

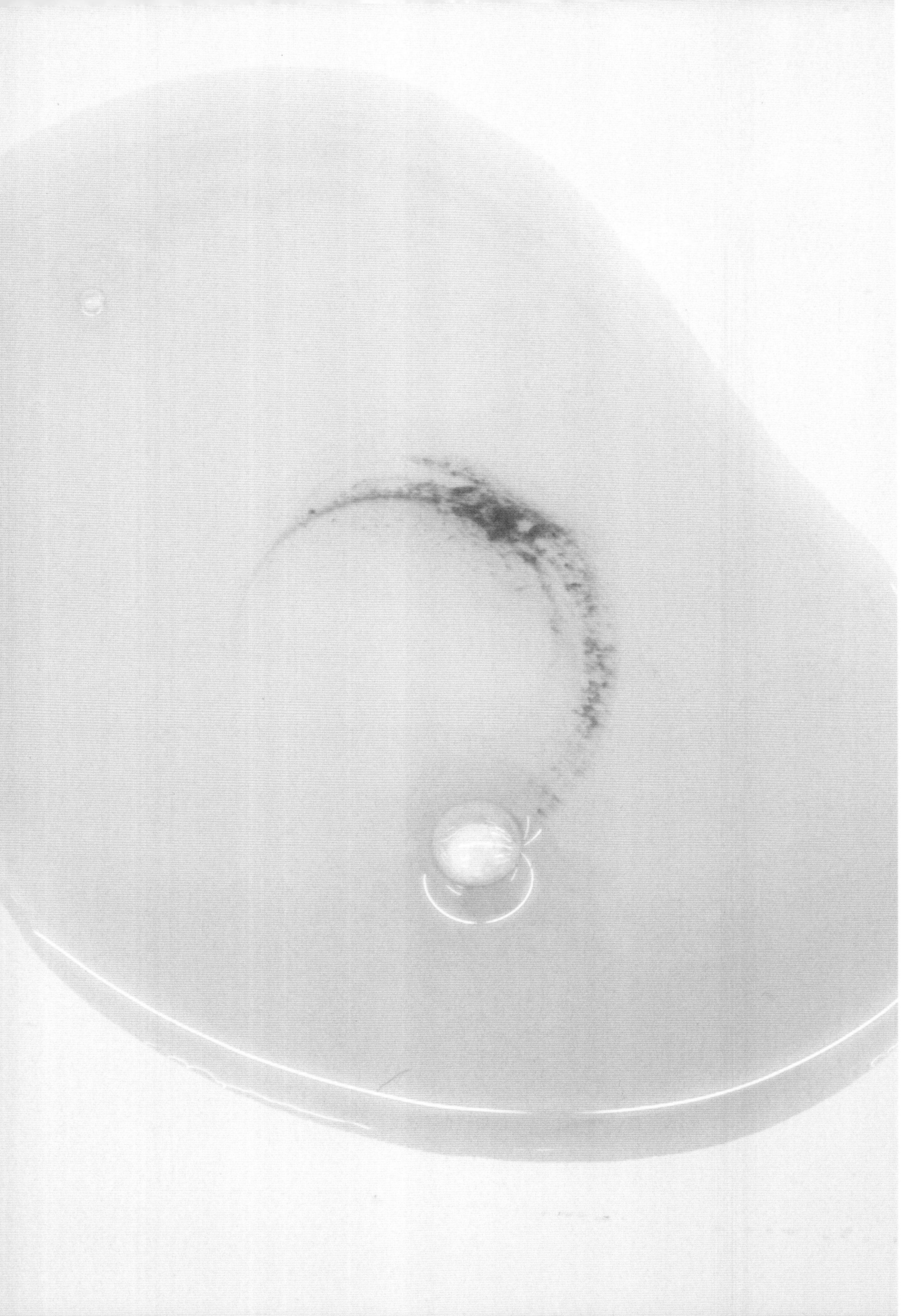

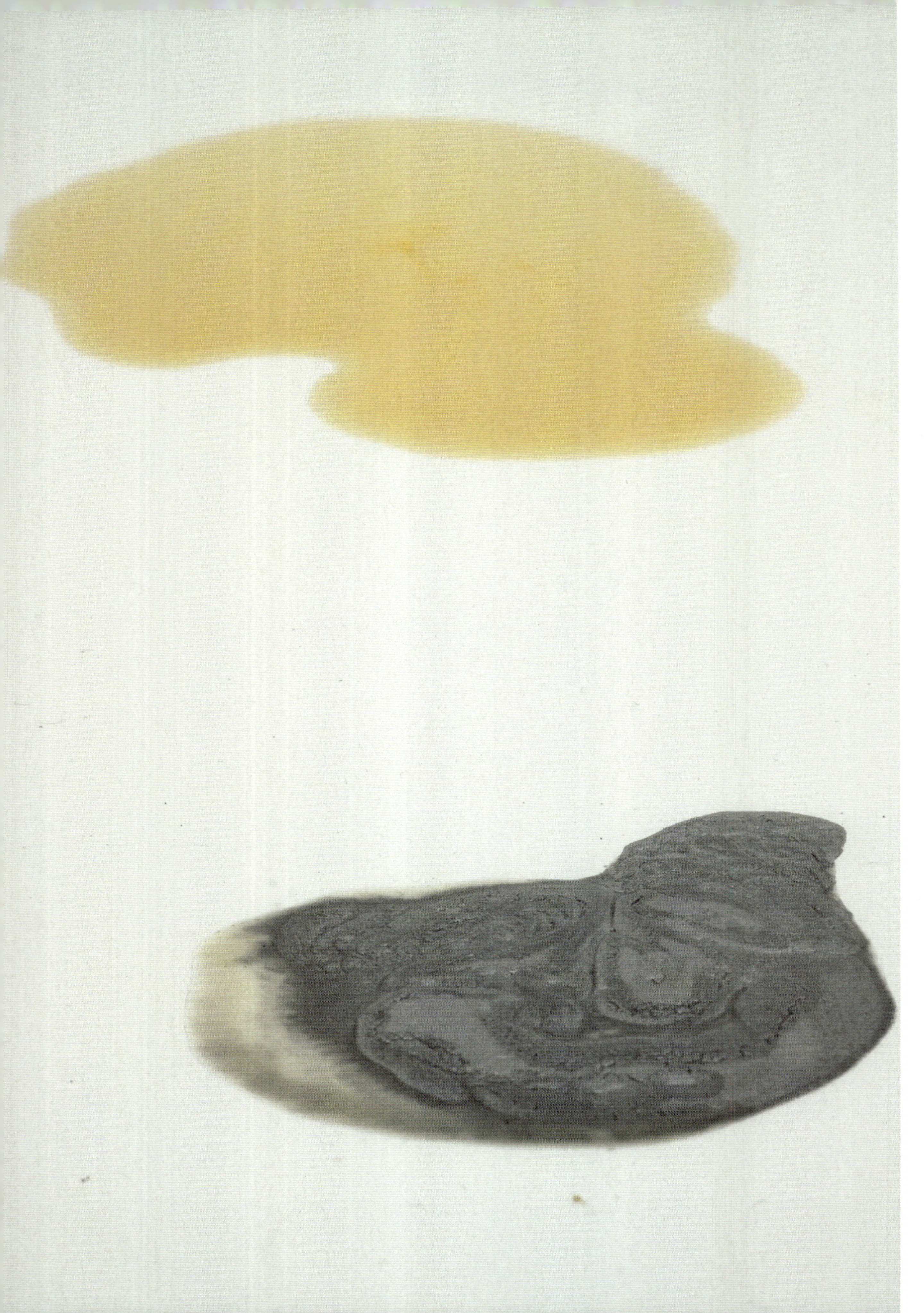

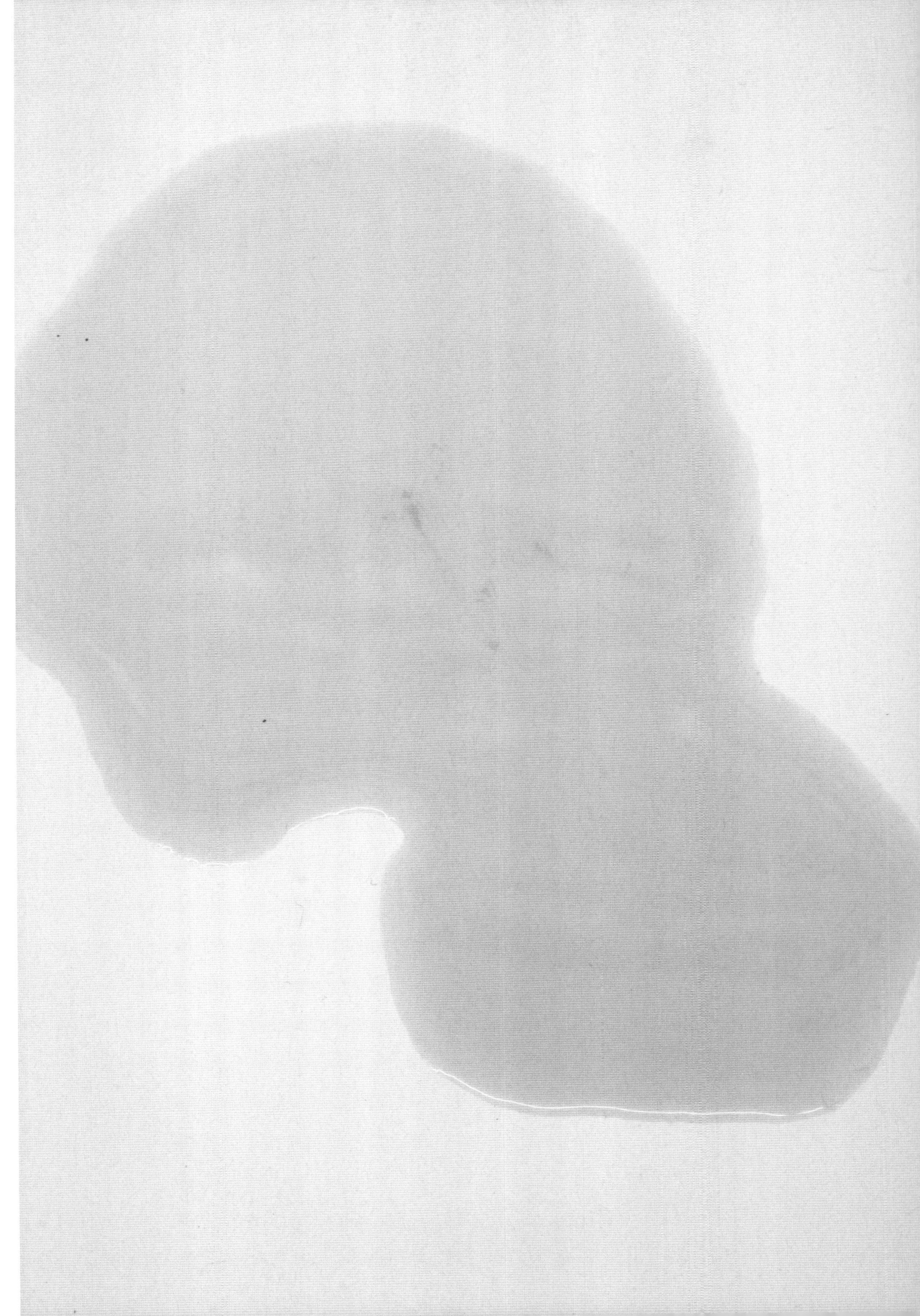

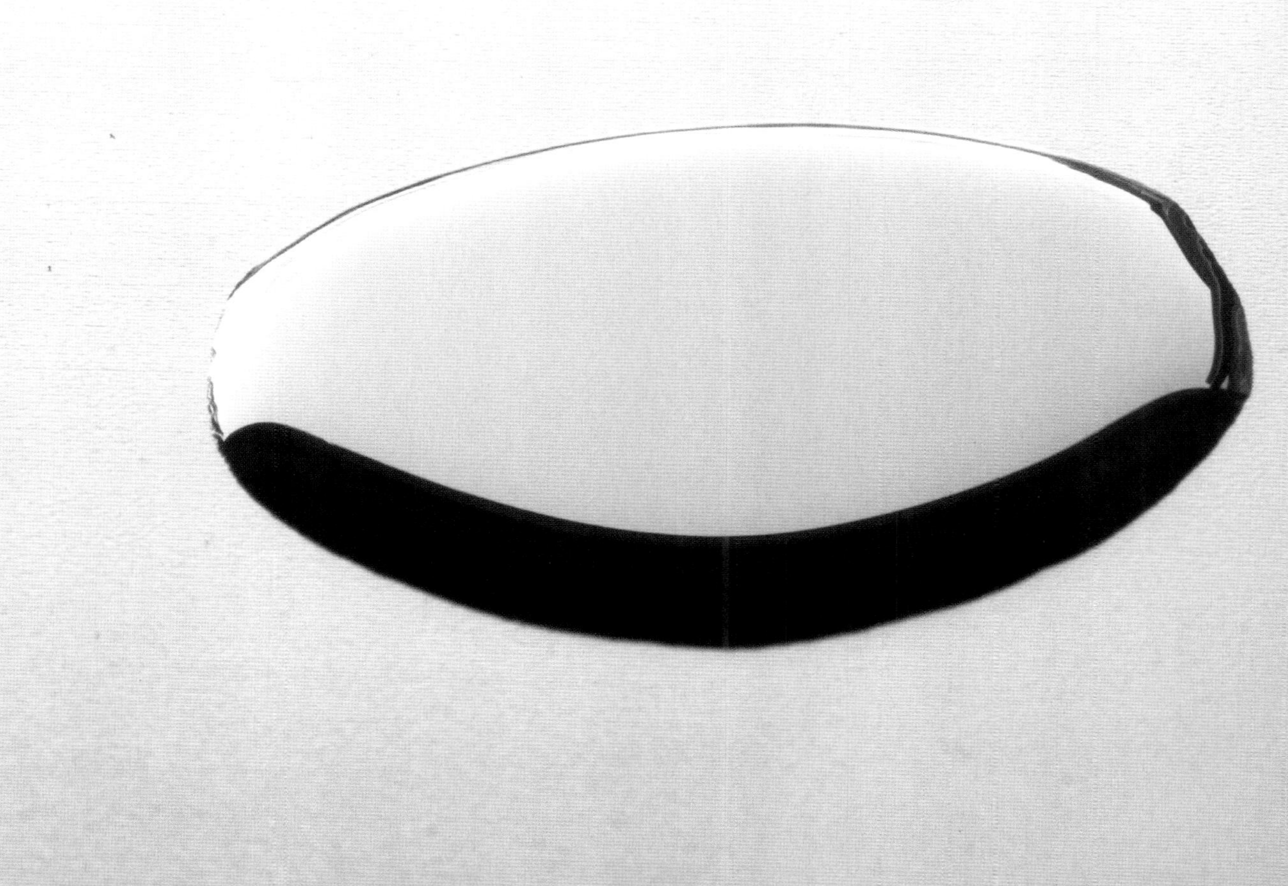

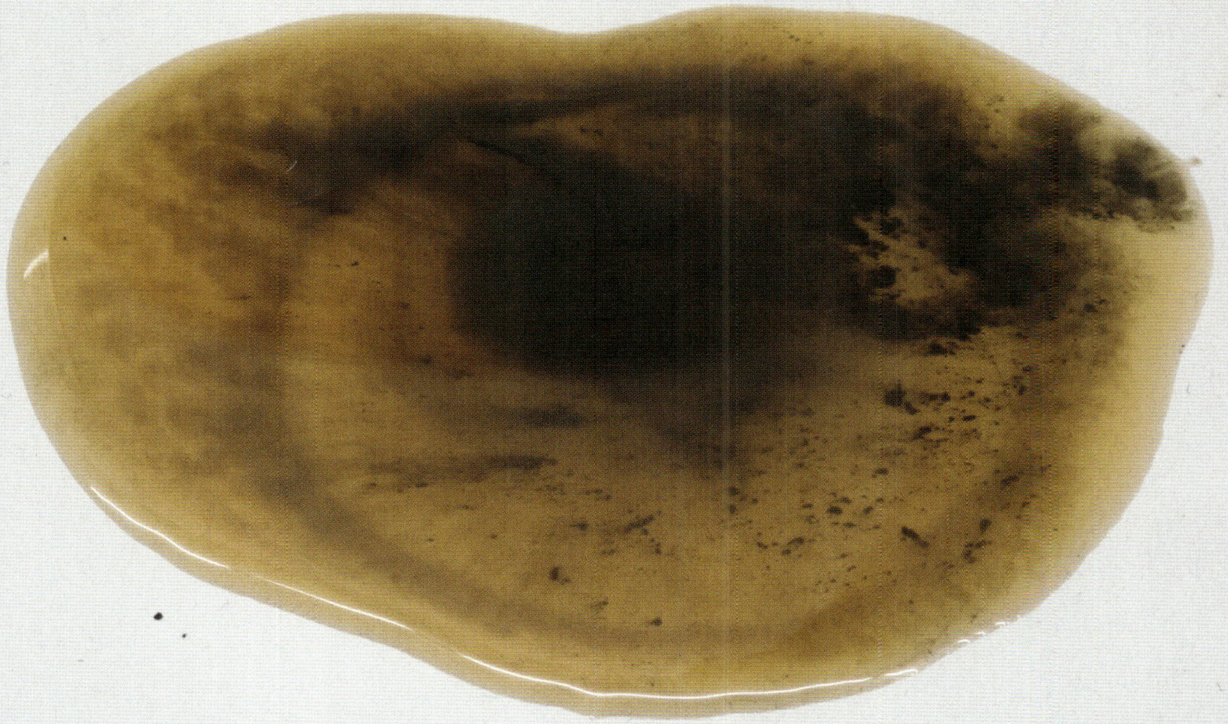

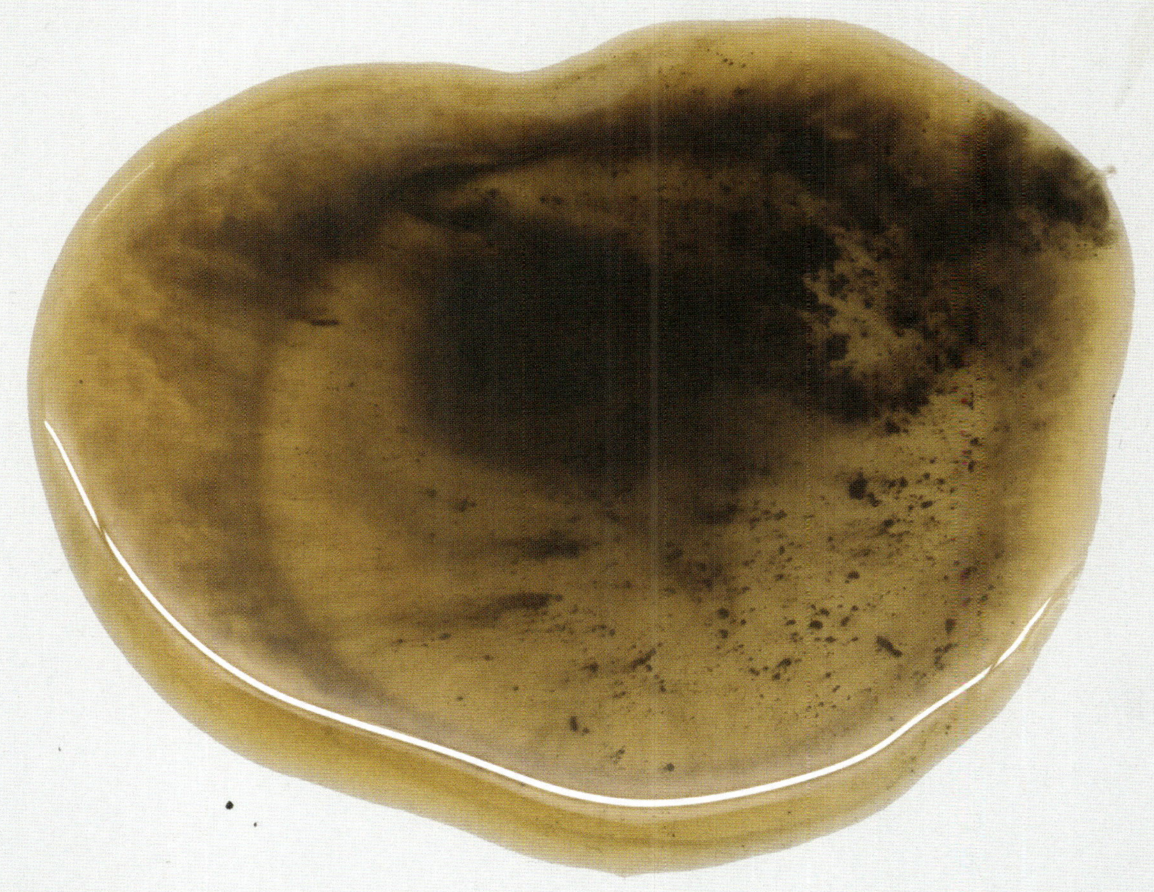

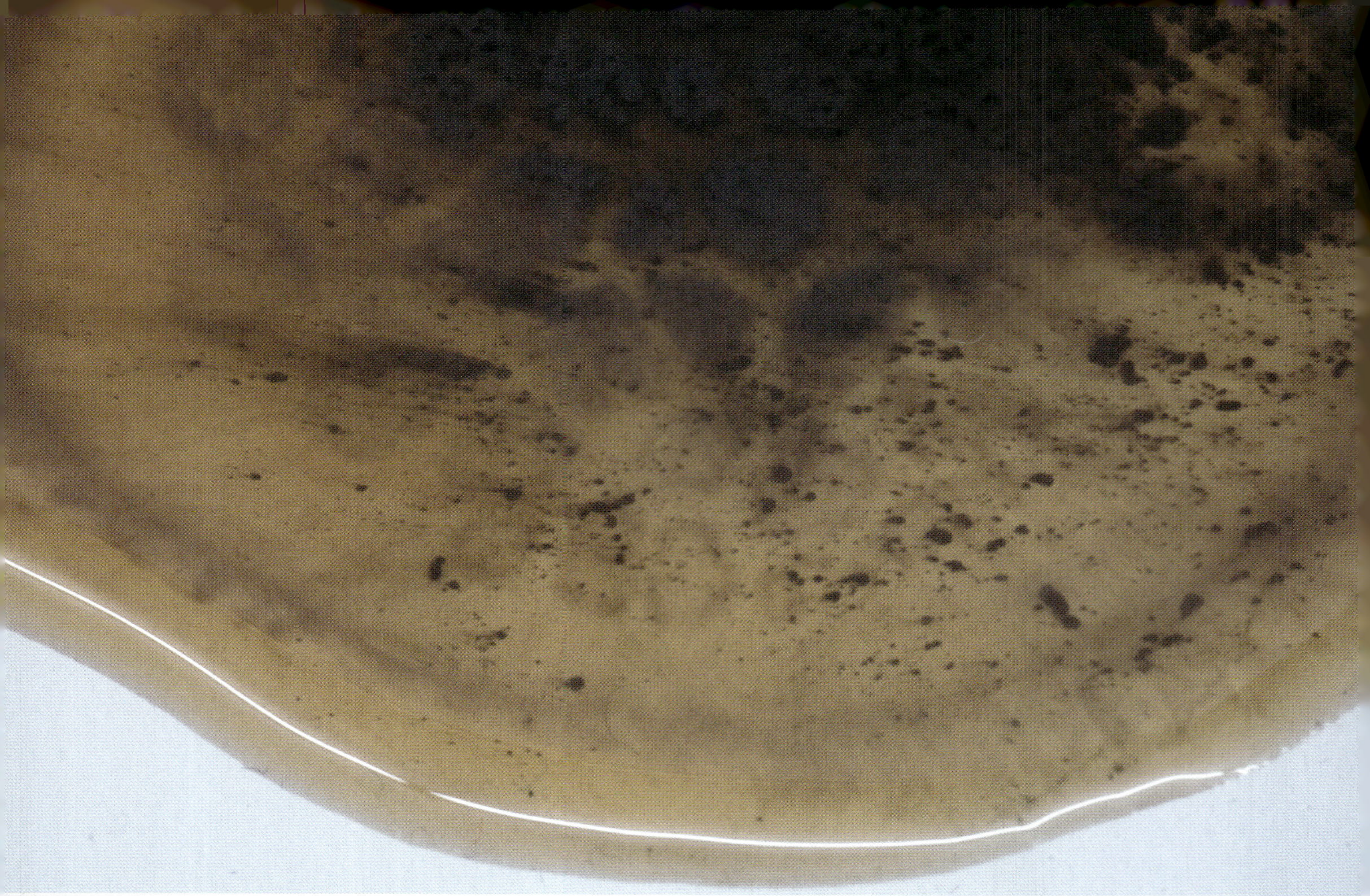

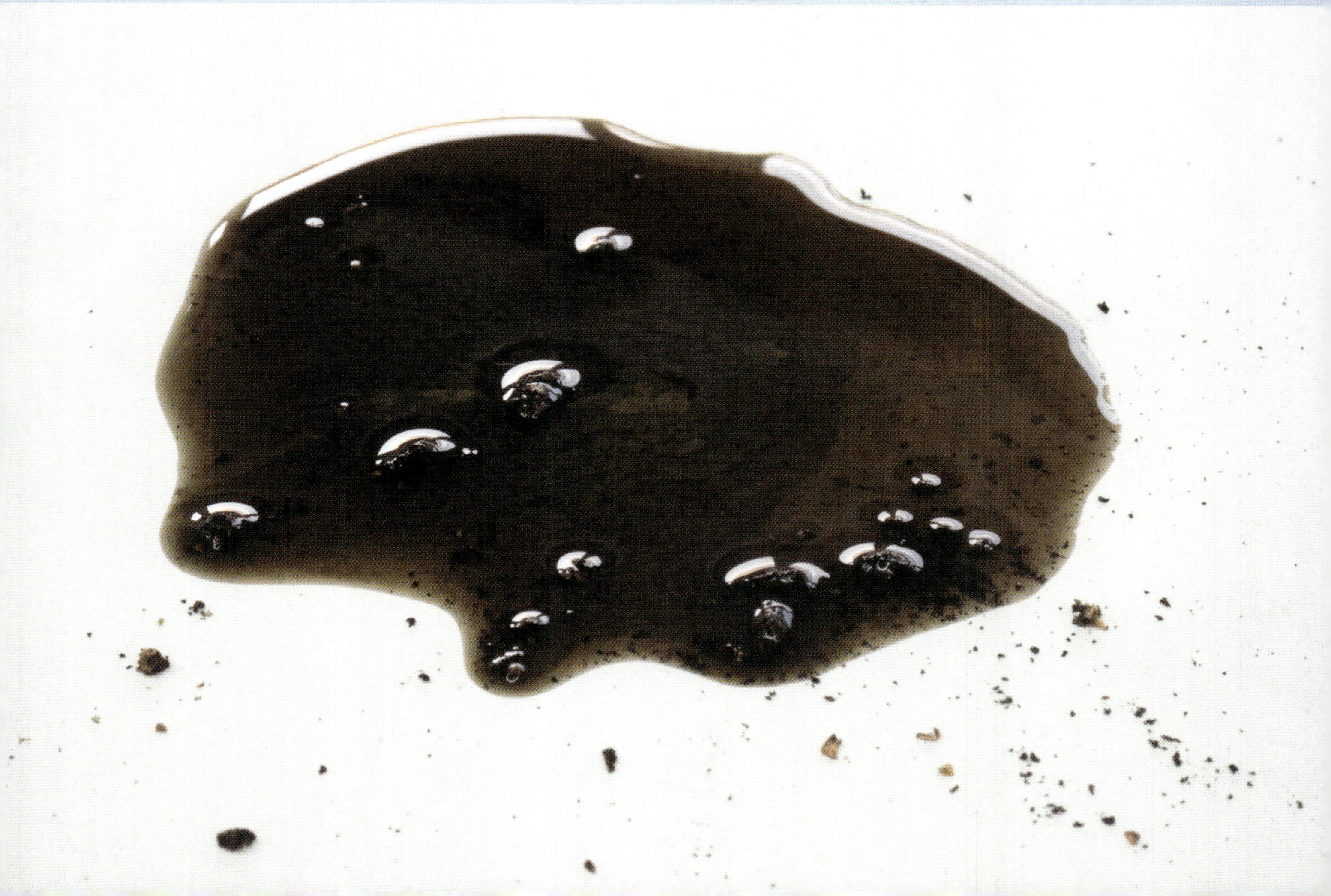

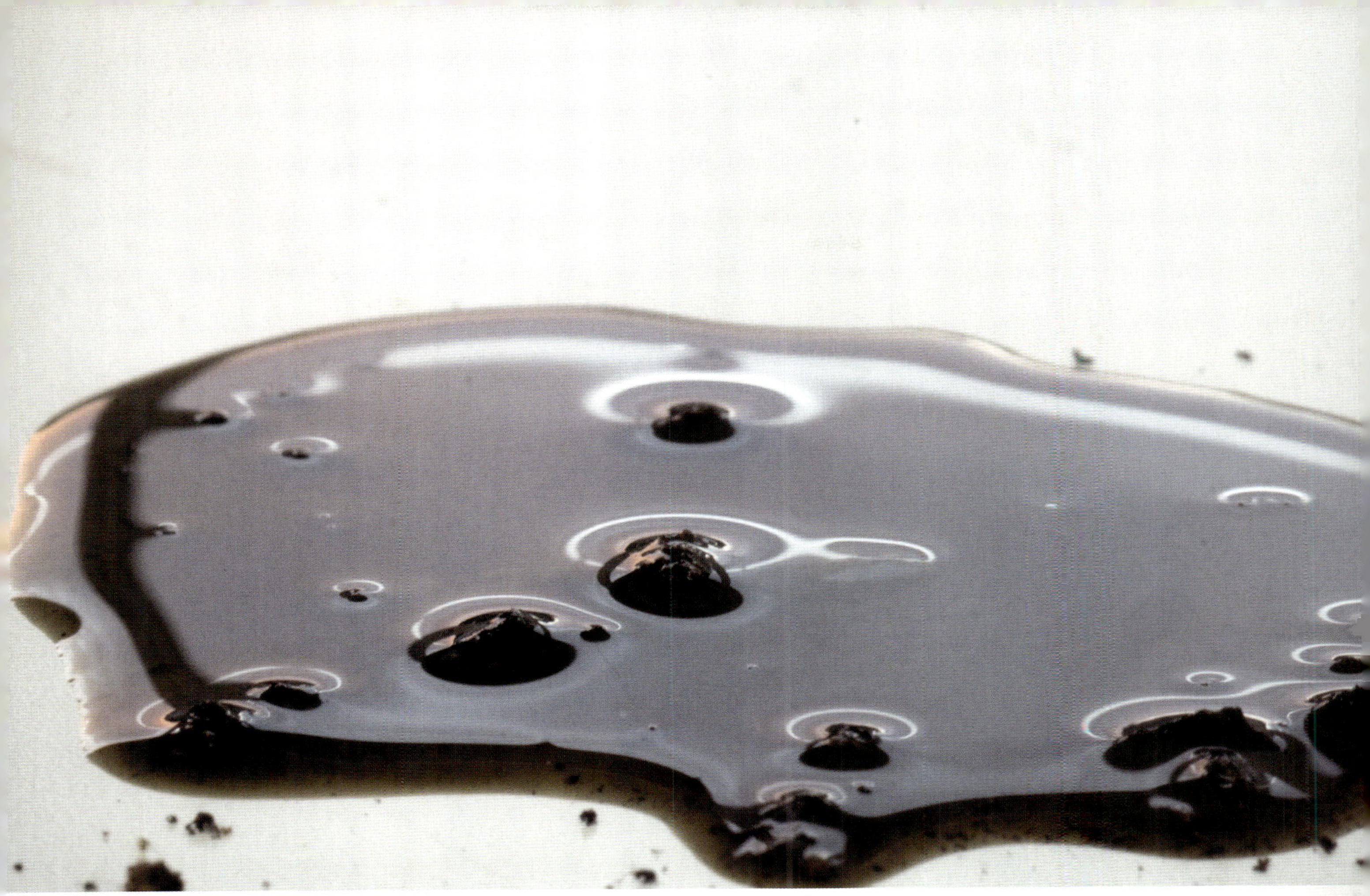

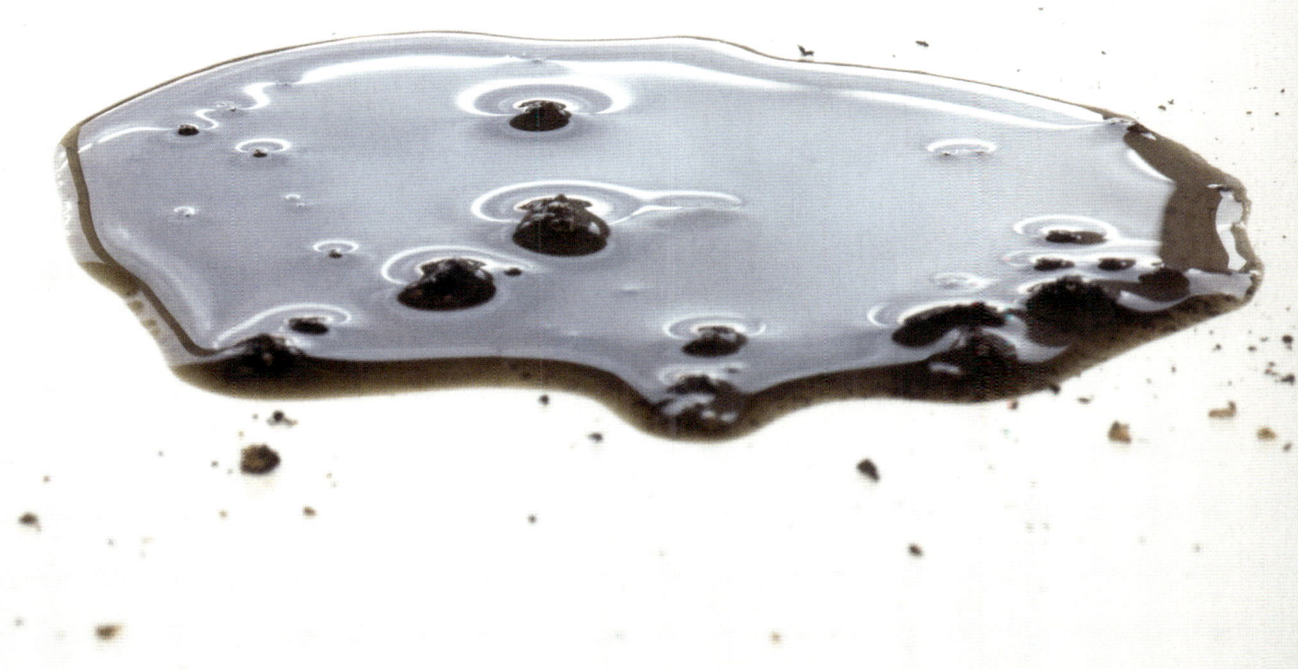

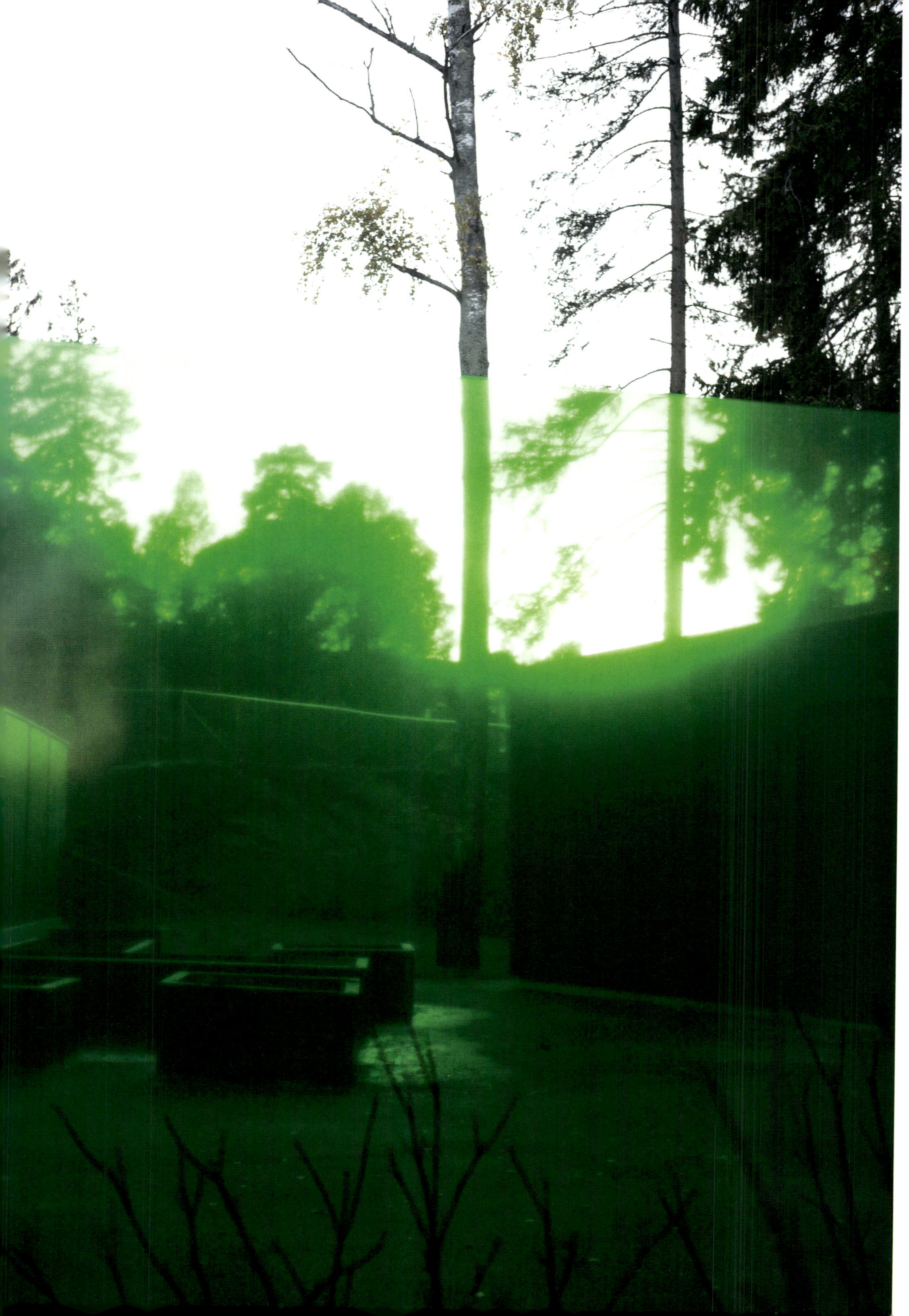

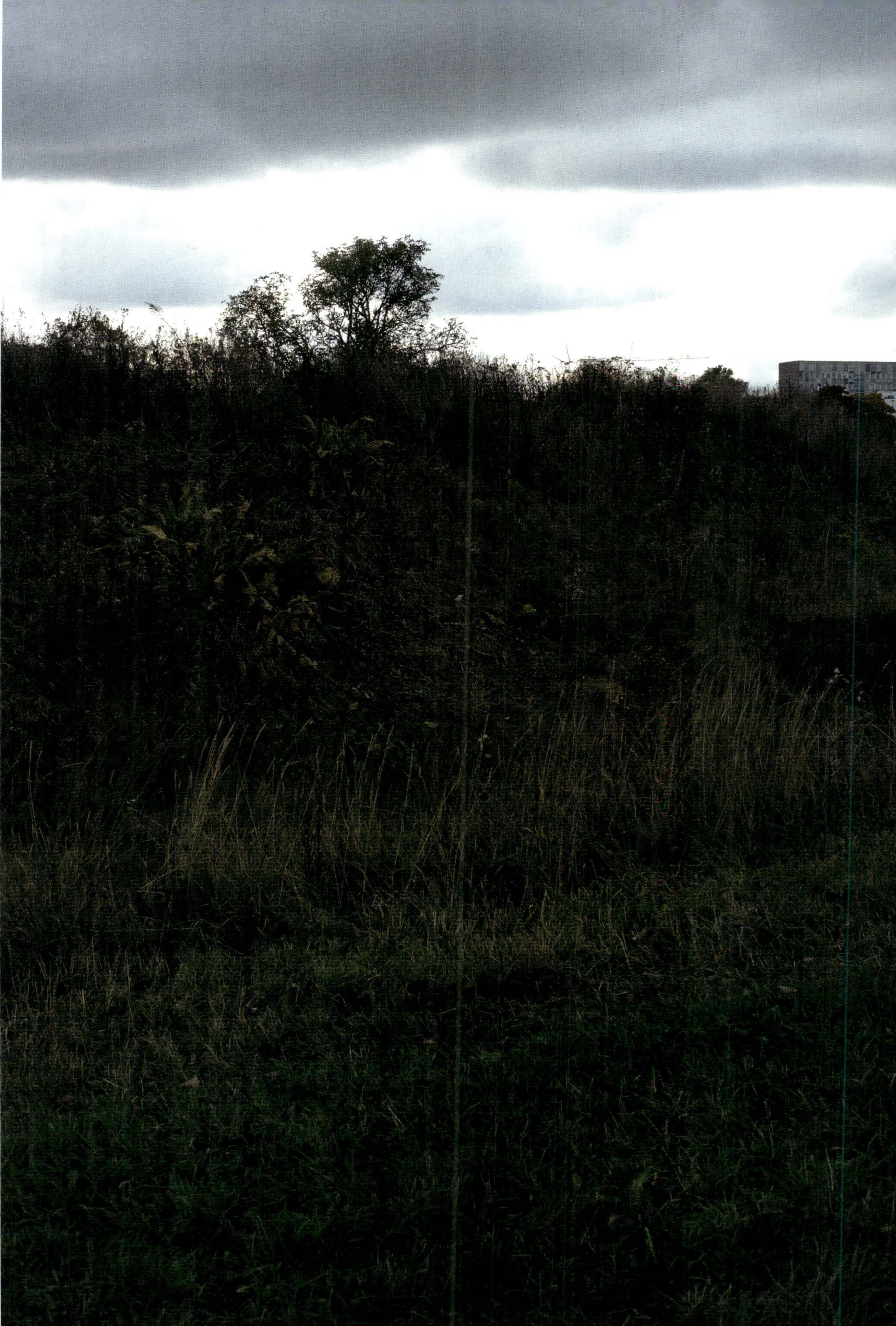

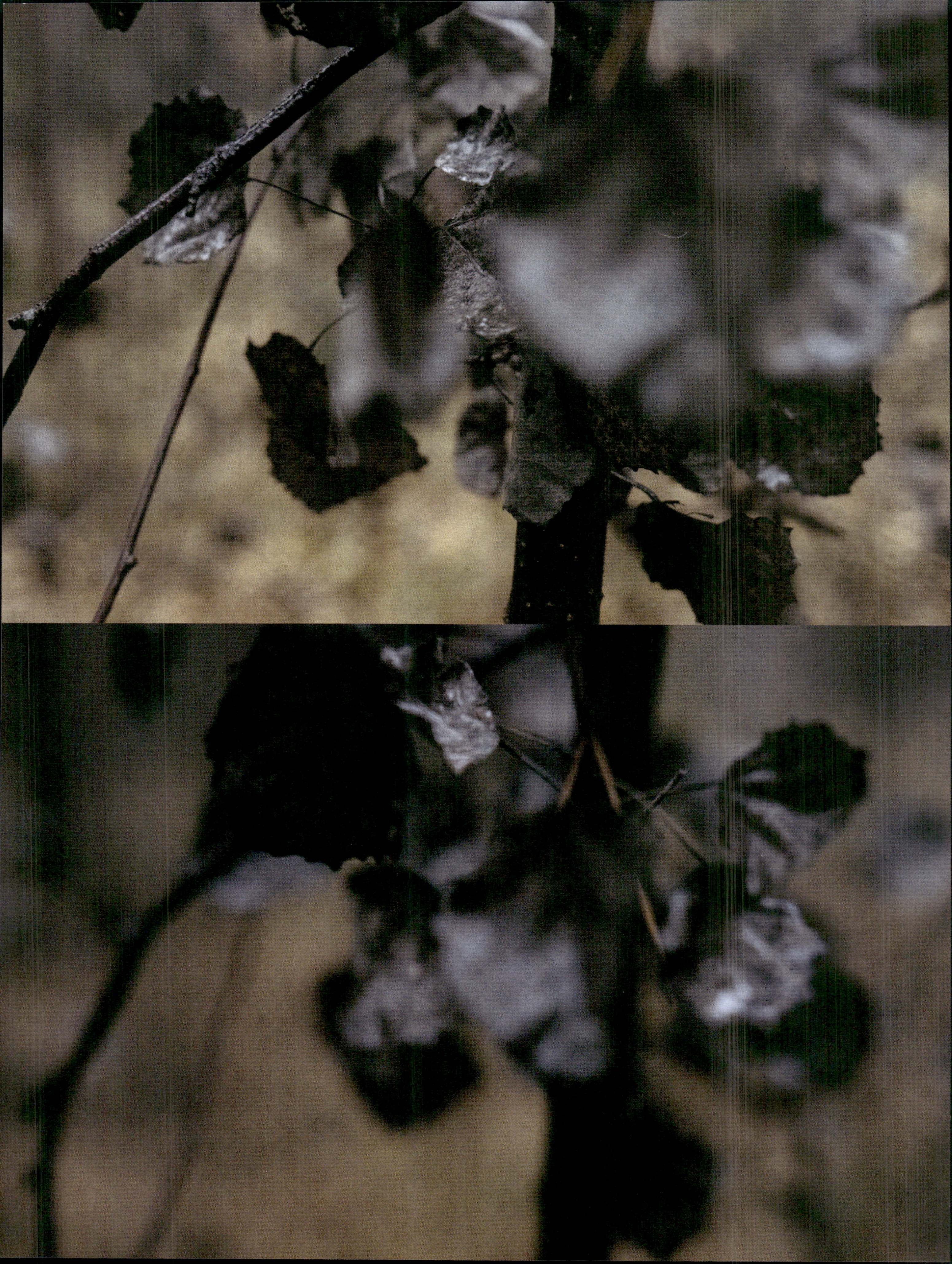

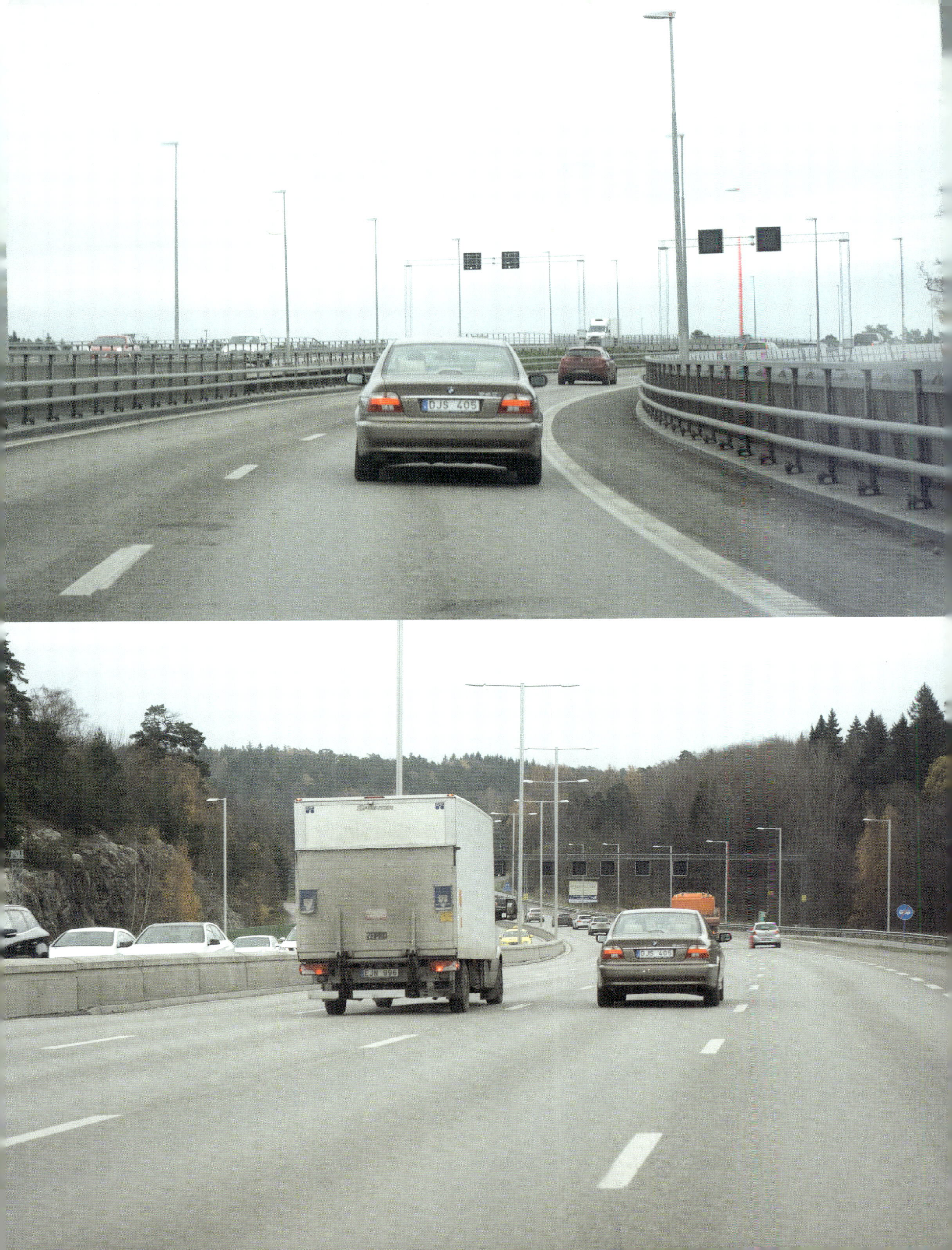

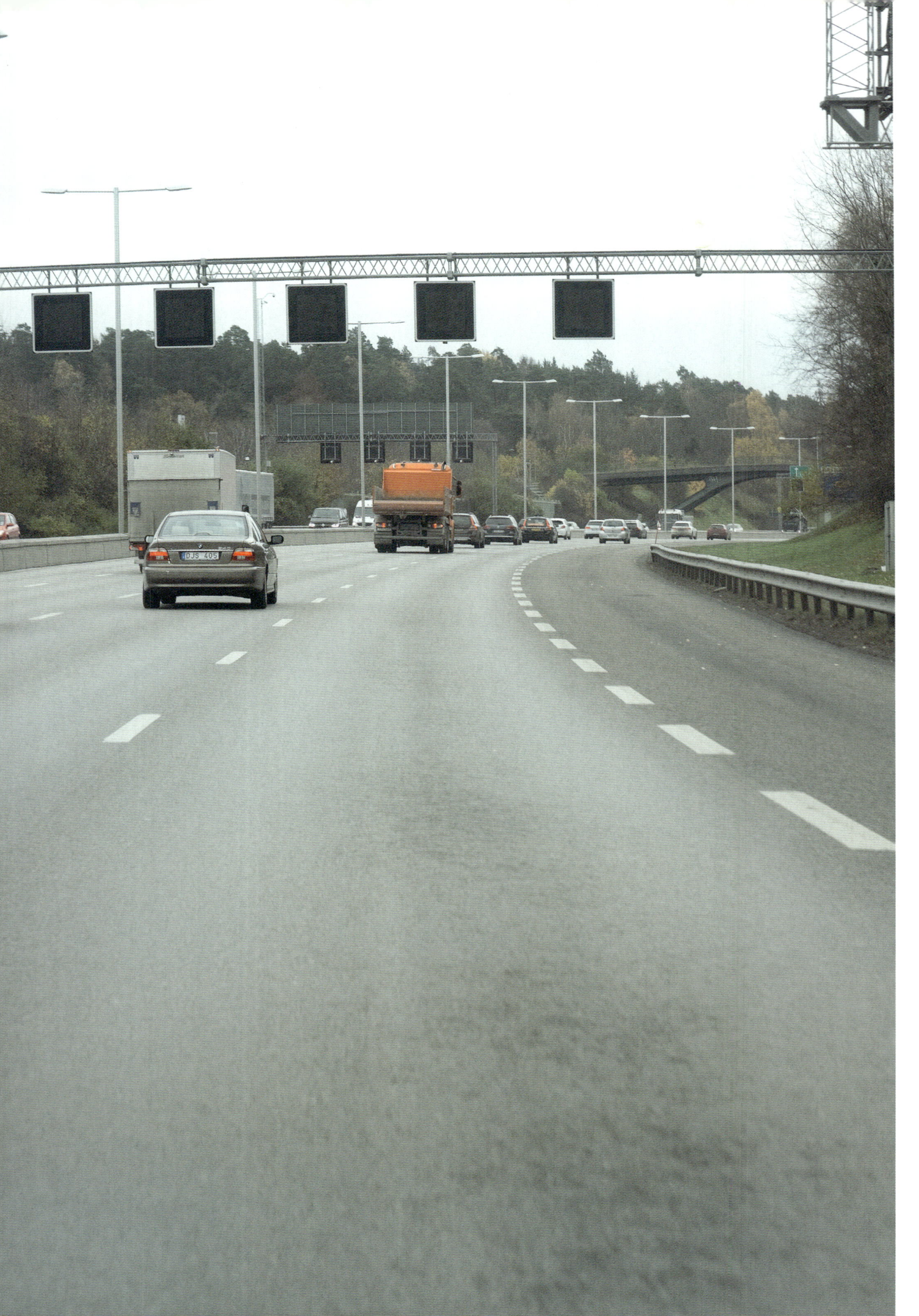

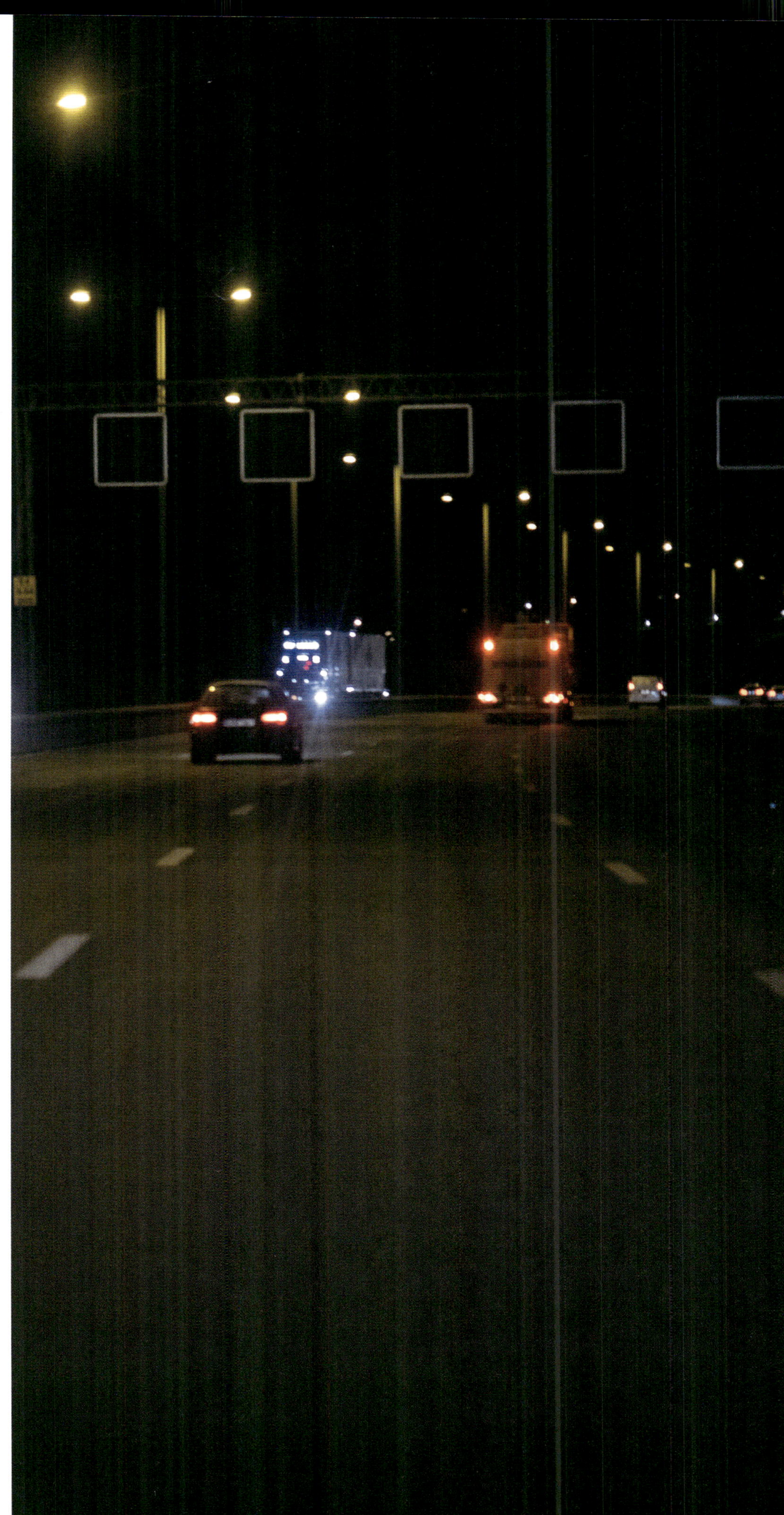

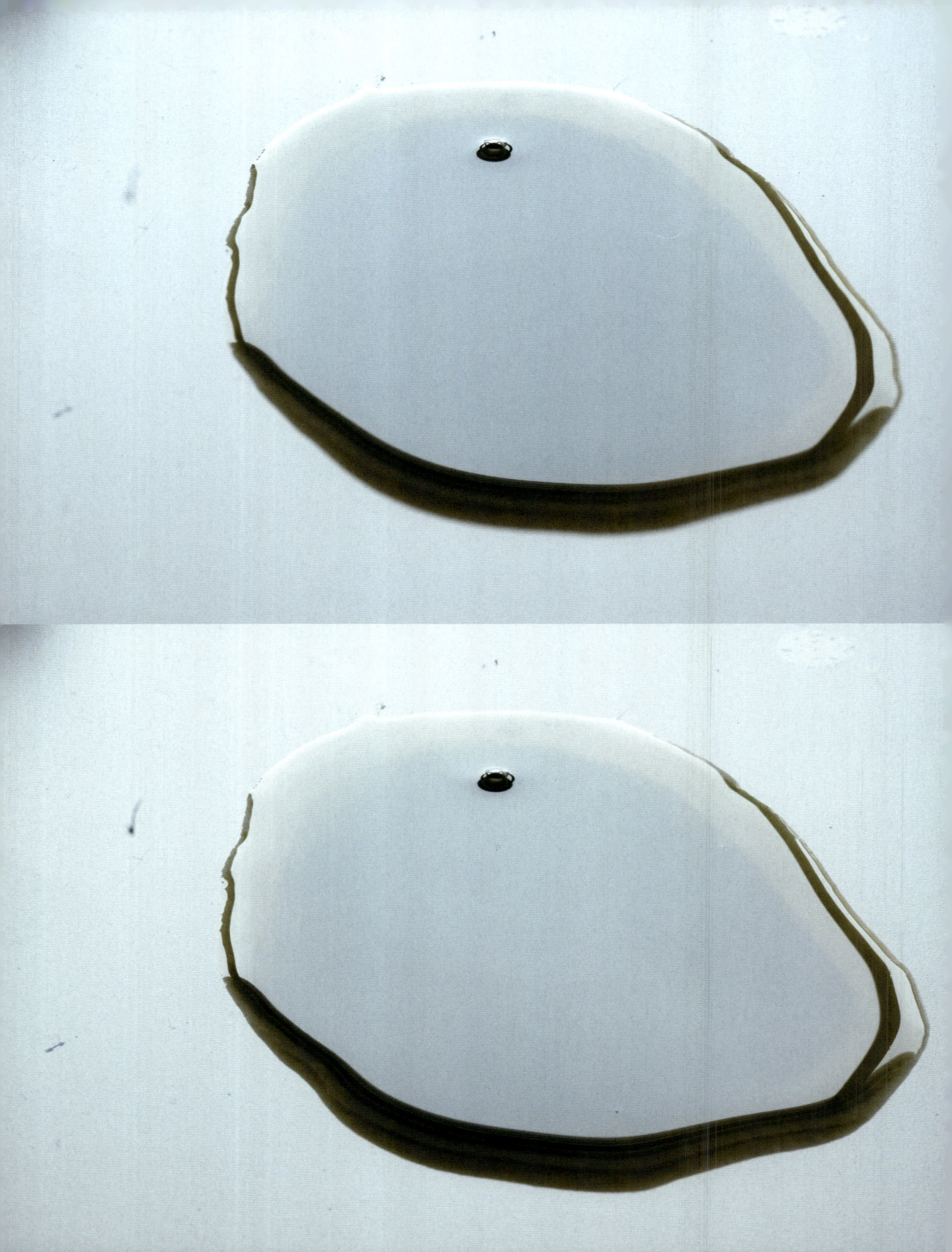

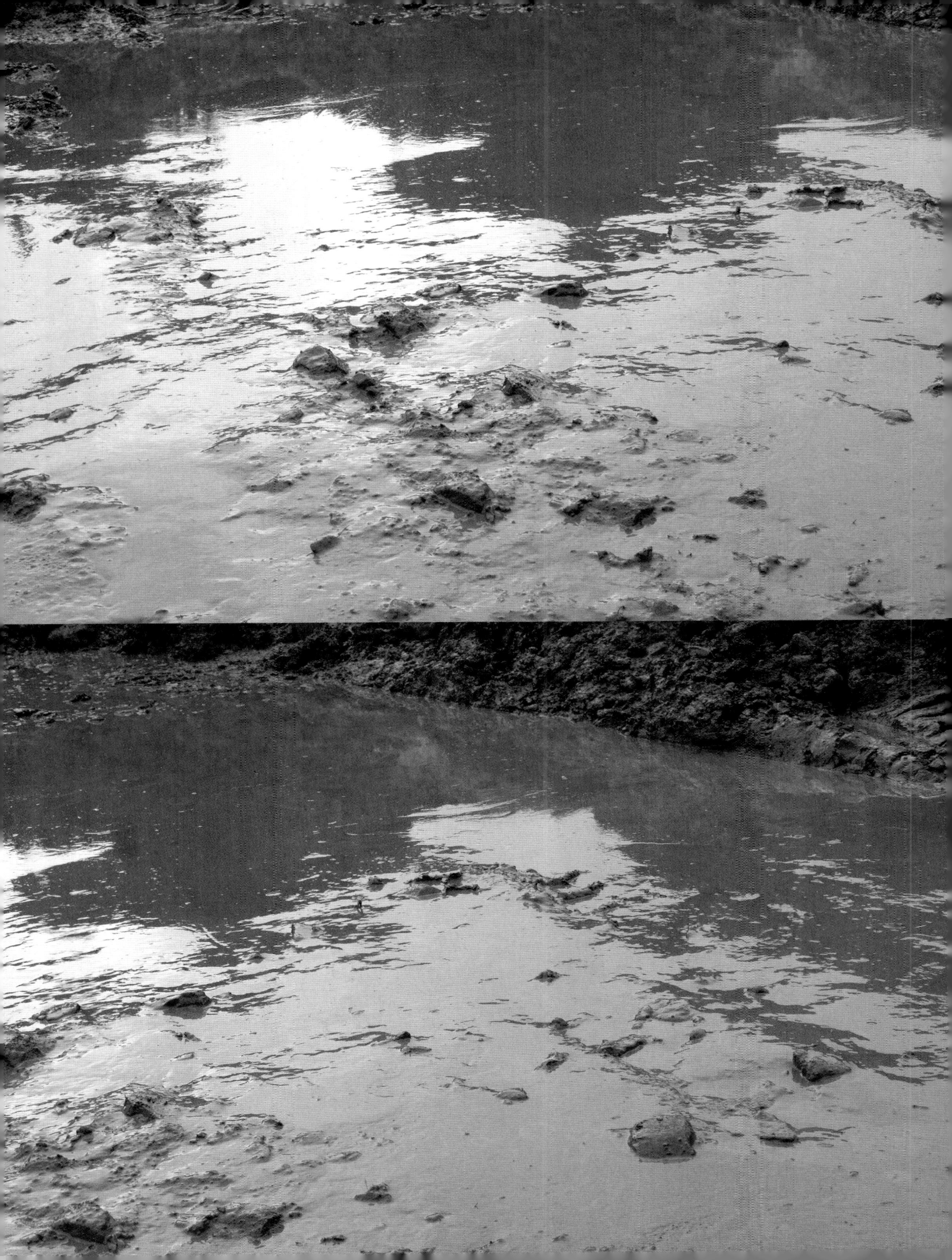

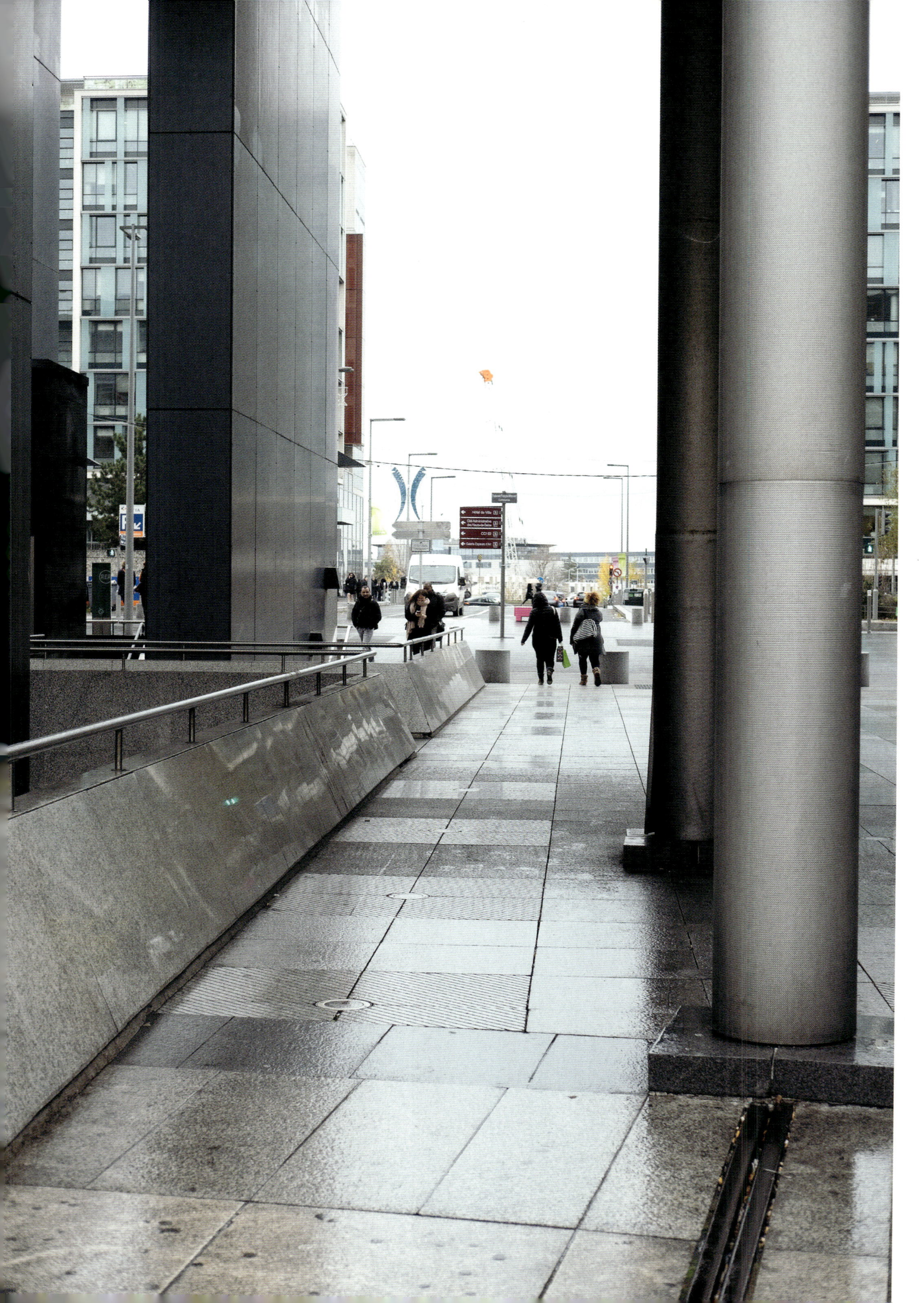

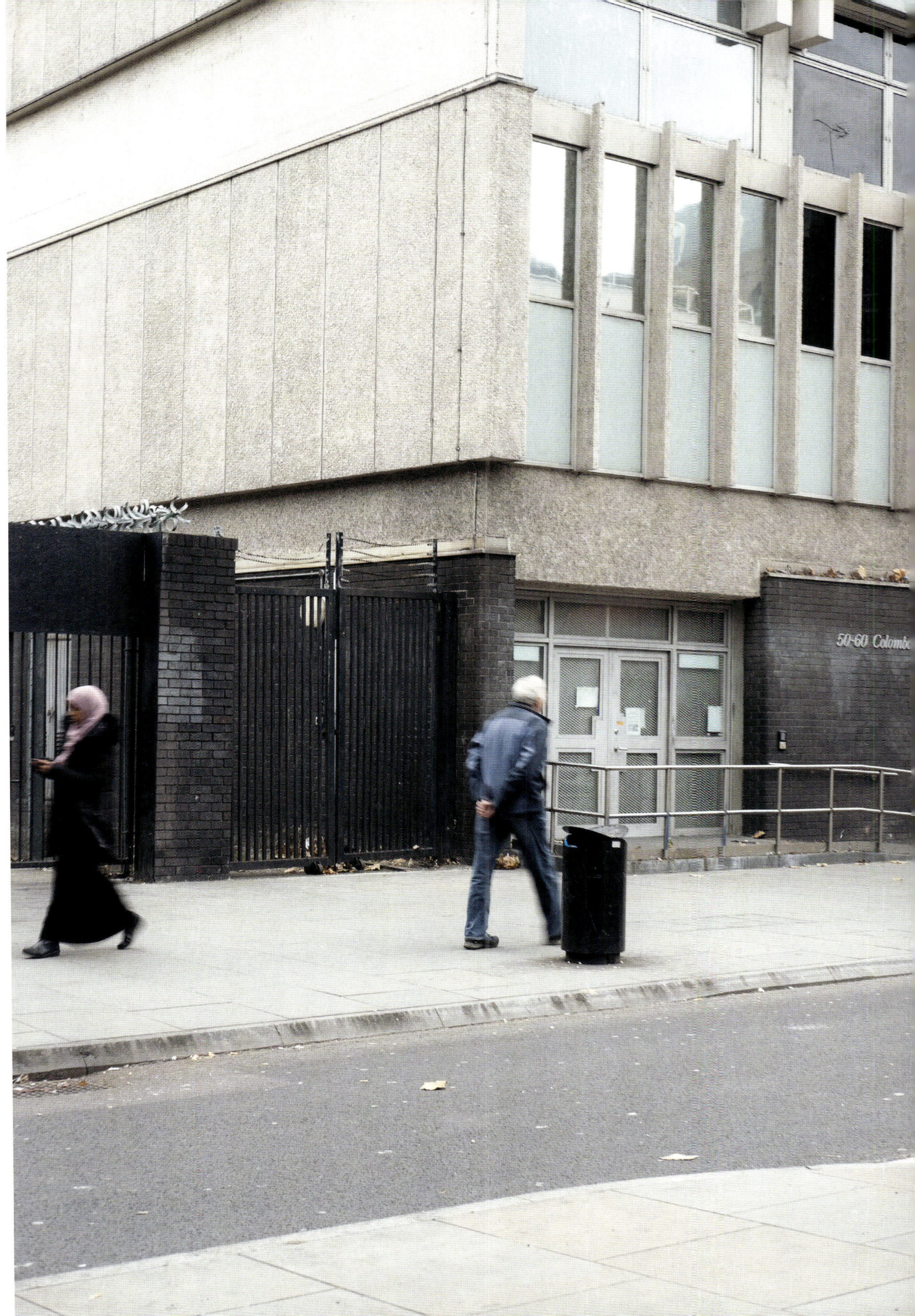

50-60 Colomb

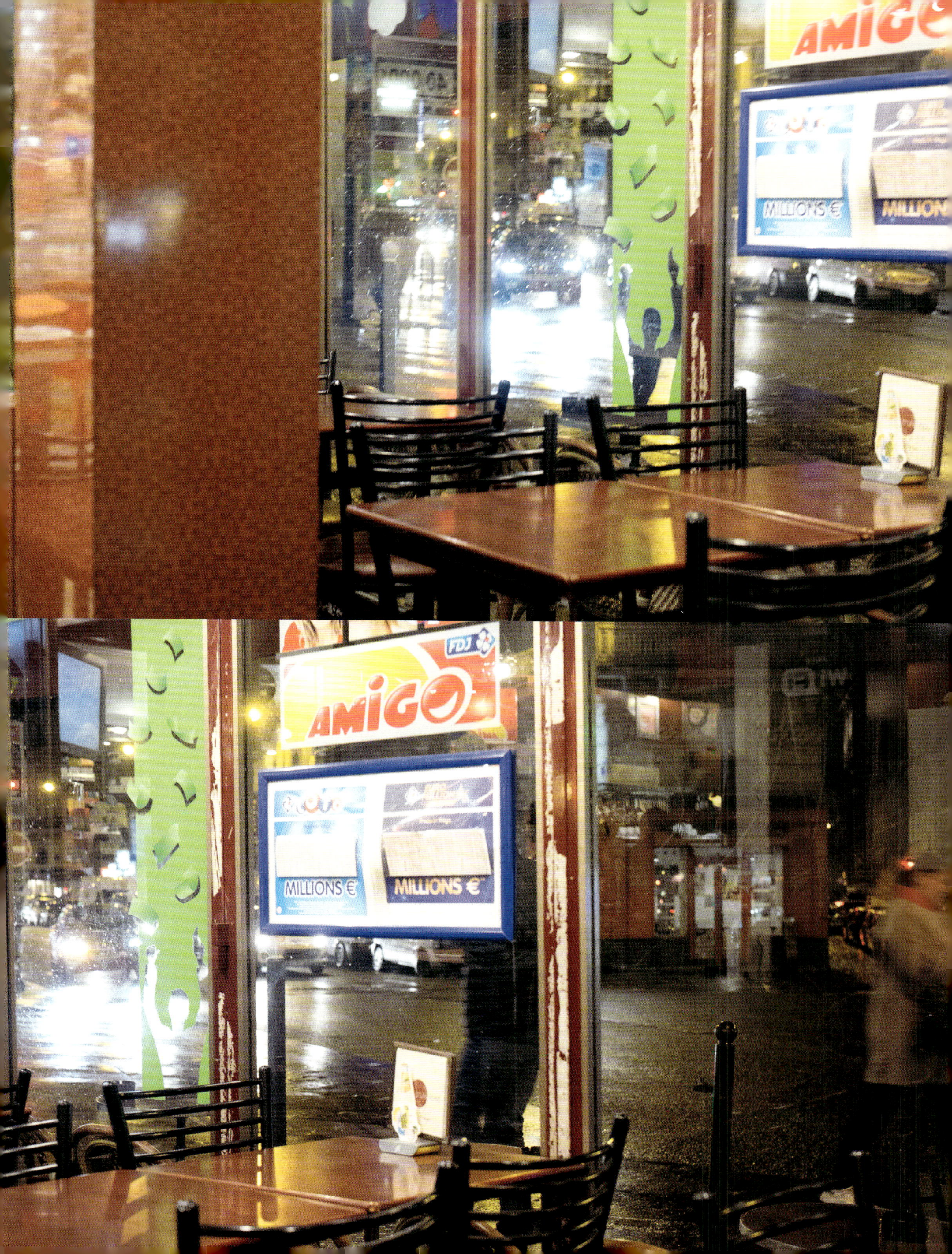

AMIGO
FDJ
AMIGO
MILLIONS €
MILLIONS €

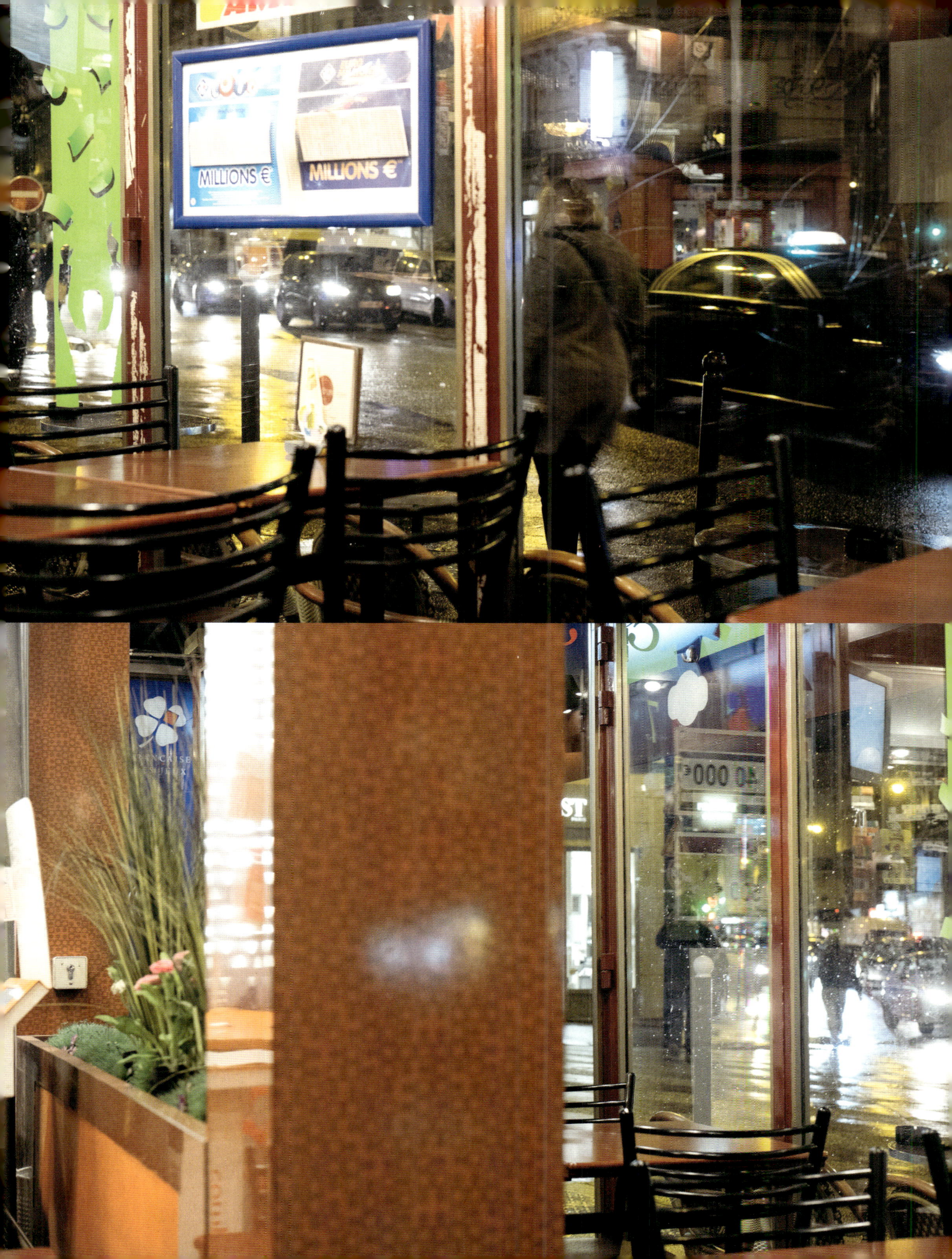

MILLIONS €
MILLIONS €

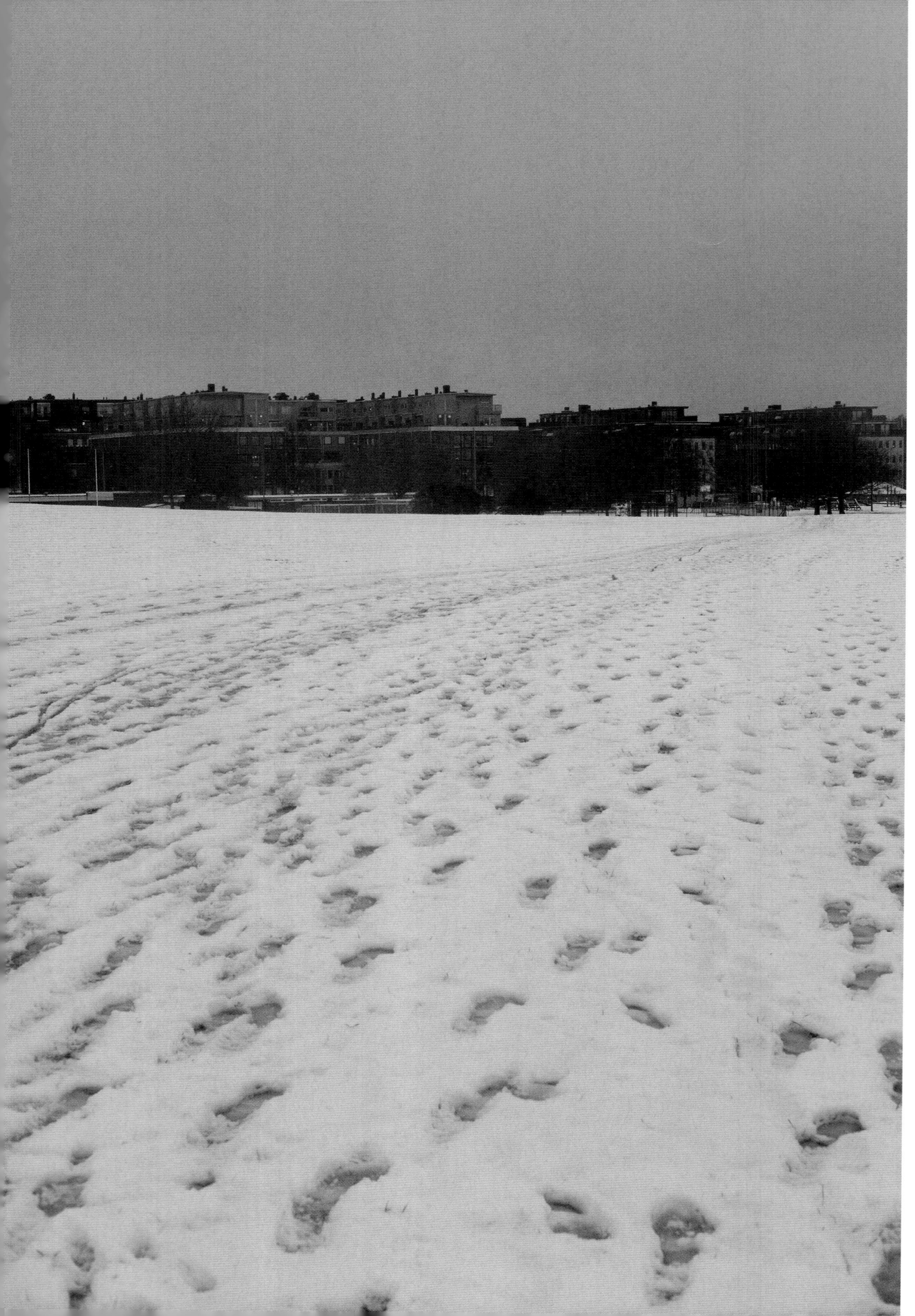

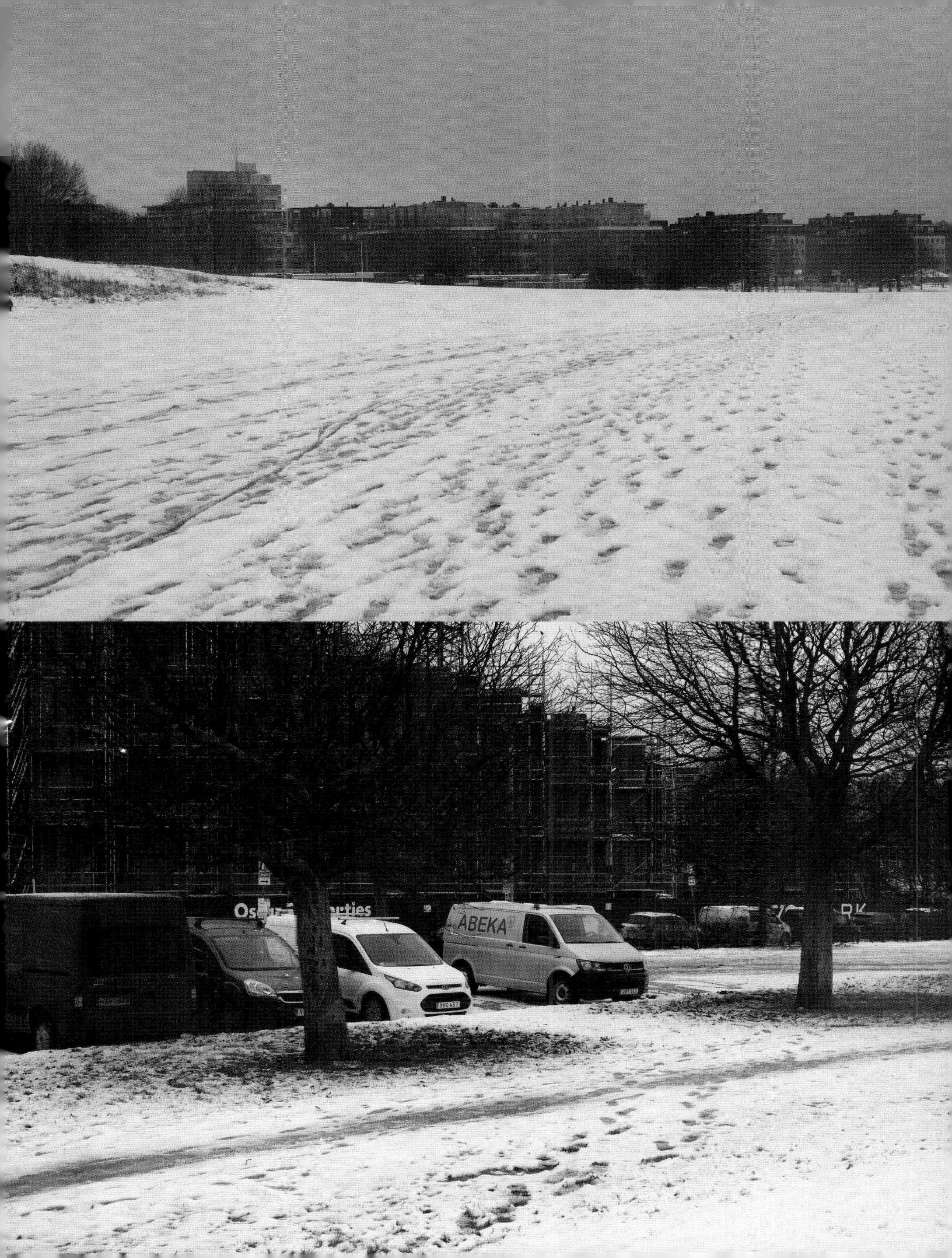
Osc properties
ABEKA
XHC 457

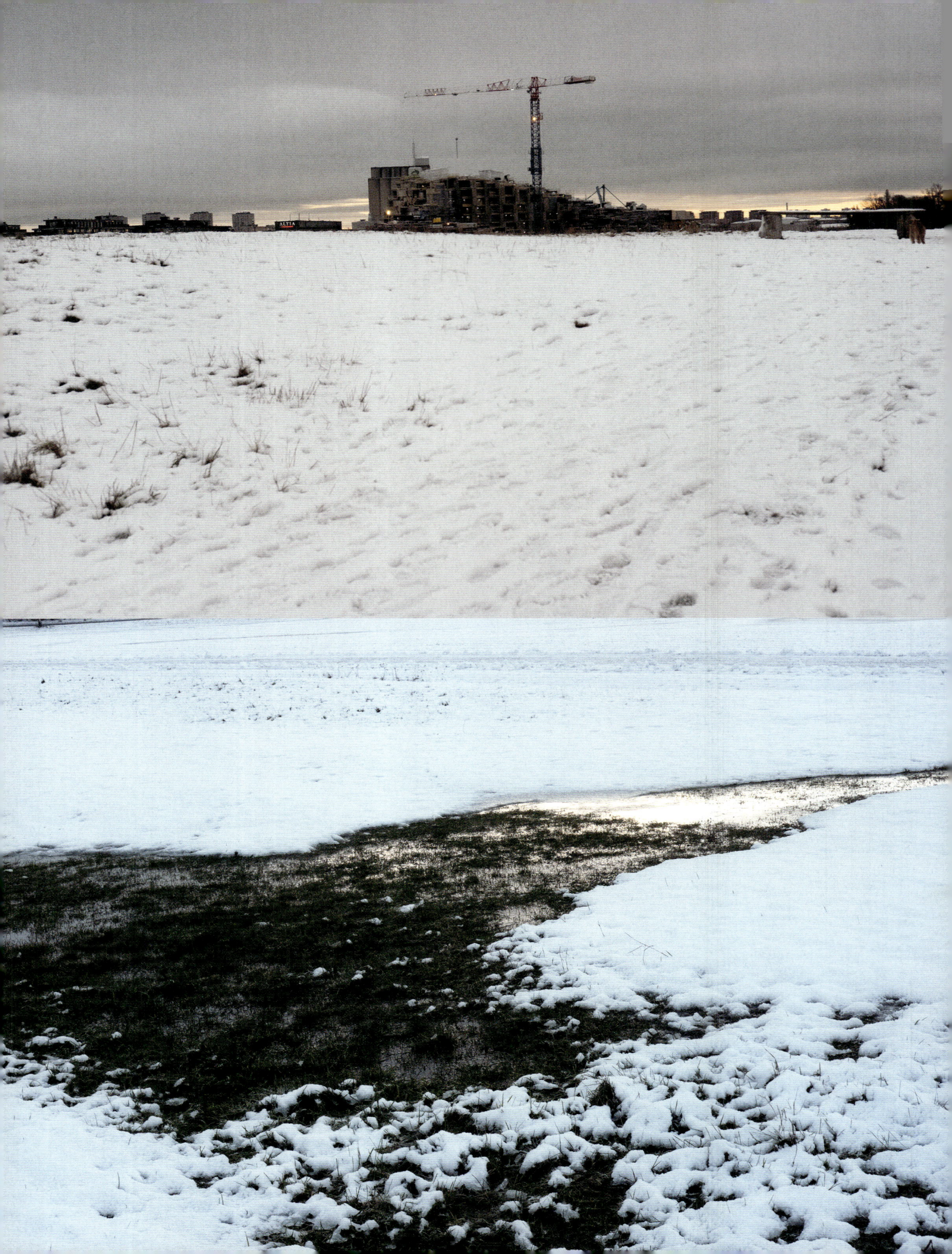
ALTIA

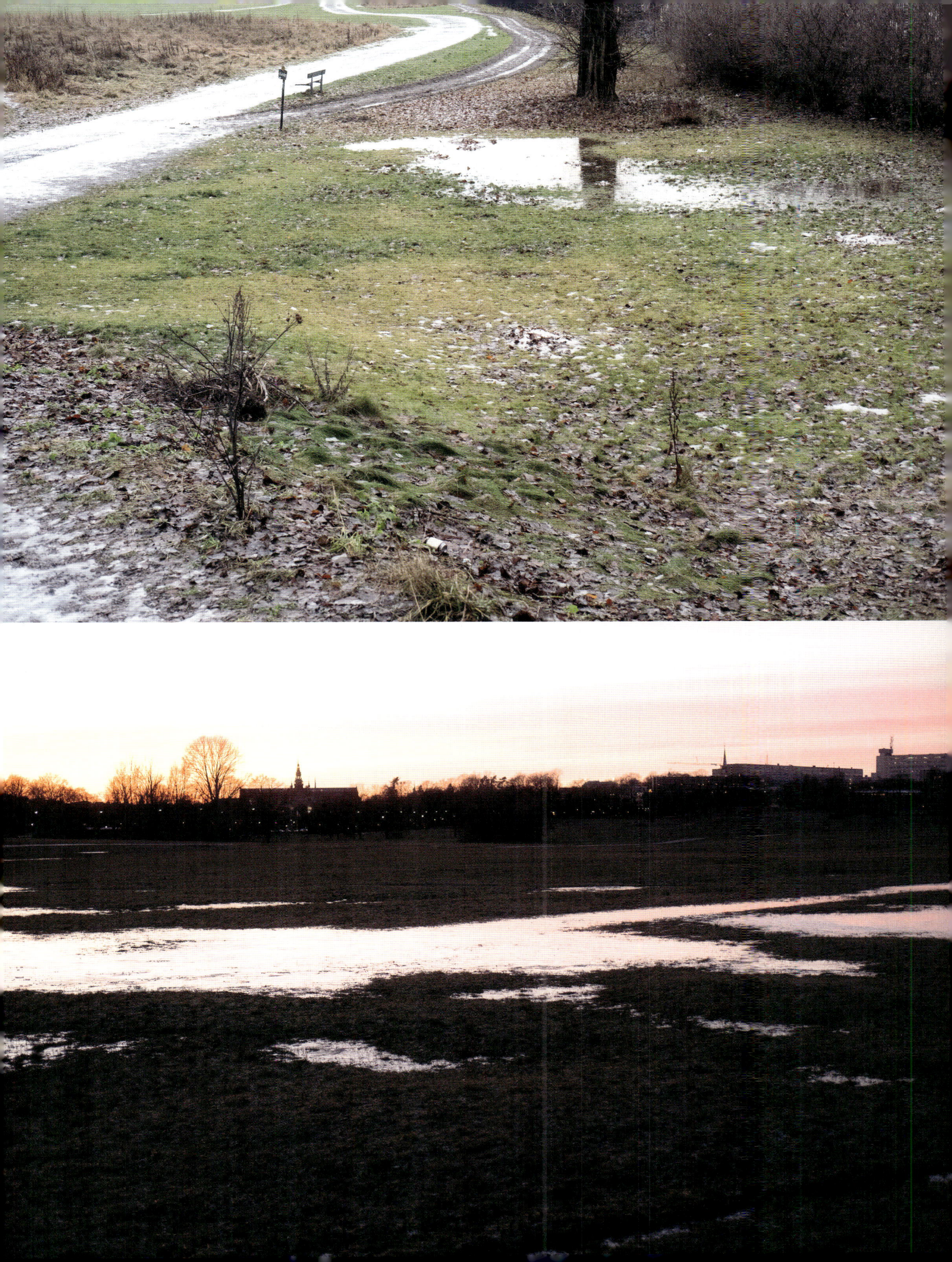

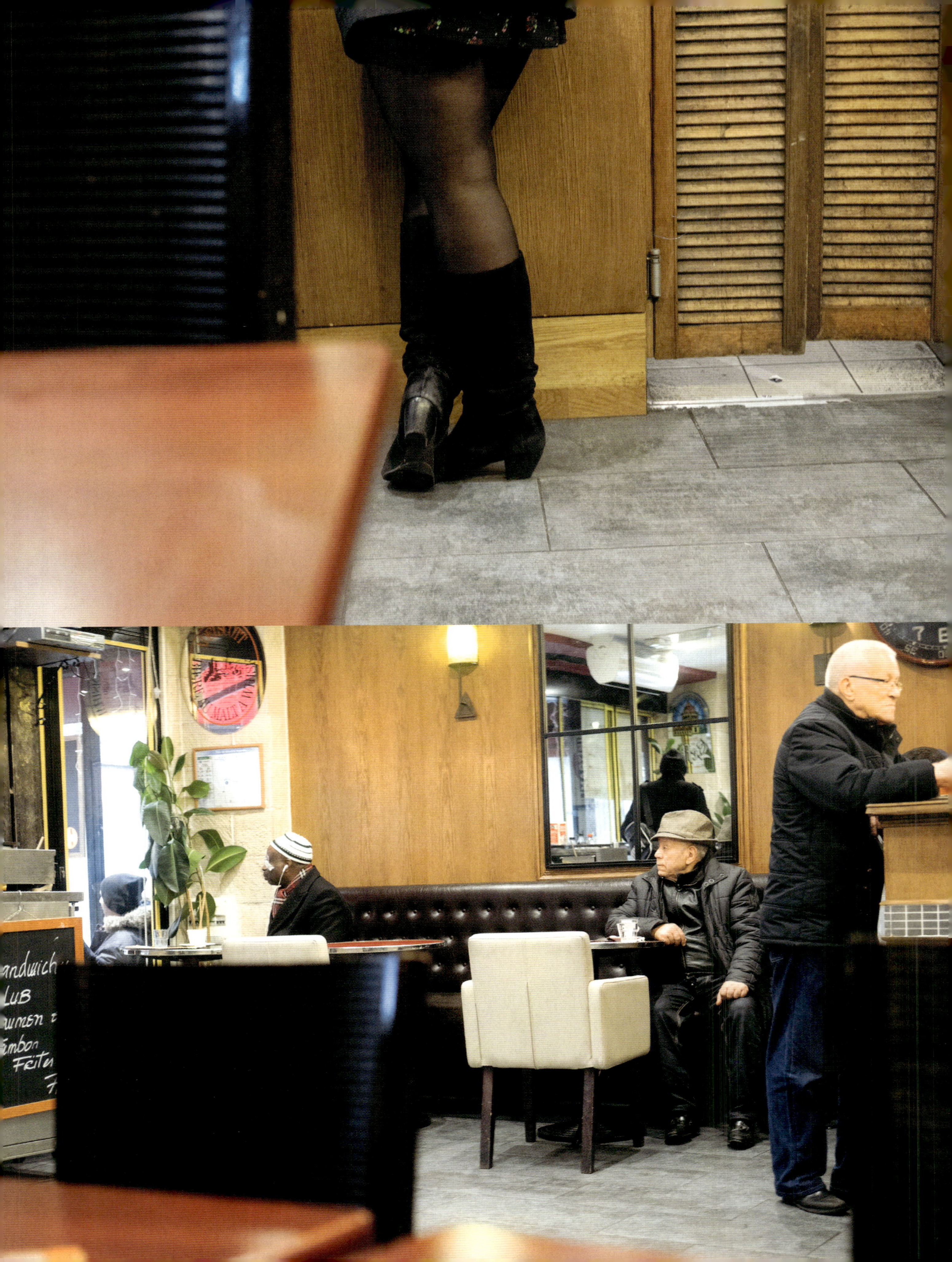

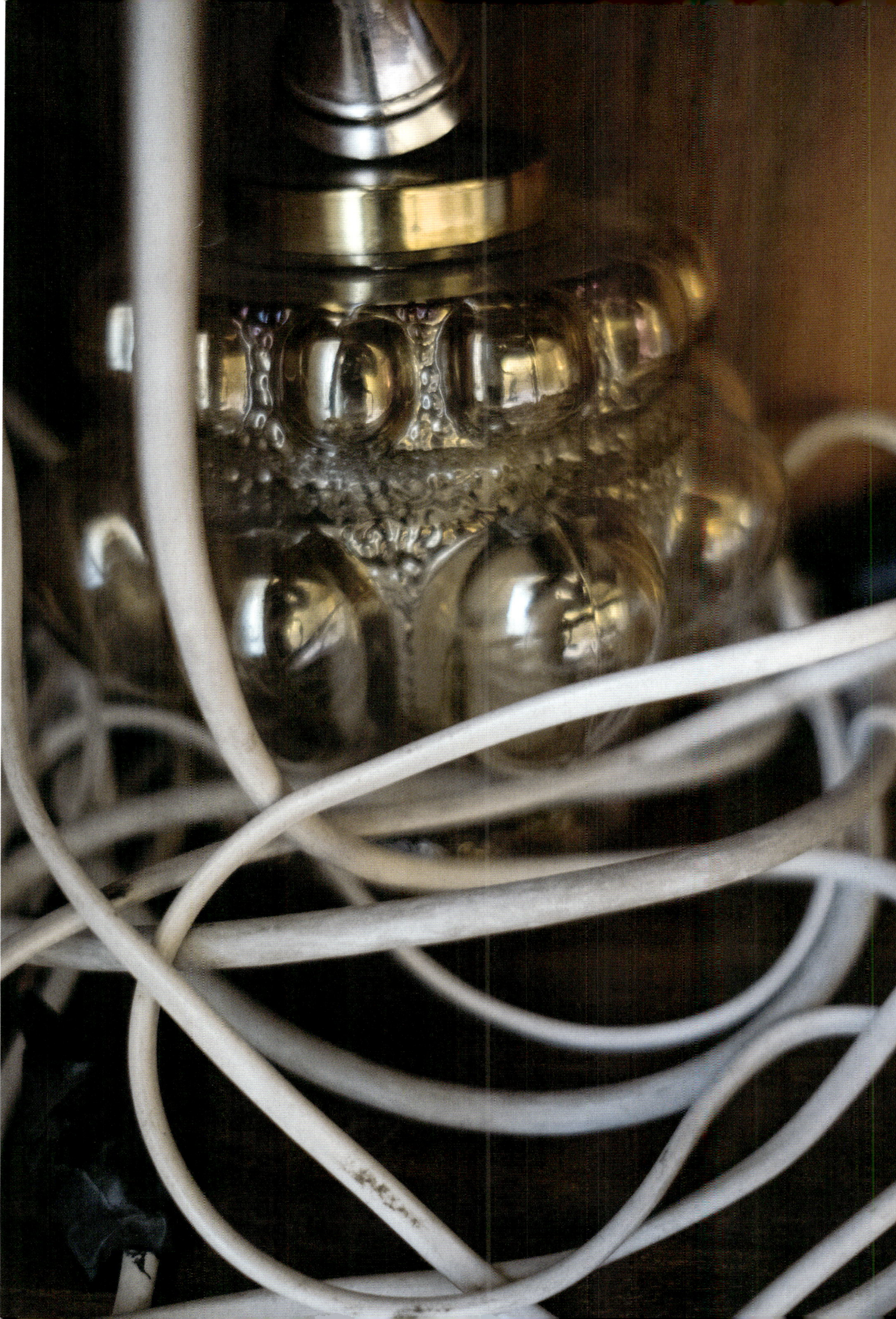

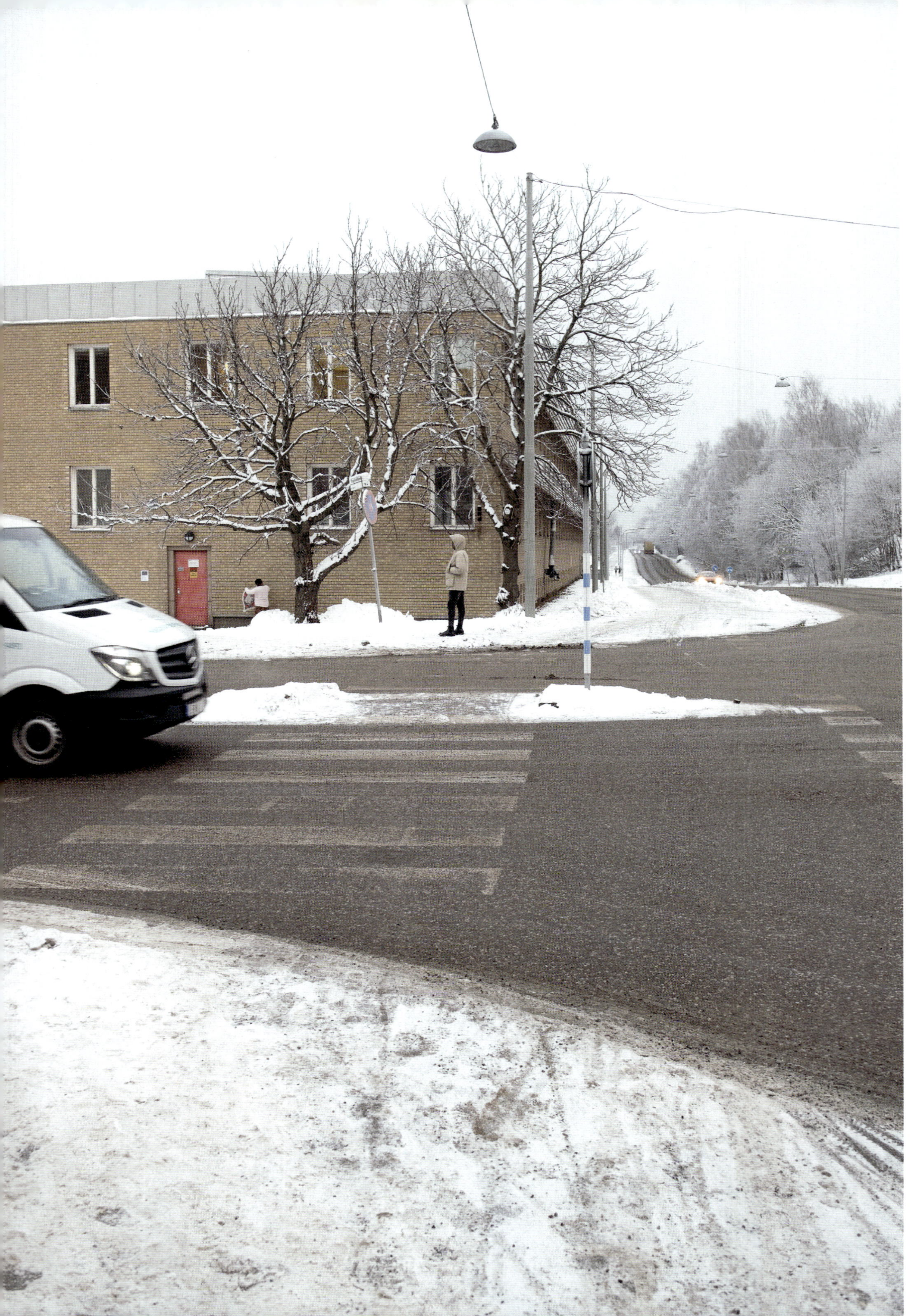

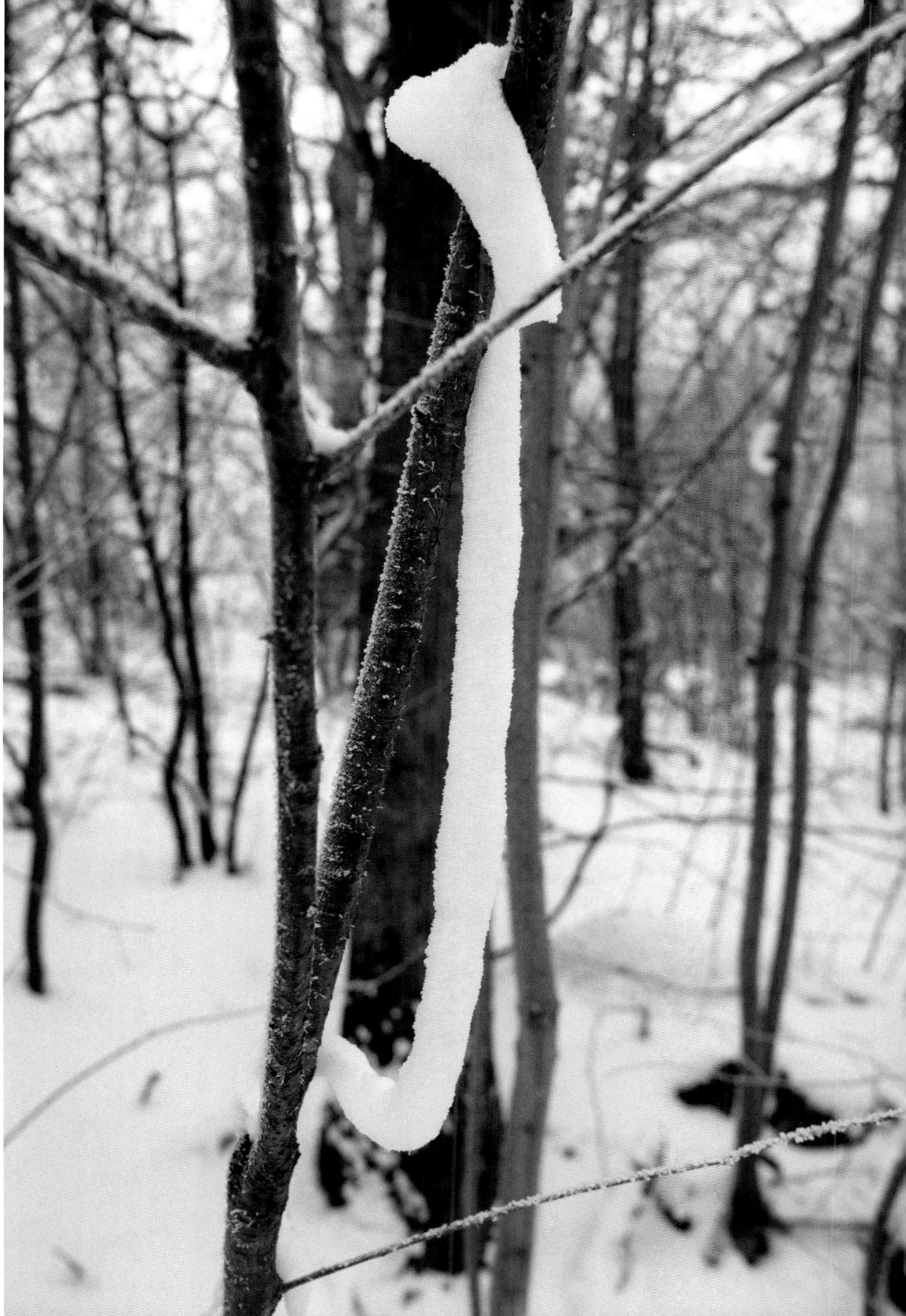

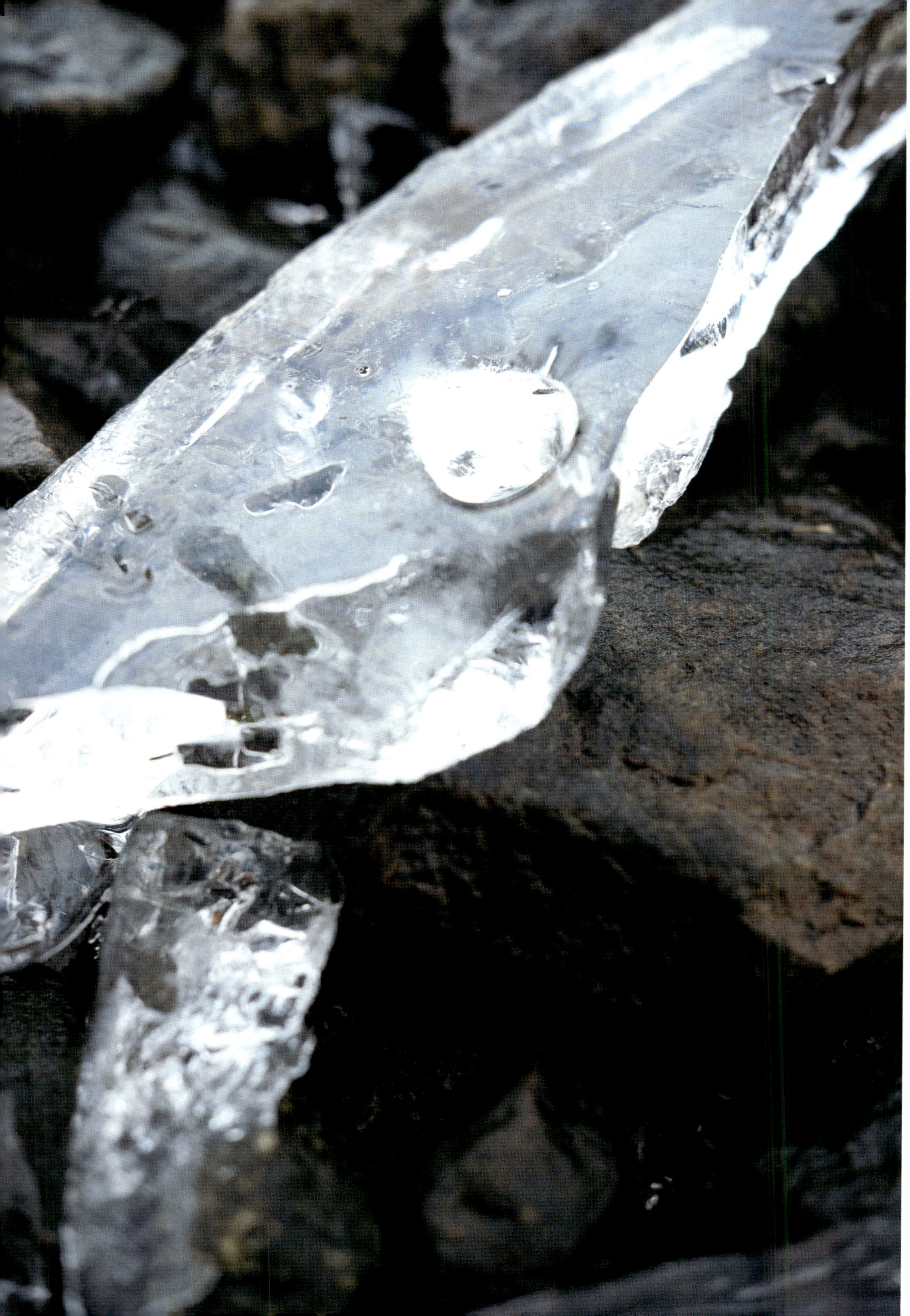

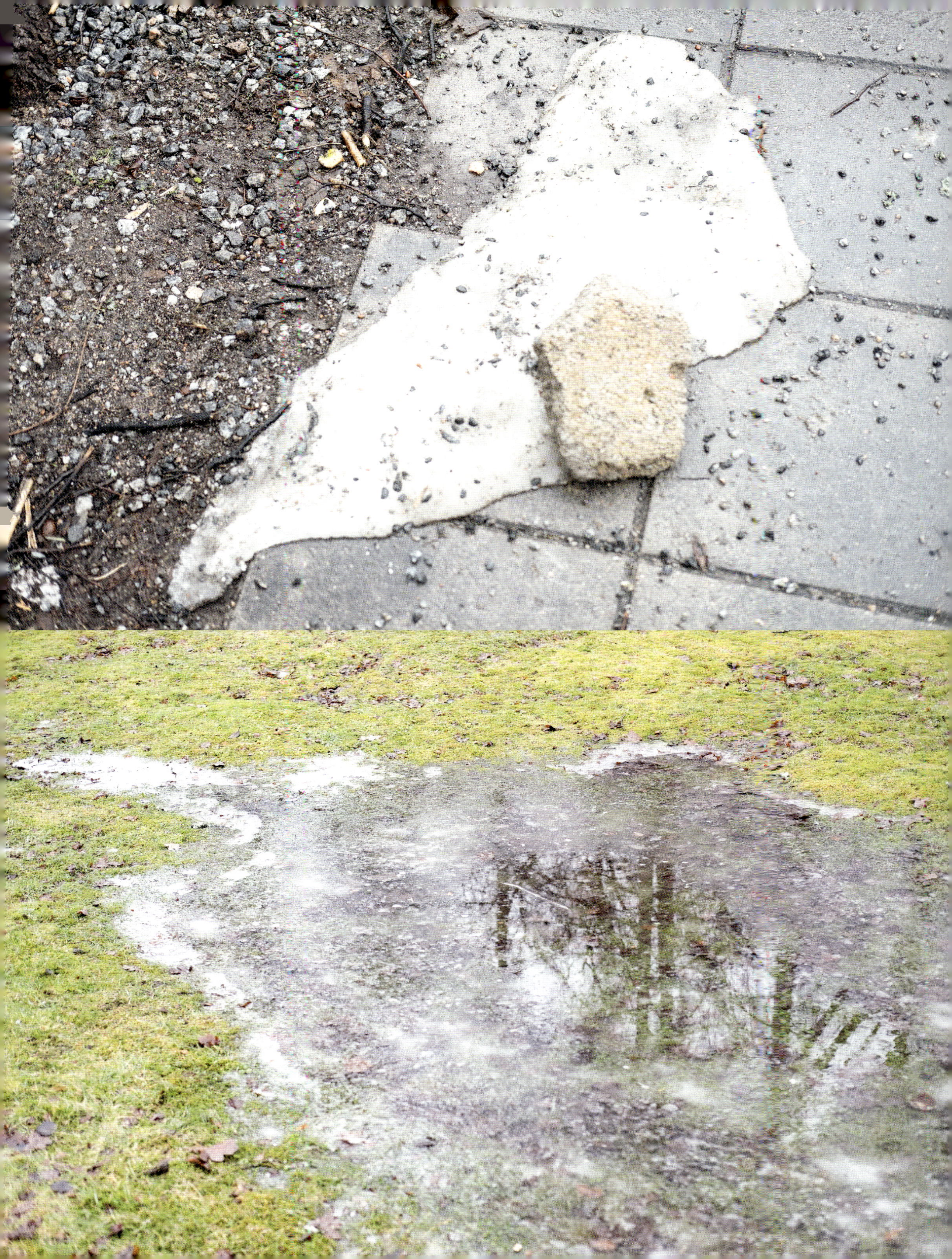

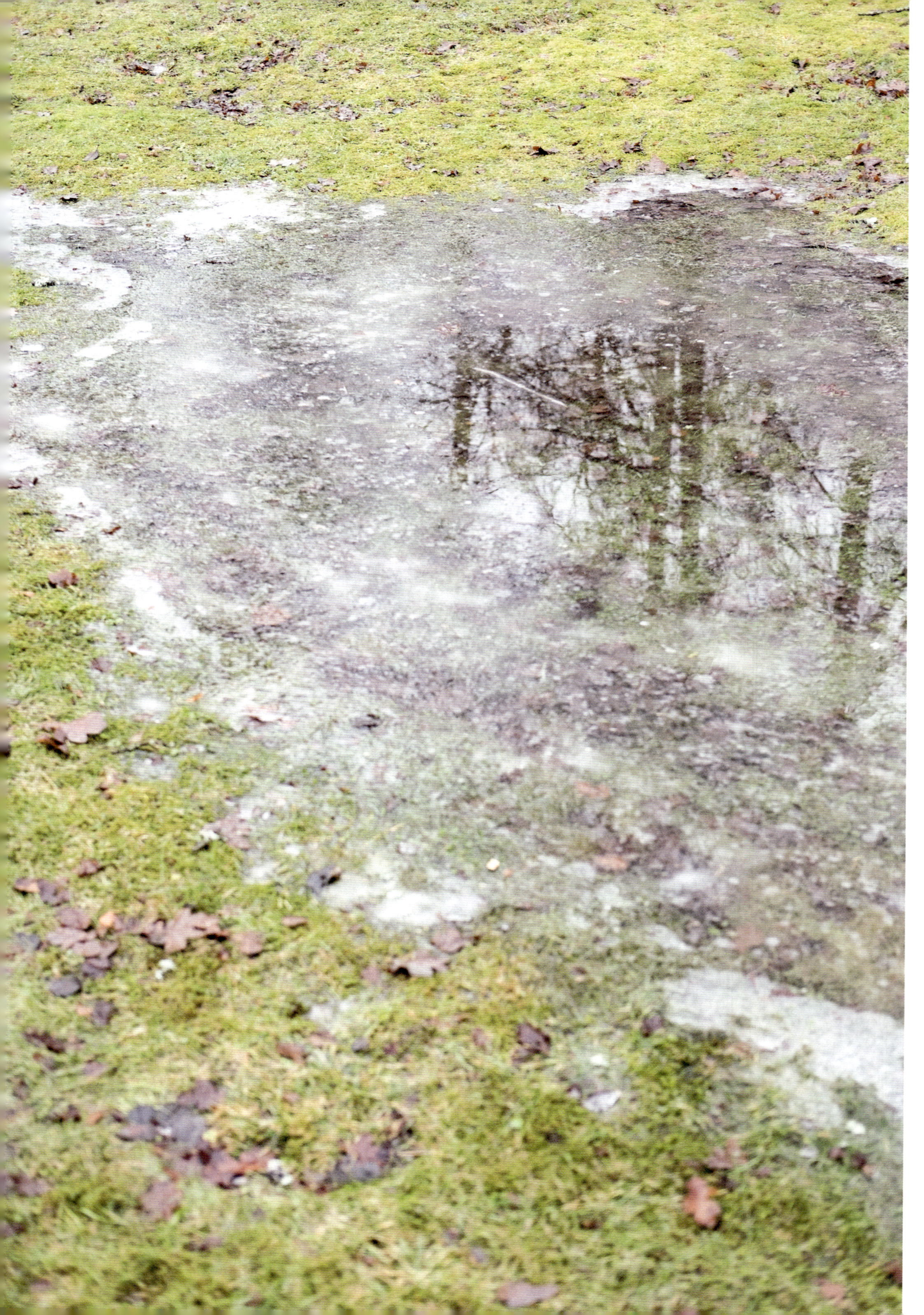

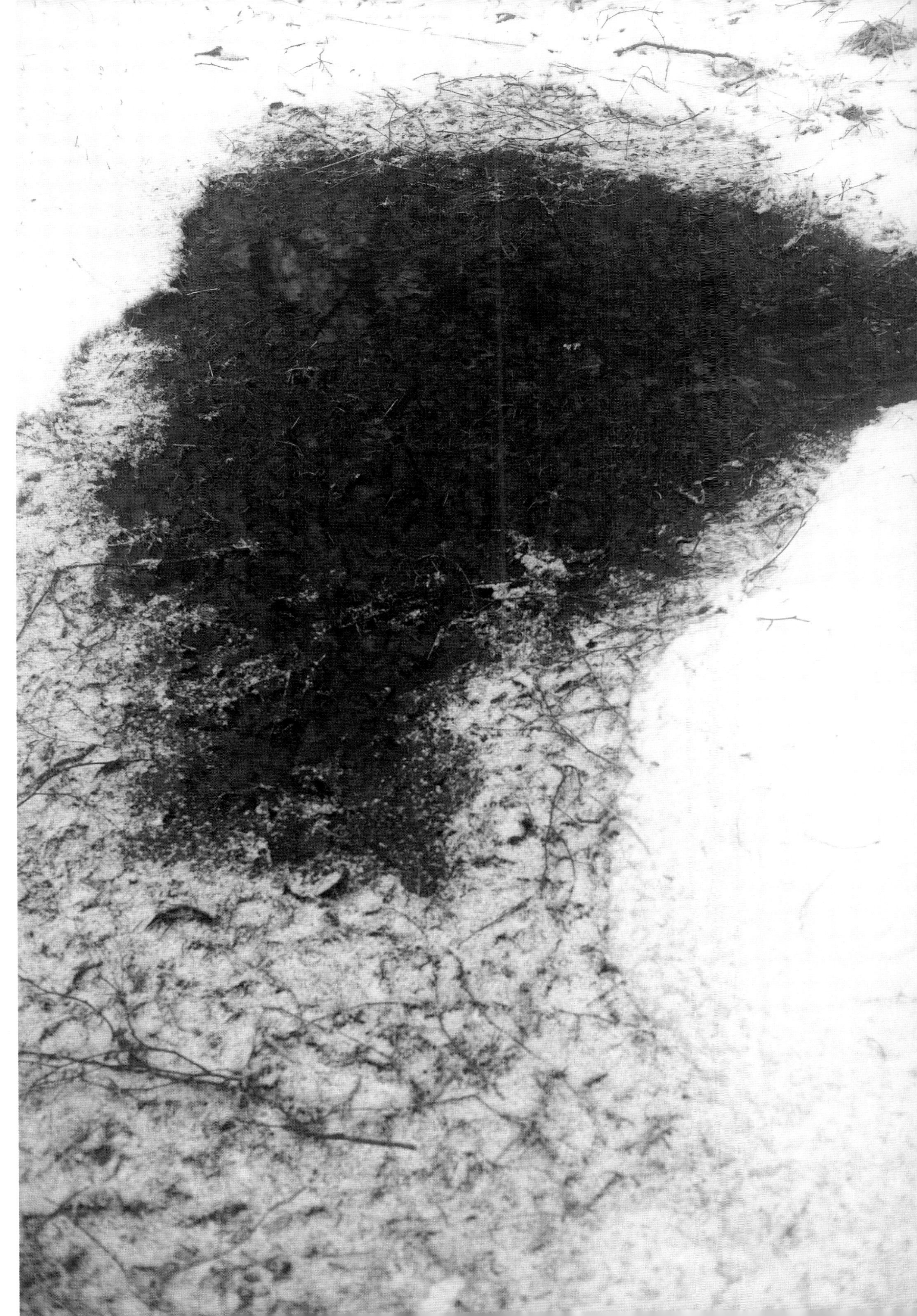

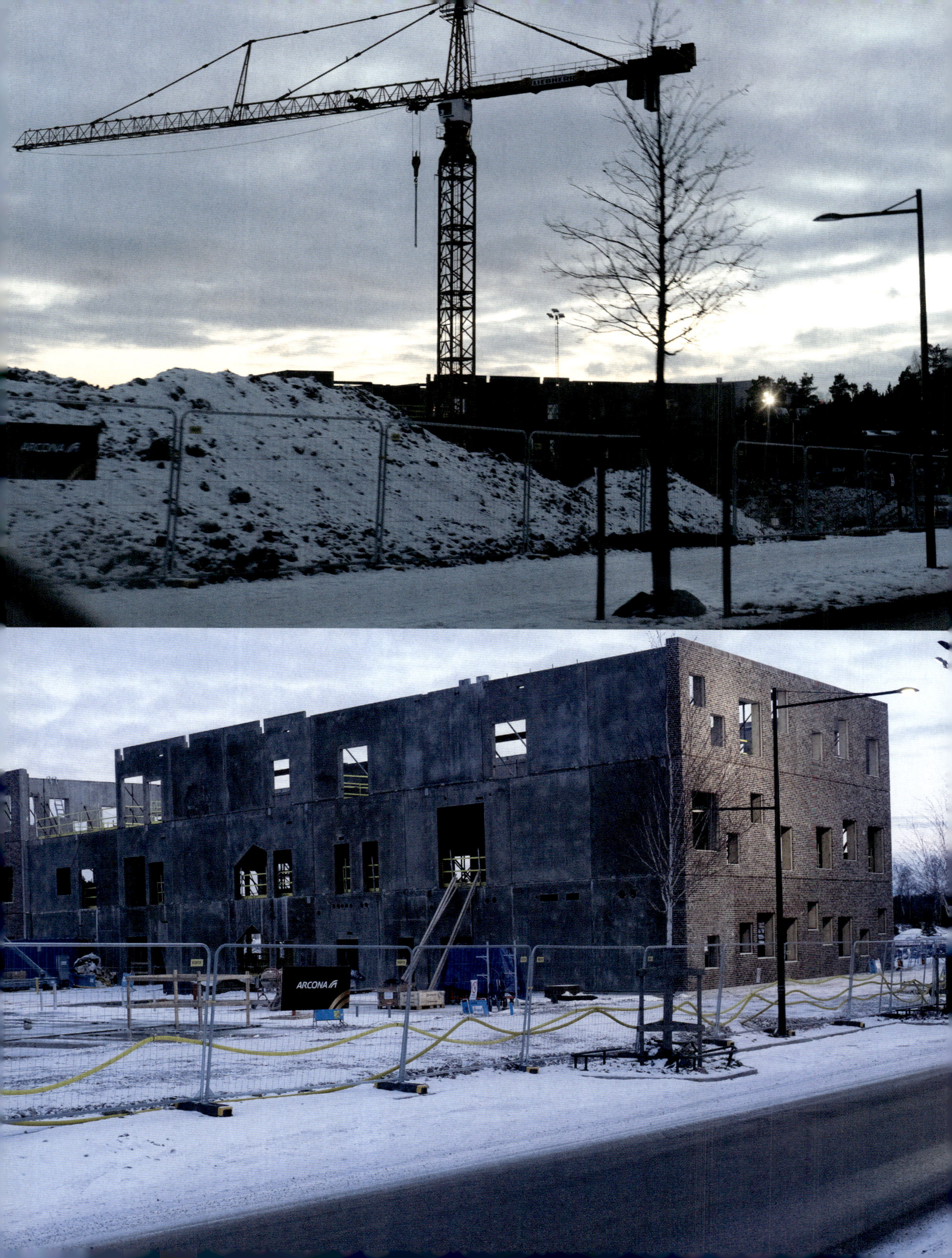

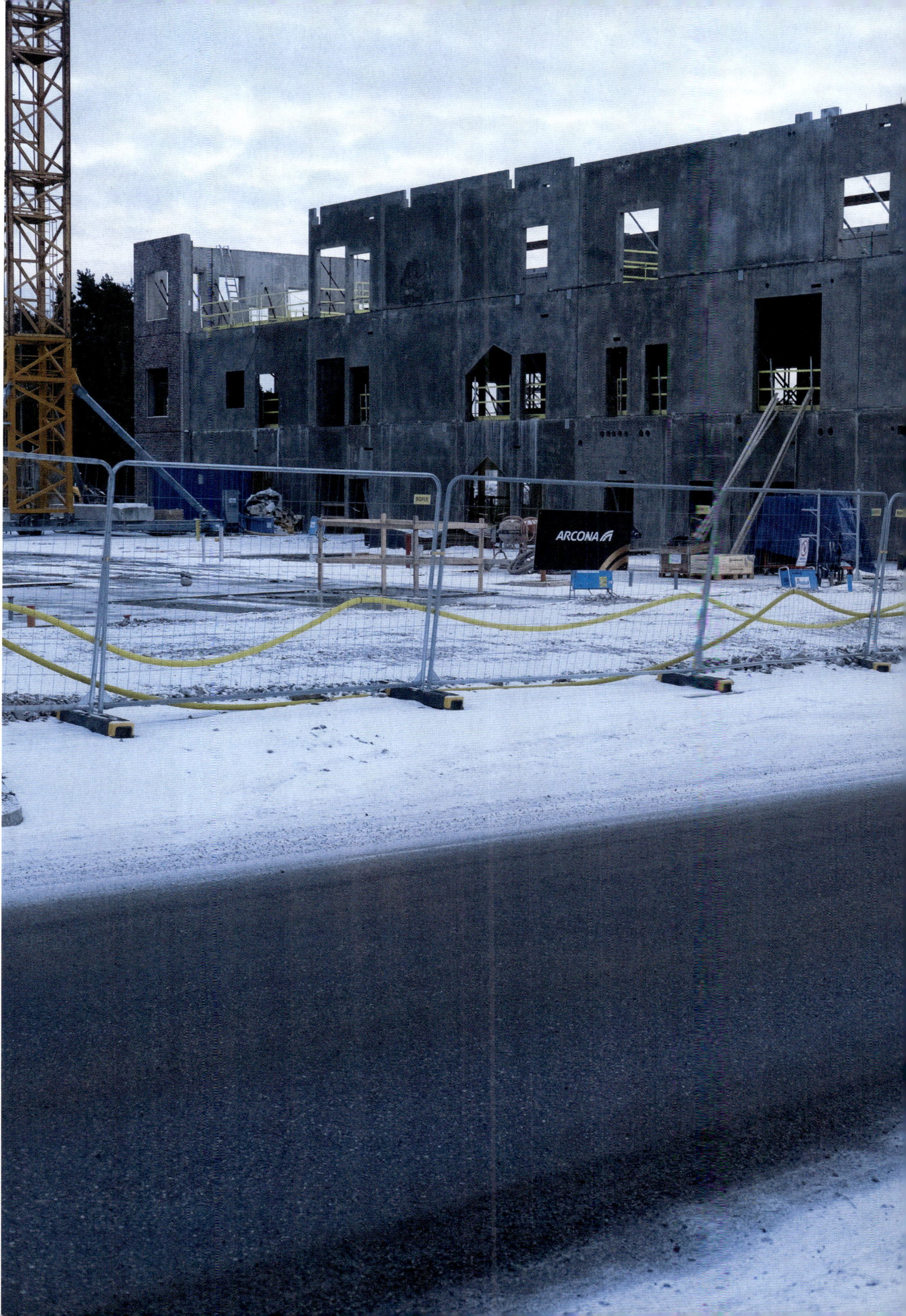

ARCONA

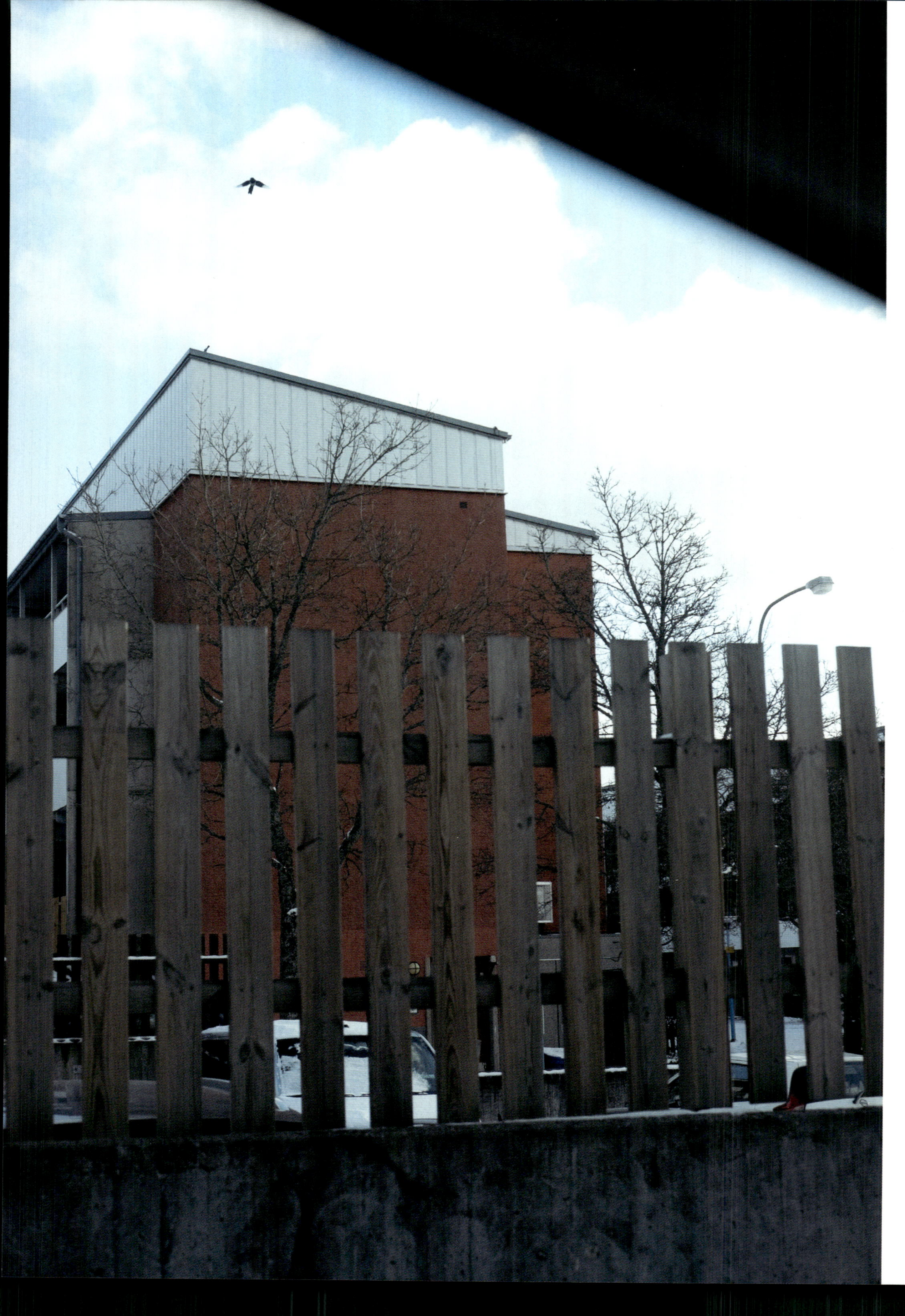

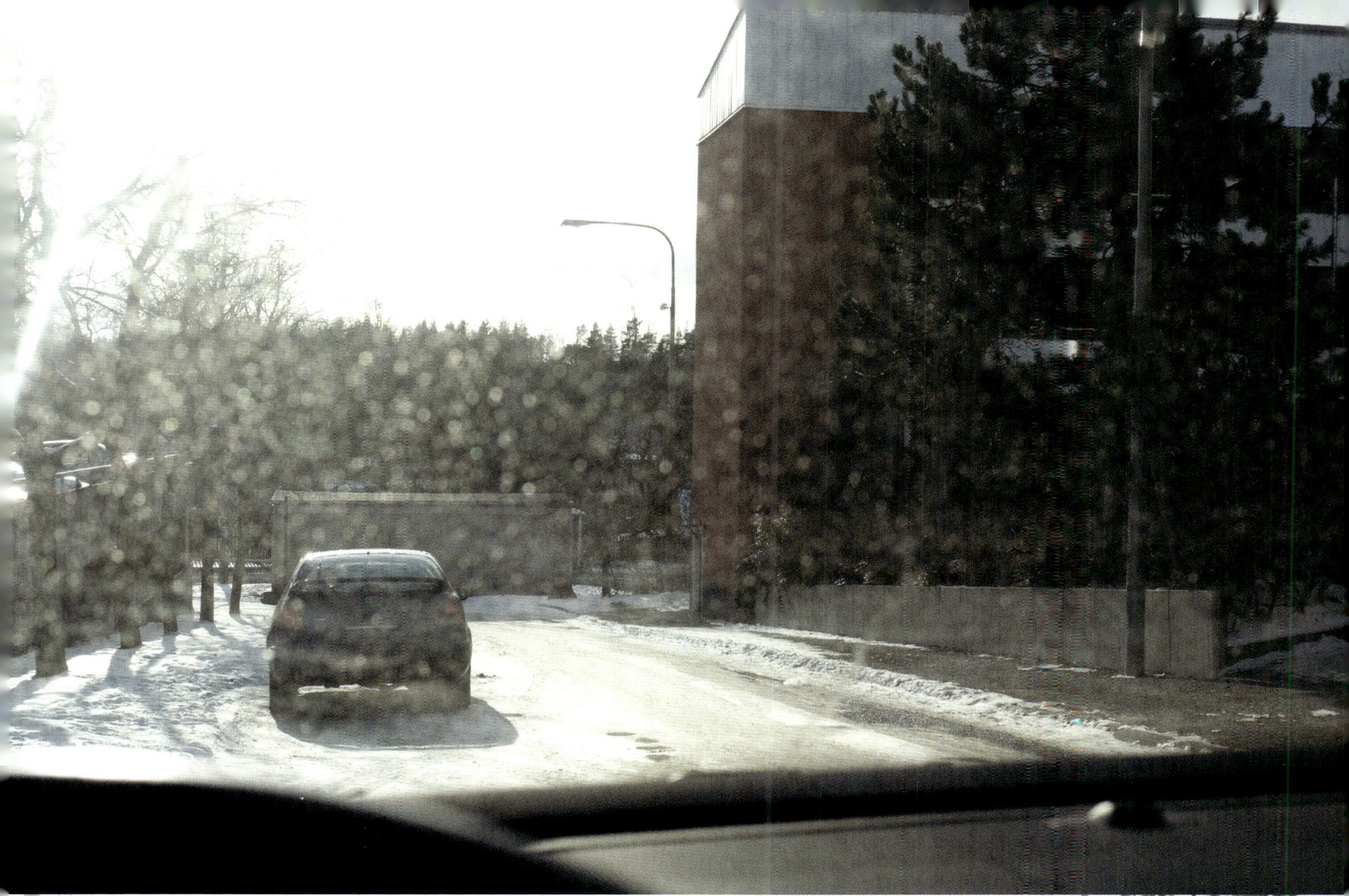

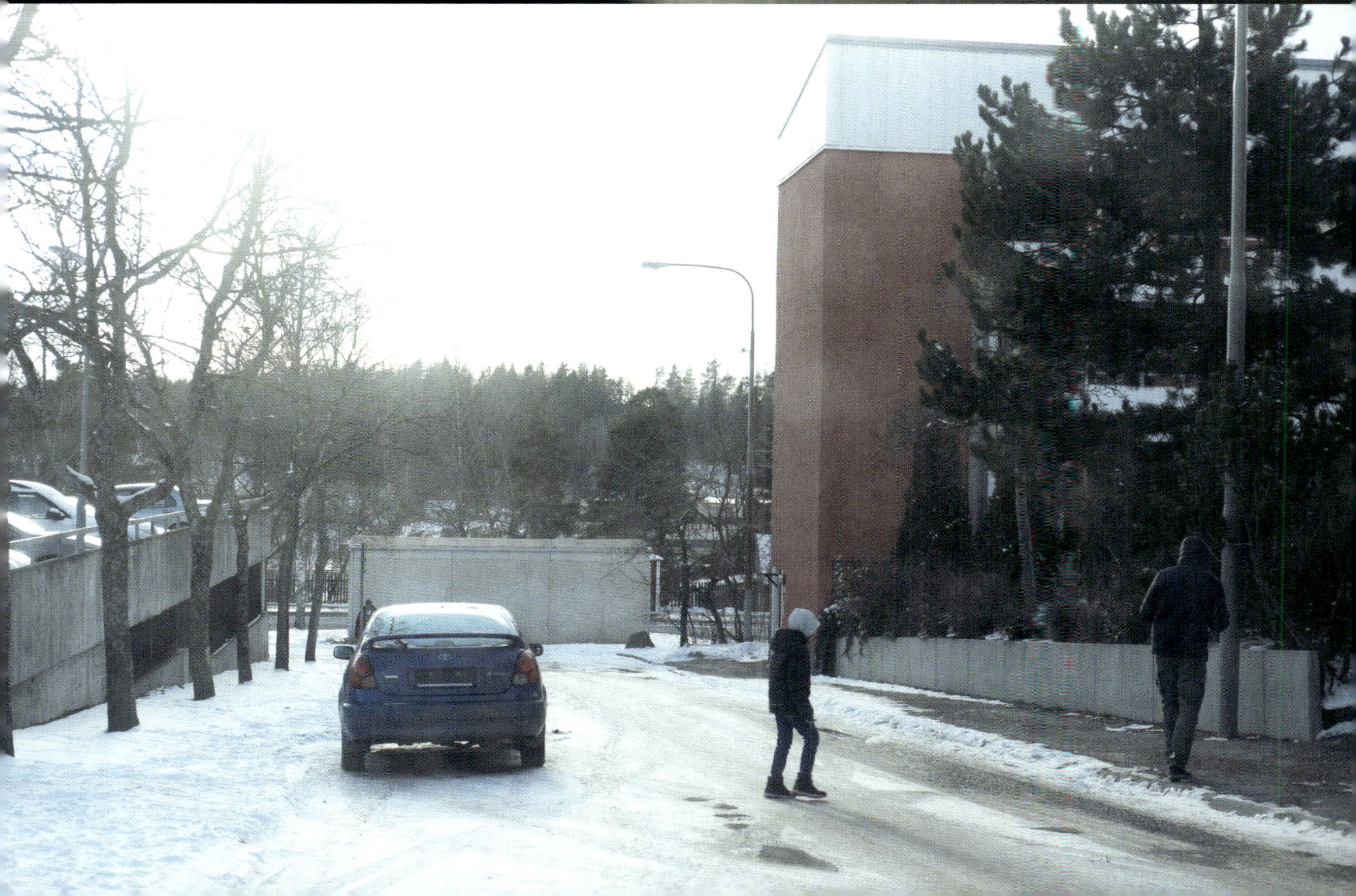

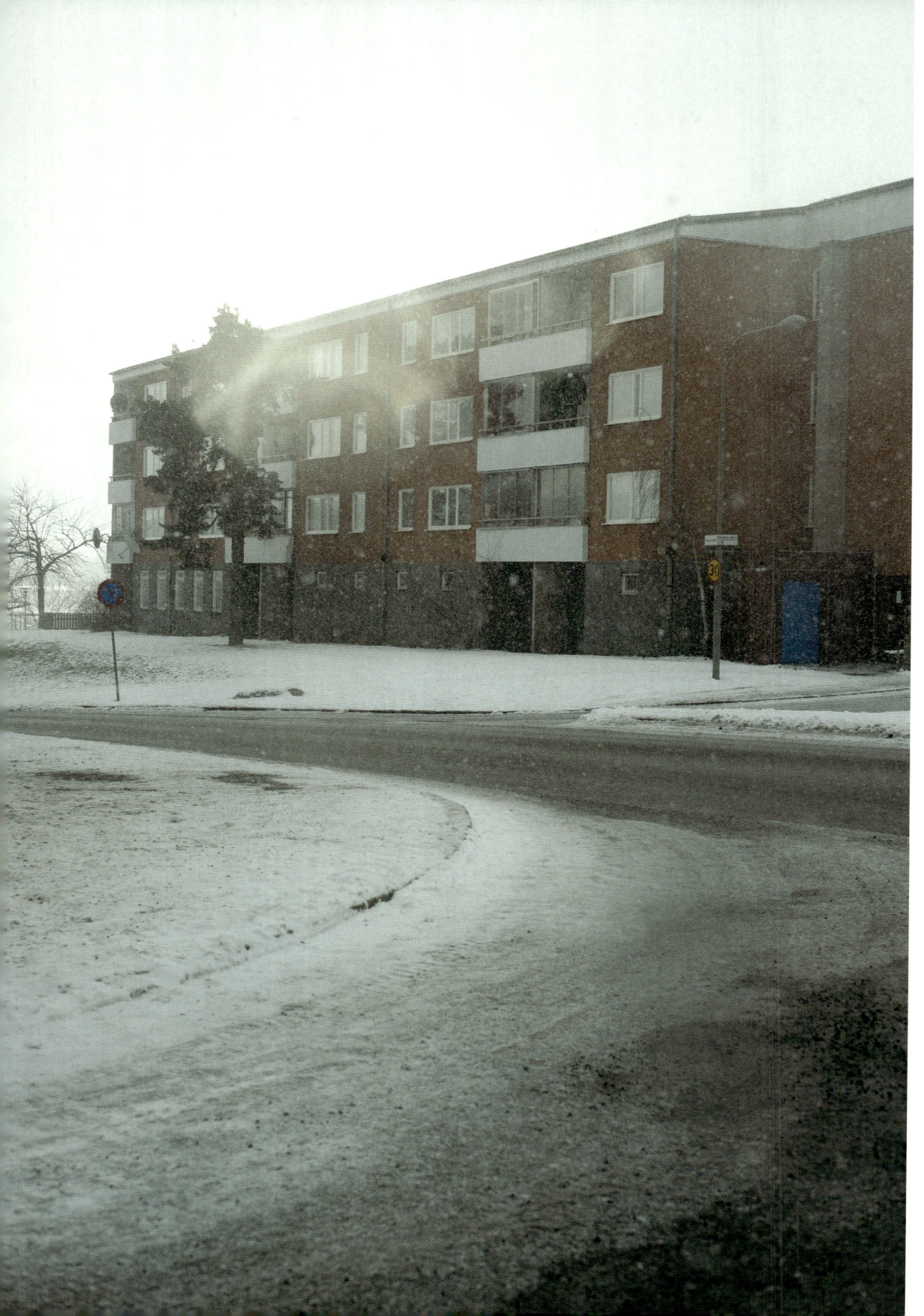

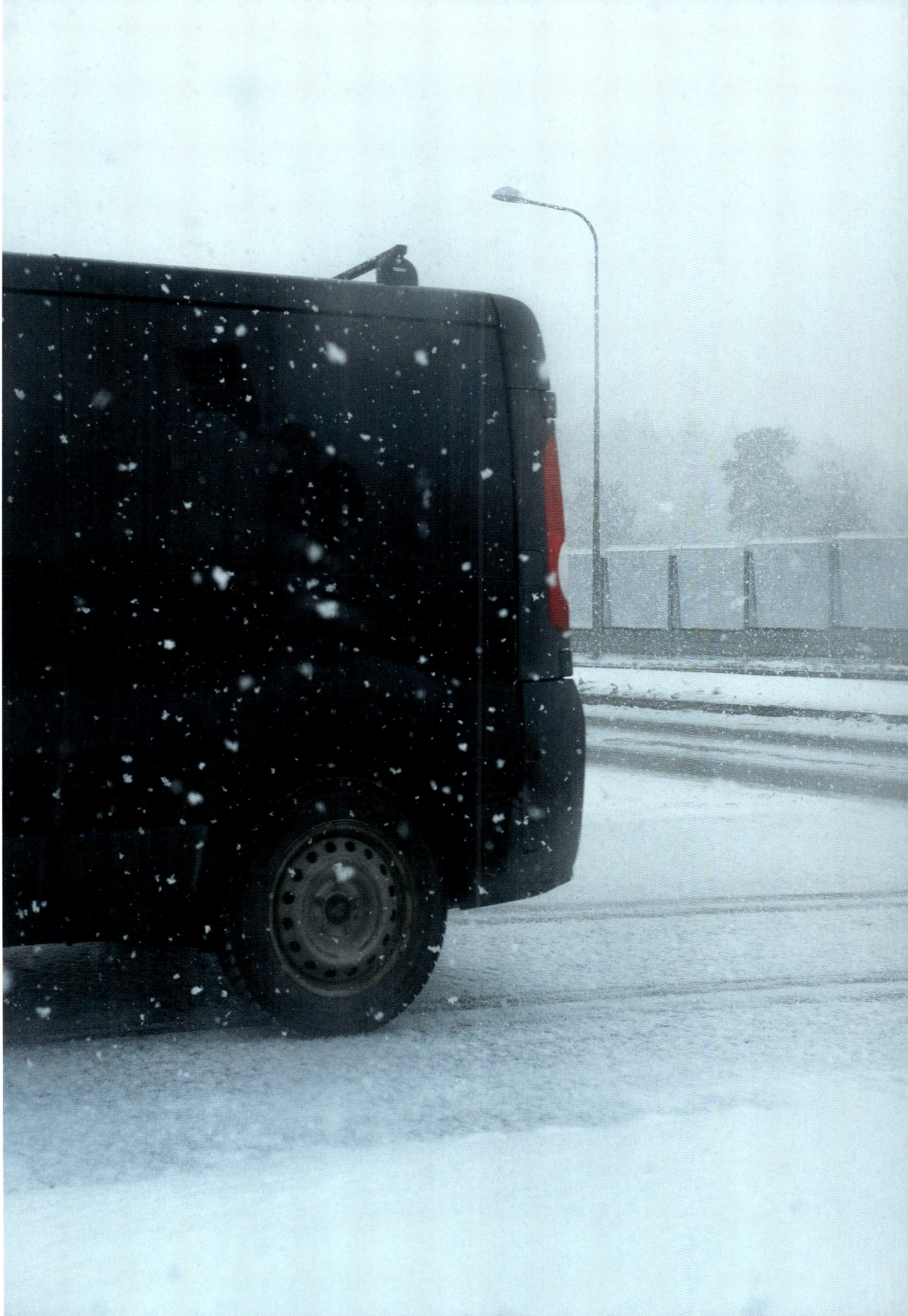

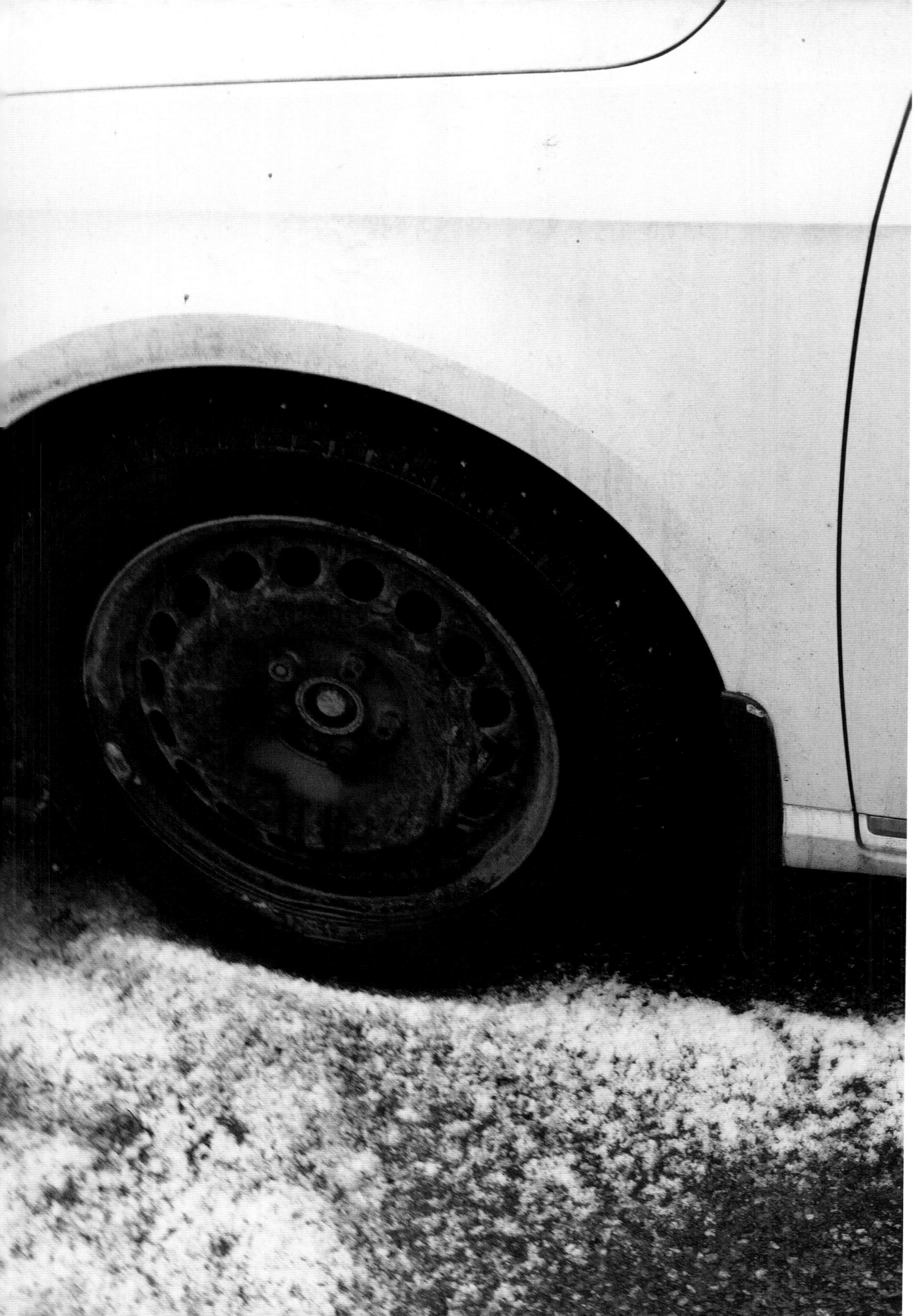

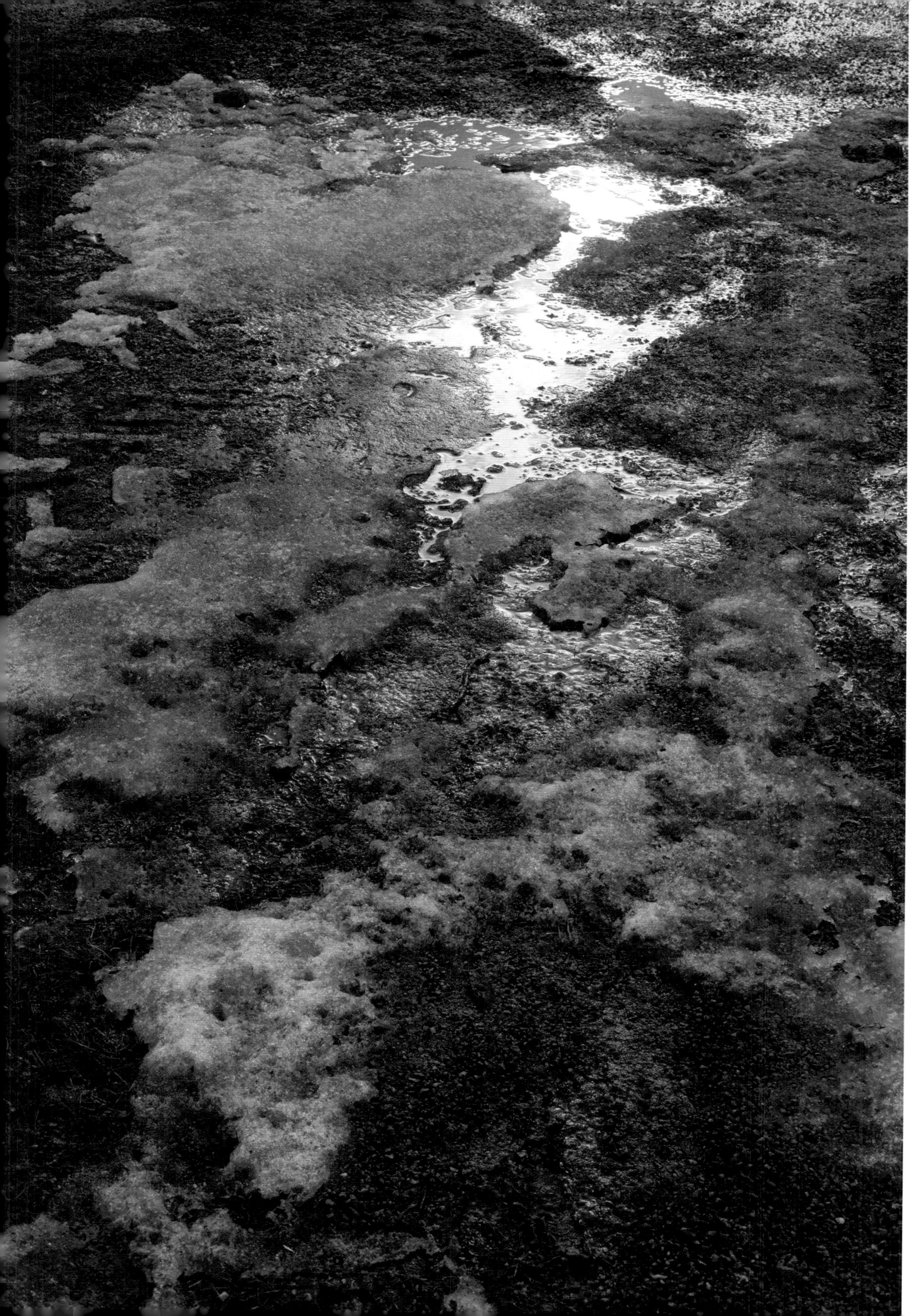

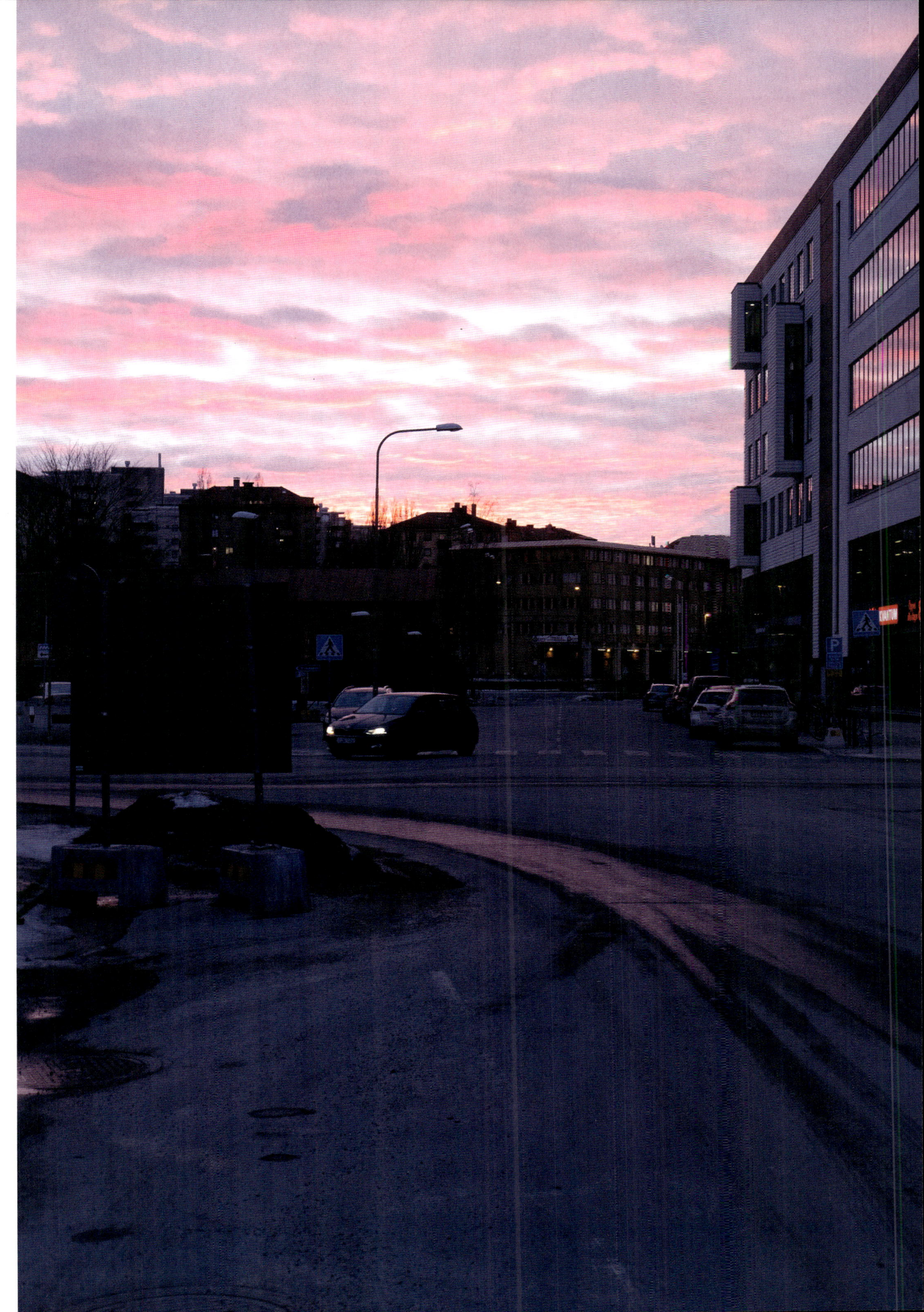

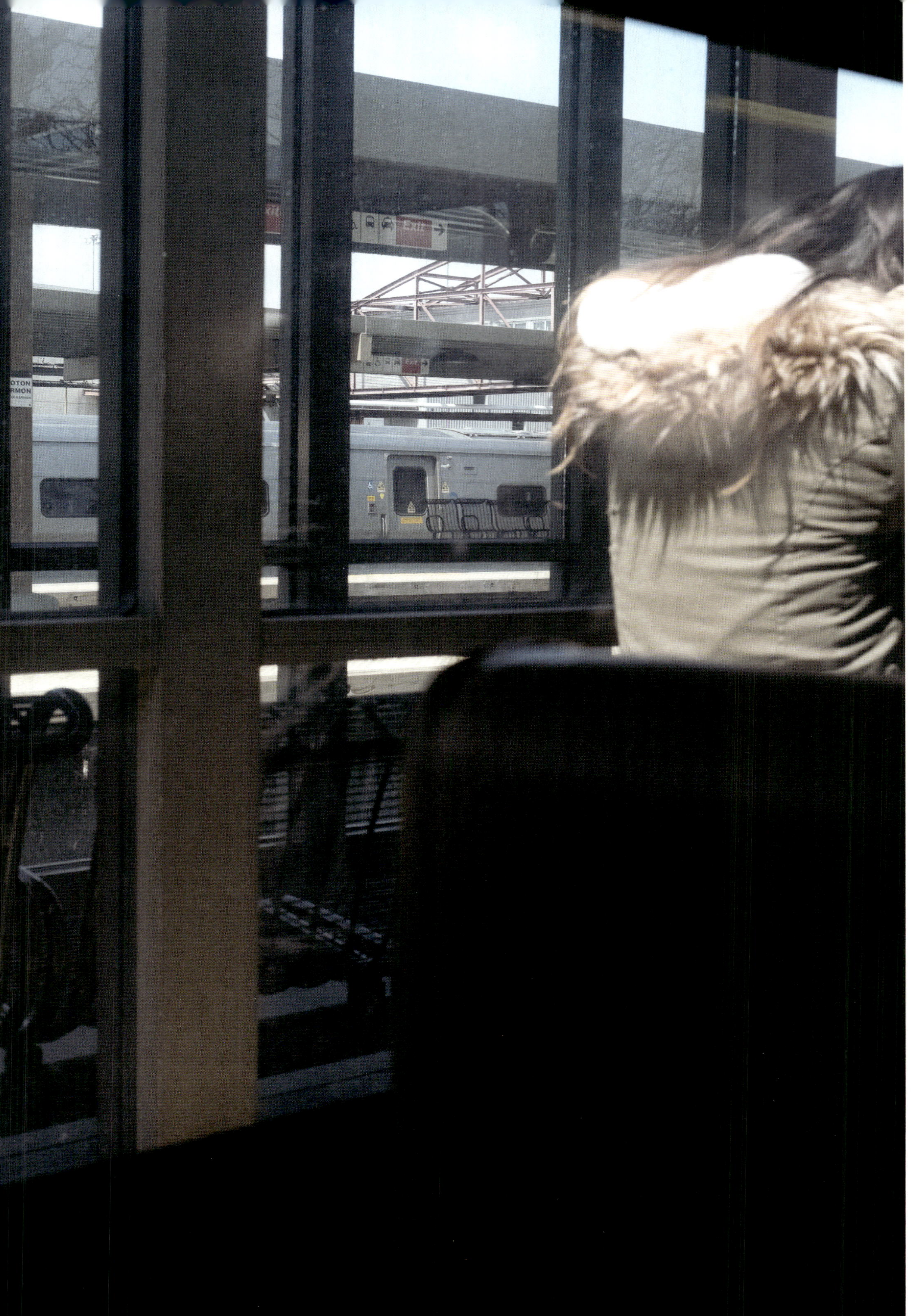
Exit →
Exit →
OTON
RMON

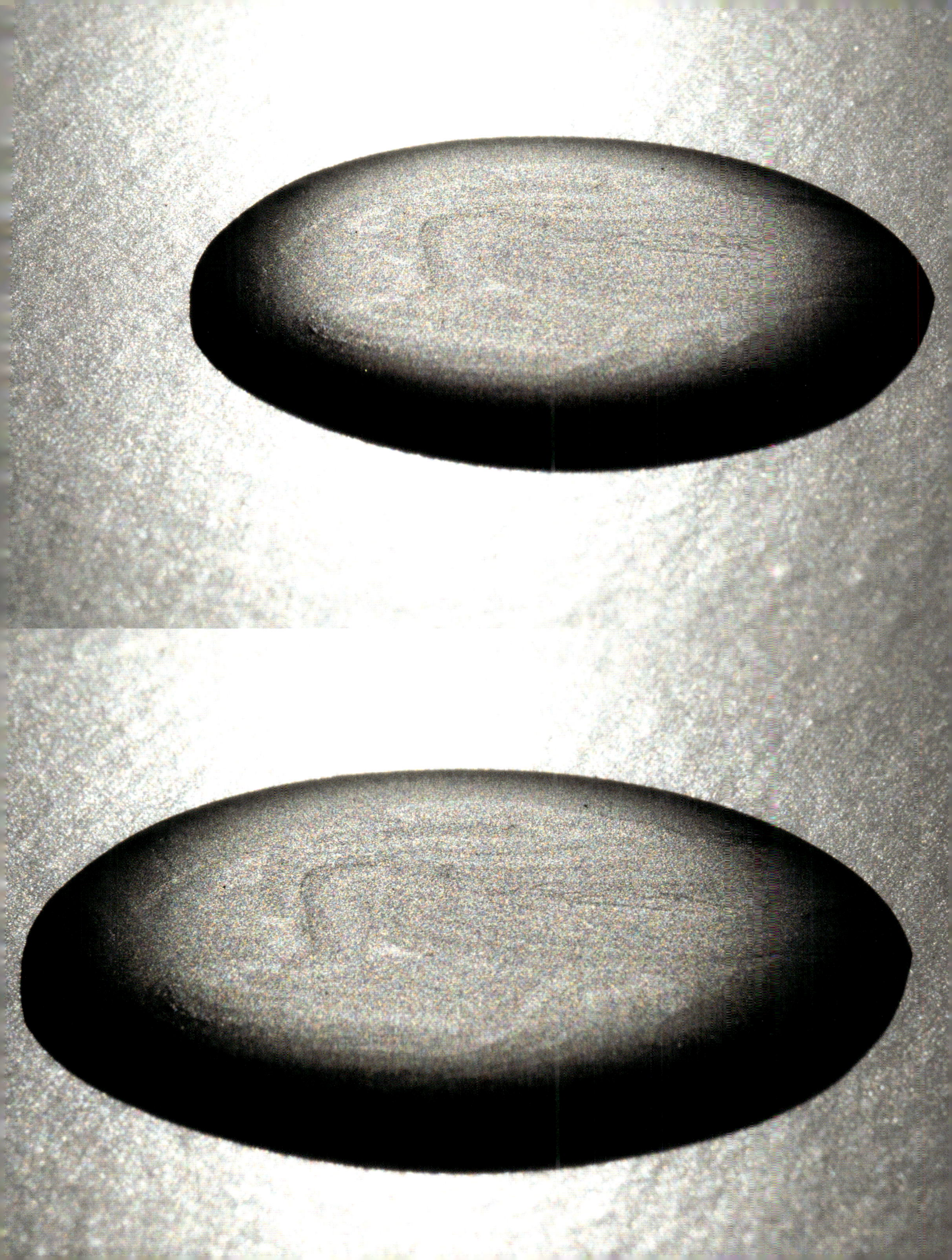

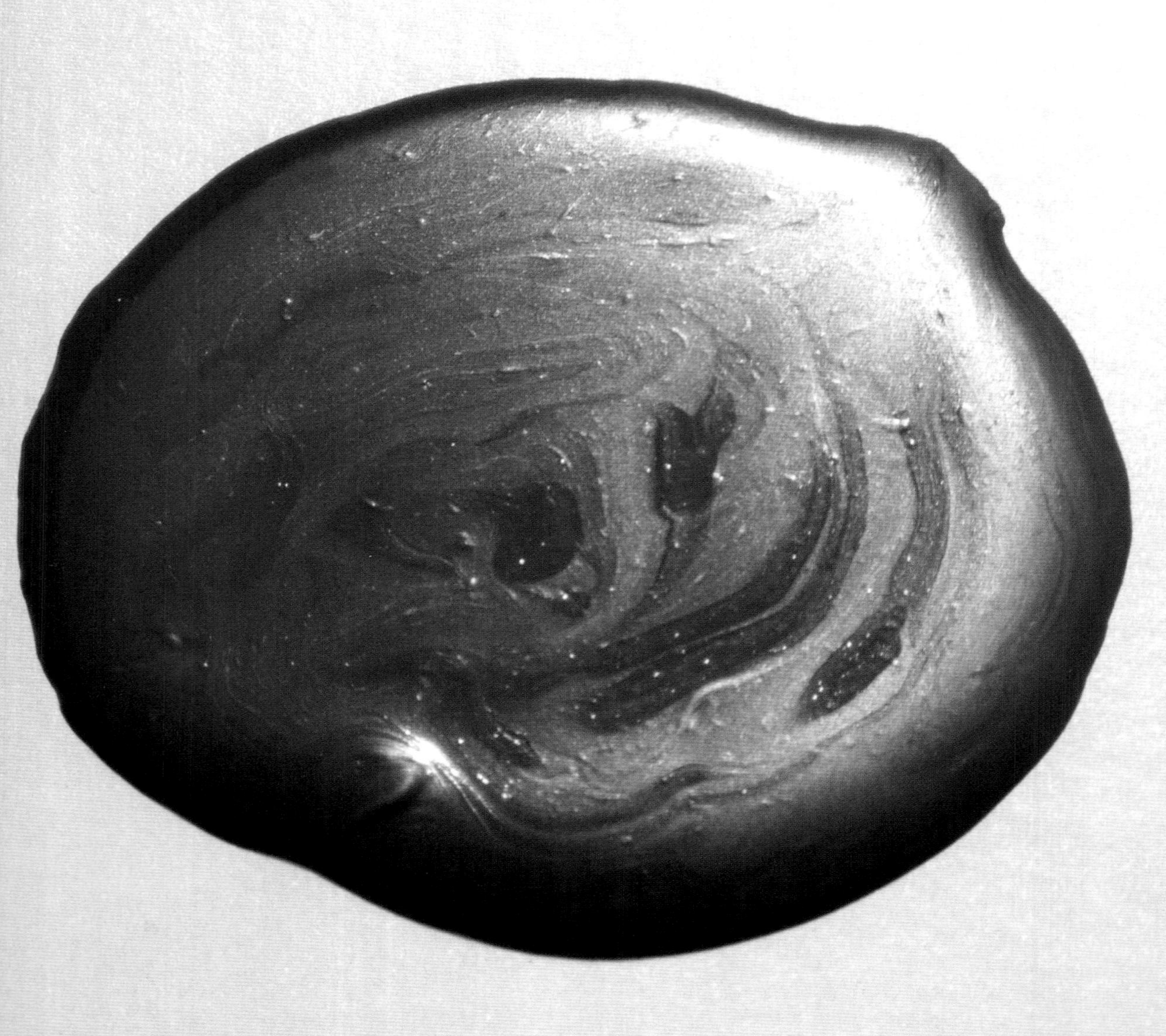

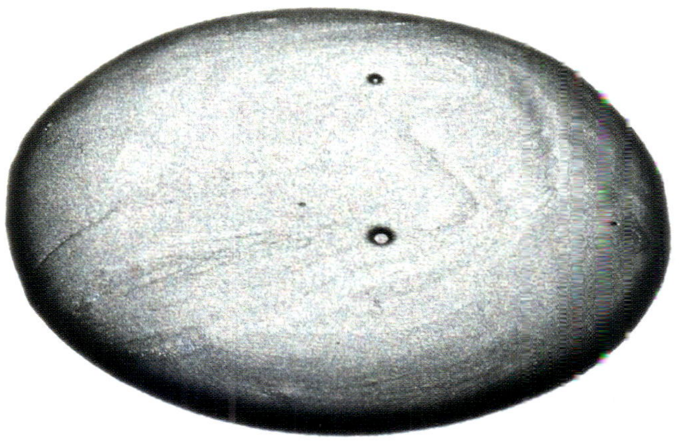

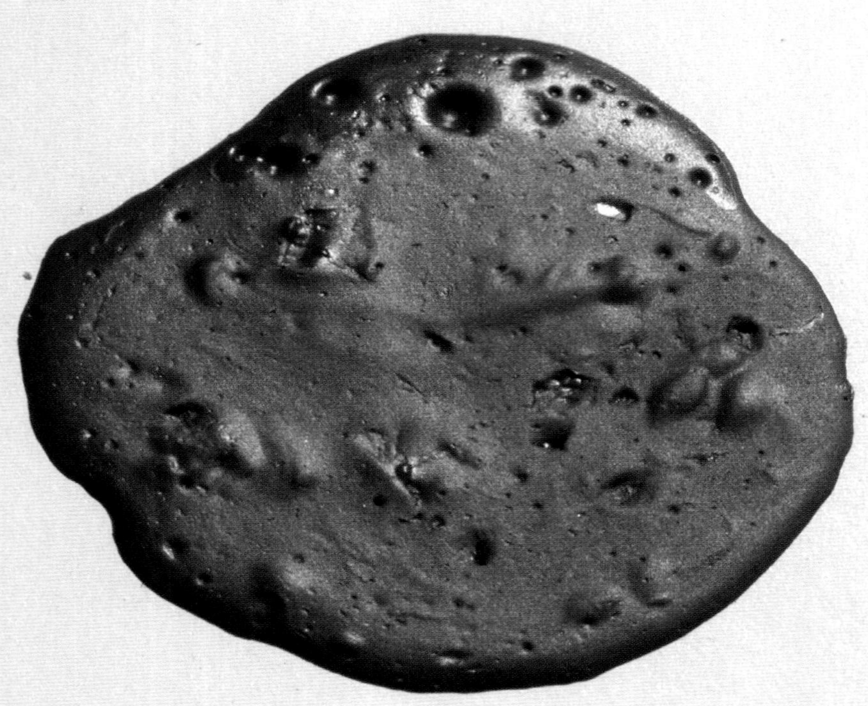

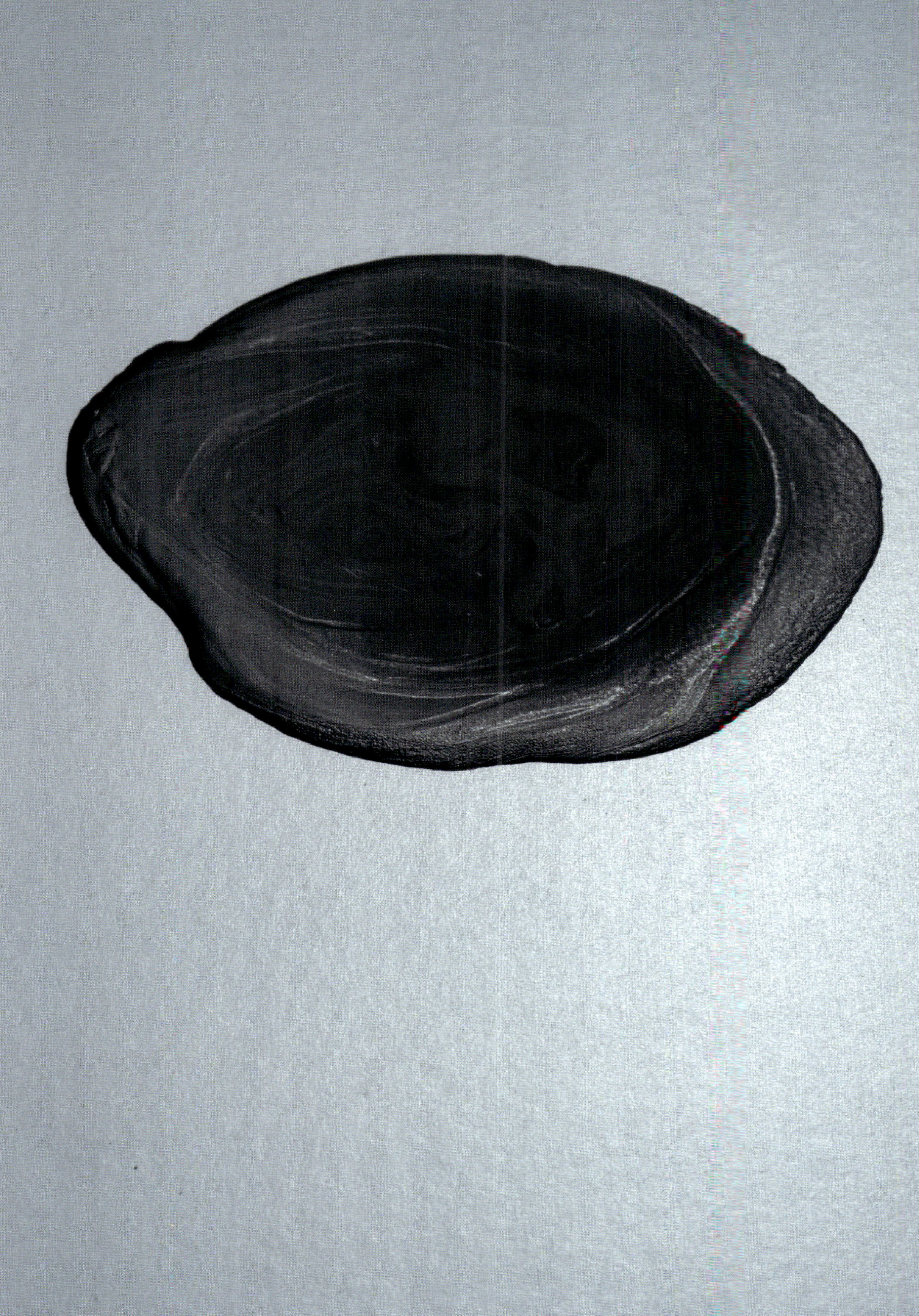

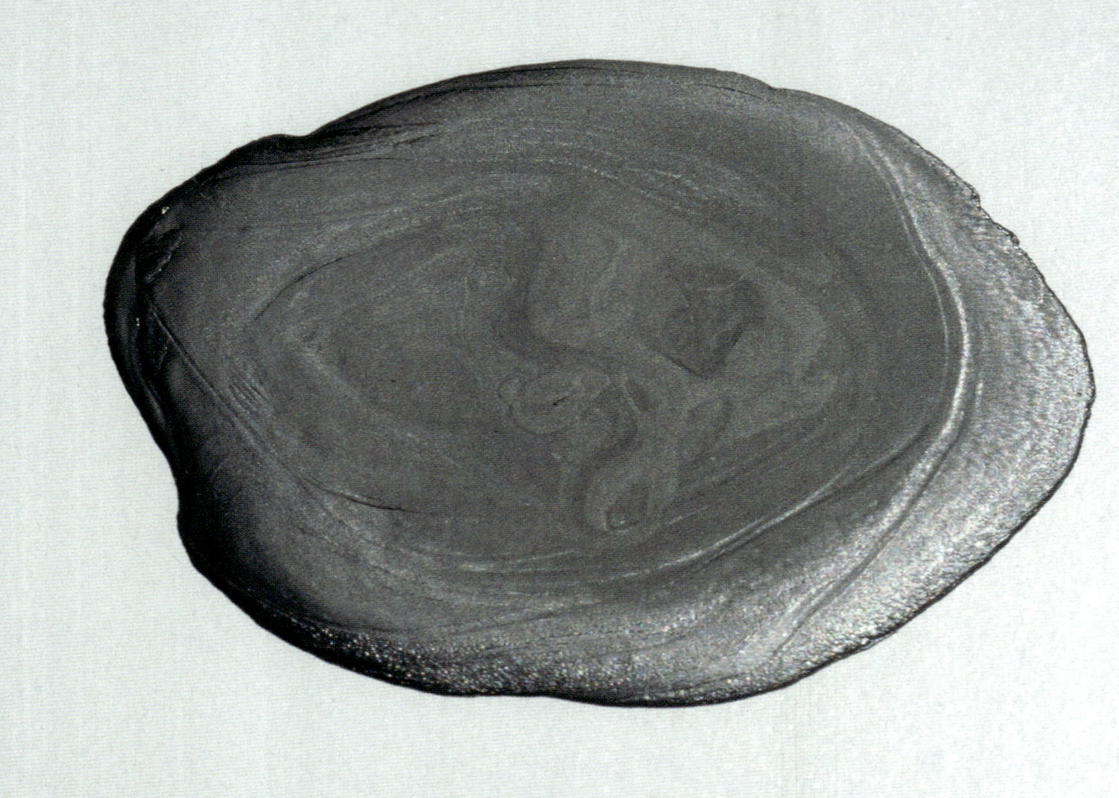

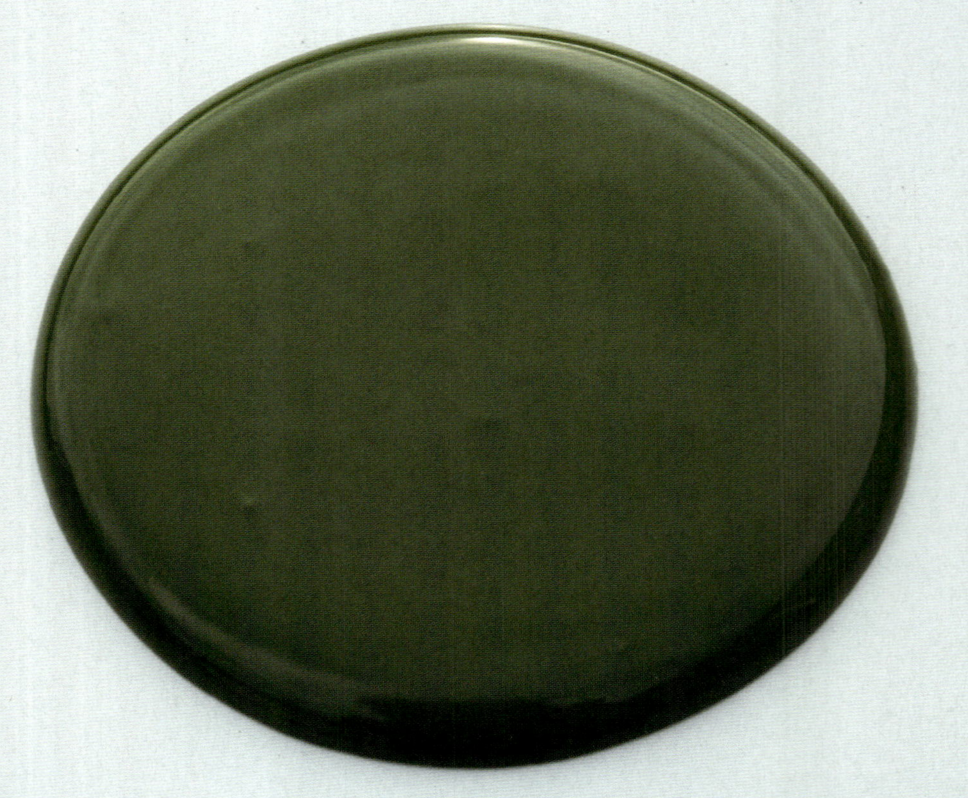

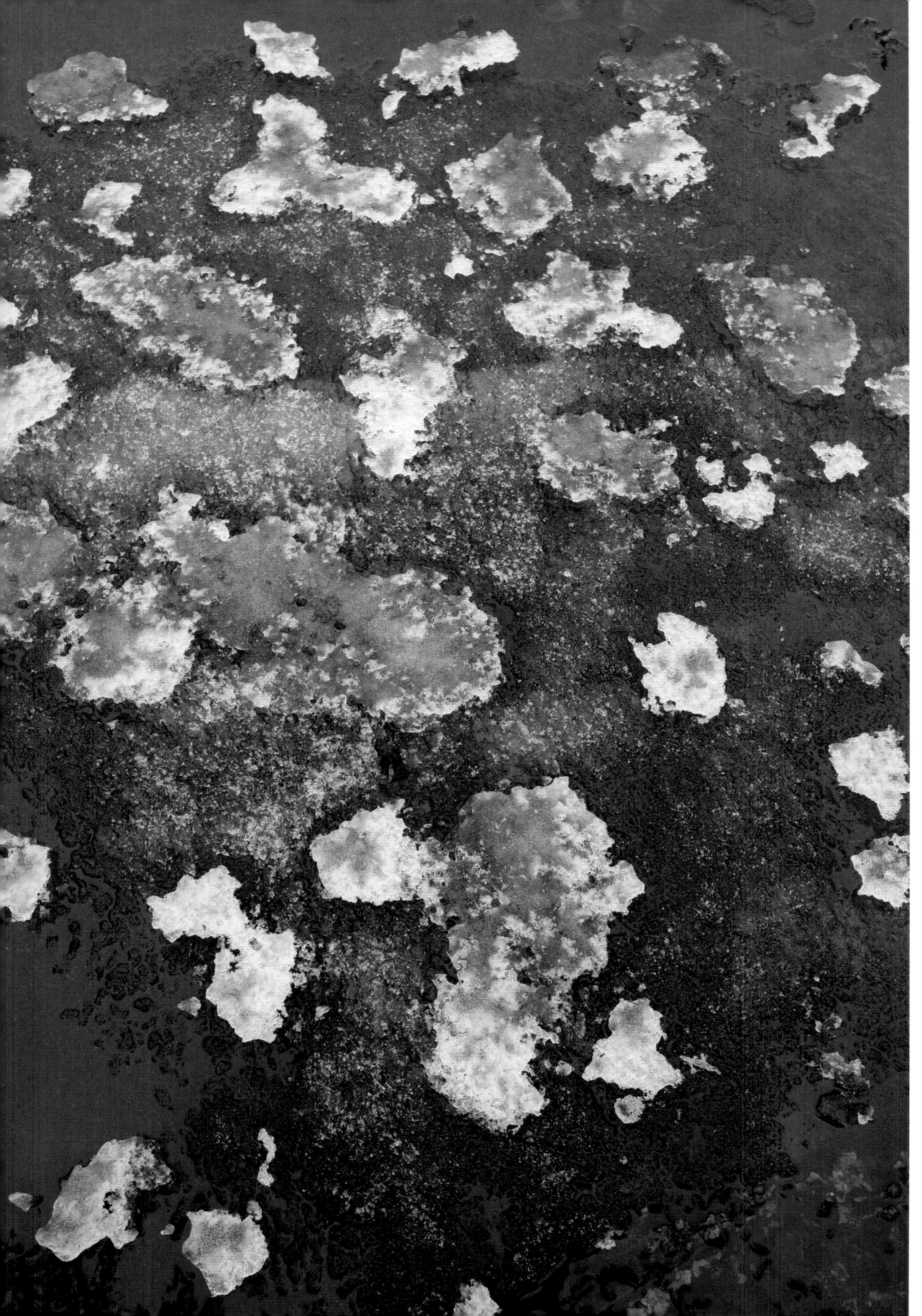

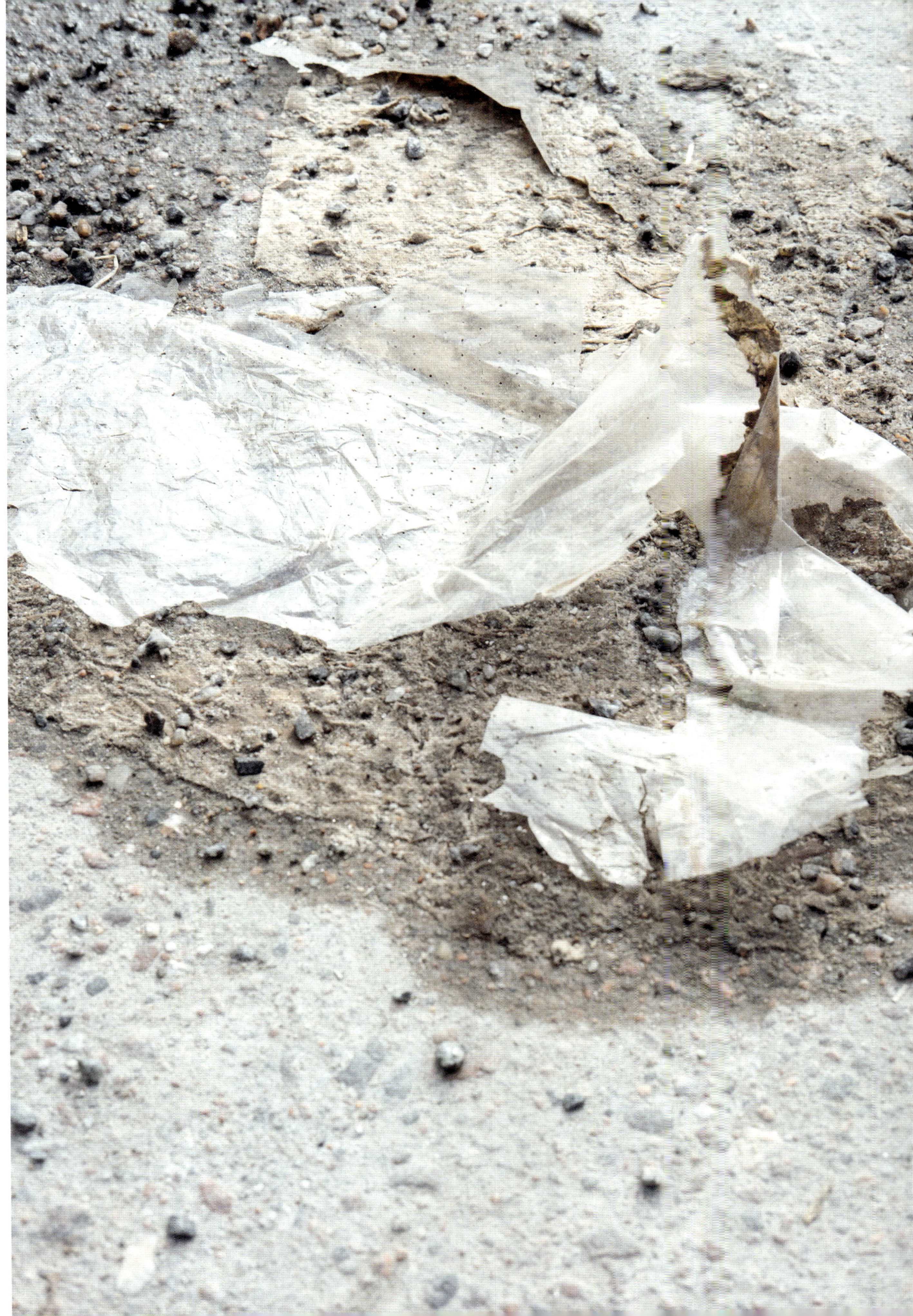

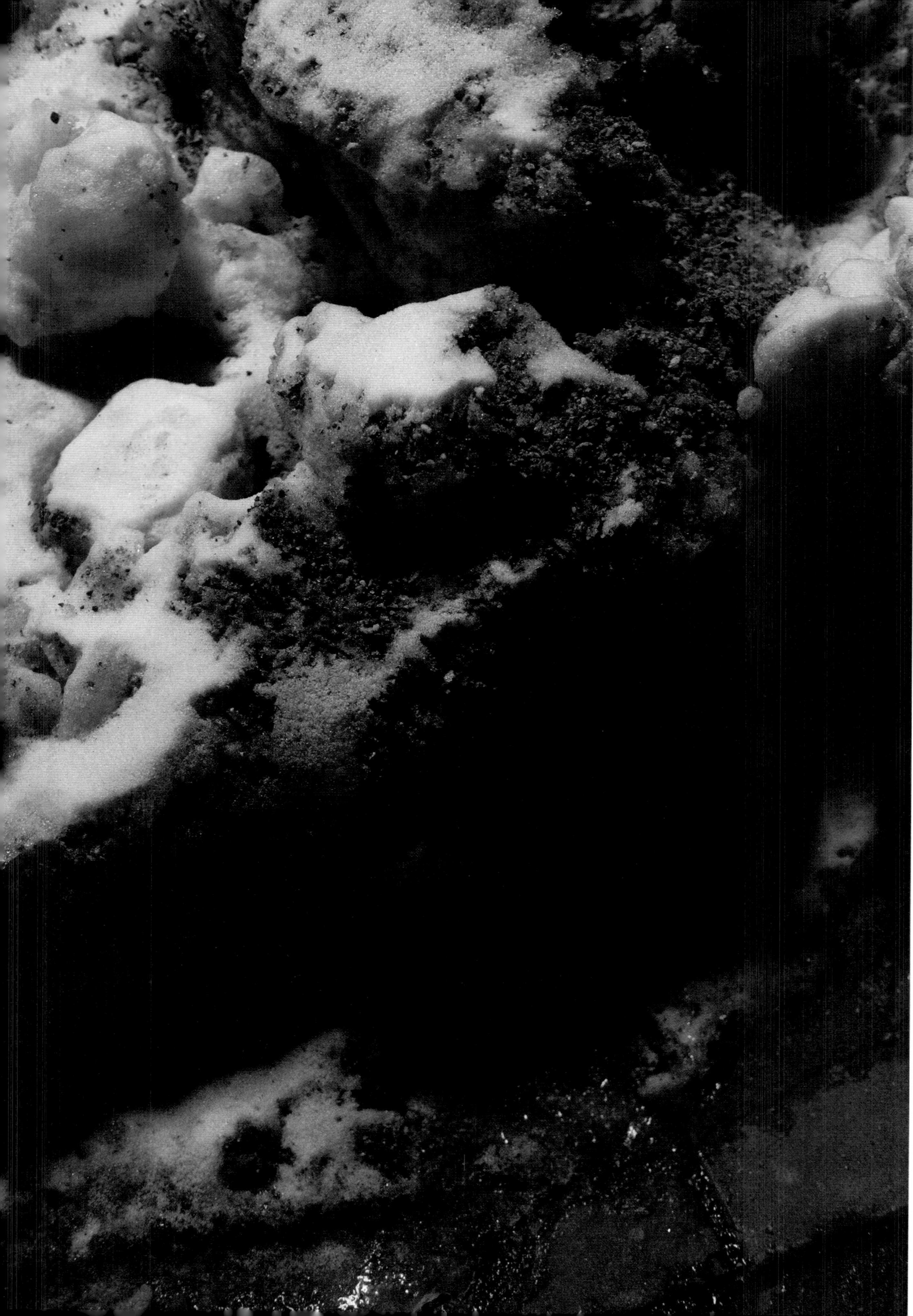

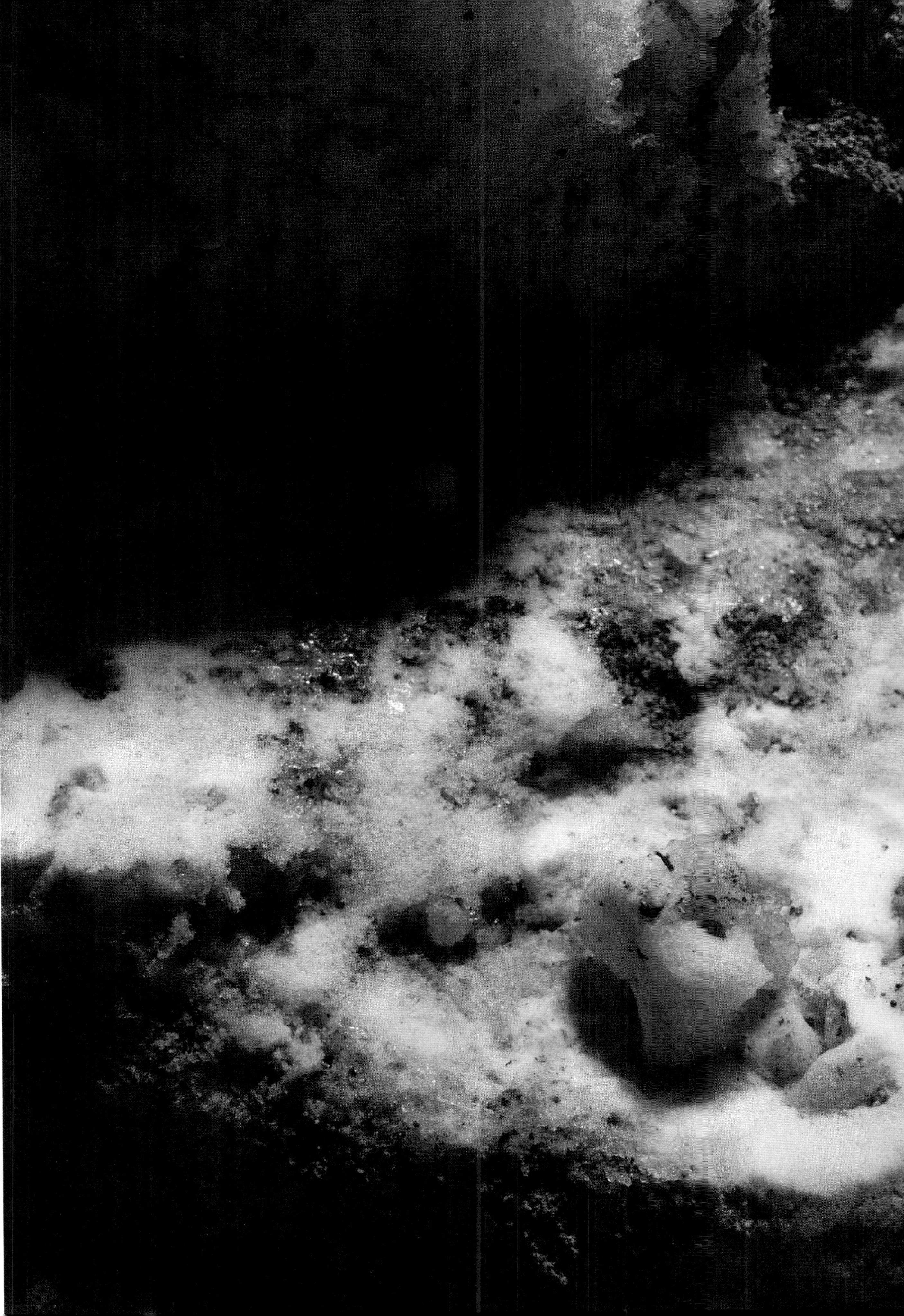

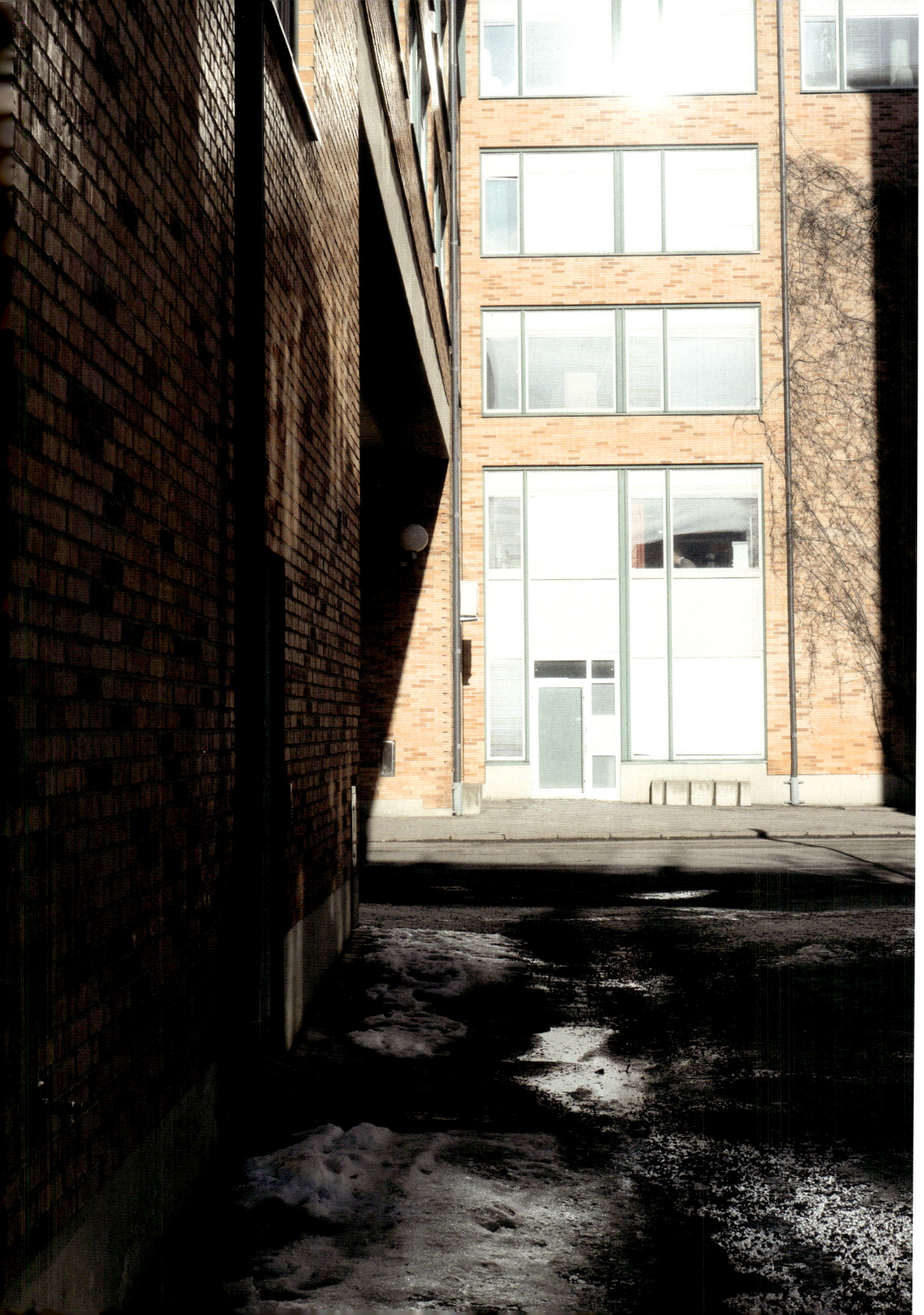

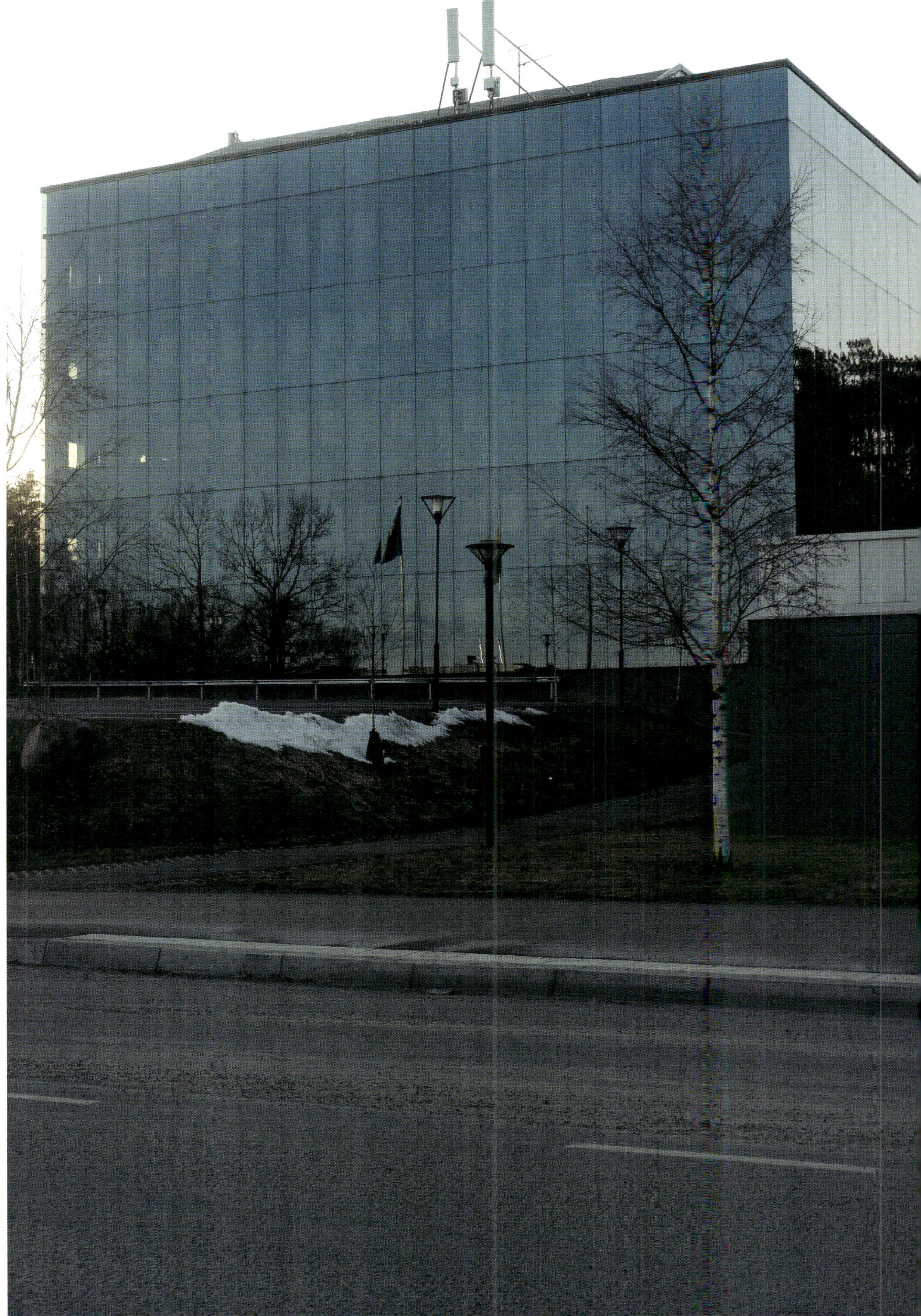

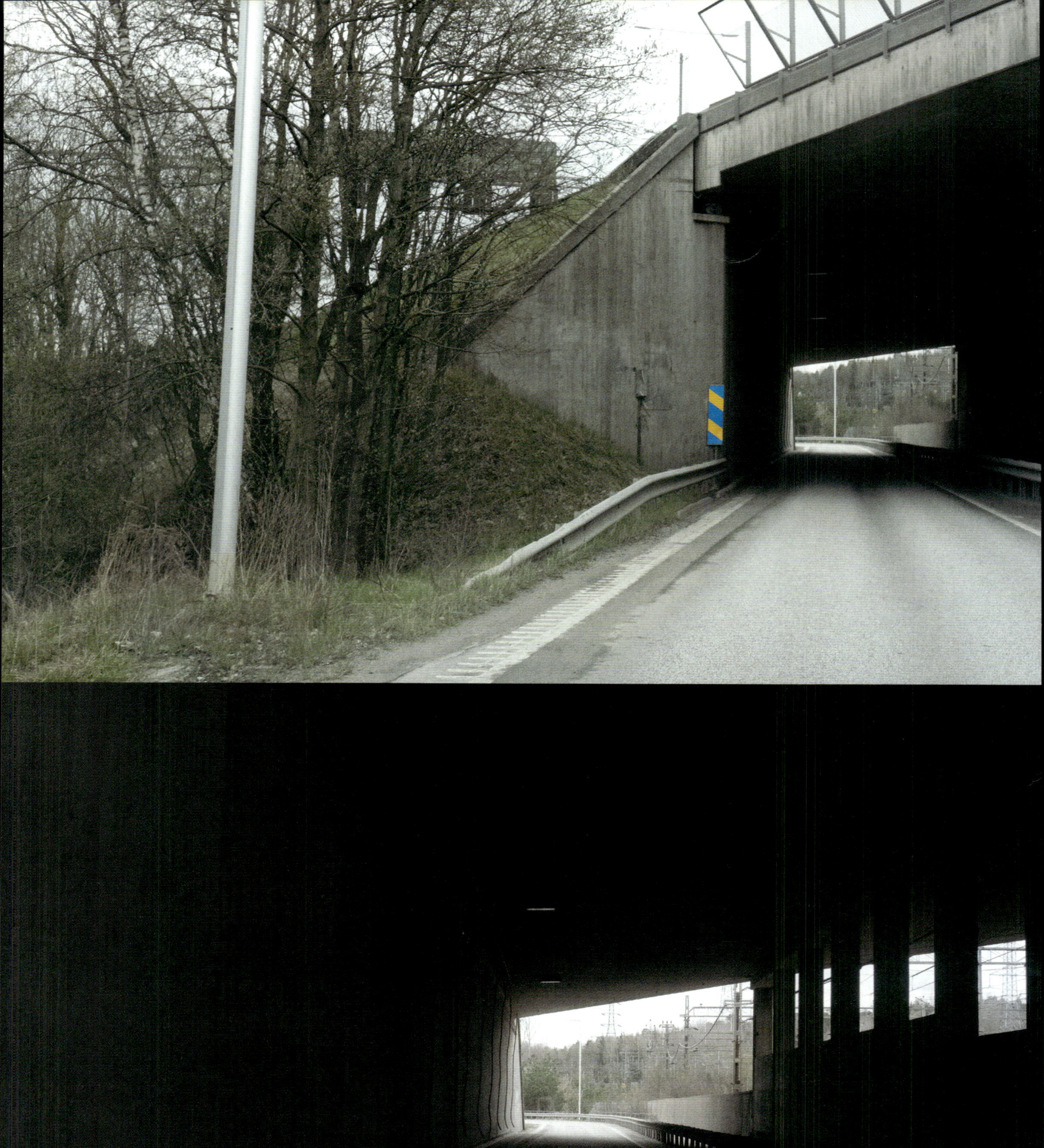

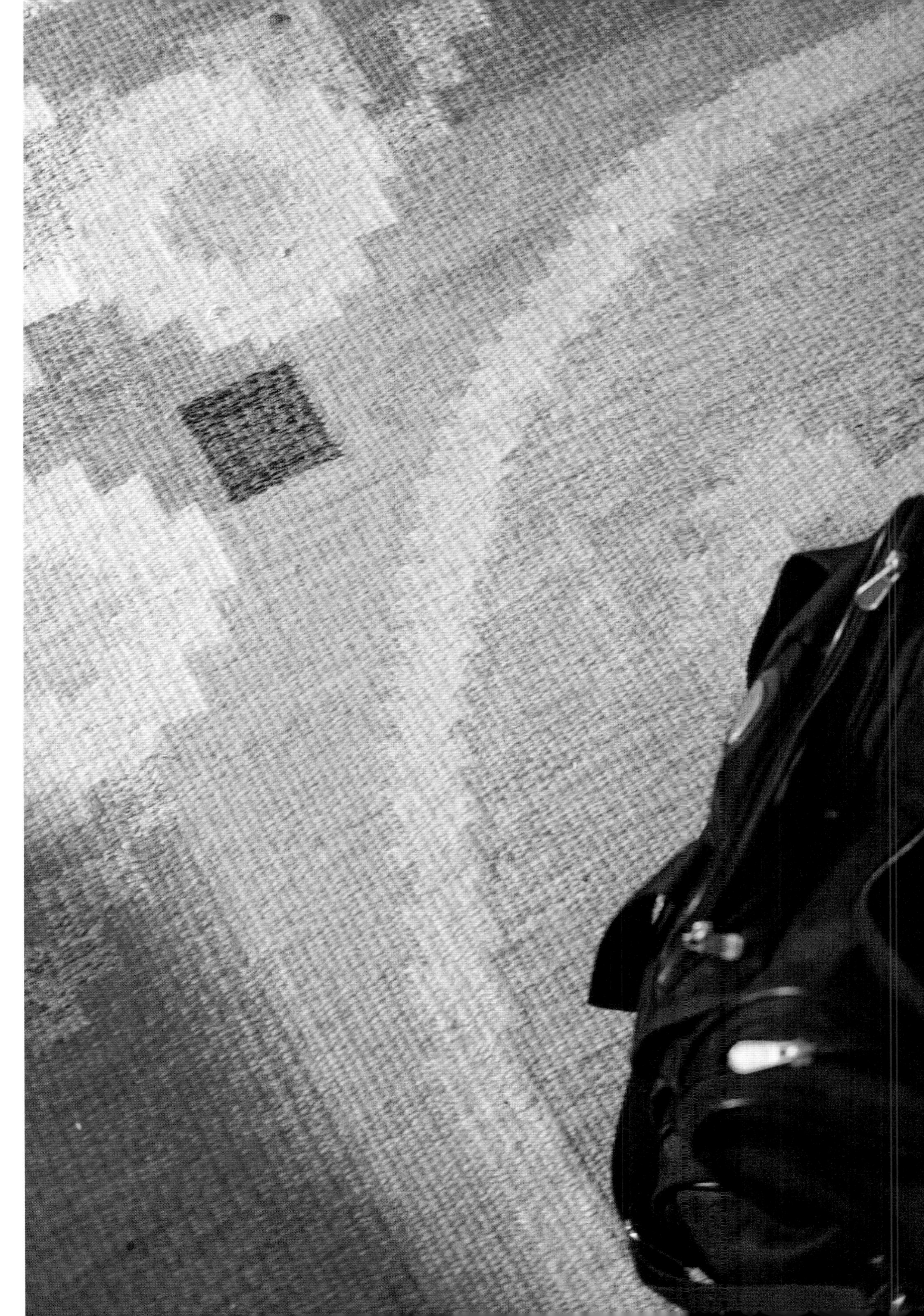

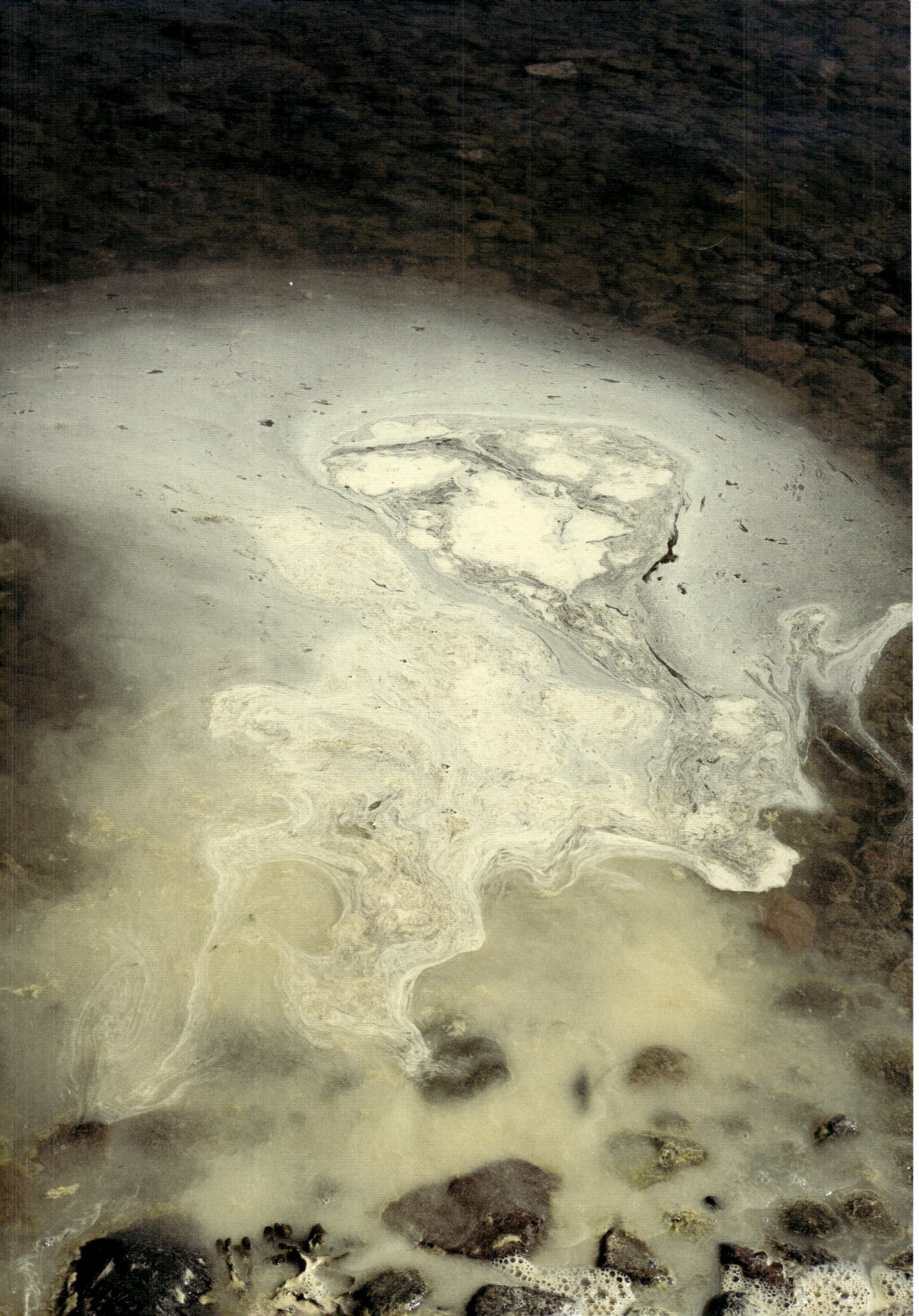

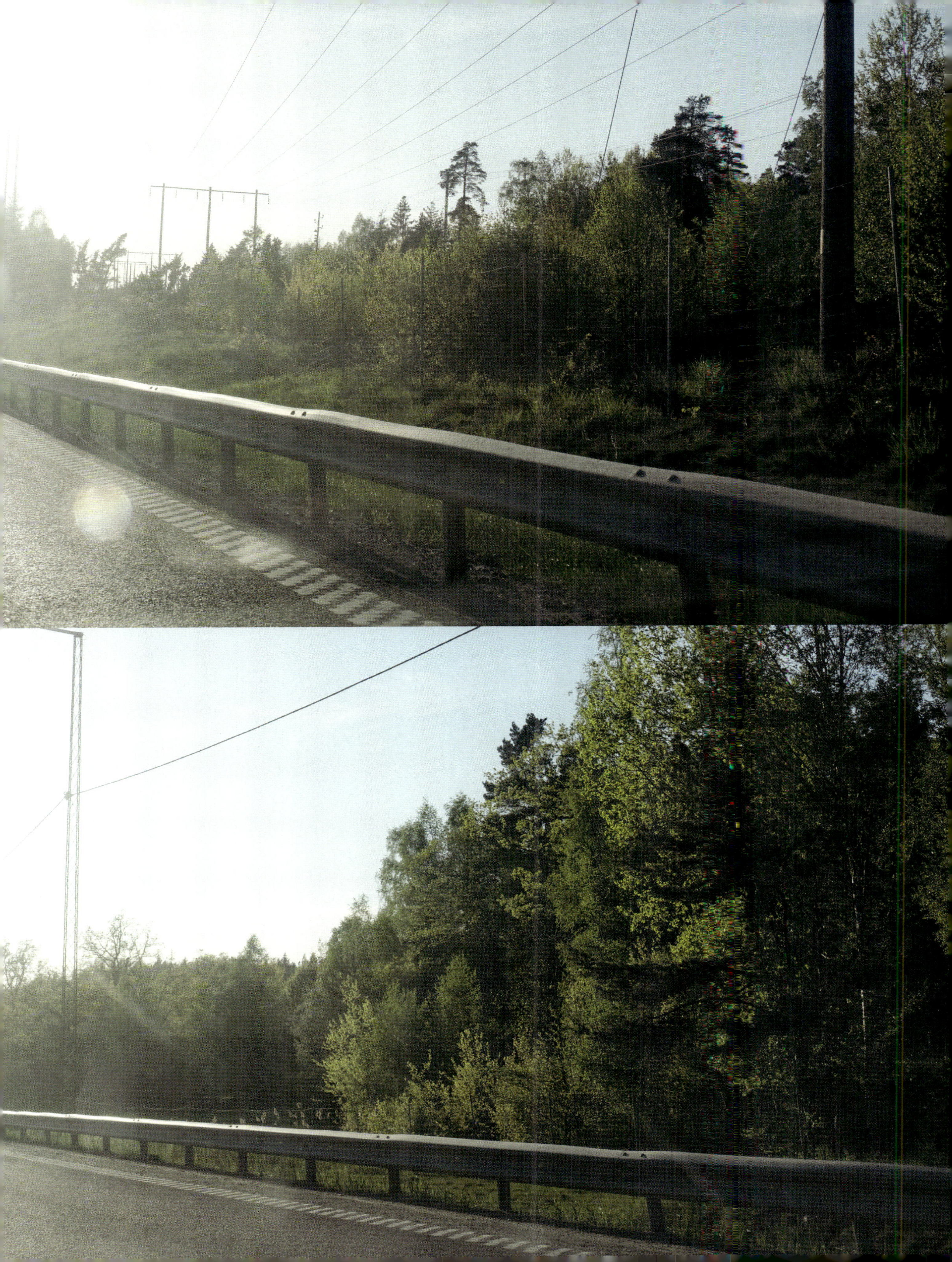

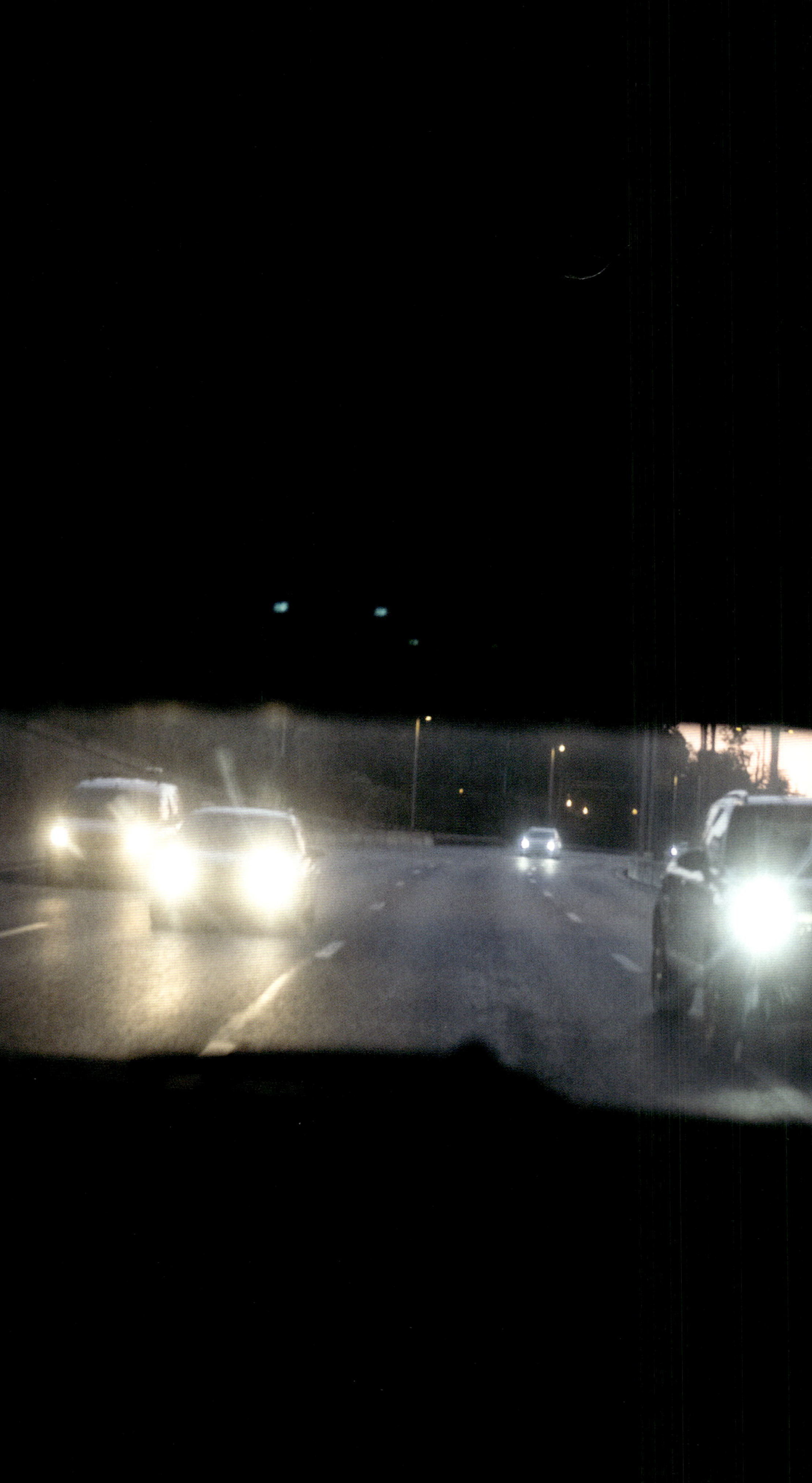

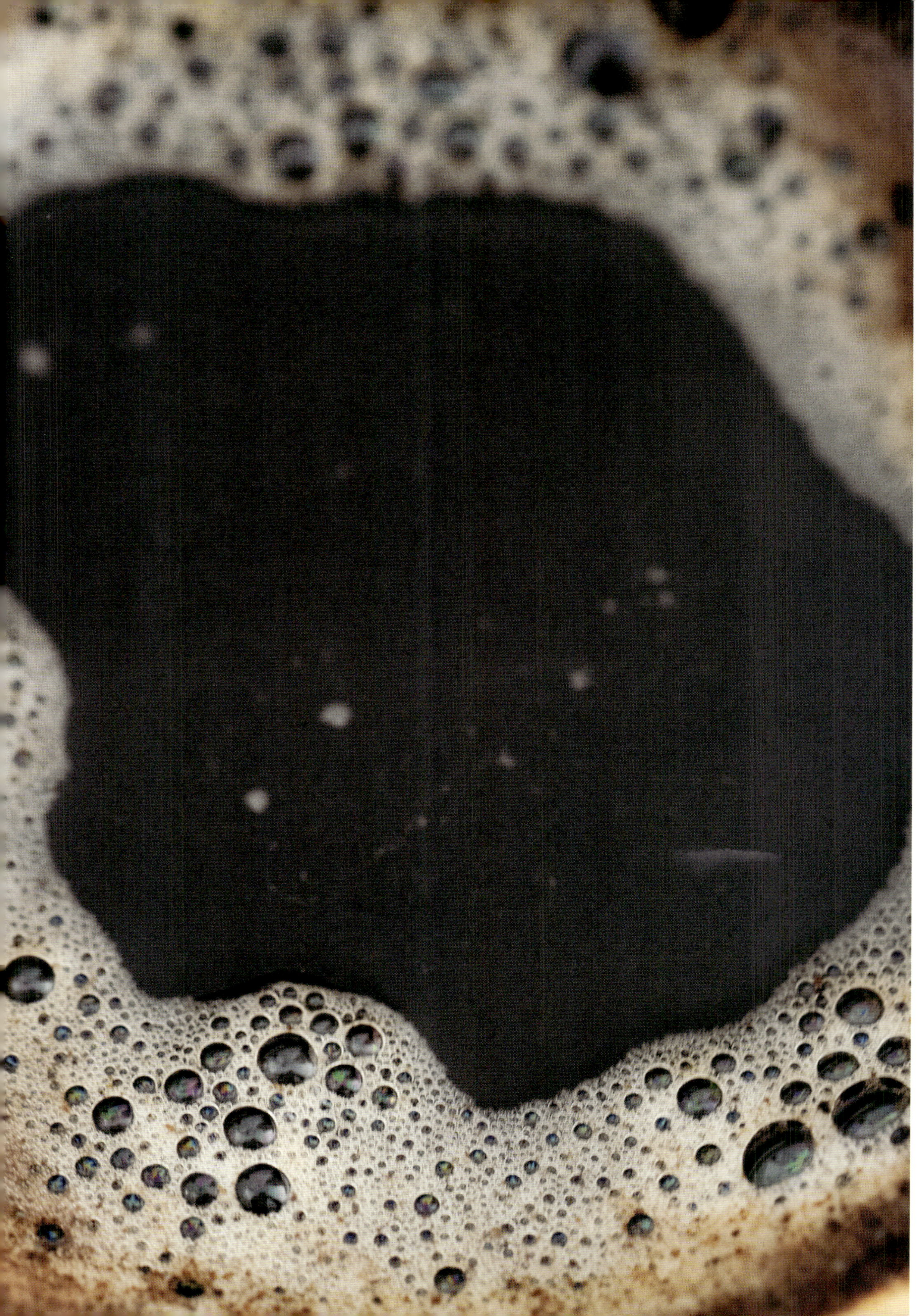

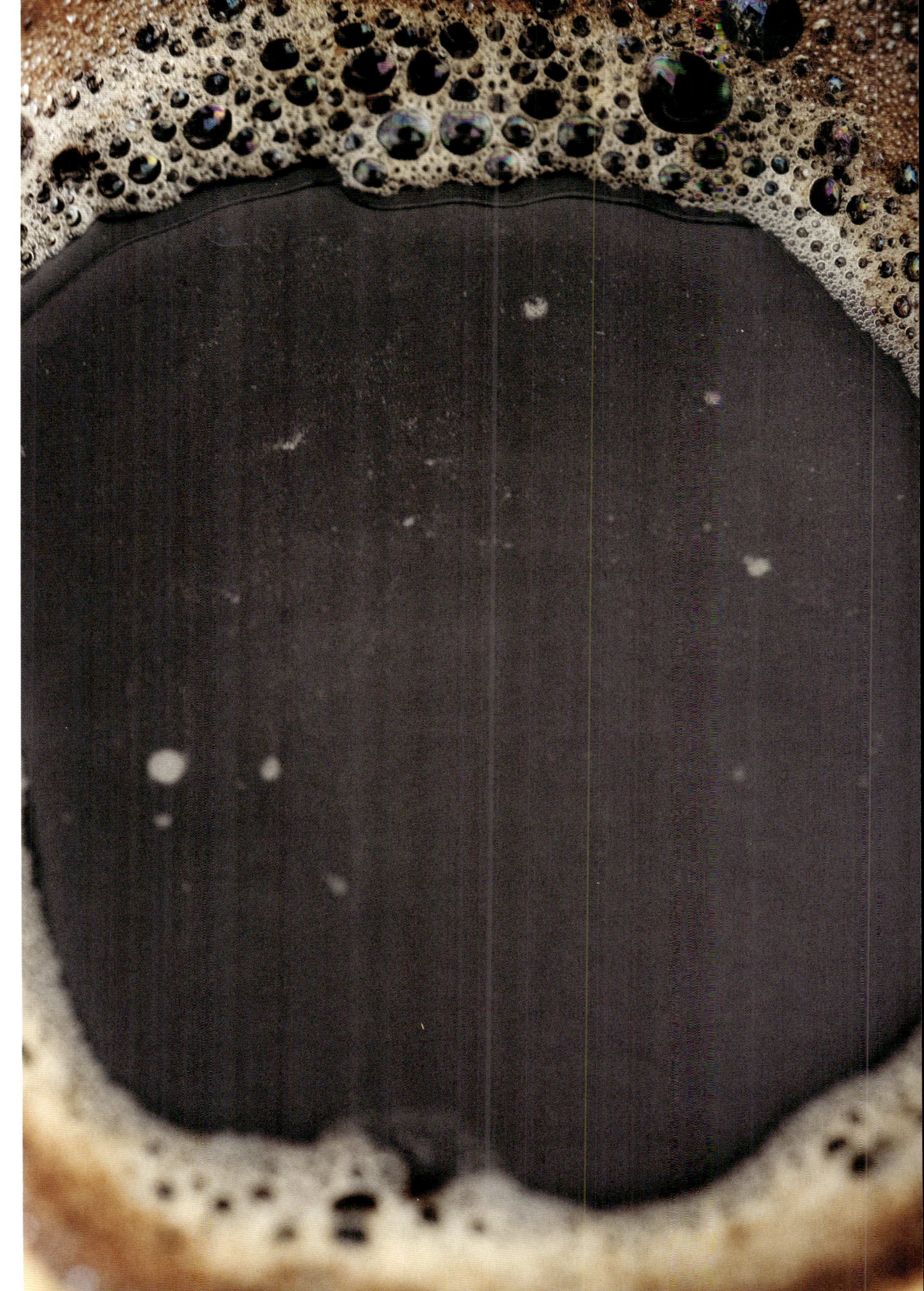

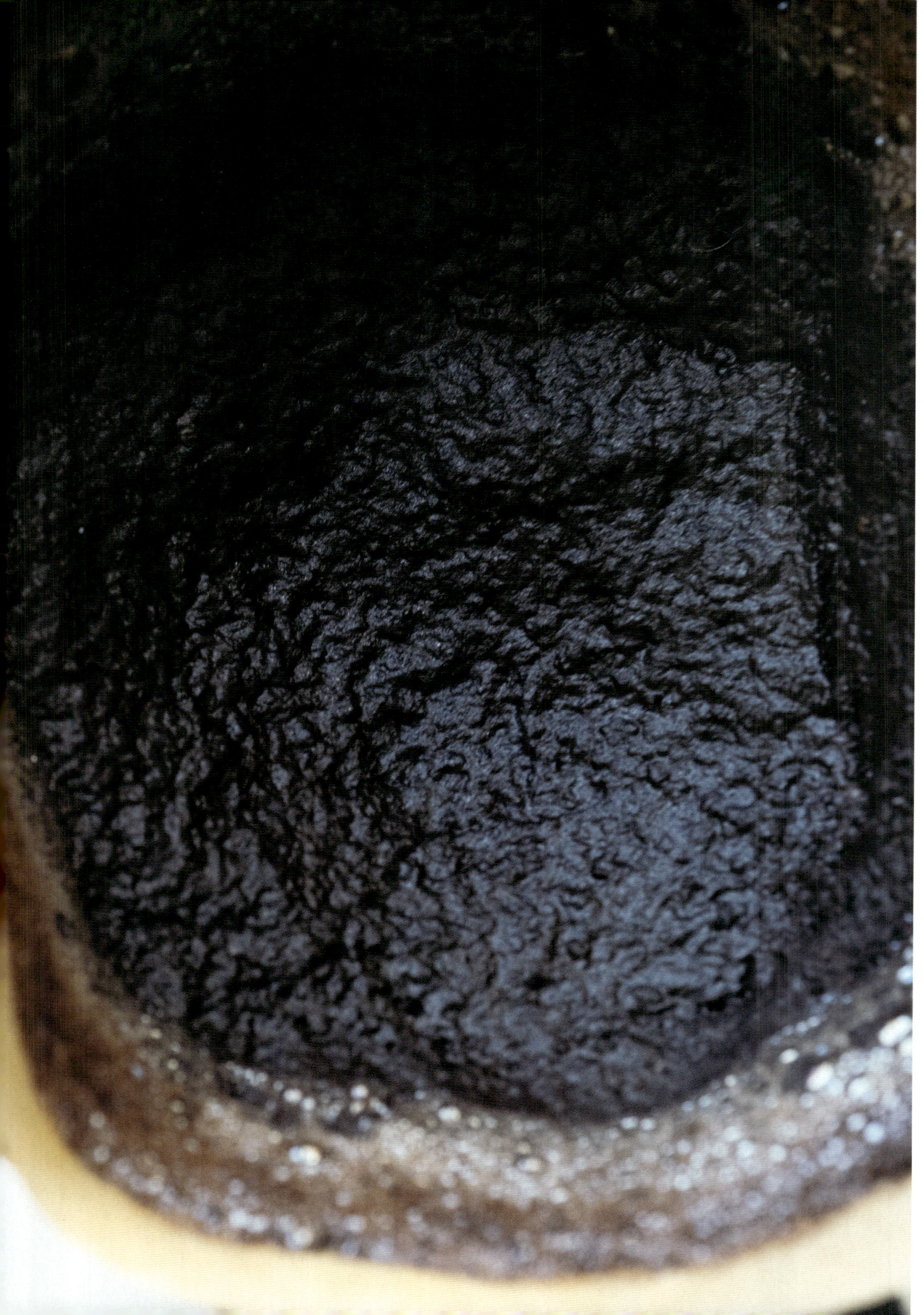

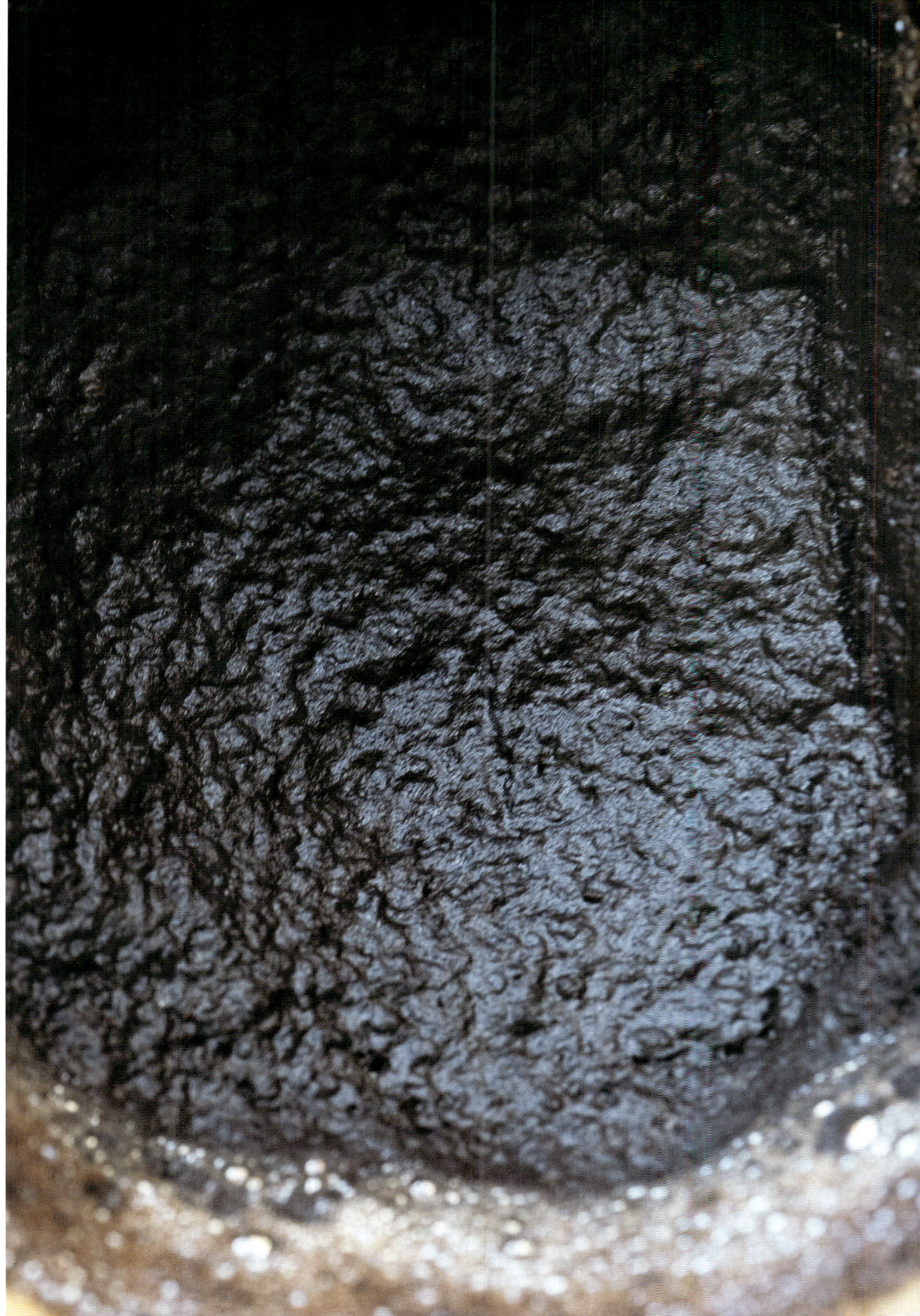

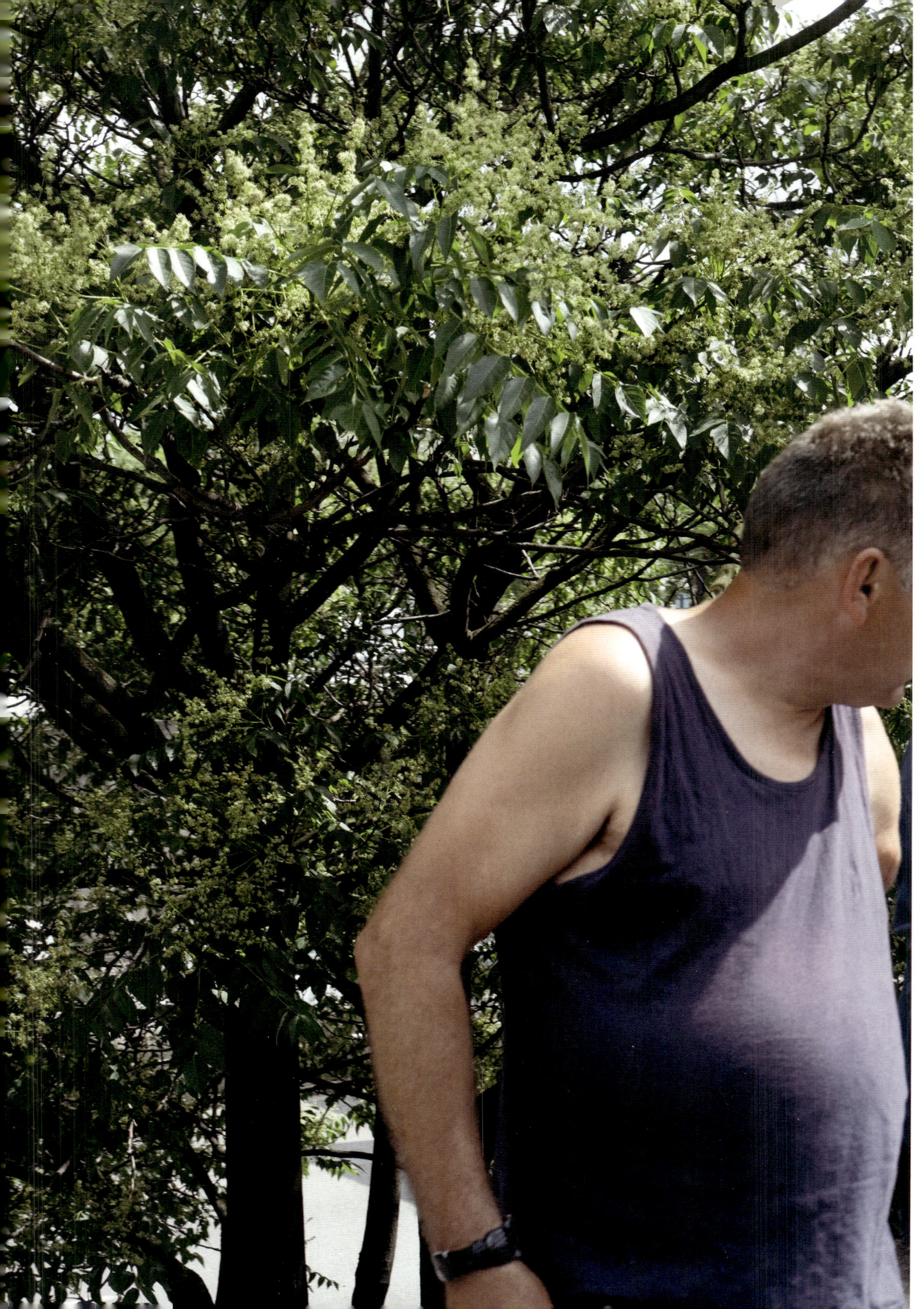

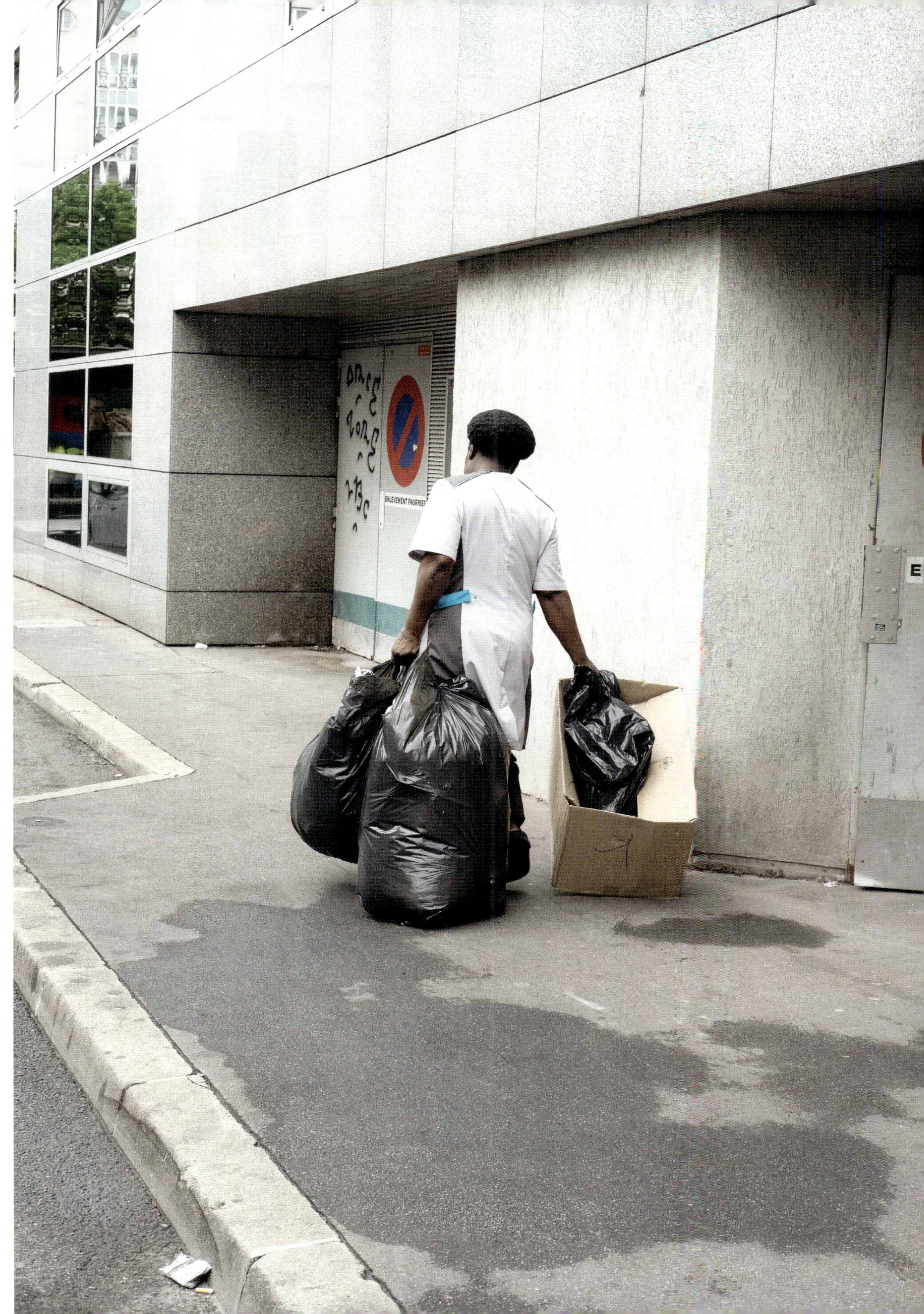
ENLÈVEMENT FOURRIÈRE

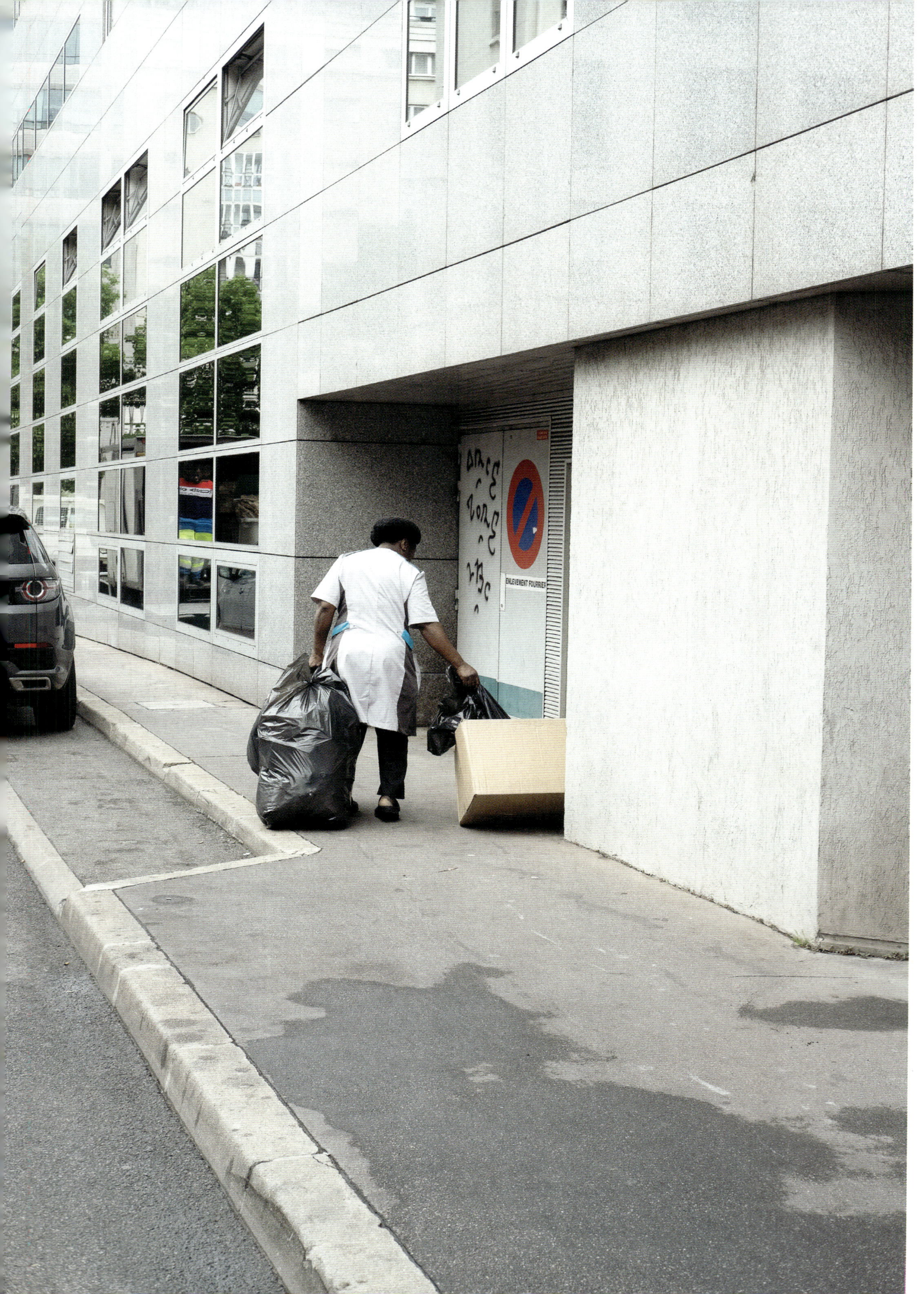

ENLÈVEMENT FOURRIÈRE

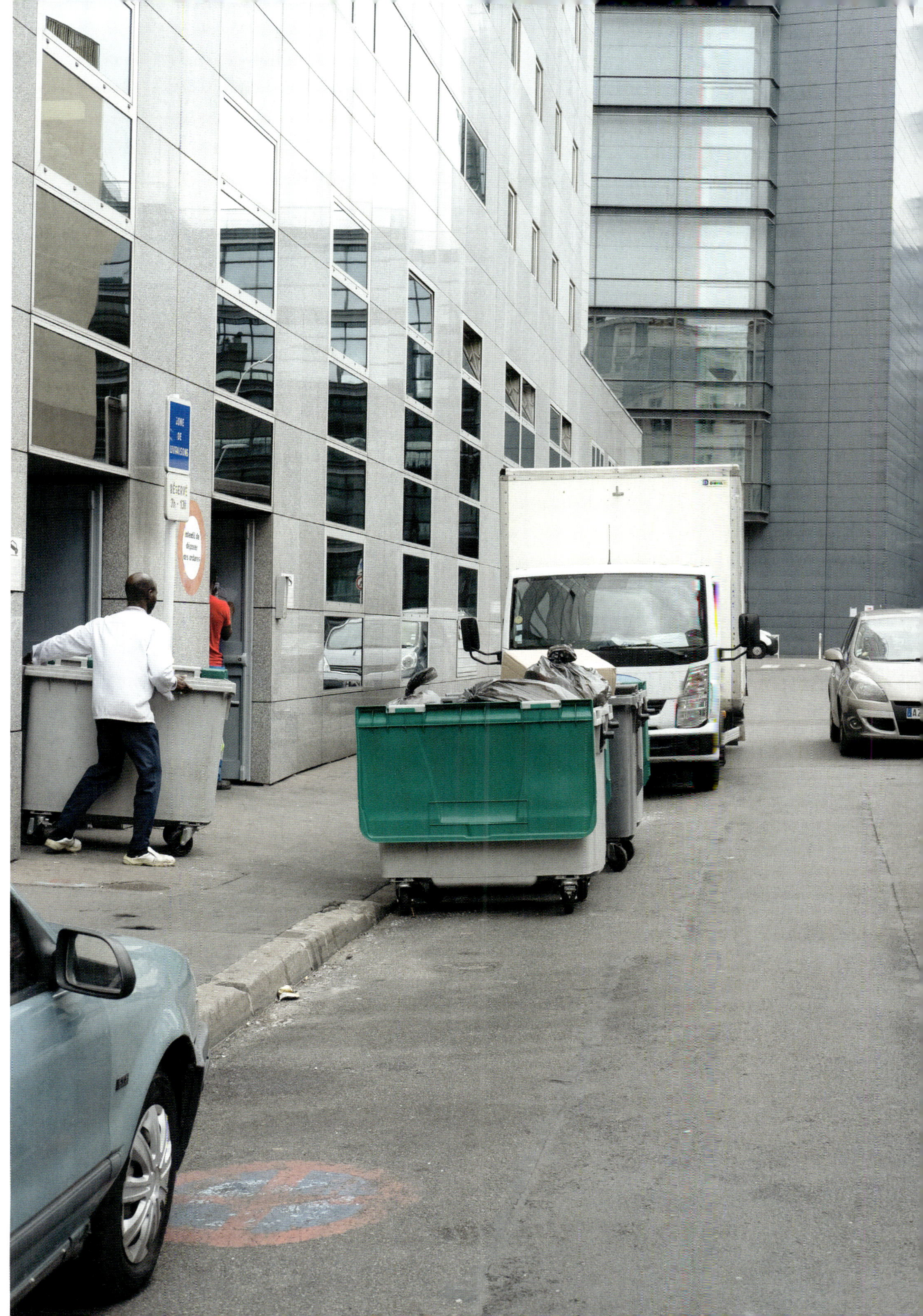

ZONE
DE
LIVRAISONS
RÉSERVÉ
7h - 13h

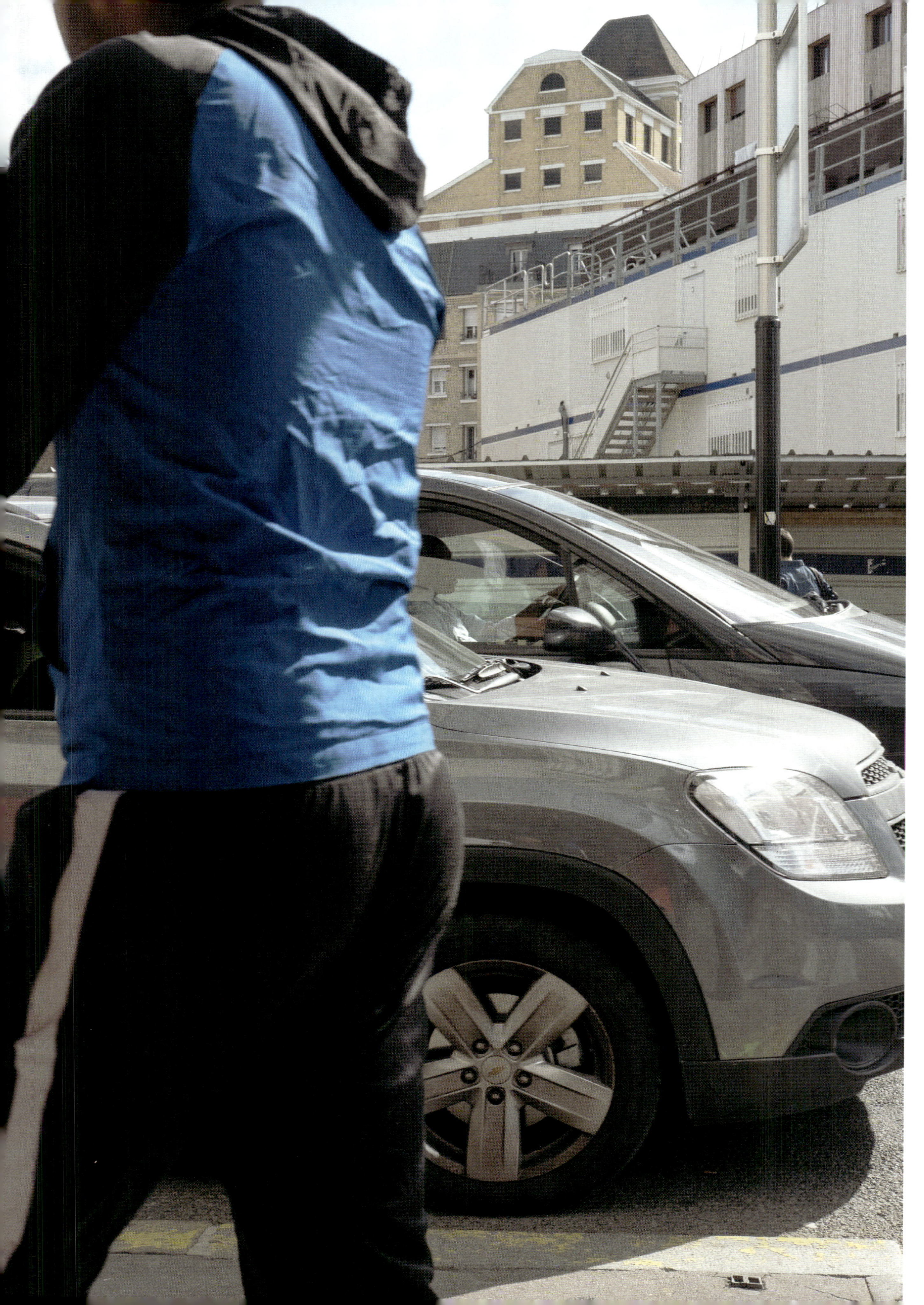

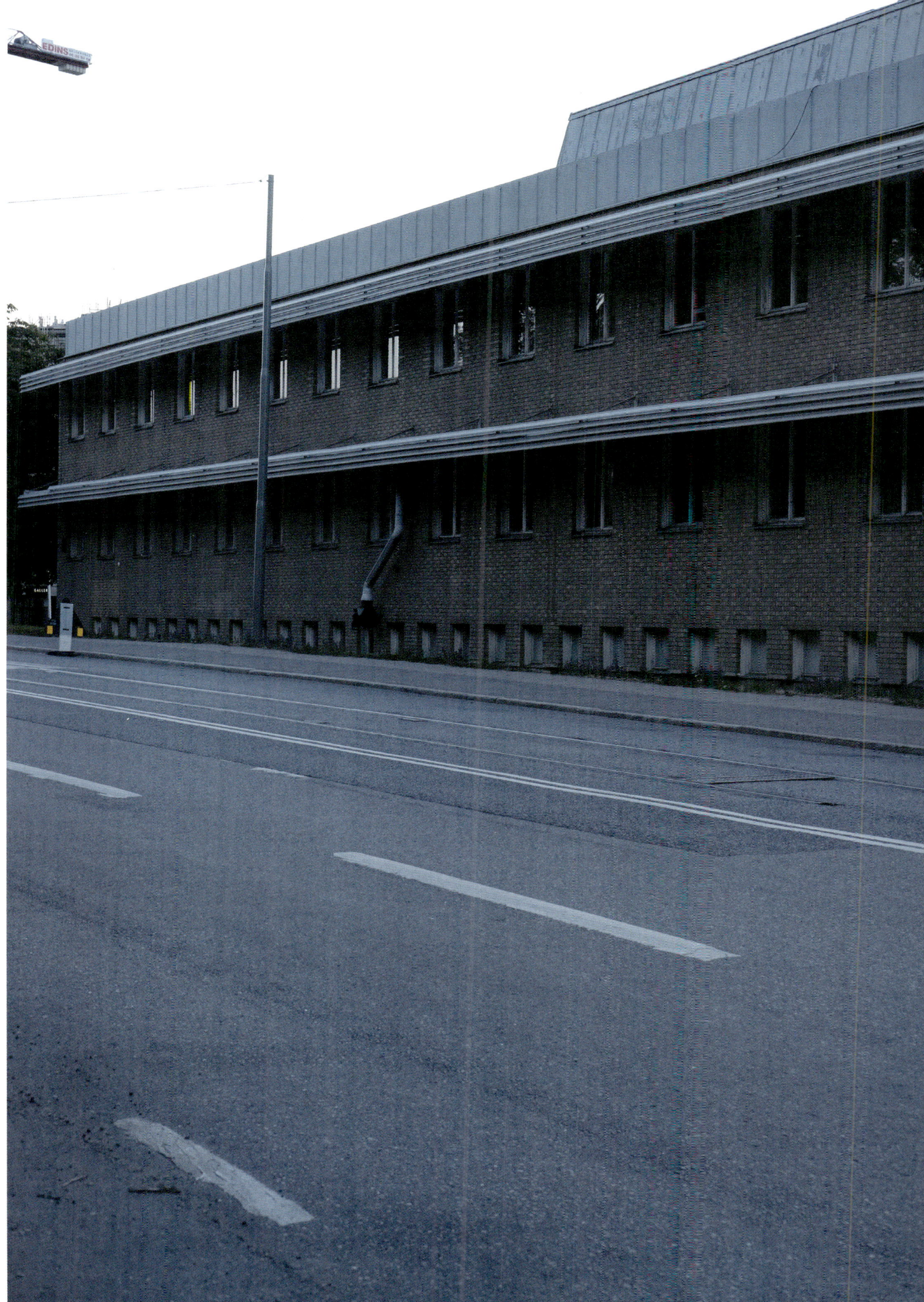
EDINS

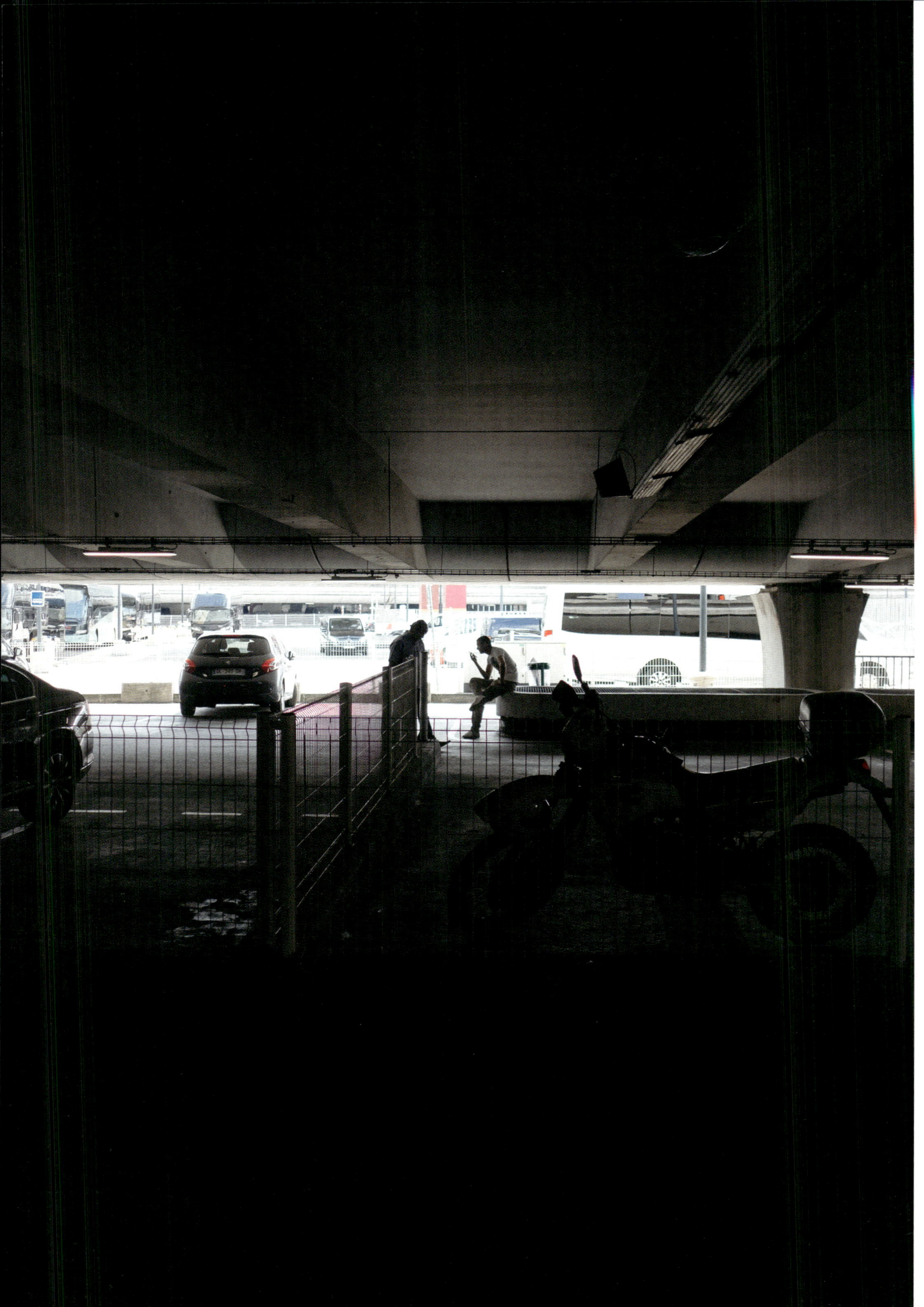

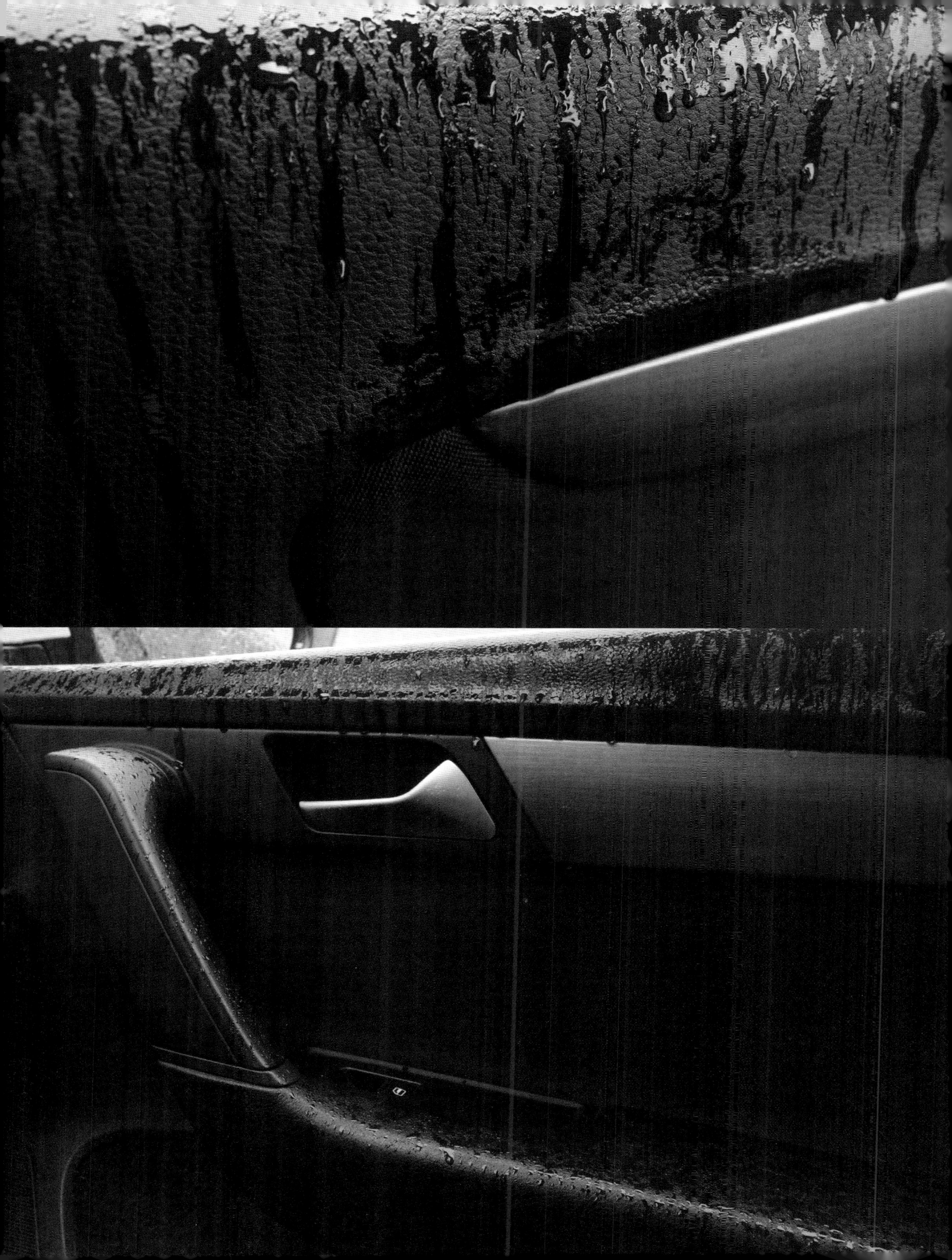

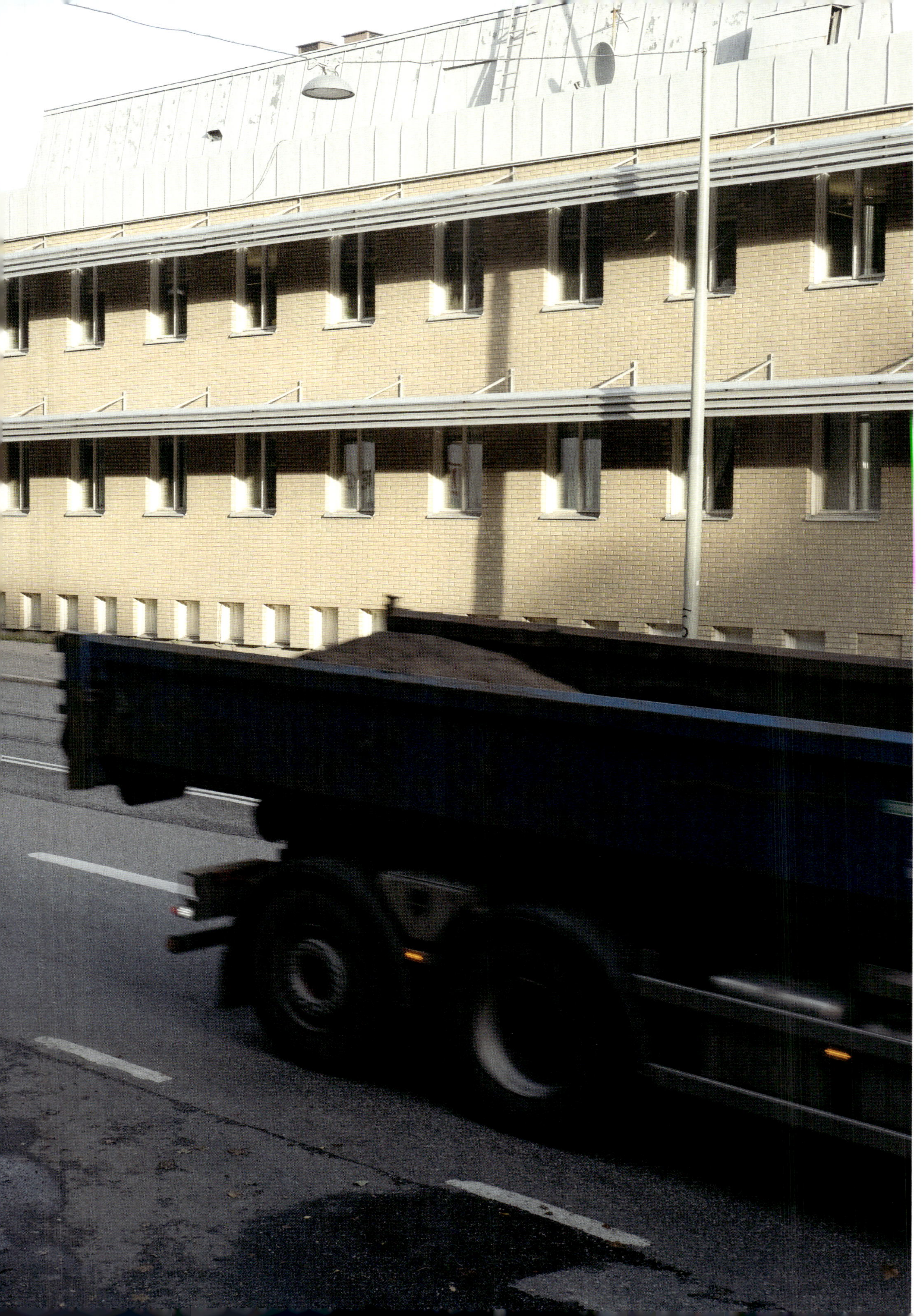

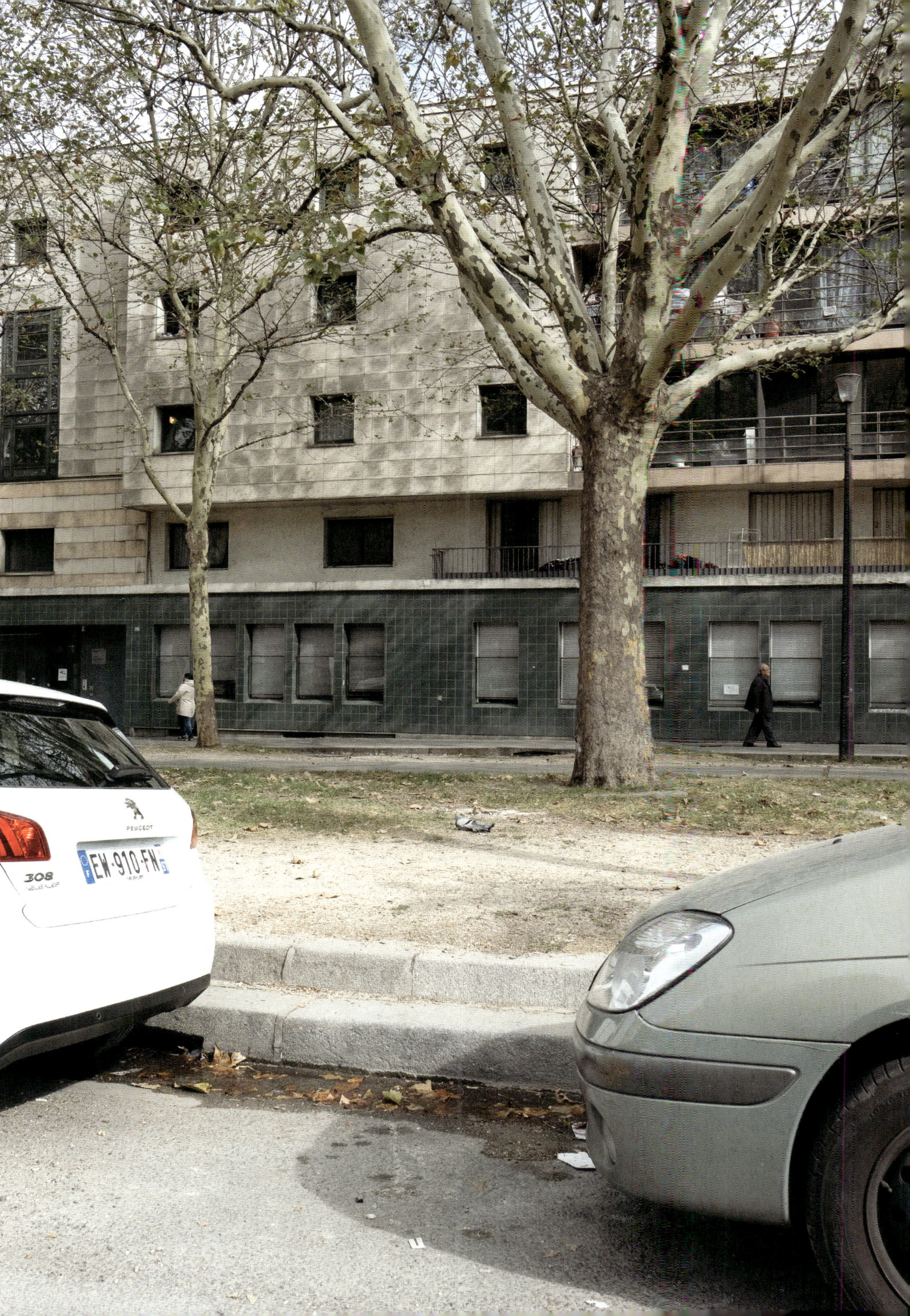

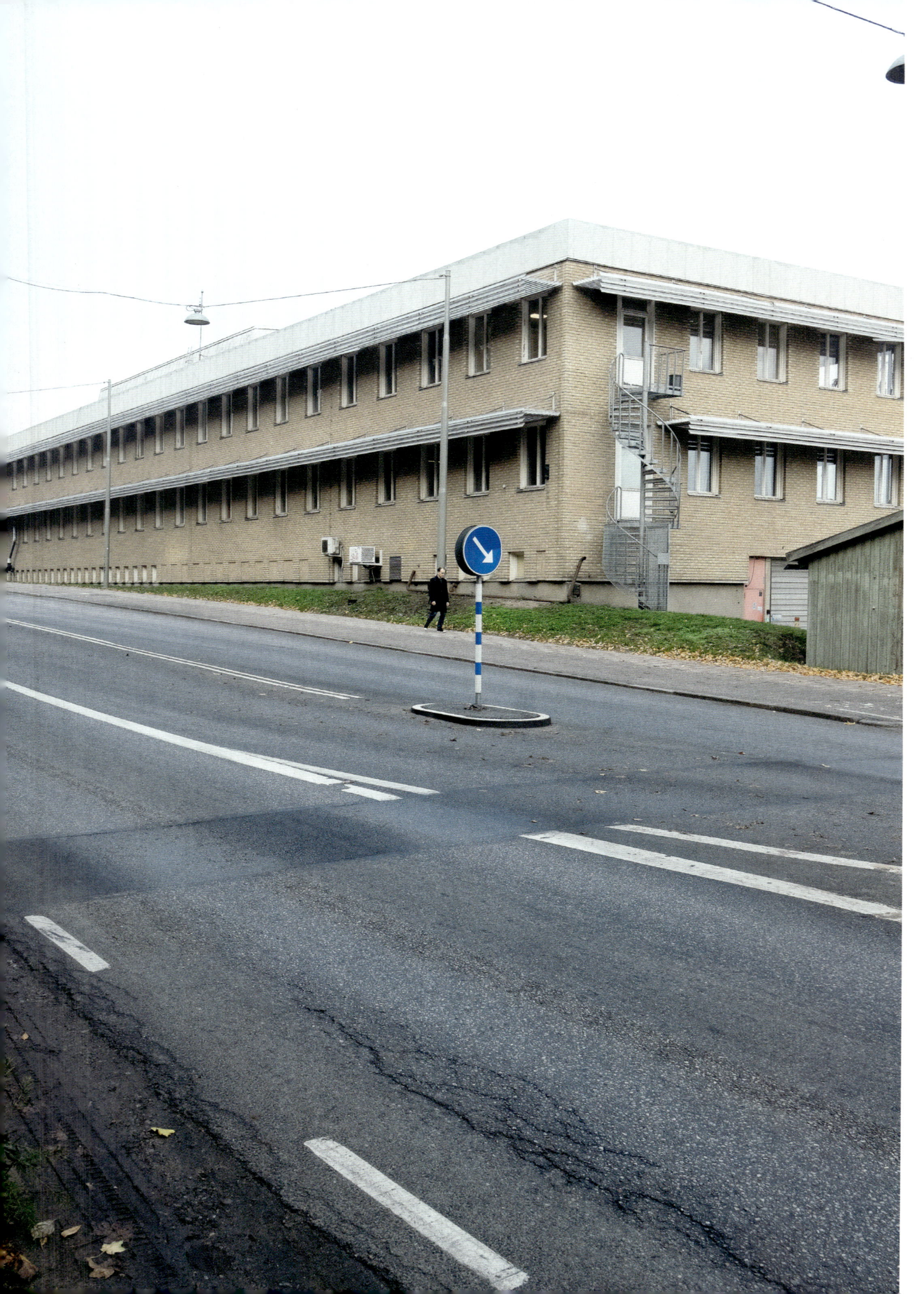

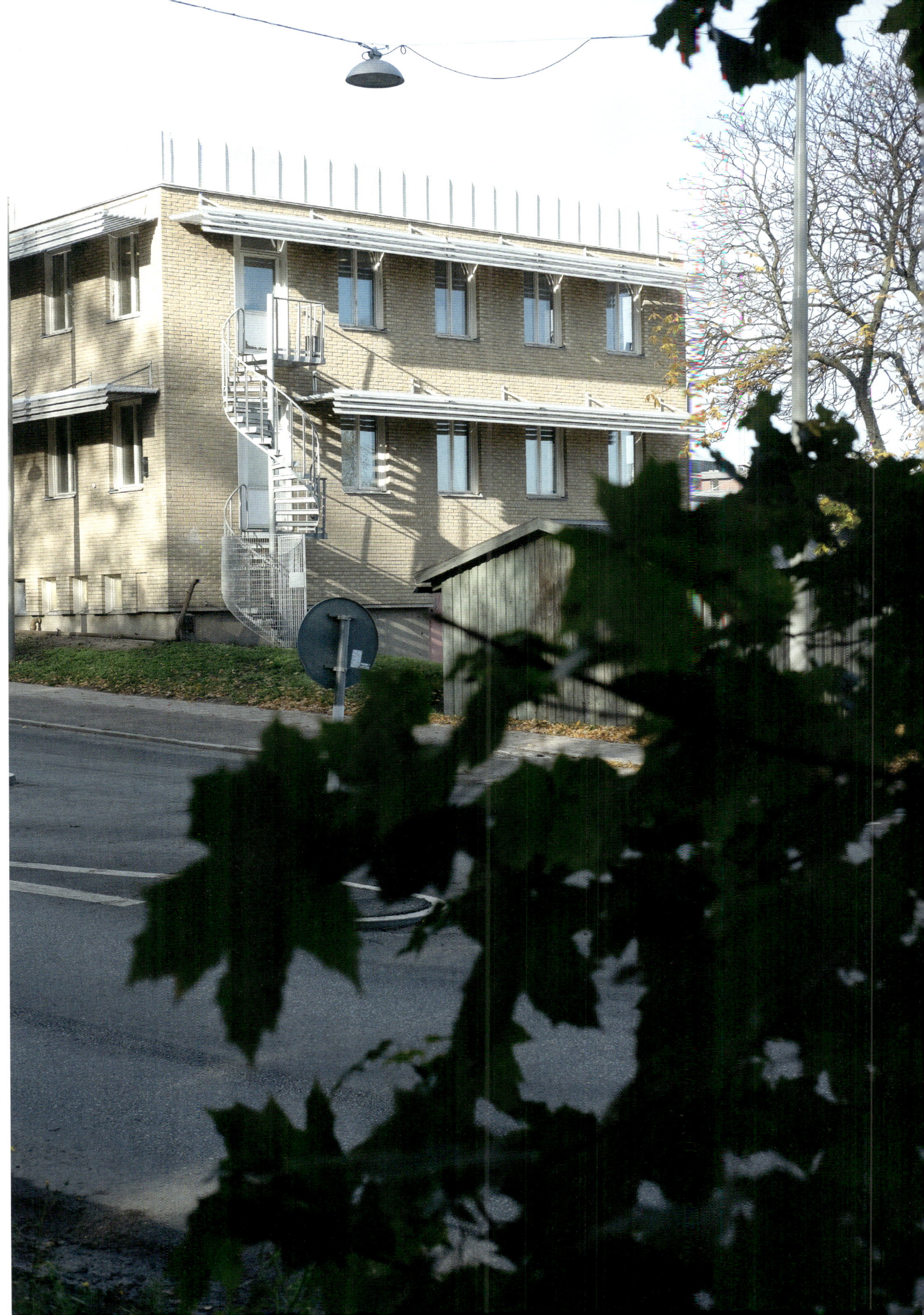

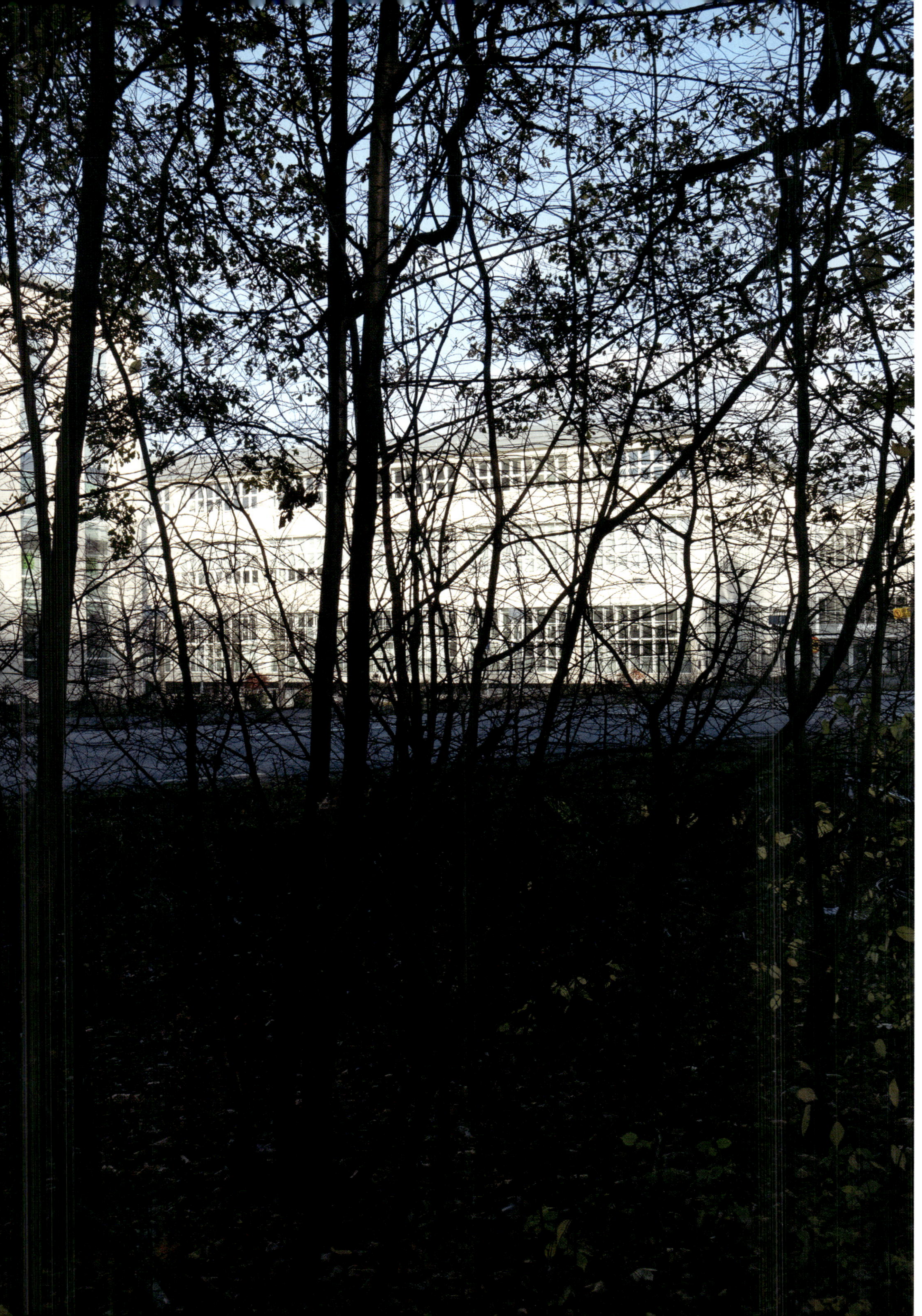

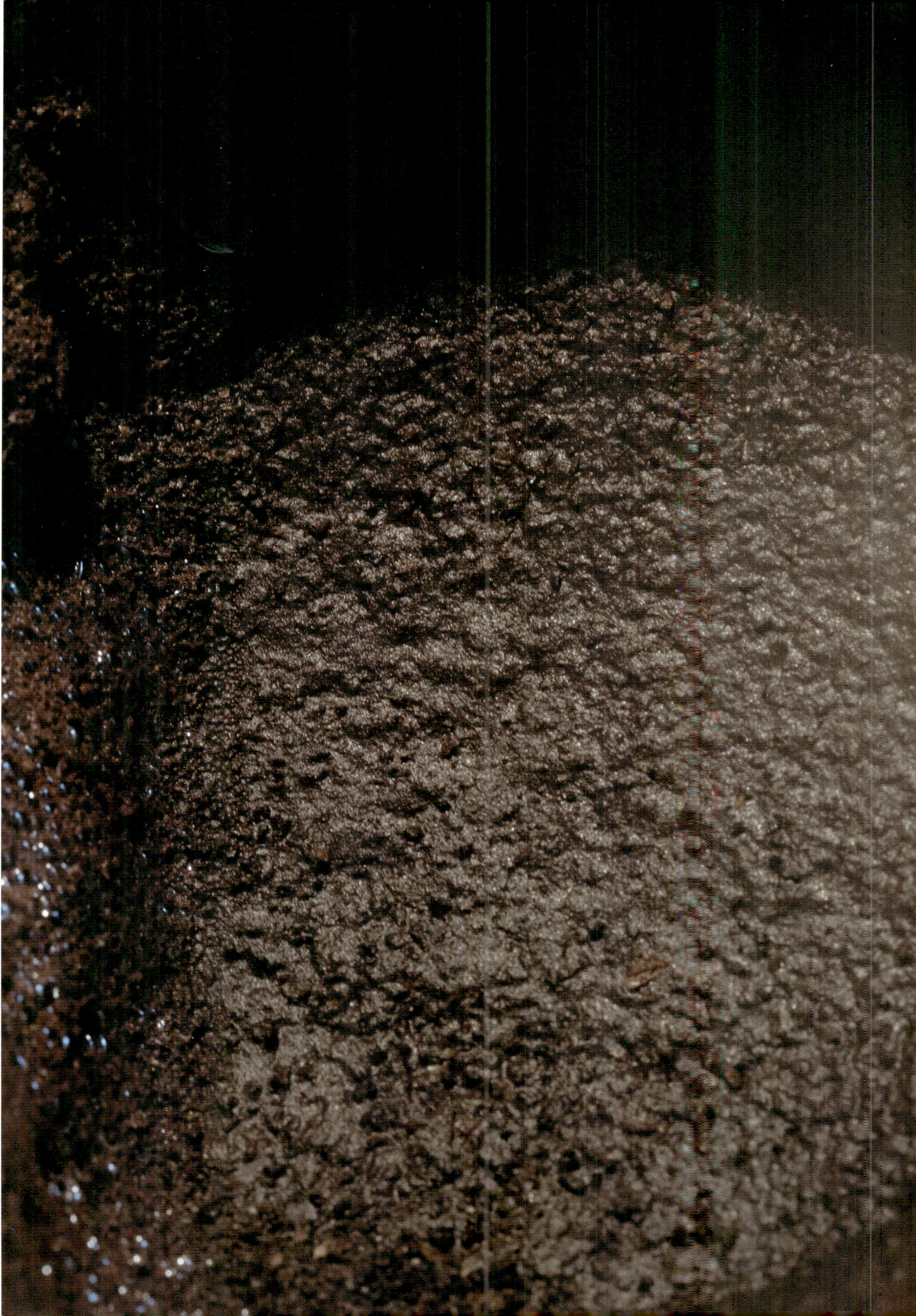

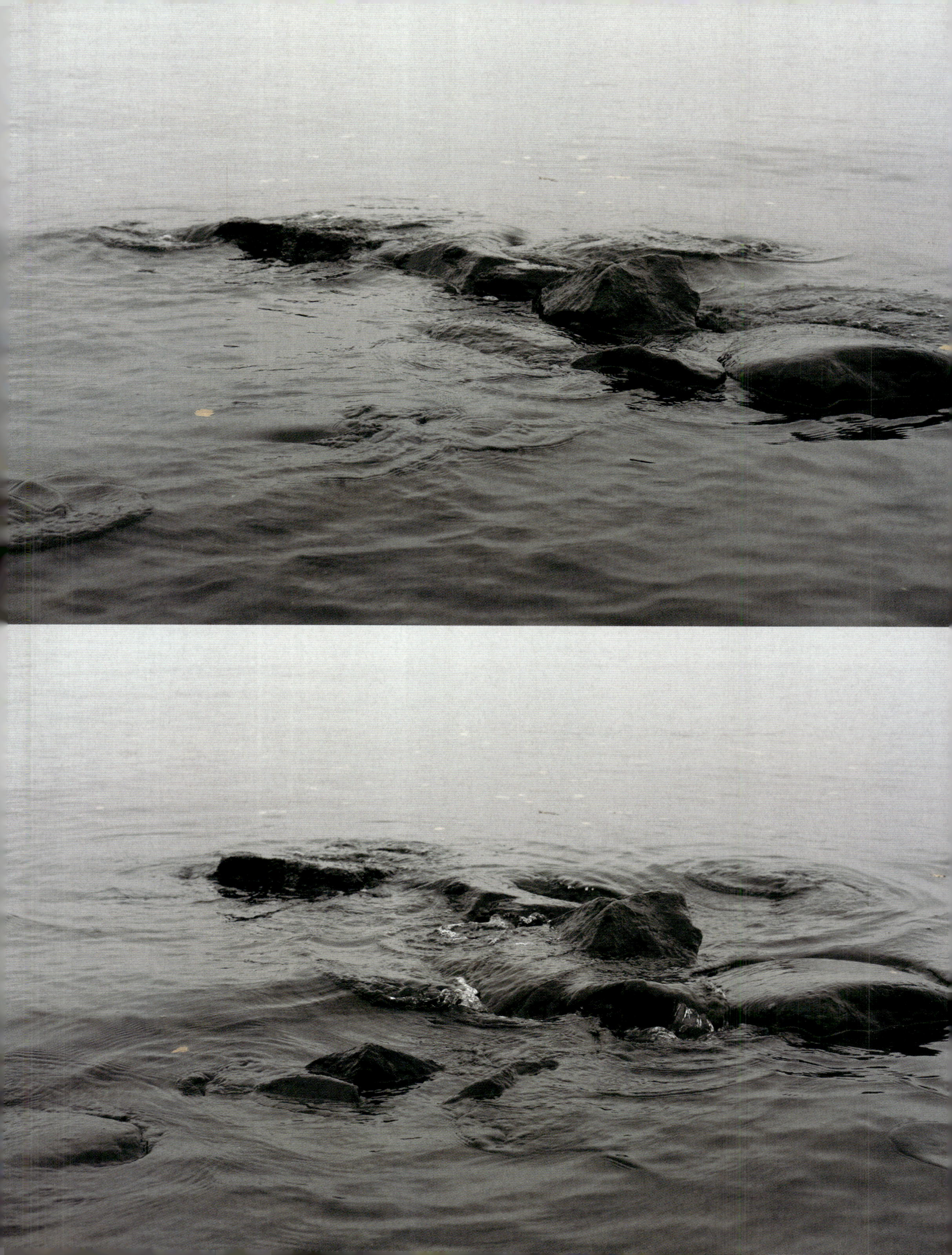

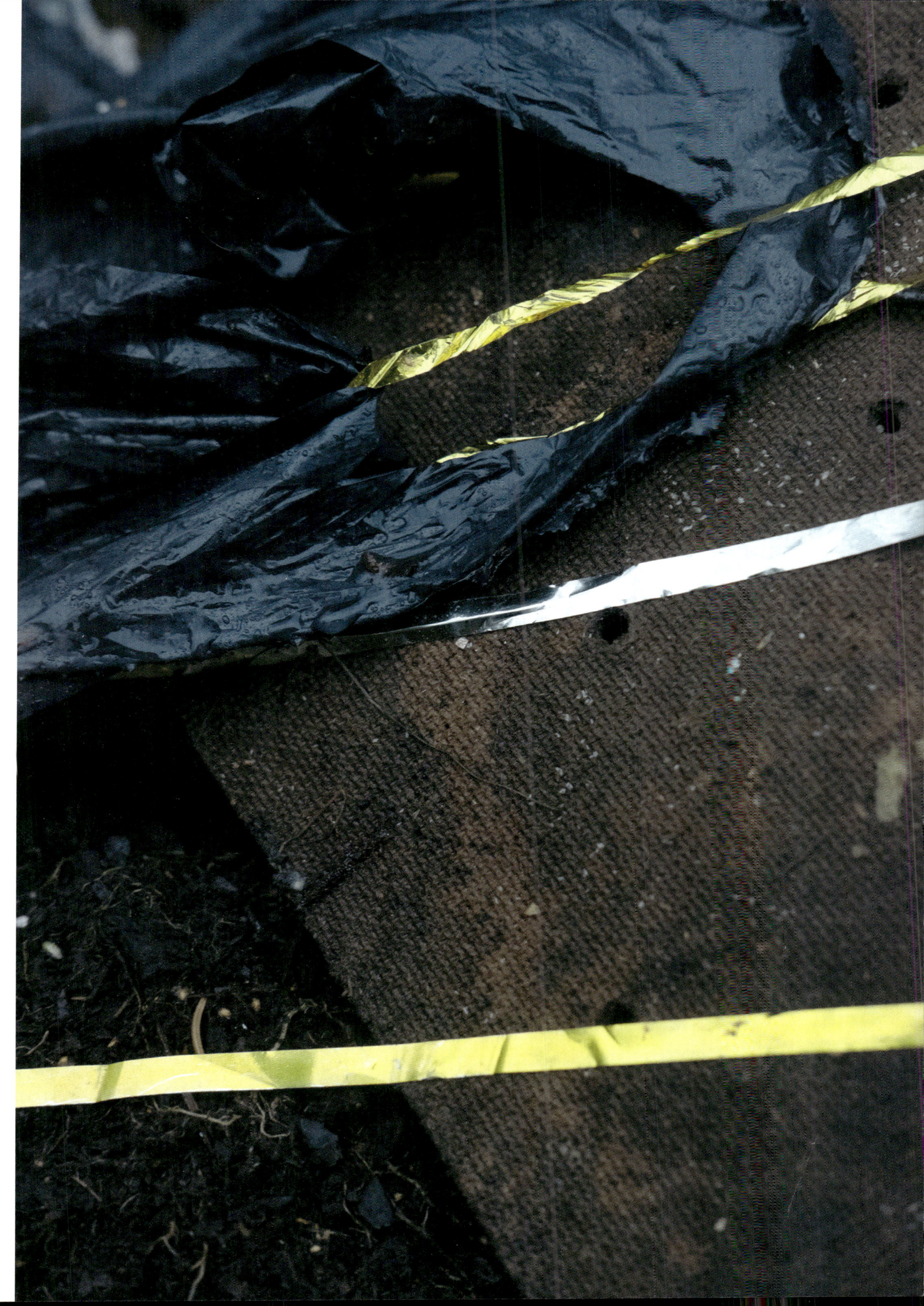

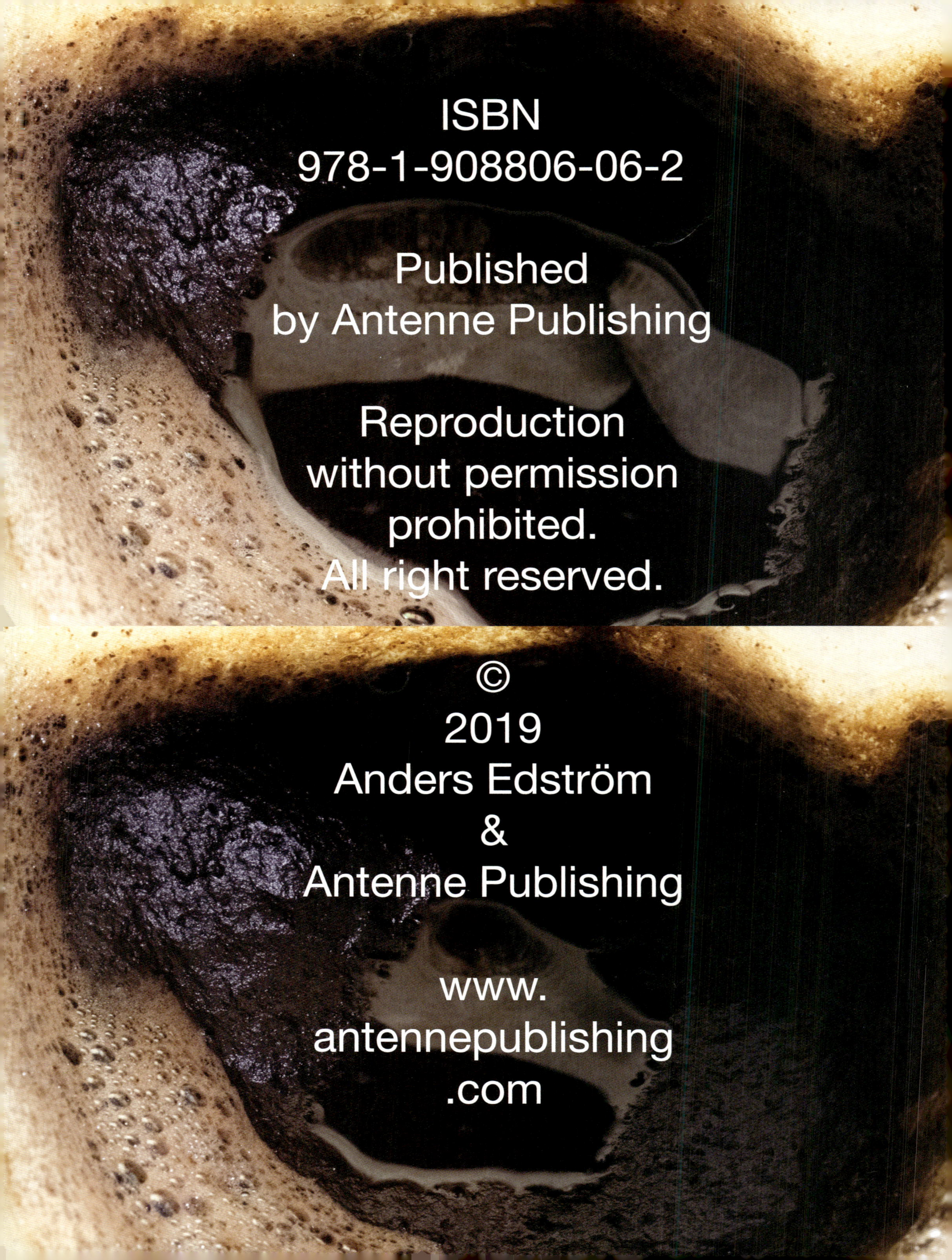

ISBN
978-1-908806-06-2

Published
by Antenne Publishing

www.
antennepublishing
.com

"*I'm into every way a poem can be done.*"

— *John Yau*

DISGUISE THE LIMIT

JOHN YAU'S COLLABORATIONS

University of Kentucky Art Museum

TABLE OF CONTENTS

FOREWORD

Collaboration is a boundary-pushing activity, built on trust and curiosity. Those who pursue it are willing to challenge the comfort of their individual habits in order to create something unexpected with a like-minded partner. The risks raise questions: What will happen? Will it be any good? When the participants are respected poet and critic John Yau and any one of a bevy of emerging and established artists, one can be assured that the process will be lively, and the outcomes significant.

This publication, *Disguise the Limit: John Yau's Collaborations,* offers the first extensive look at the paintings, drawings, prints, and unique books that he has made during the past five decades. It accompanies an exhibition with the same title, examining the intersection of Yau's poetry, criticism, and creative partnerships with others. Many of these collaborative works are being documented, exhibited, and written about for the first time.

Since the 1970s, Yau's poetry has mined aspects of his bi-racial identity, visual art, the detective genre in novels and films, city life, and mortality. He has used these subjects for varied experiments in language—anagrams, haiku, sonnets, pantoums, and free verse. Many of them were written for limited edition portfolios and artist's books before appearing in his published poetry collections.

Yau's criticism, in the form of reviews, essays, and interviews for print and online publications, has been a staple of artworld discourse since the early 1980s. Like the best of the poet-critics who preceded him, Yau is skilled in delivering thoughtful analysis and precise descriptions of the artworks under consideration.

I first encountered his writing as an art student, poring over bound copies of *Artforum*, *Art in America*, and *Arts Magazine* in the libraries at The Cooper Union and Rutgers University, arguably killing time while my paintings dried but also helping me get a handle on different aspects of the art market.

Years later, after reinventing myself as a dealer in SoHo in the early 1990s, Yau would occasionally visit my gallery and we came to know each other professionally. Since then, I have actively kept up with his prolific output, enjoying, in particular, his insightful book *A Thing Among Things: The Art of Jasper Johns*, exploring notions of contingency in the artist's iconography; his take on numerous contemporary abstract painters; and the regular weekend reports he writes for the online magazine *Hyperallergic*.

Fast forward to 2019, when I invited Yau to come to the University of Kentucky Art Museum to deliver a presentation about the history of collaborations between poets and painters. It was during this visit that he shared with me the extensive experiences he has had working with friends and like-minded peers. Learning about this treasure trove of material and realizing that much of it was unknown except to the participants (including, in some cases, publishers and printers who were an essential part of the productions), made me commit to developing this project immediately.

What follows is an attempt to celebrate and bring awareness to Yau's pursuit of unique opportunities for language generation and its usage. His collaborations are smart, audacious, parodic, and masterfully made; and I believe they should be appreciated alongside the most significant collaborative works made by poets including John Ashbery, Bill Berkson, Ted Berrigan, Robert Creeley, and Frank O'Hara, working together with some of the most acclaimed artists of their day.

In gathering information about and gaining access to these works, I have relied heavily on Yau's memory, recordkeeping, and contact lists. There is, perhaps, something about collaboration that designates it as an extremely joyful thing to do, but less fun to keep track of after the fact. That said, we appreciate the help of the artists, publishers, and collectors who have loaned the works reproduced here and those in the exhibition.

In realizing this project, we have made choices about whom and what to include. While this cannot be understood as the final reckoning of Yau's collaborative engagement with artists, we hope it is an excellent start.

—Stuart Horodner

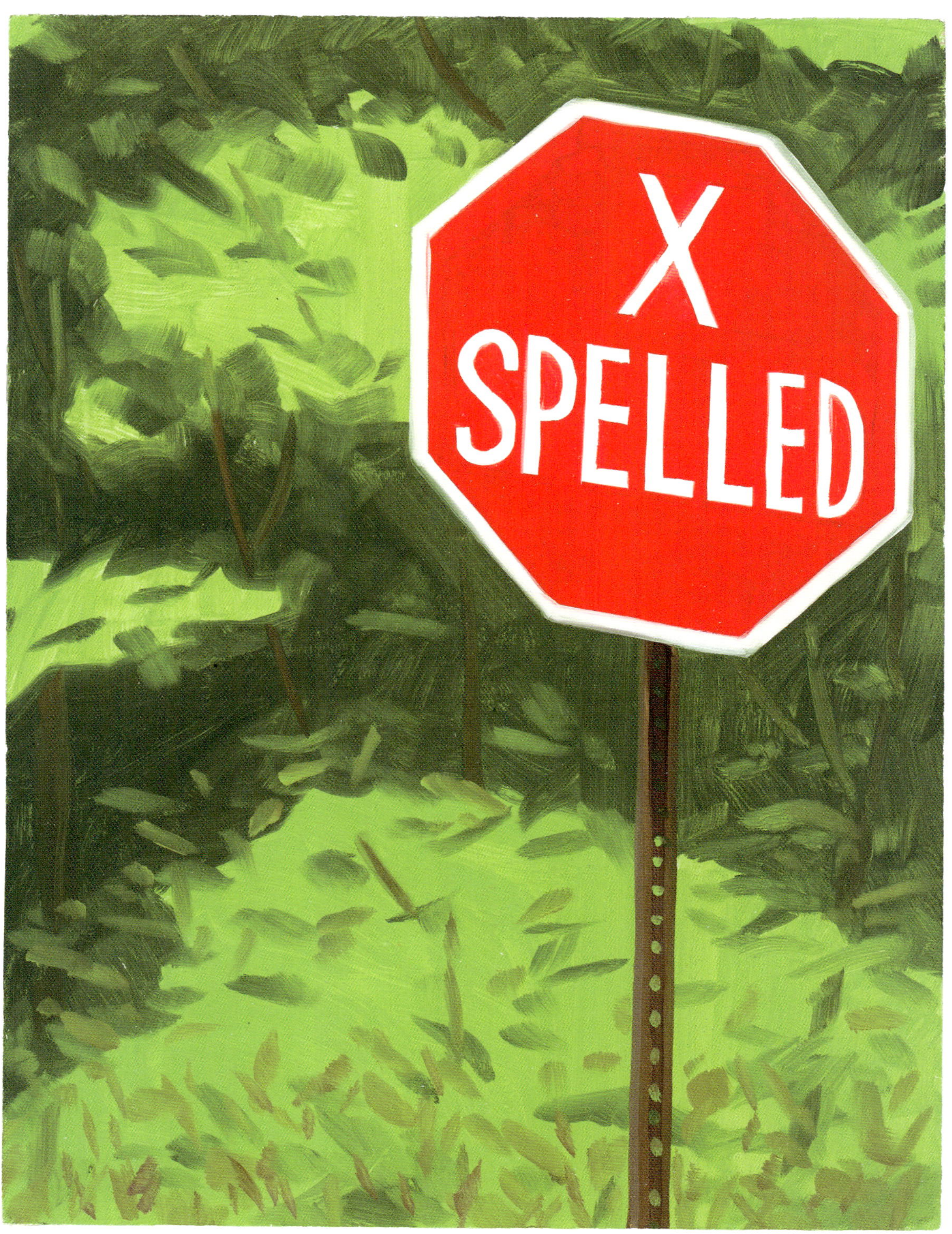

John Yau and Tom Burckhardt, *X Spelled*, 2022

DISGUISE THE LIMIT
John Yau As Poet-Critic-Collaborator

—Stuart Horodner

In the poem, "A Painter's Thoughts (5): After Thomas Nozkowski (1944–2019)," John Yau writes, "Every artist has little rules or devices that enables them to move forward."[1] This insight is in keeping with Yau's habit of consistently finding ways to challenge his own assumptions and methods. One way he keeps moving forward is by embracing Emily Dickinson's oft-quoted line, "Tell all the truth but tell it slant."[2] Yau does this by bringing together ethnicity and experimentation, constructing poems from found language and overheard phrases that he turns around, takes apart, and tweaks until they exude his unique world view. His writing is infused with irreverent humor and emotional clarity, whether he is composing odes to his desk, reminiscing about his upbringing in Boston, or offering meditations on aging.

While Yau's influences include Robert Creeley, Robert Duncan, Charles Olson, and other poets associated with Black Mountain College, he is most often slotted in the lineage that includes John Ashbery, Barbara Guest, Kenneth Koch, Frank O'Hara, and James Schuyler. This is appropriate, but he is somewhat wary of the inclusion: "As much as I'm connected to the so-called poets of the New York School, I never felt like I was part of that group . . . And I never felt like I was writing for people in that group. Maybe that isolation is me, and that's what I should write out of. Instead of trying to avoid it or overcome it or deny it. Just kind of embrace it to some degree."[3]

This accepted separateness is inextricably linked to Yau's biracial status as a Chinese-American and the double consciousness that comes with it. His writings address the complexities of looking and being looked at, investigating his own question: "What does it mean when you are not one, but two, and belong nowhere?"[4]

In his "O Pin Yin Sonnets,"[5] Yau stockpiles clichés about Chinese-ness to acknowledge the pain that comes with being understood as other[6]:

They invented fireworks, noodles, and kung fu, which hardly adds up to a civilization
They openly sneeze and snicker about it and then scatter like mice
They are nothing more than scribbled names on the flyleaf of a tattered book
They might make good sneakers but they are sneakier than snakes

He has worked the stereotype that Asian people when speaking English, confuse R's with L's (and vice versa), reveling in the sounds and spellings of words like *Bloken, Exhaust,* and *Flee Advice.* Yau attributes his sensitivity to language to the childhood experience of listening to his parents speaking a certain dialect of Chinese that he was not taught. He says, "I could understand it after a while, just through the repetition of hearing them talk. So, I heard a language that I didn't speak, but I heard the sounds of it.

I'm interested in the sounds of words and how you can stretch them out, make them sound like other words and things like that. I've always been interested in mispronunciations and language as a material thing. How if you move a letter around, one word becomes another one."[7]

Race and ethnicity are a wellspring of material for Yau, given his vested interest in unpacking marginalization and misunderstanding. "Ing Grish" offers some of his most unsparing lines[8]:

I do not know Ang Grish, but I can tell you that my last name
consists of three letters, and that technically all of them are vowels
I do not know Um Glish, but I do know how to eat with two sticks

. . .

I do not know either Cantonese or English, Ang Glish or Ing Grish.
Anguish is a language everyone can speak, but no one listens to it.

. . .

I do not know Chinese because during the Vietnam War
I was called a gook instead of a chink and realized
that I had managed to change my spots without meaning to.

Yau has written extensively from the point of view of Genghis Chan (a mashup of Genghis Khan and Charlie Chan), his doppelganger inspired by the novels (and films based on them) of Raymond Chandler and Dashiell Hammett, as well as offensive yellowface movies starring Peter Lorre and Boris Karloff (white actors playing Asian characters). He admits, "I like the slang they use. How do I access that? I'm not, you know, a white detective. So, I invented one. That opens up a space for me to explore . . . The detective—that came from watching Humphrey Bogart movies when I was in high school. There was something about the character, that kind of relentless or dogged seeking after the truth."[9] His tough guy has the requisite code of honor and justice typical of the gumshoe, but with a sensitive side. This is revealed in "Genghis Chan: Private Eye XIII," printed here in its entirety[10]:

It is hard to keep pretending
You are a yellow chink
In a hall of dusty linen

You begin believing
You are just another handkerchief
Wiping away the laundress's tears

Yau also uses the titles of artworks, artist's statements, and their signature materials as fodder for his poetry. In "830 Fireplace Road," he reworks Jackson Pollock's illuminating sentence, "When I am *in* my painting, I'm not aware of what I'm doing," until Jack the Dripper is sputtering out existential thoughts on being and doing. The name of the synthetic pigment associated with a celebrated French maker of monochromes affords Yau some anagrammatic play[11]:

Yves Klein Blue (*Interlude*)

Bevel slue inky
Been veil sulky
Bye venue skill
Bilk evenly use
Bulk eye snivel
Buys eleven ilk
Blues like envy

Since the late 1970s, Yau has led a double life as a poet and critic, and he does both with a deep understanding of precedent and a noble sense of purpose. His output is prolific and Yau is keenly aware of the pitfalls that come along with this dual identity. In "The Poet as Art Critic," he writes: "the successful poet-critic, which is to say one who regularly gets published, will most likely be dismissed or ignored by art historians, theorists, academics, and, in some cases, other poet-critics. In addition, being a successful art critic and published poet means that you have to accept that more people will read your criticism than your poetry . . . It takes a certain kind of resiliency to be a poet-critic who not only doesn't become a curmudgeon, become polemical, stop writing poetry, or start complaining about the inequity of it all, but also still manages to maintain a high level of sophistication, insight, and wit in your essays and reviews."[12]

Artists whose works have prompted Yau's ekphrastic poems and his critical writing include Francis Bacon, William Bailey, Forrest Bess, Giorgio de Chirico, Max Ernst, Suzan Frecon, Jiha Moon, Catherine Murphy, Neo Rauch, J.M.W. Turner, and Jack Whitten. The diversity of this list mirrors something that he said in appreciation of Jasper Johns: "He likes the trompe l'oeil painter John F. Peto, Marcel Duchamp, George Ohr, who was known as 'the mad potter of Biloxi,' the Victorian painter Richard Dadd, who ended up in Bedlam for killing his father, Matthais Grünewald, Edvard Munch, Juan Gris, and Barnett Newman; he likes a lot of artists that supposedly don't go together, that alone is interesting. He's not doctrinaire, but encyclopedic. It's not like he likes all the 'right' people."[13]

Mark Scroggins affirms this in the first sentences of his blurb on the back of Yau's book, *Foreign Sounds or Sounds Foreign*: "What artist hasn't John Yau looked at and thought about? What movie hasn't he seen? What poet's or essayist's works doesn't he know?"[14]

His reviews and essays are celebrated for providing fresh insights about what is in front of him and for helping to situate varied practitioners into historical contexts and traditions. Yau has been a contributor to magazines including *Art in America*, *Arts Magazine*, *Artforum*, *The Brooklyn Rail*, and in recent years, to *Hyperallergic*, where he assesses the exhibitions of emerging and established artists and advocates for those not active in the gallery system at all. He says, "I don't want to be part of a club, write only about these people and not those people. I want to have enough freedom to walk into a gallery, look at an artist, have no idea whether they went to Yale or went to Bozeman State, and write about them. And I don't have to meet them. There are other things I am interested in. I try to go to as many shows of young Asian artists as I can . . . I will write about really well-known people if I think they've been misrepresented even in their fame. They're looked at one way and they're ignored another way."[15]

Yau enjoys the rare liberty of covering whoever and whatever moves him. But there was a time when this was not so. He reveals, "For years, I was only allowed to write about artists that no one else wanted to write about."[16] This makes Yau sensitive to the gaps in representation (in exhibitions, collections, and the historical record) of artists whose gender, race, age, and sexual identity have kept them from achieving the appropriate recognition, or even worse, have rendered them undesirable or invisible. His essay "Please Wait by the Coatroom: Wifredo Lam in the Museum of Modern Art" is filled with righteous indignation: "Wifredo Lam's *The Jungle* (1943) hangs in the hallway leading to the museum's coatroom. Its location is telling. The artist's work has been allowed into the museum's lobby, but, like a delivery boy, has been made to stand and hold the package in an inconspicuous passageway near the door. By denying Lam and his work the possibility of going upstairs and conversing with Cézanne, Picasso, Matisse, Jackson Pollock, Morris Louis, and Kenneth Noland (their works are carefully arranged on the walls of the main galleries), the museum relegates both the artist and his work to secondary status."[17]

In "The Essential Importance of John Yau's Art Writing," philosopher and cultural critic David Carrier recognizes the poet-critic's relevance, stating, ". . . he matters right now because he writes clearly about a great variety of artists, and because in his practice [he] tackles issues of central importance."[18]

Yau's aversion to art world hierarchies and distinctions of "major" and "minor" achievements has informed his commitment to a third role—that of collaborator. Over the past five decades, he has dedicated himself to the good-natured and decidedly non-commercial activity of working with an intergenerational who's who of American and European artists, from those with accomplished careers to up-and-comers, including several former students. Fueled by spirited competition and camaraderie, Yau has co-created numerous paintings, mixed media drawings, prints, artist's books, broadsides, and embroidered items. He is certainly not interested in what he calls (in the admiring essay "A Few Reasons Why Poets Love Bruce Conner") "elitist paeans to capitalism,"[19] but rather, the multi-directional flow that his words can have.

It should not be a surprise, given his awareness of, and respect for, the collaborations of the past (including *Stones*, the diaristic lithographs made by Frank O'Hara and Larry Rivers; the emphatic drawings made by O'Hara and Norman Bluhm; the expository *Poem-Pictures* by Philip Guston with Bill Berkson, Clark Coolidge, and William Corbett; and Robert Creeley's nuanced publications with John Chamberlain, Jim Dine, Robert Indiana, R.B. Kitaj, Susan Rothenberg, etc.), that Yau would want to explore the possibilities of partnering with friends and like-minded peers himself.

A daily reminder to follow that impulse is evident in his review, "An Arcadian Moment in New York's Lower East Side, circa 1969." Yau explains, "Each time I leave my apartment, I look up and see a collaborative lithograph by [George] Schneeman and Ted Berrigan hanging above my front door. Under the 'ten things' Berrigan claims to do every day, I read: 'play poker, drink beer, smoke pot, jack off and curse.' He also cites O'Hara's *Lunch Poems* and Charles Reznikoff's first novel, *By the Waters of Manhattan*. Schneeman, for his part, has drawn bowling pins, a ship, and flowerpots. This was the shared culture among the writers and artists that I met when I moved to New York—not the corporate

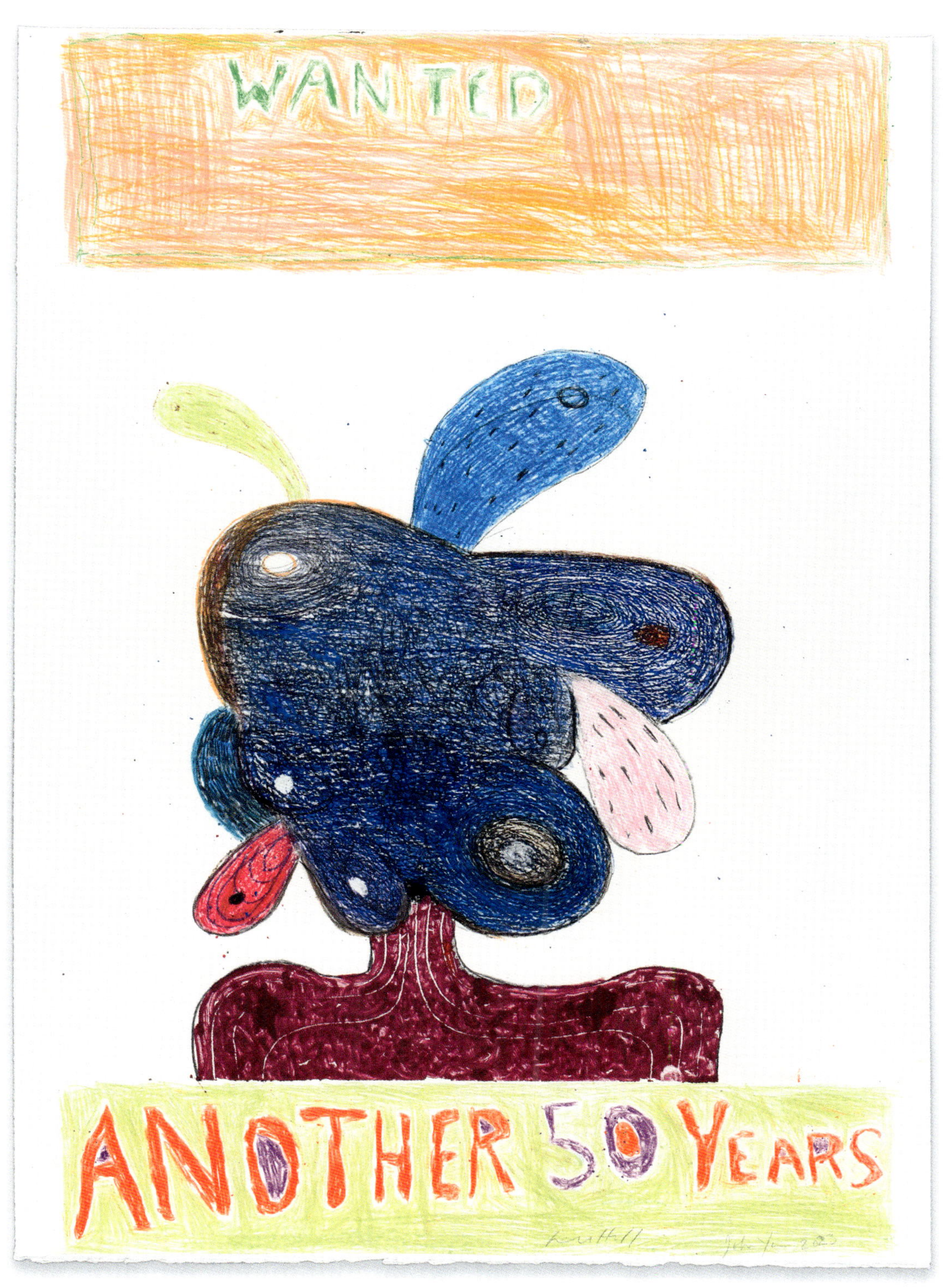

John Yau and Richard Hull, *Wanted: Another 50 Years I*, 2023

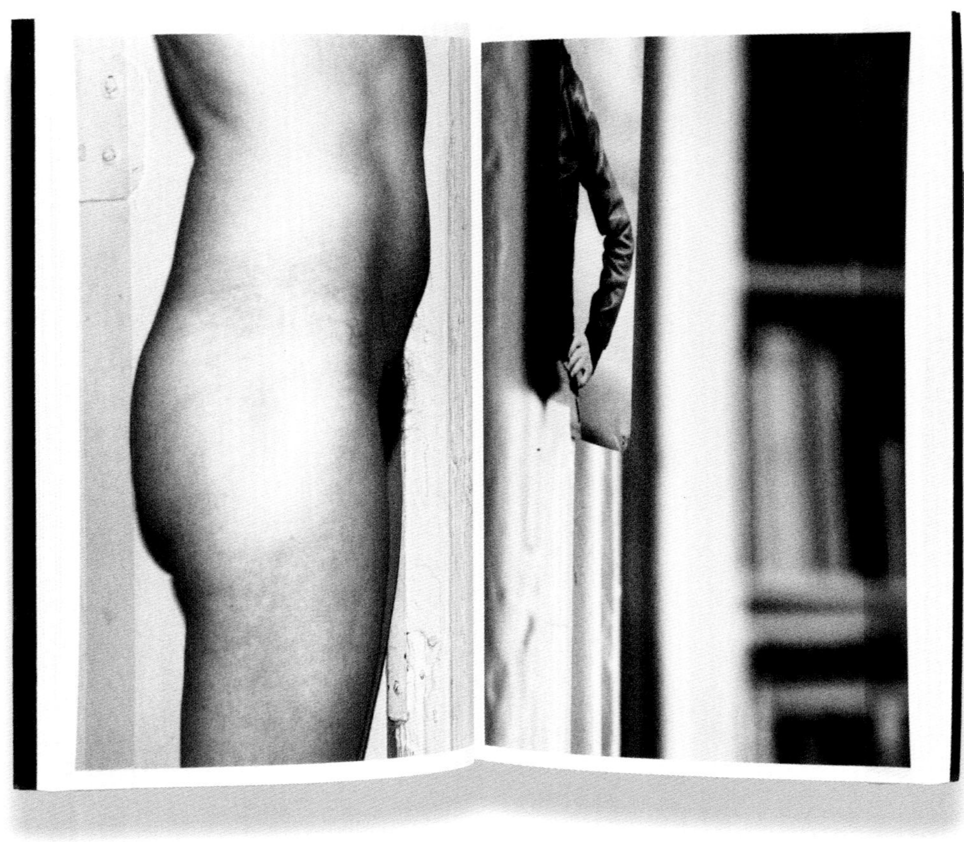

norm that so many critics and magazines find it necessary to comment on, photograph members of, and broadcast. It is this meeting of artist and poet, of the mundane, joyful and crude, that I pass under, entering the world (I would like to think) with some trace of their spirit in my head."[20]

Yau says, "I'm interested in every way a poem can be done."[21] *Disguise the Limit: John Yau's Collaborations* provides an opportunity to assess the ways that he has enjoyed two modes of collaborative activity, described by Bill Berkson as "hands on" and "hands off."[22] The distinction clarifies those works made through the direct engagement of individuals acting in the same time and place, as opposed to when a poem or drawing has been handed off to someone who responds from elsewhere. Yau has worked using both methods, aspiring to the condition that each participant acts "as the other's ideal audience."[23] He has written (and occasionally drawn) alongside artists in studios and printmaking facilities, enjoying the access to papers, paints, inks, and intimate talk; as well as through more remote means—offering nimble turns of phrase, haiku, and fragmented and completed texts for use in their variously produced and published endeavors. This includes meditations on cities (New York and Berlin) for Bill Barrette, ransom notes and road signs for Tom Burckhardt, Zen koans for Max Gimblett, "Wanted" poster information for Richard Hull, descriptions of domestic objects and weather for Justine Kurland, an occasion poem for

Judy Ledgerwood in honor of her wall painting installation, manipulating texts by Catullus for Sydney Jean Reisen, and coming up with speech bubble and thought balloon lingo for Peter Saul, to name a few.

Yau might second Franz Kline's adage, "The real thing about creating is to have the capacity to be embarrassed"[24] with his comment, "There's the kind of person that wants to show you how smart they are. I want to be the kind of person who shows you how stupid I can become."[25] Collaboration is a welcoming space for such stupidity, or perhaps "serious play" is the more appropriate term?

Archie Rand has stated, "A collaborative medium goes so against the heroic isolated macho image of what an artist is in American culture. There's a time when you have to have the generosity to merge. Collaborative work with a poet is an exhilarating democracy."[26] He appreciates the permission-giving aspects of the process, and gleefully recalls his time with Yau: "We would have stacks of paper in front of us and I would be doing an image and he would be doing a text and we would trade them back and forth. Sometimes the image came first and sometimes the text came first. It didn't make a difference. But the response had to be immediate because we were working on a real rhythm, you know? Very often, very often, I can't even imagine how many times he would do something, and I would just lose it. I would crack up. I would literally have belly laughs. I couldn't believe the things he was writing."[27]

Despite Yau's notoriety and that of several of his collaborators, their joint efforts have been rarely exhibited, sporadically documented, and occasionally made visible on websites and social media. These uniquely crafted combinations of image and text have typically languished on storage shelves or in flat files, remembered fondly by their creators but not heralded by arts professionals and institutions to the degree that is warranted. I would argue that these works were created with a focus on process and pleasure, and once completed, there was no urgency, or limited opportunities, to bring the results "to market." But it is also true that collaboration problematizes, as Rand suggests, inherited notions of the artist as a singular practitioner;[28] while challenging neat categorizations by medium (painting, drawing, print, book) that museums continue to uphold.

In a letter written in April 2023, Peter Saul addressed the unseen aspect of his collaboration with Yau in 1994: "I had a teaching job at Univ. of Texas, Austin, lasted 19 years and some time in there John Yau appeared, probably to give [a] 'lecture' about something and someone suggested we combine on a print. Probably Ken Hale, the print teacher. So we just sat right down on opposite sides of a table in the print shop and passed pieces of paper back and forth and had a few laughs. It really did take 2 hours. Actually I never thought anymore about it—pleasant experience that tends to happen to people who have 'art teacher' jobs . . . Now and then I come across our '2 hours' in my flat files, think it's pretty good and am glad you're planning to show it."[29]

While trying to find an apt title for this survey of Yau's collaborative activities, it became clear that "disguise the limit" was not only short and sweet, but sly and suggestive. These three words appear in his concrete poem, "Genghis Chan: Private Eye XXXIX (Seventh Ideogram),"[30] he has handwritten the phrase in a group of modest drawings made with Chuck Webster; and it was used for an embroidered patch designed by Carol Szymanski for a project by Emergency Eyewash. It is obviously a punning alteration of "the sky's the limit," commonly understood to mean that anything is possible, and you can achieve whatever you desire. What is Yau getting at? Clearly, he is delighting in the gap between written and spoken language, proposing that *the sky's* could easily be heard as *dis guy's* if pronounced by a wise guy from *da* neighborhood. Or is he issuing an edict to transform limits wherever one finds them? I would bet on both, and more. Yau's pun packs a wallop, prompting a smile and focusing our attention on the gap between aspirations and the glass ceilings that rein them in.

Is he addressing the limited audience for poetry? When asked about his own readership, Yau replied, "It's maybe three people. And I don't know who they are. I've always felt that way."[31] While I would argue that there are many more Yau fans out there than that, his humility is telling. In the poem "Midway" (commissioned by Gervais Jassaud for his Collectif Génération imprint), Yau posits[32]:

My poems do not travel across a landscape of cultural memory
They do not strike a dynamic balance of honesty,
Emotion, intellectual depth, and otherworldly resonance

They will not startle you out of your daily anesthesia
They do not map the deepest crevices of the interior self
They cast no light on history's margins, overlooked and neglected

And yet this is exactly what Yau's writing does. His words most certainly travel, startle, map, and illuminate. Collaboration has had a profound effect on this, and in addressing its significance, Yau stated, "The best thing, the most important thing I learned, and I think I knew what I was going to learn from the beginning, was how the line functioned. What can I do with twelve words? What can I do with eight words? How did they work? This is a lot of room to play and not a lot of room to play. It brought fun into my writing in a way that was healthy and helpful."[33]

Yau's collaborations offer him room to explore the "thingness" of words, as sounds to be heard and forms to be seen. Letters and lines are given scale and color, asserting their independence from and compatibility with abstract gestures, suggestive shapes, and recognizable imagery. He strategically uses different voices (a reminder that Yau studied dramatic monologues in college) to push at the limits of isolation he understands to be in his nature, and most creative endeavors. In "For Tom (1944–2019)," another poem dedicated to Nozkowski, he looks unflinchingly at this situation[34]:

As the years passed, trembling and crying in the dark became easier.
I don't regret my lack of social skills or how I fumble for words.
I came here to write, which means I moved to this city to be alone,
and learned that I was wrong to think that was how it was supposed to be.

By collaborating with many congenial partners (something that he shows no sign of stopping), Yau affirms his un-aloneness and embraces "the slipperiness of language and the slipperiness of living in the world."[35] In considering his various efforts, it would serve us well to remember something that he wrote in the recent monograph examining the dimensions of Joe Brainard's ebullient and hyphenate practice, all his works "must be seen as parallel and complementary to each other, even as they stand on their own as distinct bodies of work."[36]

1 John Yau, "A Painter's Thoughts (5): After Thomas Nozkowski (1944–2019) in *Genghis Chan on Drums* (Richmond, CA: Omnidawn Publishing, 2021), 79.

2 *The Complete Poems of Emily Dickinson* (Boston: Little, Brown and Company, 1960), 507.

3 John Yau, interview with the author, June 21, 2023.

4 John Yau, Introduction to *Please Wait by the Coatroom: Reconsidering Race and Identity in American Art* (Boston: Black Sparrow Press, 2023), xv.

5 *Pinyin* is the spelling out of Chinese phrases with letters from the English alphabet. This is an example of Yau playing with the sound and spelling of words; his "O Pin Yin Sonnets" are full of opinions.

6 John Yau, "O Pin Yin Sonnet (13): Don't blame the bat soup for the Wuhan virus," in *Genghis Chan on Drums* (Richmond, CA: Omnidawn Publishing, 2021), 28.

7 John Yau, interview with the author, September 27, 2022.

8 "Ing Grish" in *Ing Grish* (Philadelphia: Saturnalia Books, 2005), 62, 64, 65.

9 John Yau, interview with the author, February 26, 2023.

10 John Yau, "Genghis Chan: Private Eye XIII" in *Further Adventures in Monochrome* (Port Townsend, WA: Copper Canyon Press, 2012), 37.

11 John Yau, "Yves Klein Blue (Interlude)" in *Further Adventures in Monochrome* (Port Townsend, WA: Copper Canyon Press, 2012), 137.

12 John Yau, "The Poet as Art Critic," in *The Passionate Spectator: Essays on Art and Poetry* (Ann Arbor: University of Michigan Press, 2006), 57.

13 "John Yau with Phong Bui," *The Brooklyn Rail*, July–August 2009, https://brooklynrail.org/2009/07/art/john-yau-with-phong-bui.

14 Mark Scroggins, back cover copy in *Foreign Sounds or Sounds Foreign* (Cheshire, MA: MadHat Press, 2020).

15 John Yau, interview with the author, February 26, 2023.

16 John Yau, Introduction to *Please Wait by the Coatroom: Reconsidering Race and Identity in American Art* (Boston: Black Sparrow Press, 2023), xx.

17 John Yau, "Please Wait by the Coatroom: Wifredo Lam in the Museum of Modern Art," in *Please Wait by the Coatroom: Reconsidering Race and Identity in American Art* (Boston: Black Sparrow Press, 2023), 6.

18 David Carrier, "The Essential Importance of John Yau's Art Writing," *CounterPunch*, March 24, 2023, https://www.counterpunch.org/2023/03/24/the-essential-importance-of-john-yaus-art-writing/.

19 John Yau, "A Few Reasons Why Poets Love Bruce Conner," *Hyperallergic*, May 24, 2015, https://hyperallergic.com/209253/a-few-reasons-why-poets-love-bruce-conner/. Later published in *The Wild Children of William Blake* (Brooklyn: Autonomedia, 2017), 70.

20 John Yau, "Single Point Perspective: An Arcadian Moment in the Heart of New York's Lower East Side," *Hyperallergic* (June 8, 2014), https://hyperallergic.com/130624/single-point-perspective-an-arcadian-moment-in-the-heart-of-new-yorks-lower-east-side/. Later published in *Foreign Sounds or Sounds Foreign* (Cheshire, MA: MadHat Press, 2020), 169-170.

21 John Yau, interview with the author, September 27, 2022.

22 Bill Berkson, "Hands On/Hands Off," in *The Art of Collaboration: Poets, Artists, Books*, ed. Anca Cristofovici and Barbara Montefalcone (Austin, TX: Cuneiform Press, 2015), 77.

23 Elizabeth Licata, "Robert Creeley's Collaborations: A History," in *In Company: Robert Creeley's Collaborations*, ed. Amy Cappallazzo and Elizabeth Licata (Niagara Falls, NY: Castellani Art Museum of Niagara University; Greensboro, NC: Weatherspoon Art Gallery, University of North Carolina at Greensboro, 1999), 11.

24 Franz Kline, quoted in Musa Mayer, "Stern Conditions," in *Night Studio: A Memoir of Philip Guston by His Daughter* (New York: Alfred A. Knopf, 1988) 67.

24 John Yau, interview with the author, February 26, 2023.

26 Archie Rand, quoted in Elizabeth Licata, "Robert Creeley's Collaborations: A History," in *In Company: Robert Creeley's Collaborations*, ed. Amy Cappallazzo and Elizabeth Licata (Niagara Falls, NY: Castellani Art Museum of Niagara University; Greensboro, NC: Weatherspoon Art Gallery, University of North Carolina at Greensboro, 1999), 27.

27 Archie Rand, interview with the author, September 29, 2022.

28 Rand, in Licata, "Robert Creeley's Collaborations," 27.

29 Peter Saul, letter to the author, April 13, 2023.

30 John Yau, "Genghis Chan: Private Eye XXXIX (Seventh Idiogram)" in *Further Adventures in Monochrome* (Port Townsend, WA: Copper Canyon Press, 2012), 72.

31 John Yau, interview with the author, June 21, 2023.

32 John Yau, "Midway," in *Bijoux in the Dark* (Seattle: Letter Machine Editions, 2018), 131. "Midway" was first published as an artist's book by Gervais Jassaud under his imprint Collectif Génération. The artists who worked on separate editions are Kathy Berry, Astrid Sylwan, Claude Viallat, and Chuck Webster.

33 John Yau, interview with the author, February 26, 2023.

34 John Yau, "For Tom (1944–2019)" in *Genghis Chan on Drums* (Richmond, CA: Omnidawn Publishing, 2021), 127.

35 Yau, interview with the author, June 21, 2023.

36 John Yau, *Joe Brainard: The Art of the Personal* (New York: Rizzoli Electra, 2022), 66.

Opening Up the Space of Reading
—Barry Schwabsky

How far back in time should one go in considering the historical context for artist/poet collaborations? One idea might be to start where the artist and the poet happened to be the same person—with William Blake, who wrote, illustrated, and printed all his books. In 2017, John Yau published a collection of critical writings called *The Wild Children of William Blake*. It was titled after a piece that had first appeared the previous year, in which he emphasized certain contemporary artists' affinity with the contrarian nature of Blake's enterprise—in particular, their propensity for devising heretical cosmologies. Although Yau has not followed Blake in attempting to take all aspects of his creative production—verbal, visual, and material—into his own hands (and indeed very few since Blake have gone so far in that direction) I suspect he would not be averse to our intuition that he, too, should be counted among the wild children of William Blake. In his collaborations with artists, Yau often does what he once praised the painter Philip Hanson for doing: He observed that Hanson, incorporating a poem by Emily Dickinson into some of his works, "has entwined the separate experiences of looking and reading in a way that requires us to untangle them, which opens up the space of reading."[1] When I first read that I had to stop and wonder, was the word I'd just read "untangle" or "entangle," and how could I tell the difference in practice? Wasn't that self-questioning opening up my space of reading?

But aside from the English-language tradition of which Blake is a contrarian part, Yau is also a child of French modernism and the international avant-garde that arose in its wake. It's this tradition—yes, I'm quite aware that some may detect an irony in the idea of an avant-garde tradition—that offers a more immediate (and populous) background to Yau's collaborations with artists. By general consensus, modern painting begins with Édouard Manet, though I sometimes think it would be better to backdate it to Gustave Courbet. (Here I should probably provide an at least provisional definition of modernism, but instead I will take refuge in Supreme Court Justice Potter Stewart's test of obscenity: I know it when I see it.) And take note, in the crowded scene of Courbet's 1855 magnum opus *L'Atelier du peintre. Allégorie réelle déterminant une phase de sept années de ma vie artistique et morale* (The Painter's Studio: A real allegory summing up seven years of my artistic and moral life), of the figure on the far right, absorbed in a book: the poet Charles Baudelaire. I can't help wondering if Courbet isn't indulging in a bit of irony at his friend's expense, showing the poet as someone who doesn't really look at painting but transmutes it by way of a text. Nonetheless, Courbet clearly placed Baudelaire among "all the shareholders" in his enterprise, or as we might say today, his *allies*, "that is, friends, workers, and art lovers."[2] The poet-critic tends not to pose as a disinterested judge, but to become immersed in the work of certain artists and take their side; their critical writing was already in itself a sort of collaborative exercise. As Frank O'Hara observed, "Poets who have distinguished themselves as critics—Baudelaire, Apollinaire—talked it over with the painters first and made a work out of it."[3]

Just as one might ask whether or not Courbet was quite what's meant by the word "modern," it's possible to agree with the literary-minded music critic Ian Penman in his recent remark that although Baudelaire "was declared the first modernist, . . . he didn't feel 'modern' in the way Rilke or Jarry or Apollinaire did," being as he was "a poet with a capital P, writhing in the coils of Church and Satan, Evil and Beauty, Sin and Damnation."[4] But about Manet, there are no such doubts, and he was devoted to Baudelaire; it's been said, "It was Baudelaire's friendship that gave Manet the encouragement to plunge into the unknown to find the new, and in doing so to become the true painter of modern life."[5] There's a mirrorical (Marcel Duchamp's word) complementarity in the fact that the poet is pictured at the right of Courbet's studio and at the left (as a barely discernable smudge, and yet—yes—that's undoubtedly him) of Manet's *Music in the Tuileries Gardens*, painted just seven years later.

Courbet was less clearly a modernist than his successor Manet, and the same could be said of Baudelaire in relation to his successor, Stéphane Mallarmé. And as much as Manet admired Baudelaire, he was closer to Mallarmé, of whom he painted a ravishing portrait in 1876. Just as important as the portrait was their collaboration the same year on the limited-edition publication of Mallarmé's poem *L'après-midi d'un faune* (The Afternoon of a Faun), using a font designed for the occasion (though not an artist himself, Mallarmé could be just as particular about the visual impact of his work as Blake

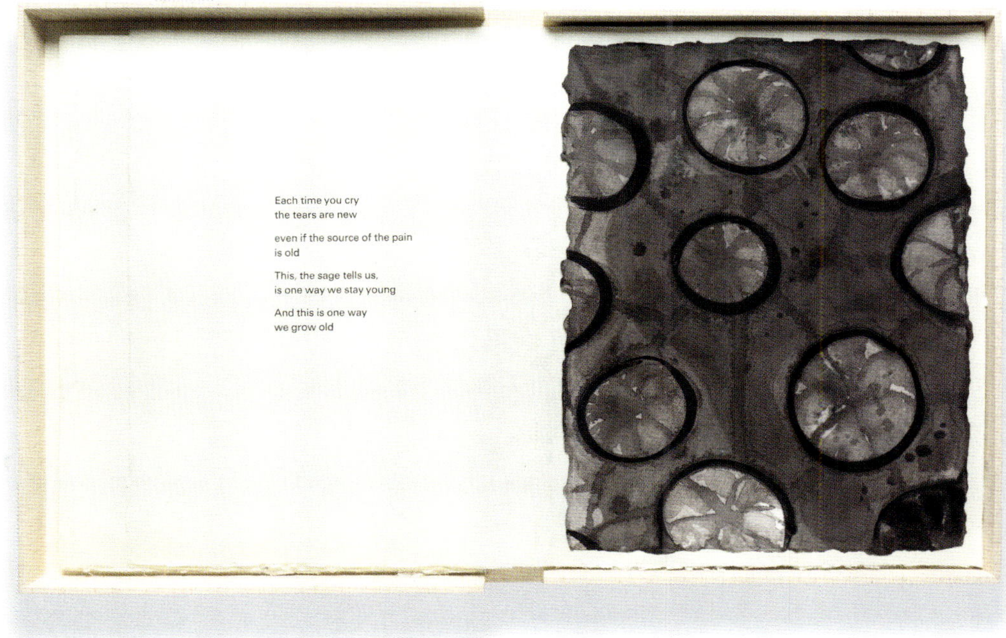

John Yau and Max Gimblett, *A Book of Millennium Koans*, 1988–2001

had been). Manet provided "four wood-engraved embellishments that were printed in black and hand tinted in pink by Manet himself."[6] That's as good a place as any to mark the beginning of modernist collaborations between painters and poets—poets who might also take on the role, as Mallarmé occasionally did, of art critics. (The year 1876 was also when Mallarmé published, in English, his great essay "The Impressionists and Édouard Manet."[7])

Baudelaire's friendships with Courbet and Manet should be considered an outgrowth of what Harrison and Cynthia White called the dealer-critic system. In their sociological analysis of the transformation of the French art world in the nineteenth century, the Whites saw the gradual displacement of the earlier academic system. While the latter was geared toward the evaluation of isolated works, the new system "dealt with an artist more in terms of his production over a career."[8] Now, "the individual painting was a piece of the whole," which in the case of the Impressionists could be understood as "the painter's interpretation of nature."[9] It was the critic—and especially, I'd add, the poet-critic—who could illuminate that vision.

This brief essay is hardly the occasion to offer an overview of the vast number of collaborations since 1876 between painters and poets who were also art critics. In the twentieth century, Dada and Surrealism alone—with their unusually close association between pictorial and textual invention—would supply material for a thick volume, or perhaps several, especially if one were to look beyond France to their manifestations around the world, from Chile to Egypt and elsewhere.[10] Something similar could be said of Expressionism and Futurism, which likewise flourished internationally after coming to birth in Germany and Italy respectively. All the avant-garde movements of the early twentieth century produced rich harvests of artist-poet collaborations.

Lacking the space (and erudition) to elaborate on all that, I want instead to fast-forward to midcentury Manhattan, where, as in nineteenth and early twentieth-century Paris, tremendous artistic ferment coexisted with a remarkable literary outpouring. And the poets who came to be dubbed, semi-facetiously, the New York School—John Ashbery, Barbara Guest, Kenneth Koch, Frank O'Hara, and James Schuyler, soon joined by others including a whole "second generation"—were all excited and inspired by what was going on in painting in postwar New York. They admired not only the work of the Abstract Expressionists but of others as well, especially the painterly realists (Jane Freilicher, Alex Katz, Fairfield Porter) who'd learned from Abstract Expressionism but took their own work in a different direction. Only Koch, of the five poets I mentioned, did not venture deeply into art writing. None of those poet-critics was committed to a given mode of art-making or a specific historical narrative intended to justify one form or style over others. In fact, as Ashbery once said, "This might be one definition of the New York School—its avoidance of anything like a program."[11] That same attitude animated such second-generation New York School poets as Bill Berkson, Ted Berrigan, Bernadette Mayer, Ron Padgett, David Shapiro, and Marjorie Welish, some of whom also became art critics or even practiced as artists themselves.

Yau was a student of Ashbery's, and he picked up on that programmatically unprogrammatic agenda. The New York School attitude or sensibility or whatever you like to call it was, given its antiprogrammatic nature, never considered an "ism," and this is probably why those who were casting

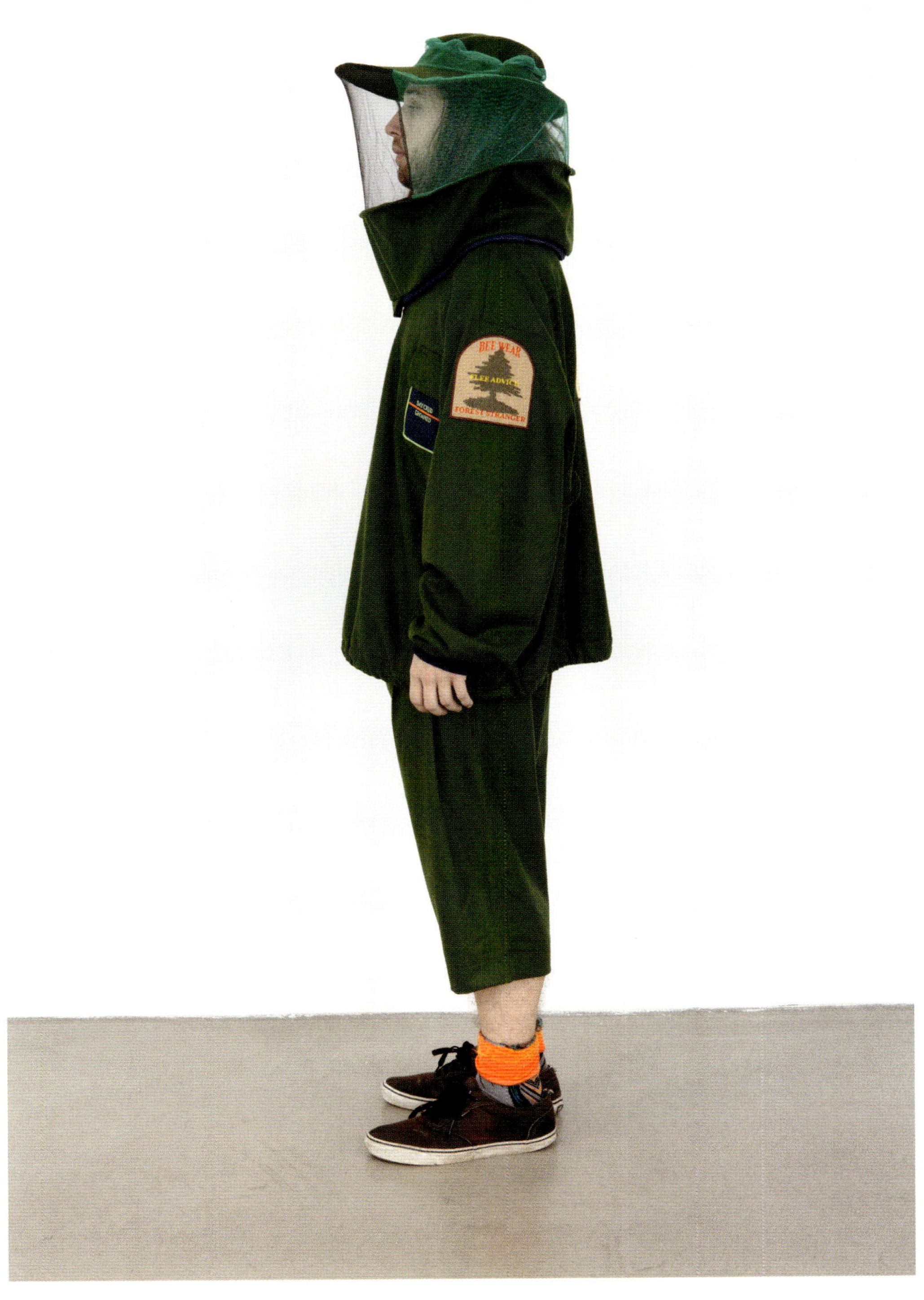

Emergency Eyewash with John Yau, Siv Støldal, and Carol Szymanski, *Bee Wear*, 2017/2023

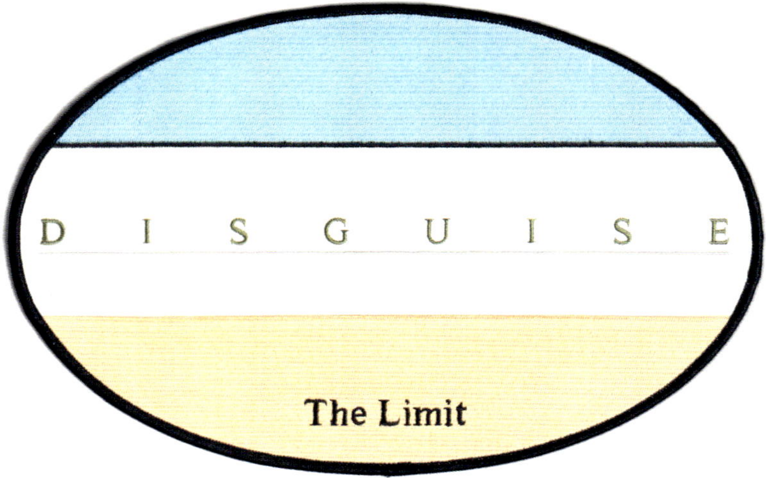

Emergency Eyewash with John Yau, Willa Schwabsky, and Carol Szymanski, *Emergency Eyewash Patch*, 2017

about for a name for it resorted to the equally but less obviously inappropriate designation of it as a "school." In any case, this is why I think David Lehman was mistaken in calling his book about the New York School poets *The Last Avant-Garde*.[12] They were programmatically—I insist on the word—non-avant-garde because the most important thing about any avant-garde was typically its manifesto, that is, the credo around which a collective could crystallize; whatever was not true to the manifesto had to be rejected as passé. The avant-gardes were, paradoxically as it may seem, following in the footsteps of the late nineteenth century art critic-theorists who, as Pierre Bourdieu pointed out in his lectures on Manet, "were fighting for the monopoly that the state and the minister of fine arts had previously held" under the old academic system, namely, "to be able to say: 'What I am doing is what should be done, and it is the only thing that should be done; I am the legitimate authority.'"[13]

Nothing could be further from the sensibility of an Ashbery or O'Hara. They did not want to claim authority, legitimate or otherwise. They replaced the avant-gardists' commandments, "You must do this; you must not do that," with some good advice: You can also do this; you don't have to do that. I suppose it was the permissiveness of this attitude that led the conservative critic Hilton Kramer—as Irving Sandler recalls—to decry Ashbery, among others, of betraying the "high purposes and moral grandeur of modernism."[14] Ashbery's sensibility has something in common with that of Joe Brainard, a remarkable writer who as an artist was one of the second-generation New York School's favorite illustrators, a peerless collaborator. The poet Geoffrey O'Brien recently remarked (in a review of Yau's monograph on Brainard) how Brainard's writing (but the same is true of his visual art) "served as an instant and almost innocent deflation of every sort of grandiosity, literary and otherwise" in an exposition of his "experience of being in the world and in his body in discrete flashes of perception, at once startling and hilarious and frank, and often most mysterious when contemplating the obvious."[15]

Yau himself has observed, "In his collaborations, Brainard rejected the commonplace art world model of art as a commodity created by a single individual. By definition, collaboration requires that at least two people be involved, with neither of them being dominant," undermining conventional ideas of authorship.[16] It almost goes without saying that in this, Yau is declaring his own idea of collaboration as well as Brainard's—I should call it, really, his own *ethic* of collaboration. He declares it again in writing of another postwar group of artists and writers, this time on the West Coast, the circle around Wallace Berman and his magazine *Semina*: "Instead of trying to assimilate into the art or literary world, the contributors to *Semina* granted themselves authority over their own work and gave each other both mutual permission and support."[17]

Because Yau's idea of collaboration is a deeply held ethic, an exhibition (and book) such as this one that surveys the whole range of ways that he has made work together with visual artists amounts to more than just an intriguing sidelight on the work of a prominent poet and art critic, or a way of gathering works by many artists under the banner of the alliance with him that they all share: It shows something essential about Yau, something very particular to him. What I mean by that is very simply explained: I don't believe that any poet, any art critic, any writer of any sort, today or in the past, writing in English or in any other language, has so assiduously engaged in processes of collaboration with so many artists, and moreover, with artists of so many different sorts; not even O'Hara, who most enthusiastically "assumed the role of the friend of artists" to the extent that "attention was of vital significance to artists; it literally sustained them," comes close. [18]

And the writing that Yau has produced for these occasions is equally varied. Is it that the multiplicity of artist-collaborators and the different modes and moods their disparate visions embody stimulate Yau to find different tones and forms that he might not otherwise have resorted to? In that vein, Yau quotes Robert Creeley saying that collaboration helps get you "out of the habits of your own thinking."[19] Or is it rather that he sought out such dissimilar working partners precisely in order to generate enough different contexts for the many sides of his literary personality, the various ways of thinking he already knew to be in him?

The poignant "millennium koans" with which Yau accompanied the ink drawings of the New Zealand painter Max Gimblett—with lines like "Each time you cry / the tears are new / / even if the source of the pain / is old / / This, the sage tells us / is one way we stay young / / And this is one way / we grow old"—maintain the same meditative spontaneity as Gimblett's images which, with their fluid look and evanescent imagery in shades of gray, seem to confirm Yau's statement that the artist has long been "a serious student of Japanese ink painting."[20] Those poems provide a distinct contrast with, for instance, the raucous tone of the short pieces Yau composed for the many watercolors he made with Archie Rand. Rand himself is an inveterate collaborator with poets, having also worked with, among others, Ashbery, Clark Coolidge, Robert Creeley, and Anne Waldman; although this hasn't been noted by critics, Brainard is one of Rand's icons, and he's said that seeing a 1967 Brainard collaboration with Kenward Elmslie "blew me away and remains influential on my painting."[21] Some of Yau's poems for these watercolors are one-liners, others might be something more like incongruously brassy haiku ("I am the violin of lust / I made the night / soft and round, red"), and all were apparently dashed off on the spot, just like Rand's gleefully boisterous but often disquieting images, as poet and painter handed paper back forth between them—working in the moment like a couple of jazz soloists trading fours.

I could go on: With Richard Tuttle, Yau created *The Missing Portrait*, a sort of book-as-sculptural-object that exceeds the conventional boundaries of the codex, and the text itself, unusually for Yau's work, follows in the tradition of Mallarmé's landmark work of 1897, *Un coup de dés jamais n'abolira le hasard* (A throw of the dice will never abolish chance) with its simultaneity of different streams of writing distinguished typographically and through spatial placement. With Tom Burkhardt, on the other hand, Yau's verbal imagination gets encapsulated in a sequence of road signs, so that the shape of the imagined structures Burkhardt depicts become the words' container. In working under the aegis of Emergency Eyewash, the "conceptual brand" I established with Carol Szymanski in order to foment art/text collaborations, Yau supplied punning texts to adorn patches, designed by Szymanski, to be applied to a fanciful bee-keeper's outfit created for the occasion by Norwegian menswear designer Siv Støldal. Among the expressions he came up with was this one: DISGUISE THE LIMIT. There's a lesson there. There's always a limit, but if you can carry on as if it weren't there, then who knows? The sky's the limit.

Yau the collaborator contains multitudes—or rather, doesn't contain them, but quite the opposite, generates them, releases them, disseminates them. This is, in the end, more than a purely artistic matter; it is a reflection of his capacity for friendship. That's part of the tradition too. The mutual recognition between literarily sensitive artists and visually minded poets, like that between Manet and Mallarmé, was the source more than the result of their having worked together. Manet wasn't Mallarmé's only painter friend, by the way. Another was Edgar Degas, about whom there's an oft-repeated story: Degas, who had some writerly ambitions of his own, complained to the poet that although he had some marvelous ideas for sonnets, he somehow couldn't bring them off. "But my dear Degas," Mallarmé is supposed to have replied, "poems are made of words, not ideas." Did he really say that? Who knows. But if so, one thing it proves is that friends enjoy each other's snappy retorts, whose deeper truth may be mysterious, or just moot; and yet they open up the mind, helping both parties break of their habits of thought. (And some of Yau's collaborations with artist friends can feel like sequences of witty zingers.) But truly, Mallarmé knew very well that poems are made of more than words. "Philosophically," he wrote, "verse makes up for what languages lack."[22] The collaboration of artists and poets demonstrates both the autonomy of each art—it is only because they are distinct that they can be combined without confusion—and its incompleteness: They need each other to make up for what they lack. One of Yau's poems asks, "What happens when words (or sounds) become colors, and a thunderclap descends into swirls of red?"[23] One wants to find out. Words *do* become colors, colors *do* become words, but the mode of translation or transmutation is not given in advance, must be invented anew each time. In the same poem we read, "I could not have written these words until I played the game of second-guessing," and perhaps we can understand working alongside a second person wielding a parallel art as a form of that second-guessing; and then the poem continues, "Every word is a stab in the dark, a treatise about a parallel conclusion."[24] These parallel conclusions are what open the space of reading, of seeing.

1 John Yau, "Late Bloomer: Philip Hanson's Recent Paintings," in *The Wild Children of William Blake* (Brooklyn: Autonomedia, 2017), 223-24. Originally at Hyperallergic, April 13, 2014, https://hyperallergic.com/120123/ late-bloomer-philip-hansons-recent-paintings/.

2 Gustave Courbet, quoted by Michael Fried, *Courbet's Realism* (Chicago: University of Chicago Press, 1992), 57.

3 Ian Penman, quoted by Irving Sandler, *A Sweeper-Up After Artists: A Memoir* (London: Thames & Hudson, 2004), 40.

4 Ian Penman, "Brussels Pout," *London Review of Books* 45, no. 6 (March 16, 2023): https://www.lrb.co.uk/the-paper/v45/n06/ ian-penman/brussels-pout.

5 Alan Bowness, Poetry & Painting: Baudelaire, Mallarmé, *Apollinaire and their Painter Friends* (Oxford: Clarendon Press, 1994, quoted at A&A art and architecture, http://www.artandarchitecture.org.uk/fourpaintings/manet/ life/baudelaire.html#:~:text=Baudelaire%20died%20in%201867.,true%20 painter%20of%20modern%20life.

6 Julie L. Mellby, "Stéphane Mallarmé and Édouard Manet," Graphic Arts: Exhibitions, acquisitions, and other highlights from the Graphic Arts Collection, Princeton University Library (February 1, 2011), http:// www.princeton.edu/~graphicarts/2011/02/stephane_mallarme_1842-1898_ la.html.

7 The essay appeared in The Art Monthly Review and Photographic Portfolio 1, no. 9 (September 30, 1876), 117-122. For more information on it, see Margaret Werth, "Mallarmé and Impressionism in 1876," Non-Site 27 (February 11, 2019), https://nonsite.org/mallarme-and-impressionism-in-1876/.

8 Harrison C. White and Cynthia A. White, *Canvases and Careers: Institutional Change in the French Painting World* (Chicago: University of Chicago Press, 1993), 98.

9 White, 118.

10 A good place to begin exploring the history of collaborations in French Surrealism is Renee Riese Hubert, *Surrealism and the Book* (Berkeley: University of California Press, 1988).

11 John Ashbery, "The New York School of Poets," in *Selected Prose*, ed. Eugene Richie (Ann Arbor: The University of Michigan Press, 2004), 113.

12 David Lehman, *The Last Avant-Garde: The Making of the New York School of Poets* (New York: Doubleday, 1998).

13 Pierre Bourdieu, *Manet: A Symbolic Revolution: Lectures at the Collège de France* (1998-2000), trans. Peter Collier and Margaret Rigaud-Drayton (Cambridge: Polity Press, 2017), 134.

14 Sandler, *A Sweeper-Up After Artists*, 320.

15 Geoffrey O'Brien, "Joe Brainard's Communal Intimacy," *The New York Review of Books* 70, no. 7 (April 20, 2023): 23

16 John Yau, *Joe Brainard: The Art of the Personal* (New York: Rizzoli Electa, 2022), 12.

17 John Yau, "Wallace Berman & His Circle," in *The Wild Children of William Blake*, 26. Originally published as "Semina Culture: Wallace Berman and His Circle," in *The Brooklyn Rail* (April 2007), https://brooklynrail.org/2007/ 04/artseen/ semina-a.

18 Sandler, *A Sweeper-Up After Artists*, 207.

19 John Yau, "Some Things I Know About This Artist," *Hyperallergic* (April 1, 2012), https://hyperallergic.com/49328/ max-gimblett-gary-snyder-gallery/.

20 Yau, "Some Things I Know About This Artist."

21 Sam Jablon, "Painting and Poetry: In Conversation with Archie Rand," *Hyperallergic* (April 21, 2014), https://hyperallergic.com/121615/painting-and-poetry-in-conversation-with-archie-rand/.

22 Stéphane Mallarmé, "Crisis in Poetry," in Mary Ann Caws, ed., *Manifesto: A Century of Isms* (Lincoln: University of Nebraska Press, 2001), 25.

23 John Yau, "A Painter's Formulas, An Alchemist's Notes, and an Unknown Convict's Ravings found on a Blacke Calendar," in *Bijoux in the Dark* (Tucson: Letter Machine Editions, 2018), 14.

24 Yau, "A Painter's Formulas," 14.

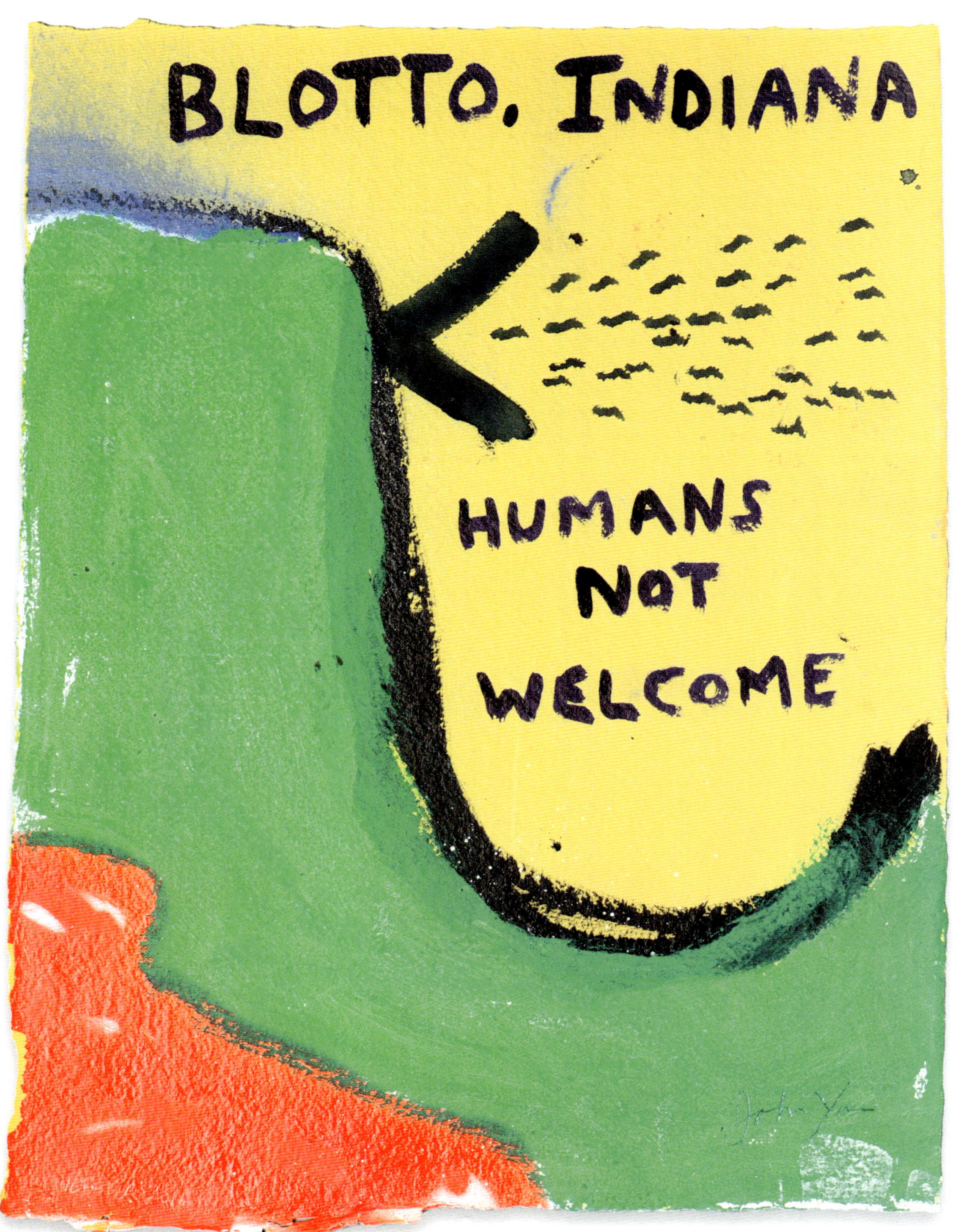

John Yau and Chuck Webster, *Blotto, Indiana*, 2016

FEAR OF LAUGHTER
John Yau's Persistent Humor

—*Sharon Mesmer*

Mark Twain said, "Humor is mankind's greatest blessing."[1] True, unless you're a poet. For poets, humor is a neglected off-ramp on the interstate of contemporary American poetry that spits the scribe out into an obscure, unincorporated, tumbleweed-y area that GPS doesn't pick up. Poets who want to be considered "serious" don't go there.

Sure, there's Kenneth Koch's "Variations on a Theme by William Carlos Williams," Allen Ginsberg's "America," and Frank O'Hara's "Ave Maria" and "Autobiographia Literaria." Beginning in the early aughts, the 30+ poets of the Flarf Collective used random word searches to mine the internet for juxtapositions—as filthy and disturbing as they were funny—churned up by Google's algorithm. Included as well are certain works by Edwin Torres, Todd Colby, Melissa Broder, Paul Violi, Shane Allison. And there's Ted Berrigan:

Tompkins Square Park

All my friends in the
park speak Latin: when
they see me coming, they
say, "Valium"?

(from *The Collected Poems of Ted Berrigan,* University of California Press, 2007) [2]

It's not like poets never use humor, but many seem to feel it's . . . well, . . . sus. In an April 7, 2012, post on the Best American Poetry blog, funny poet Jennifer Knox quoted poet Kazim Ali: "I don't think funny poetry is valid. I know that I'm wrong, but I still feel that way."[3]

Run away, bards, and fast! But despite how some versifiers may feel, comedy and poetry do share a muse—Thaleia, also one of the Graces. Comedians wield well-crafted language (like hairpin-turn juxtapositions delivered with impeccable timing) and fearless vulnerability; so do poets. But poets seem to equate humor with misbehavior. "American poetry's biggest problem right now is that it wants so badly to be good," writes Julie Carr in her essay "The Good the Bad and The," which appears in the winter 2023 issue of the literary magazine *Fence*.[4] "It wants to be a lot of kinds of good: spiritual, material, political, crafty, accessible, marketable. But above all, it seems to me, American poetry wants to be *morally* good."

She ends her essay with this statement:

" . . . the best American poets have always been the ones who are willing to be bad."

Enter John Yau.

Yau has always taken the off-ramp, and gleefully. His humor is often so deadpan and clothed in "reality" that readers may be fooled—for a second—into believing he's being (gasp!) *serious*. To deploy that humor, he takes on personae; a particular voice—often a vulnerable one—carries a poem to places other poems aren't going. In fact, one might wonder who, exactly, is speaking in some of his poems, and where that speaker is speaking from:

> *I am writing to you from the bedroom of my ex-wife, where I have been stenciling*
> *diagrams on sheets and ceiling, intricate star charts of the paths modern soldier*
> *ants take to reach the lips waiting at the end of their long journey. . .*
>
> *I am writing to you from the bedroom my ex-wife keeps in her bedroom . . .*
>
> *I am writing to you from the sleeping car temporarily disabled in the bedroom of my ex-wife . . .*

("Unpromising Poem," from *Ing Grish*, Saturnalia Books, 2005)[5]

Whose representative experience is that? Whose affective, individual voice? And in what bonkers time-space continuum does that bedroom exist? As in André Breton's "Free Union," where the wife (in Breton's case) is described as a creature possessed of a sex like a platypus and breasts haunted by the ghosts of roses,[6] Yau describes persons and places similarly possessed of polyvalent qualities and identities. The increasingly strange spiral of descriptions wedded to playful, euphonic language creates the humor:

> *I used to be a plastic bottle*
> *I used to be scads of masticated wattle*
> *I used to be epic spittle, aka septic piddle*

("Confessions of a Recycled Shopping Bag" from *Further Adventures in Monochrome*,
Copper Canyon Press, 2012)[7]

In "Screen Name" (also from *Ing Grish*), the poet riffs on the question of qualities and identities[8]:

> *John Yau is calling, his name has come up on the screen of my cell phone. This*
> *makes me uneasy because I am John Yau, and I would like to believe that I am always answering to myself*

. . . It is Wednesday, and the long-necked geese have
  started returning to the chimneys of my hometown.

There's a cottage-y, European-y flavor to the last line that upends the Twilight Zone-y, contemporary poetry-y speculations that begin the poem. These upendings are where his humor is often located. They feature in many of his poems and are surgically delivered. In "Domestic Bliss" (from *Borrowed Love Poems*, Penguin Books, 2002)[9], the poet starts out small, pivots, and ends up large:

If I am as cute as a button
why have you spent the past hour
hunting for the one that rolled down your sleeve

onto the aluminum siding bus
carrying rows of disillusioned tourists . . .

Sometimes multiple quick shifts occur, in the moves from one section to the next, taking us from shifting personae . . .

At night, I dive onto the breeze
fermenting above the dirt

and dream that I am a crocodile
a tin of shoe polish, an audience of two

In the morning, before the smallest yawn
becomes a noodle, I am offered

a ribbon of yellow smoke

. . . to the detritus of our technology, then the stars, and finally back to Earth:

I am one of the last computer

chain errors to be illuminated I tell you there are rooftops

on which the moon stops
being a cold jewel

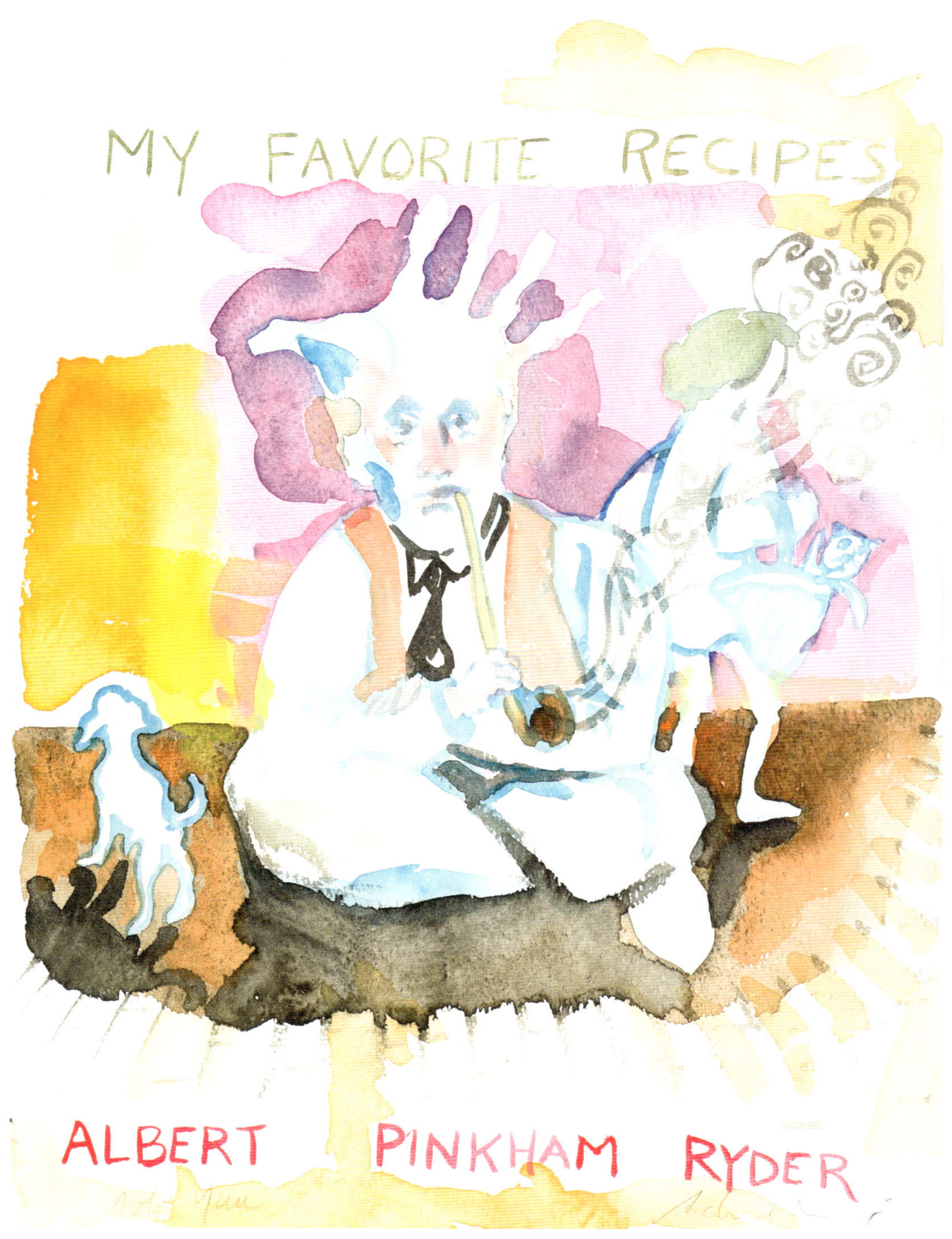

John Yau and Archie Rand, *My Favorite Recipes*, 1987

And one by one the mountains

begin their descent from

the chambers of a lost book

("A Sheaf of Pleasant Voices," from *Paradiso Diaspora*, Penguin Books, 2006)[10]

These shifts and turns, whether phrase by phrase, line by line, or section by section, bring to mind what Allen Ginsberg termed "eyeball kicks." In *Howl: Original Draft Facsimile, Transcript, and Variant Versions, Fully Annotated by Author*, Ginsberg defined eyeball kicks as " . . . the juxtapositions of disparate images to create a gap of understanding which the mind fills in with a flash of recognition . . . "[11]

Yau's collaborations with painters are marked by these "eyeball kicks," produced by the running of the poet's burlesque/gallows/epigrammatic/hyperbolic humor up against the bawdy visuals to produce that flash of recognition—and then laughter, like the best Rodney Dangerfield one-liners ("My wife and I were happy for twenty years. Then we met") which are also well-crafted, fearlessly vulnerable, impeccably timed. To wit (ha!), some of Yau's funniest collaborations:

With Archie Rand:

In Rand's vivid, anarchic watercolors with text/titles by Yau, a *Revised Idiot* is sexually stimulated by eating bees. A baby elephant turns blue looking at donut water seeping from a penis, in a scene deemed *Death by Donuts*. In *The Fly Who Came In From the Cold*, a penis may be an ear horn coming out of a nose. In *I Upgrade the Sublime*, a Samuel Johnson-looking dude wears a puppy hat and is accompanied by a woman wearing a Martian. And in *My Favorite Recipes*, Albert Pinkham Rider, smoking a long tobacco pipe, has a hand for a head. In each, a central figure captures the eye and urges it toward the text, where the recognition flash + laugher occurs. In some, the combinations of image + text act like covers of the weirdest books ever writ. What *are* Albert Pinkham Rider's favorite recipes?

With Peter Saul:

These black and white drawings on paper—which resemble a vulgar (in the very best way) graphic novel —suggest that if UFOs brought us donut stones, toilet paper, Head Hatchet™, and ham (which gave us copious diarrhea, and thus the toilet paper), then what the aliens really gave us is the knowledge that charred poodle steak is very, very wrong. Yau's text functions like graphic novel elements such as thought balloons ("the pig dwipper," as ruminated by a pig) and captions ("charred poodle steak," "You make my hamburger all nervous and melty").

With Chuck Webster:

Apparently in Blotto, Indiana, humans are not welcome. That may not be a bad thing. In these stark, colorful watercolors on paper, Yau's words act as captions for the blocky, rough and ready figures: like the bear that morphs into the Keebler cookie elves' hollow tree, wearing the Tin Man's oil can suit. Once that bear (or tree . . . whatever) gets in the house and plods down the basement stairs, watch out: the smell of baking will never go away. And beware: those elves can hear in the dark. And they are willing—nay, happy—to be bad and slightly undefined, like things seen in dreams. You never will believe where those Keebler cookies come from!

In his collaborations with painters, Yau reprises a signature activity of the first-generation New York School Poets: confluence with the art world in life and work. Four of the five canonical NYSPs (John Ashbery, Barbara Guest, Frank O'Hara, and James Schuyler), regularly contributed reviews to *ARTnews*, for which Ashbery was an executive editor, after being the magazine's Paris correspondent. Schuyler and O'Hara both worked at the Museum of Modern Art, and O'Hara's poetry contains references to his friendships with, and the works of, Jane Freilicher, Grace Hartigan, and Larry Rivers, among others. One of his most well-known poems, "Why I Am Not a Painter," contains a classic O'Hara name-check:

> *. . . Mike Goldberg*
> *is starting a painting. I drop in.*
> *"Sit down and have a drink" he*
> *says. I drink; we drink. I look*
> *up. "You have SARDINES in it."*
> *"Yes, it needed something there."*

(from *Selected Poems of Frank O'Hara,* Knopf, 2009)[12]

Despite Yau's own involvement with the art world—he's written criticism for *ARTnews*, *Artforum*, *Art in America*, and *Vogue*, served as art editor for *The Brooklyn Rail*, and was guided to criticism by Ashbery while studying with him in the Brooklyn College MFA poetry program—he isn't easily situated among the New York School's many antecedent schools, so populous within the literary landscape. He's his own thing. There's the Dangerfield-like vulnerability and timing that sets him apart . . .

> *I used to date a mannequin in a space suit*
>
> *Whenever I look out the porthole*
> *I can see the planet that ejected me*

("I Heard a Man Say," from *Bijoux in the Dark*, Letter Machine Editions, 2018)[13]

. . . as well as the slightly dirty personae (perhaps) not his own, which persist in the face of calls for "authenticity":

I have started a list of the costumes I want to be buried in, beginning with horny centaur

("After I Turn Sixty-Nine" from *Genghis Chan on Drums*, Omnidawn, 2021)[14]

Asked if he'd ever received pushback for his humor, and his stubbornness in deploying it, Yau answered in an email:

"Yes. Someone once said after I read, 'I didn't know you had a sense of humor.' Her facial expression conveyed her displeasure. Another time, after I read in Berkeley, the person who introduced me said he didn't think I was serious enough—I did not write socially relevant poetry. And a *Publisher's Weekly* reviewer dismissed my work for its 'puerile humor.'"[15]

And yet he persisted. Why?

In a 2003 *Brooklyn Rail* interview with Joan Waltemath, Yau gave his reasons:
"The idea of a poem being funny was a big taboo for literature and Kenneth Koch or Frank O'Hara clearly were laughing and how could this be? Also, Wallace Stevens said of poetry: 'It must give pleasure' . . . We don't want to know that art can give us pleasure. Some people seem to think pleasure is a mortal sin. I am not one of them."[16]

1 Mark Twain, quoted in Albert Bigelow Paine, *Mark Twain, A Biography: The Personal and Literary Life of Samuel Langhorne Clemens* (New York: Harper & Brothers Publishers, 1912), 3: 1556.
2 *The Collected Poems of Ted Berrigan* (Oakland: University of California Press, 2007) 606.
3 "Conversating with Kazim Ali: Is Funny Valid? Starring Don Knotts as Emily Dickinson," *Best American Poetry*, April 7, 2012, https://blog.bestamericanpoetry.com/the_best_american_poetry/2012/04/conversating-with-kazim-ali-is-funny-valid.html.
4 Julie Carr, "The Good the Bad and The" in *Fence* 40, vol. 22, no. 1 (winter 2023), 169.
5 John Yau, "Unpromising Poem," in *Ing Grish* (Philadelphia: Saturnalia Books, 2005), 18.
6 André Breton, "Free Union" trans. Louis Simpson. *Harvard Review*, no. 9 (1995): 59–60. http://www.jstor.org/stable/27560477.
7 John Yau, "Screen Name," in *Ing Grish* (Philadelphia: Saturnalia Books, 2005), 9.
8 Yau, "Domestic Bliss," in *Borrowed Love Poems* (New York: Penguin Books, 2002), 80.
9 Yau, "A Sheaf of Pleasant Voices," in *Paradiso Diaspora* (New York: Penguin Books, 2006), 40.
10 Allen Ginsberg, *Howl: original draft facsimile, transcript and variant versions, fully annotated by author, with contemporaneous correspondence, account of first public reading, legal skirmishes, precursor texts and bibliography* (New York: Harper & Row, 1986), 130.
11 Frank O'Hara, "Why I Am Not a Painter," in *Selected Poems of Frank O'Hara* (New York: Alfred A. Knopf, 2009), 112.
12 Yau, "I Heard A Man Say," in *Bijoux in the Dark* (Tuscon: Letter Machine Editions, 2018), 42.
13 Yau, "After I Turn Sixty-Nine," in *Genghis Chan on Drums* (Richmond, CA: Omnidawn Publishing, 2021), 103.
14 John Yau, email message to author, June 25, 2023.
15 "John Yau with Joan Waltemath," *Brooklyn Rail*, April–May 2003, https://brooklynrail.org/2003/04/art/john-yau-with-joan-waltemath.
16 "John Yau with Joan Waltemath," *Brooklyn Rail*, April–May 2003, https://brooklynrail.org/2003/04/art/john-yau-with-joan-waltemath.

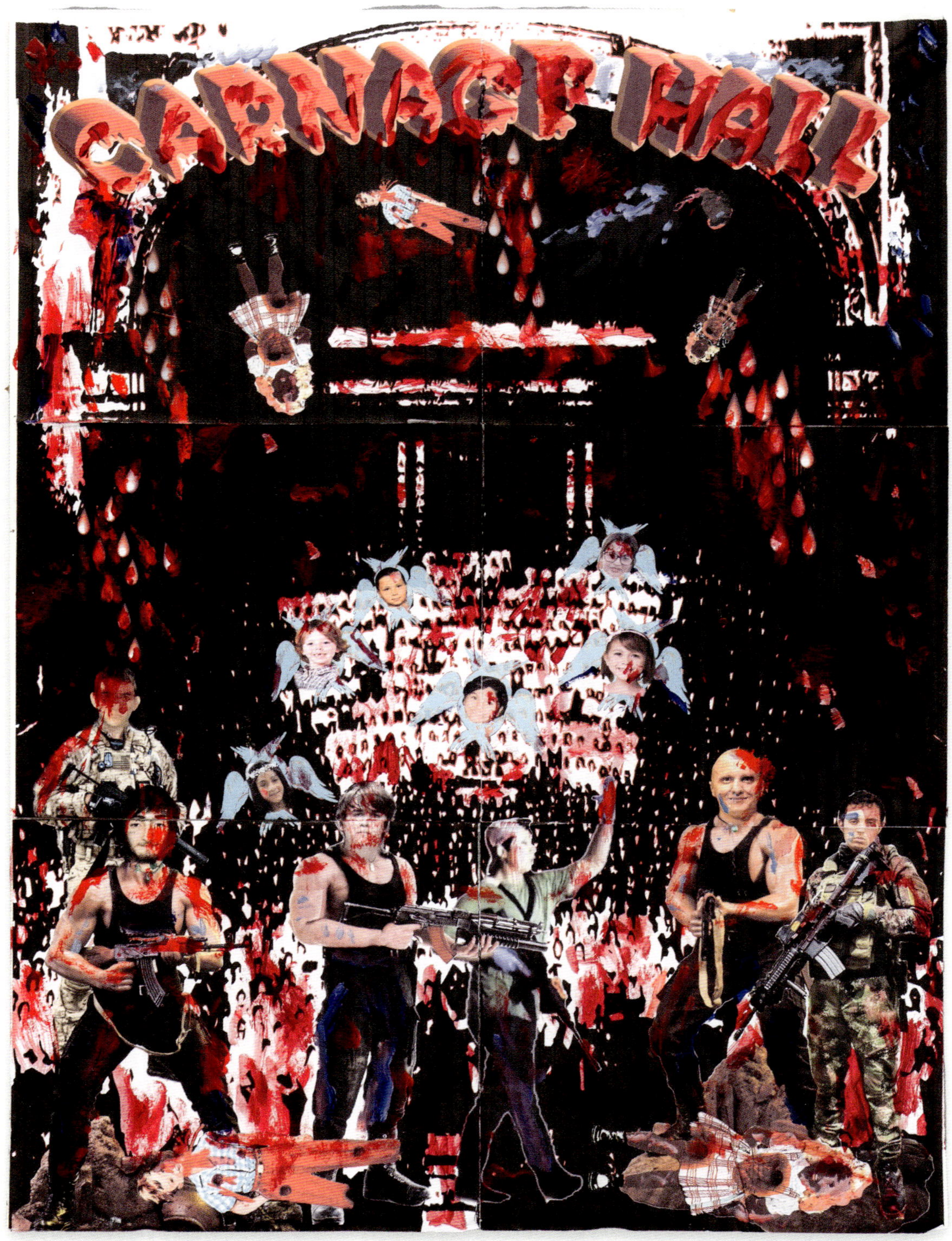

John Yau and Phil Allen, *Carnage Hall*, 2023

PHIL ALLEN

American, born 1952

Many of Yau's collaborations find him in the role of deft and playful wordsmith, exploring the mutability of language in smart-alecky and surreal ways. But in his work with Phil Allen, the words are a response to horrific shootings in Kenosha, Wisconsin, and Uvalde, Texas, in particular, and the state of American life in general.

Yau recalled, "They're pretty gloomy and kind of disturbing. At one point I sent him the word Carnage Hall, after Carnegie Hall, and he sent back the image. We both lamented and said, 'This is not showable in a way, you know what I mean? Who's going to want to show this?' And then we wrote back and forth about the idea of making work that someone might not want to show. Does that have a value? We decided it did."[1]

Allen writes that he was deeply affected by the killings and tried his best to "convey the horror and idiocy of these events, collaging the faces of dead children and the Rambo-outfitted killers"[2] on the stage of the venerable concert venue.

Yau has written several poems that rail against the woeful inadequacy of politicians who issue platitudes in response to mass shootings. Here is "The President's Telegram," printed in its entirety[3]:

No child or teacher should ever feel terrible in an American school
My prayers should feel safe to the victims of a terrible child
My condolences to the families of anyone else
Should anyone feel unsafe in school, my condolences
Should anyone feel unsafe in a family, my prayers
Should anyone else ever feel unsafe, my prayers and condolences
Should my prayers feel unsafe, my condolences to the terrible school
Unsafe child and unsafe teacher feel my prayers

(February 14, 2018)

---

[1] John Yau, interview with the author, September 27, 2022.

[2] Phil Allen, email message to author, April 5, 2023.

[3] John Yau, "The President's Telegram," in *Genghis Chan on Drums* (Richmond, CA: Omnidawn Publishing, 2021), 48.

BILL BARRETTE

American, born 1947

In the late 1980s, Bill Barrette was making box-like sculptures that incorporated optical devices, found objects, and early daguerreotypes of various sitters having their portraits made. Yau reviewed an exhibition of these works at Fiction/Nonfiction Gallery in *Artforum* in 1990, and he included the artist's work in *Diverse Representations*, a group show that he curated at the Morris Museum in New Jersey, that same year.

Acts of looking and appreciating the passage of time are brought together in the two book projects that the men made together. Yau writes, "Bill showed me photographs he had taken of New York City—abandoned, burned out cars is one set of images I remember. They were for a book that Jane Timken, of Timken Publishers, was going to do. They were looking for a text to go with it and began talking to me about writing poems to accompany the photographs. I thought it was a wonderful challenge . . . When I looked at the people-less photographs—all of them stark black-and-white images against a gray sky—I decided to take a documentary approach. At the time, Suzanne McClelland was helping me do research for the Andy Warhol book I was working on. I began asking her to do some about different aspects of New York and learned about Countee Cullen and other figures."[1]

After the publication of *Big City Primer*, Barrette met the German publisher Stefan Weidle, who was interested in producing a book about Berlin. Yau recalls, "Stefan invited us to collaborate, as well as introduced us to the poet and translator Joachim Sartorius . . . I believe Bill and I went at least three times for extended stays. We got to know Berlin, both the East and West, and went to Leipzig and Dresden. I became interested in street signage and the mixture of German and English that stores used to advertise their specialties."[2]

Yau met the Romanian-German poet Oskar Pastior (a member of the Oulipo group, known for their constrained writing techniques) during one of these visits. Inspired by his sestinas, Yau decided to translate them by sound rather than meaning, and these constitute some of the texts in *Berlin Diptychon*. His writing exudes the kind of observations and insights that only a stranger can have in an unfamiliar city.

Both publications have a haunted quality made manifest by Barrette's black-and-white images and Yau's sensitivity to the architecture, histories, and bizarre facts he learned along the way. He writes, "I began the poem "E is for Enema" after Bill told me about pharaonic remedies for constipation. I researched different remedies, the different links people made between feces and bad health, and the role it played in thinking about racial purity."[3]

---

[1] John Yau, email message to author, December 12, 2023.

[2] Yau, email to author, December 12, 2023.

[3] Yau, email to author, December 12, 2023.

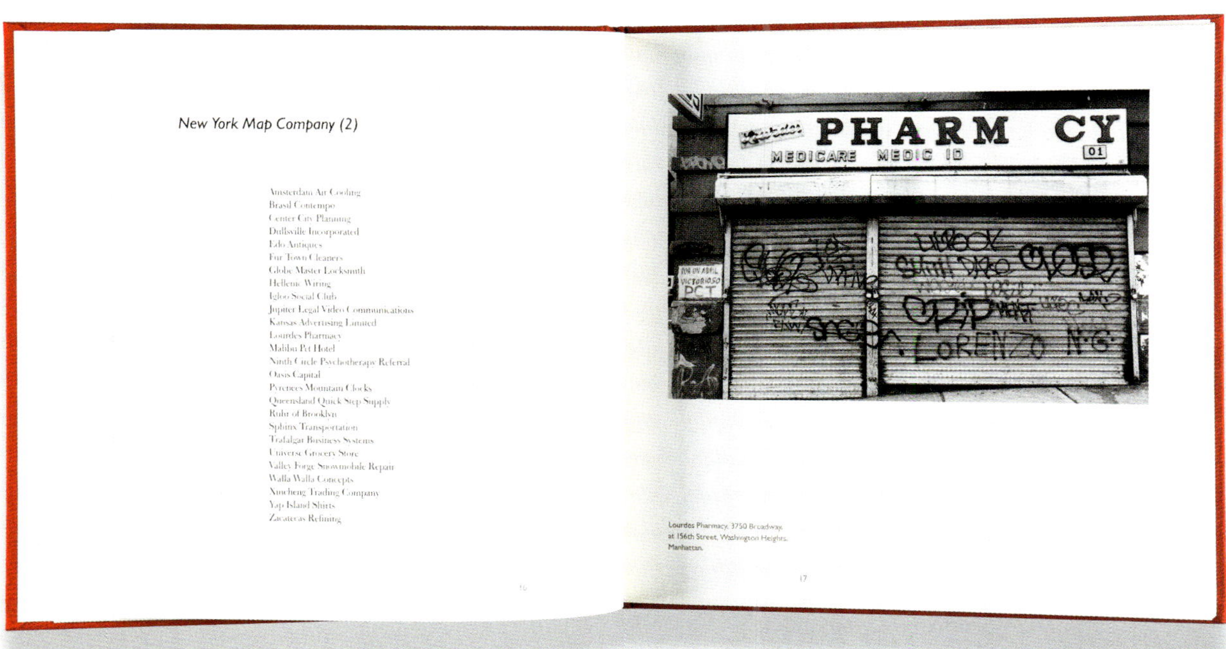

John Yau and Bill Barrette, *Big City Primer: Reading New York at the End of the Twentieth Century*, 1991

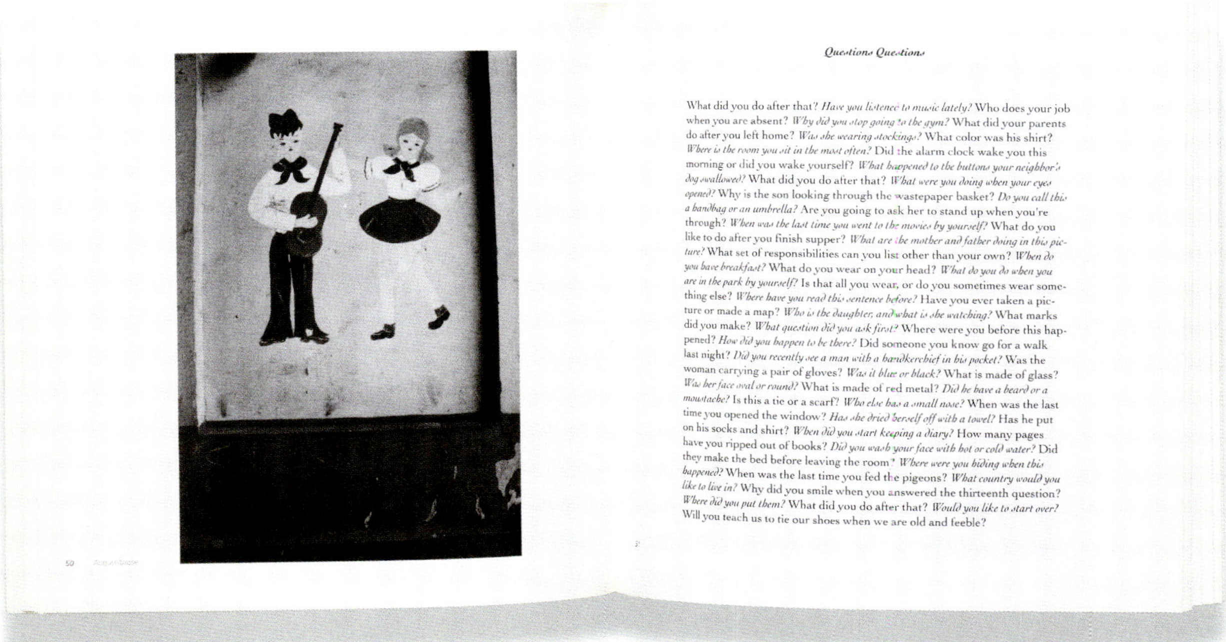

John Yau and Bill Barrette, *Berlin Diptychon*, 1995

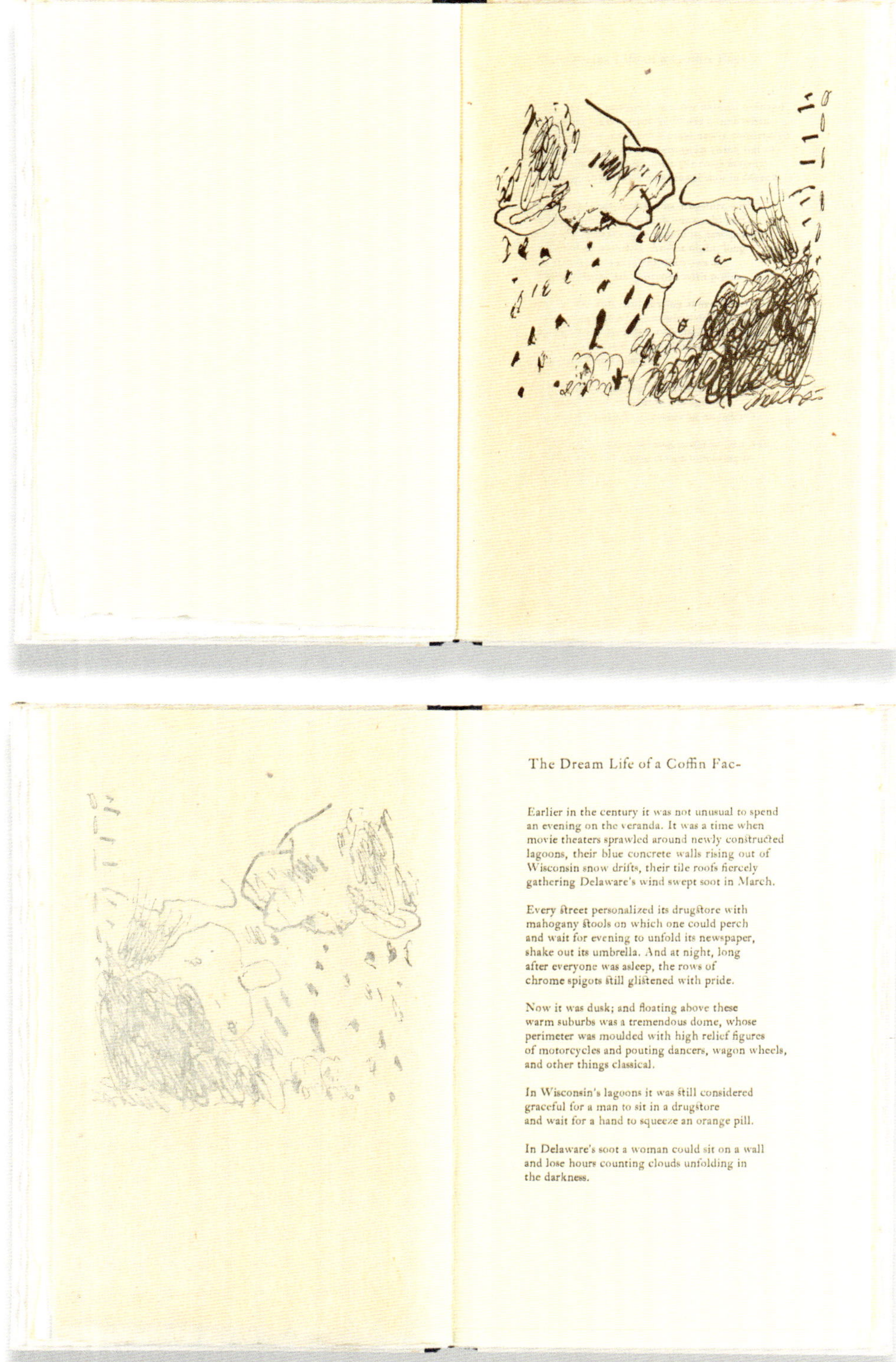

The Dream Life of a Coffin Fac-

Earlier in the century it was not unusual to spend
an evening on the veranda. It was a time when
movie theaters sprawled around newly constructed
lagoons, their blue concrete walls rising out of
Wisconsin snow drifts, their tile roofs fiercely
gathering Delaware's wind swept soot in March.

Every street personalized its drugstore with
mahogany stools on which one could perch
and wait for evening to unfold its newspaper,
shake out its umbrella. And at night, long
after everyone was asleep, the rows of
chrome spigots still glistened with pride.

Now it was dusk; and floating above these
warm suburbs was a tremendous dome, whose
perimeter was moulded with high relief figures
of motorcycles and pouting dancers, wagon wheels,
and other things classical.

In Wisconsin's lagoons it was still considered
graceful for a man to sit in a drugstore
and wait for a hand to squeeze an orange pill.

In Delaware's soot a woman could sit on a wall
and lose hours counting clouds unfolding in
the darkness.

John Yau and Jake Berthot, *Notarikon*, **1981**

JAKE BERTHOT

American, 1939 – 2014

Throughout his career, Jake Berthot made paintings that situate a particular form within an evocative surrounding space. This includes the rectangular bars, ovals, and lozenges that occupied his abstract canvases, and the trees and mountain ridges anchoring his late representational works.

Reviewing an exhibition by the artist in *Artforum* in 1988, Yau wrote, "Berthot has overcome his own tendency toward refinement. The paintings are simultaneously sensual and brutish, with surfaces that seem raw and unfinished, and in which various kinds of namelessness are allowed to emerge and comment on each other."[1]

This could easily describe the skittish and diaristic drawings Berthot also produced, using ink, graphite, and enamel on paper. They include figures and skulls near illegible cursive handwriting and enigmatic doodles.

In their collaborative book, *Notarikon*, Yau's poems are accompanied by examples of Berthot's lively drawings, a reminder that the book's title comes from the Latin word *notarius* or "shorthand writer," a system of abbreviations for the shortening of words (as in the speedy writing of a stenographer).

This is in keeping with Yau's interest in linguistic compression and manipulation, as when he takes a familiar phrase and hijacks its meaning by changing a letter or two, such as this stanza from the poem "Late Night Movies II" [2]:

Don't wire until you see the fights of their eyes.
Introduced in the doorway of a hotel. Pine tree
moonlight. Tonight, a bird in the band is worth
two in the hush; the hush surrounding
a lifetime of guarantees.

---

[1] John Yau, "Jake Berthot," *Artforum* 26, no. 10 (Summer 1988): 134.

[2] John Yau, "Late Night Movies II," in *Radiant Silhouette: New & Selected Work, 1974 – 1988* (Santa Rosa, CA: Black Sparrow Press), 99-100.

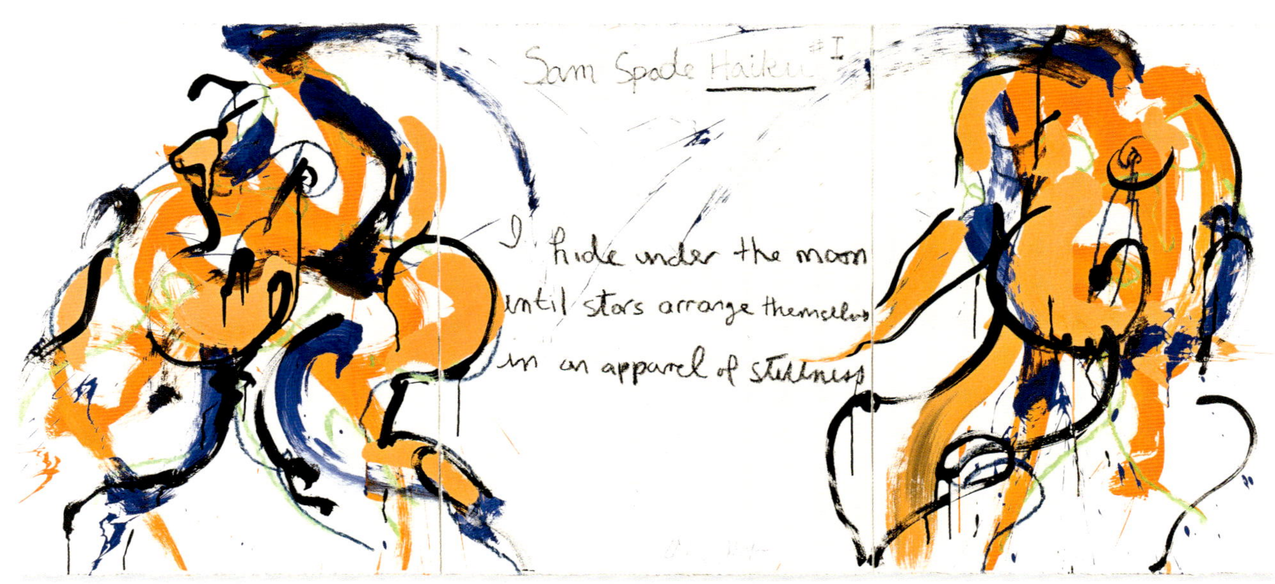

John Yau and Norman Bluhm, *Sam Spade Haiku #1,* **circa 1988**

NORMAN BLUHM

American, 1921 – 1999

When Yau met Norman Bluhm in the 1980s, he was very aware of the painter's achievements in the heyday of Abstract Expressionism, including the fact that he'd partnered with poet Frank O'Hara to create one of the classic collaborations of post-war American art. They made twenty-six drawings together in 1960, with O'Hara contributing lines that sound like snippets of overheard conversation and Bluhm making bold gestures in gouache and watercolor. "It was all instantaneous, like a conversation between friends," the artist recalled in a magazine article. "You know, going back and forth. Quick and playful. There were no big thoughts, no idea that anyone would be interested in it or that it would ever be shown or published."[1]

Yau remembers his own activity with the artist: "When Norman suggested that we collaborate, he said, 'It has to be different from the way I did it with Frank. We'll do everything in color. We will use good paper.' He wanted our collaboration not to be connected to Frank. He wanted to make a break."[2]

The two men worked with motifs that occupied them at the time. For Bluhm, it was using a nude female model as source for exuberant, gestural painting; for Yau, it was creating lines for a haiku dedicated to Sam Spade, the fictional detective made famous by Dashiell Hammett's 1930 novel, *The Maltese Falcon*.

Perhaps the form of haiku, with its precise syllabic structure and revelatory "aha" moment, reminded Yau of the solving of a crime. His description, "Her perfect oval of dark intermissions," is the kind of phrase that might come to Spade while sizing up a beautiful and secretive female client entering his office.

In 1987, Cone Editions published a series of Yau and Bluhm collaborative silkscreen prints, that were exhibited that year. In the accompanying brochure, Yau wrote, "We've collaborated while watching TV, or been more ambitious and worked in the studio. Huge sheets of paper stapled to the walls. It has been a way to get over inhibitions. After all, you feel pretty silly standing around having an existential crisis about what to write or paint, when there's someone else in the room."[3]

---

[1] Norman Bluhm, "26 Things at once: Bluhm on O'Hara, the poem paintings, the art & the scene," in *lingo: A Journal of the Arts 7: Poem Paintings, Frank O'Hara, Norman Bluhm*, ed. Jonathan Gams and Peter Occhiogrosso (West Stockbridge, Massachusetts: Hard Press, Inc., 1997), 11.

[2] John Yau, interview with the author, September 27, 2022.

[3] John Yau, introduction to *Poem Prints: Norman Bluhm & John Yau* (South Lunenburg, Vermont: Meriden Stinehour Press, 1987). Published in conjunction with an exhibition of the same title, organized and presented at Cone Editions, New York, October 14 – November 14, 1987.

TOM BURCKHARDT

American, born 1967

Tom Burckhardt's drawings and paintings exploit various aspects of modernism, including the mixing of organic and machine-like forms, experiments in pictorial depth, and an affection for collage. Yau appreciates the artist's sensibility, and they share an interest in the generative capacities of working within prescribed limits. They have dedicated themselves to what Yau describes as "making something that doesn't look like something either of us would've done on our own."[1]

"Tom said, 'I've been painting road signs in Maine. Why don't you think about doing some?'" Yau recalled. "And my first thought was, 'Road sign, I can't do anything with a road sign. It's such a fixed form and format.' But then I kept thinking, 'Well, you can make up your own road signs.' I would send him how I would want the words arranged, but I left everything else up to him."[2]

These signs use the colors and shapes familiar to travelers on our highways and roads. But instead of clear warnings of construction, directional information, and specific regulations, Yau offers humorous and head-scratching language that requires sorting out. Burckhardt has painted them in lush rural environments, using a casual realist style akin to the landscapes of Fairfield Porter and Jane Freilicher.

A red octagonal sign typically tells a driver to "stop" but in this case, the phrase X SPELLED is stated. Is the driver meant to consider themselves expelled from the locale and never allowed to return? Or given the ways the letter is used in everyday life, we might read the X as a form of cancellation, or a kiss at the end of a message.

Consider the message in black letters on an orange diamond spelling out A VOID GOING BACK. Should one not revisit their past, or if one does, is a void waiting there? Yau might be paying tribute to Georges Perec and his *La disparition* (translated into English and published as *A Void*), a 300-page novel written without using the letter "e."

Yau came up with the concept of artist bars, perhaps in recognition of the significance of watering holes and cafes throughout art history; where artists and writers would meet, drink, form alliances, argue, and flirt. He created names and related marketing language for places honoring (and poking fun at) Yves Klein, Meret Oppenheim, Georges Seurat, and Andy Warhol. Burckhardt carefully rendered the signage for each establishment as if pitching the concepts to potential investors.

The two men have explored other formats, including the ransom note with letters cut out from different printed materials, as well as limited-edition publications. In *The Autumn Fields of a Young Art Handler*, Burckhardt pictures the process of packing and moving artworks at studios and galleries while Yau provides practical and absurd comments from the point of view of paint rollers, artifacts, a cordless drill, etc.

---

[1] John Yau, interview with the author, February 26, 2023.

[2] Yau, interview with author, February 26, 2023.

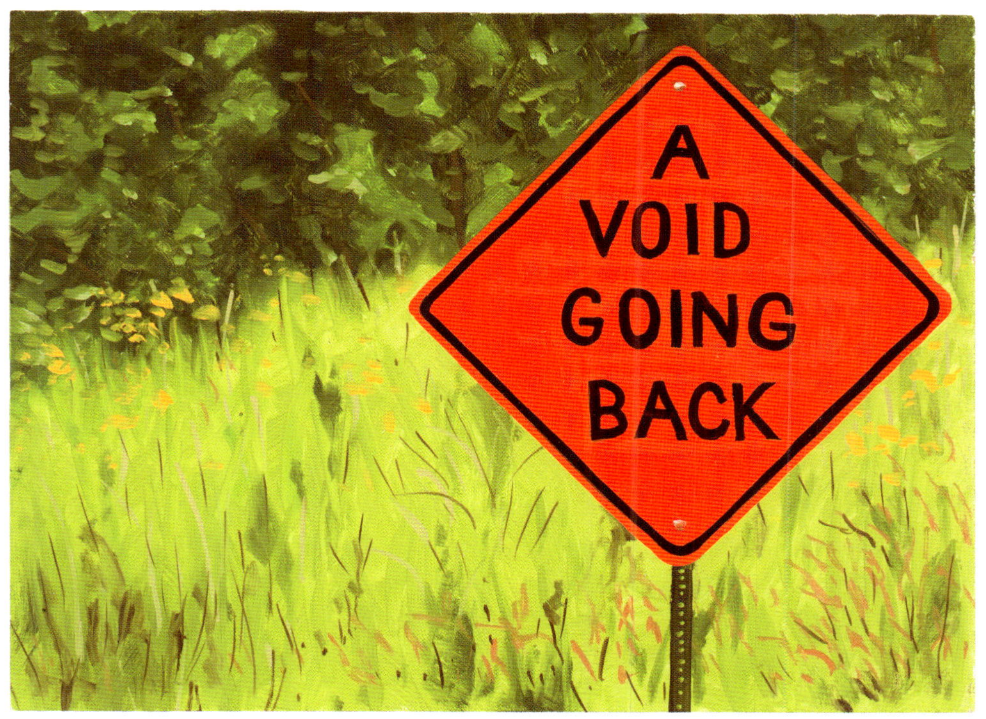

John Yau and Tom Burckhardt, *A Void Going Back*, 2022

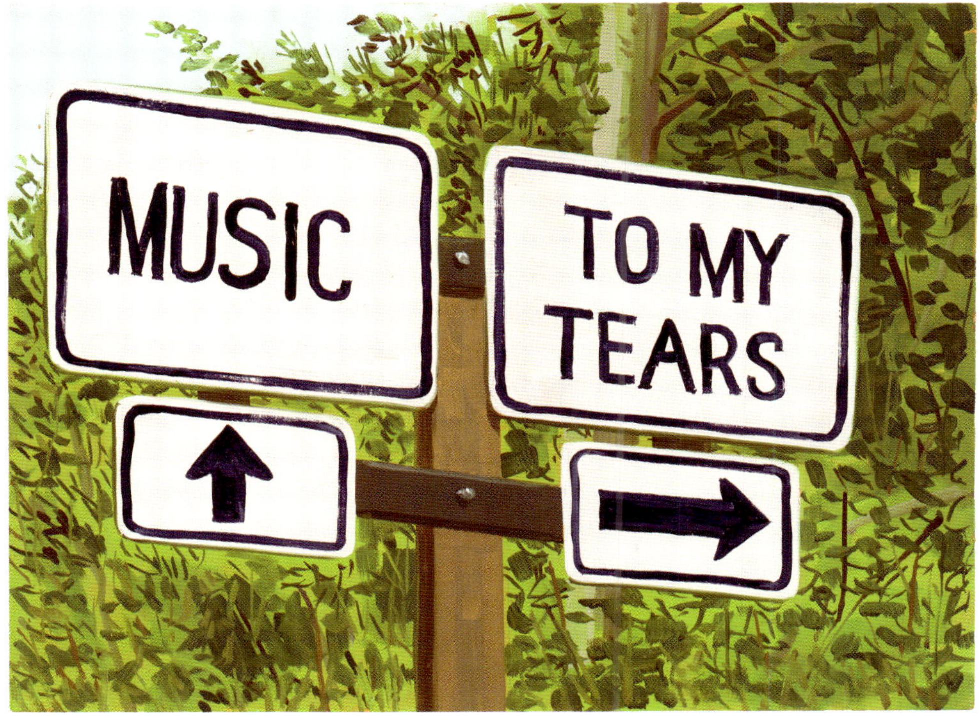

John Yau and Tom Burckhardt, *Music to My Ears*, 2022

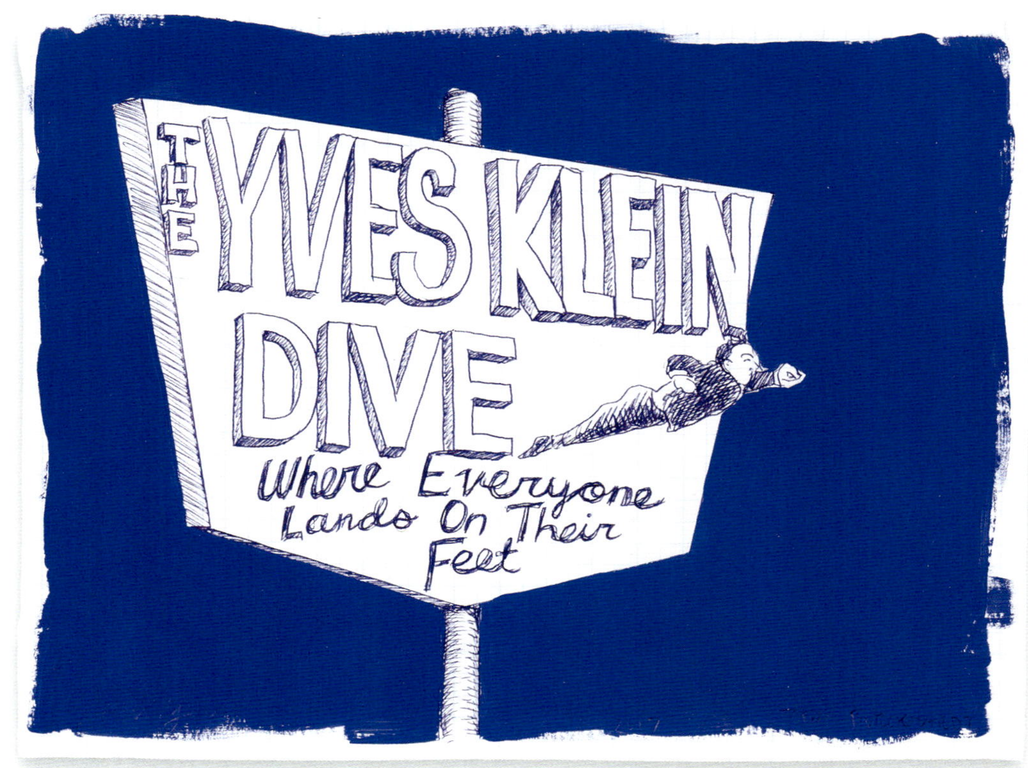

John Yau and Tom Burckhardt, *The Yves Klein Dive*, **2017**

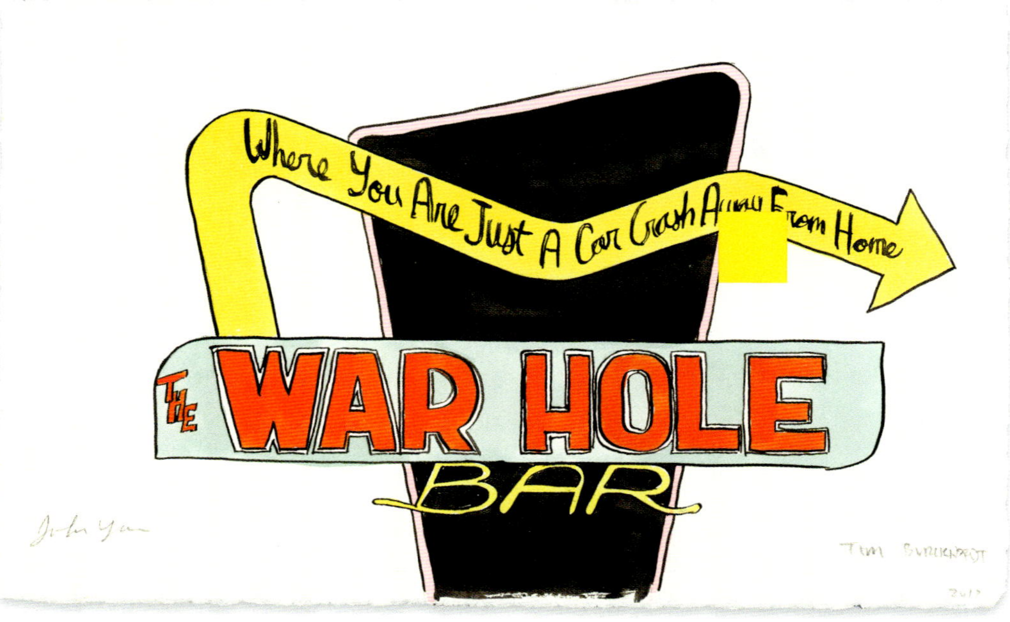

John Yau and Tom Burckhardt, *The War Hole Bar*, **2017**

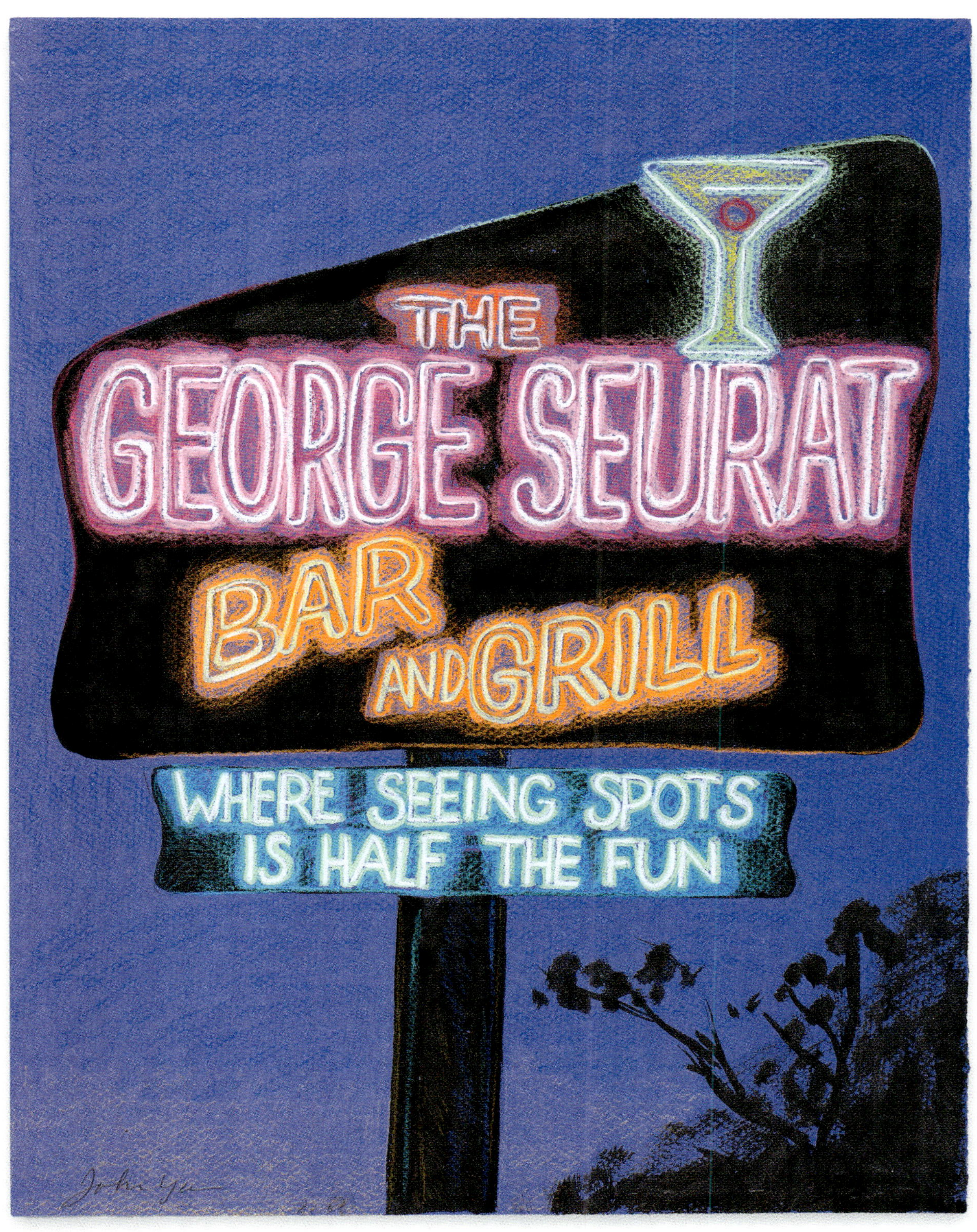

John Yau and Tom Burckhardt, *The George Seurat Bar and Grill,* 2018

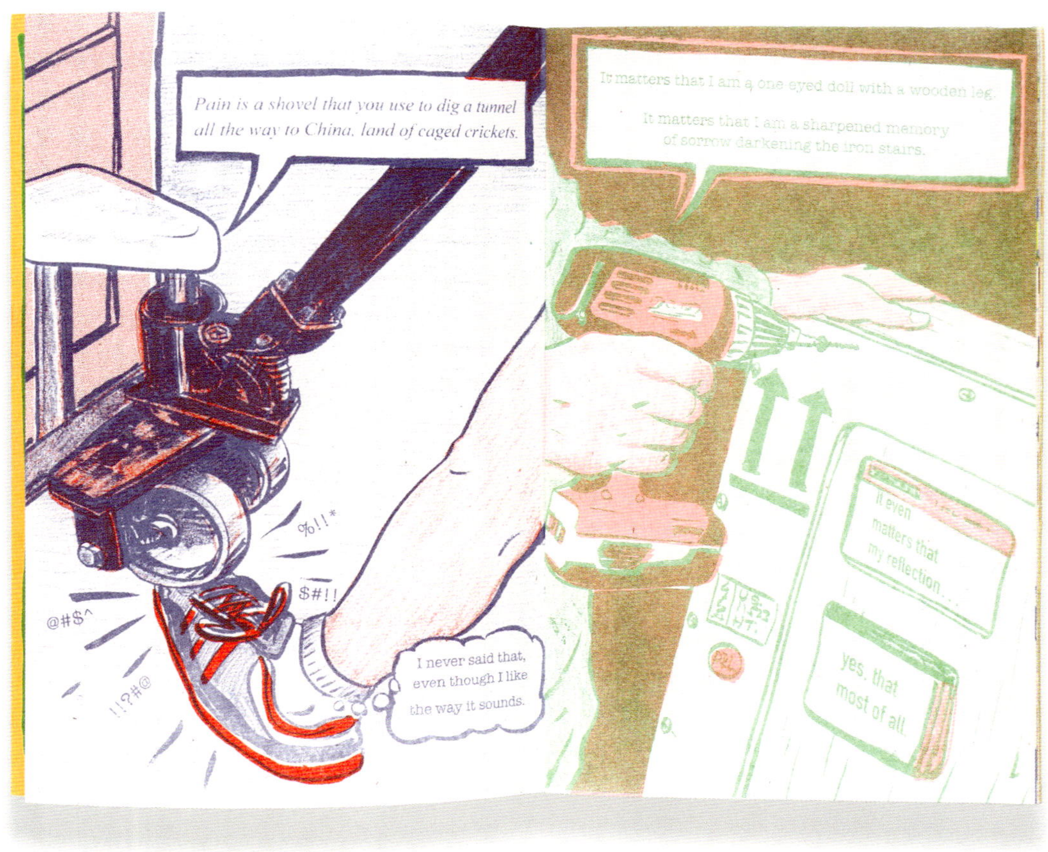

John Yau and Tom Burckhardt, *The Autumn Fields of a Young Art Handler*, **2019**

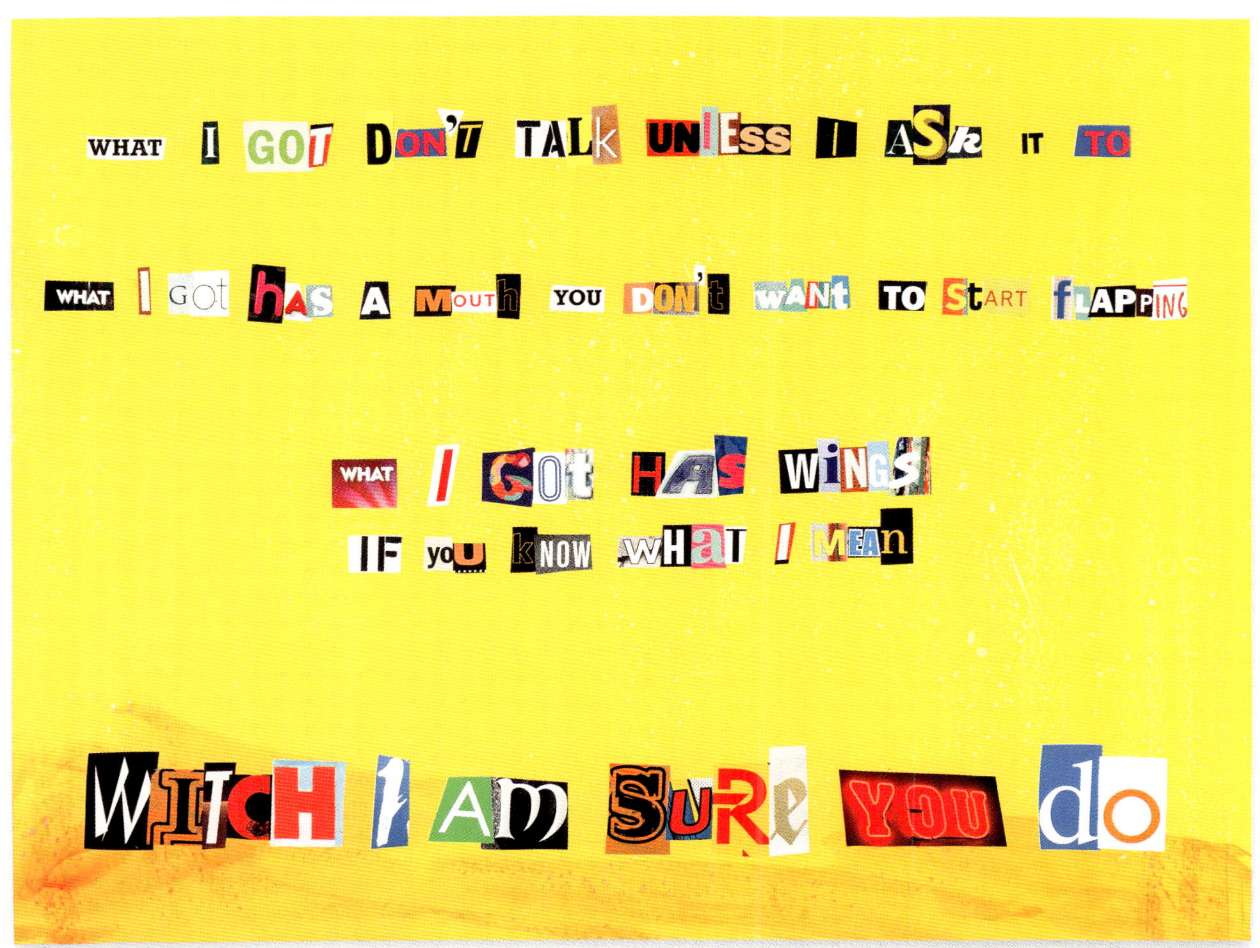

John Yau and Tom Burckhardt, *What I Got Don't Talk*, 2016

MARSHA BURNS

American, born 1945

MICHAEL BURNS

American, born 1942

RANDY HAYES

American, born 1944

The works of Marsha Burns, Michael Burns, and Randy Hayes were brought together in 1987 for the exhibition, *Cities*, curated by Chris Bruce at the Henry Art Gallery at the University of Washington. The artists were longtime friends with studios near each other in the Pioneer Square district in downtown Seattle and had visited cities including Berlin, Frankfurt, Los Angeles, and New York to explore image-making opportunities.

Bruce saw the connections between their works and used the opportunity to create a project that would allow them to travel to Rome together to continue their investigations of urban style and various subcultures. Marsha and Michael Burns both made new photographs, and Hayes created large photo-based pastel drawings. They drew inspiration from the Roman context, including dramatic lighting in Caravaggio paintings and historic Roman destinations like the Spanish Steps and Pantheon.

As a catalog collaboration, *Cities* combines the representational skills of the three artists with Yau's poems that examine conditions of portraiture, including presence, place, and light. "Radiant Silhouette V," printed here in its entirety, contains a mercurial internal monologue[1]:

> *"I wanted to speak to the side of me*
> *aimed away from the sun*
>
> *arrive face to face with the instant*
> *before light outlines my contour*
>
> *makes me into the shadow I am"*

---

[1] John Yau, "Radiant Silhouette V," in *Cities* (Seattle: Henry Art Gallery, University of Washington, 1987), 12.

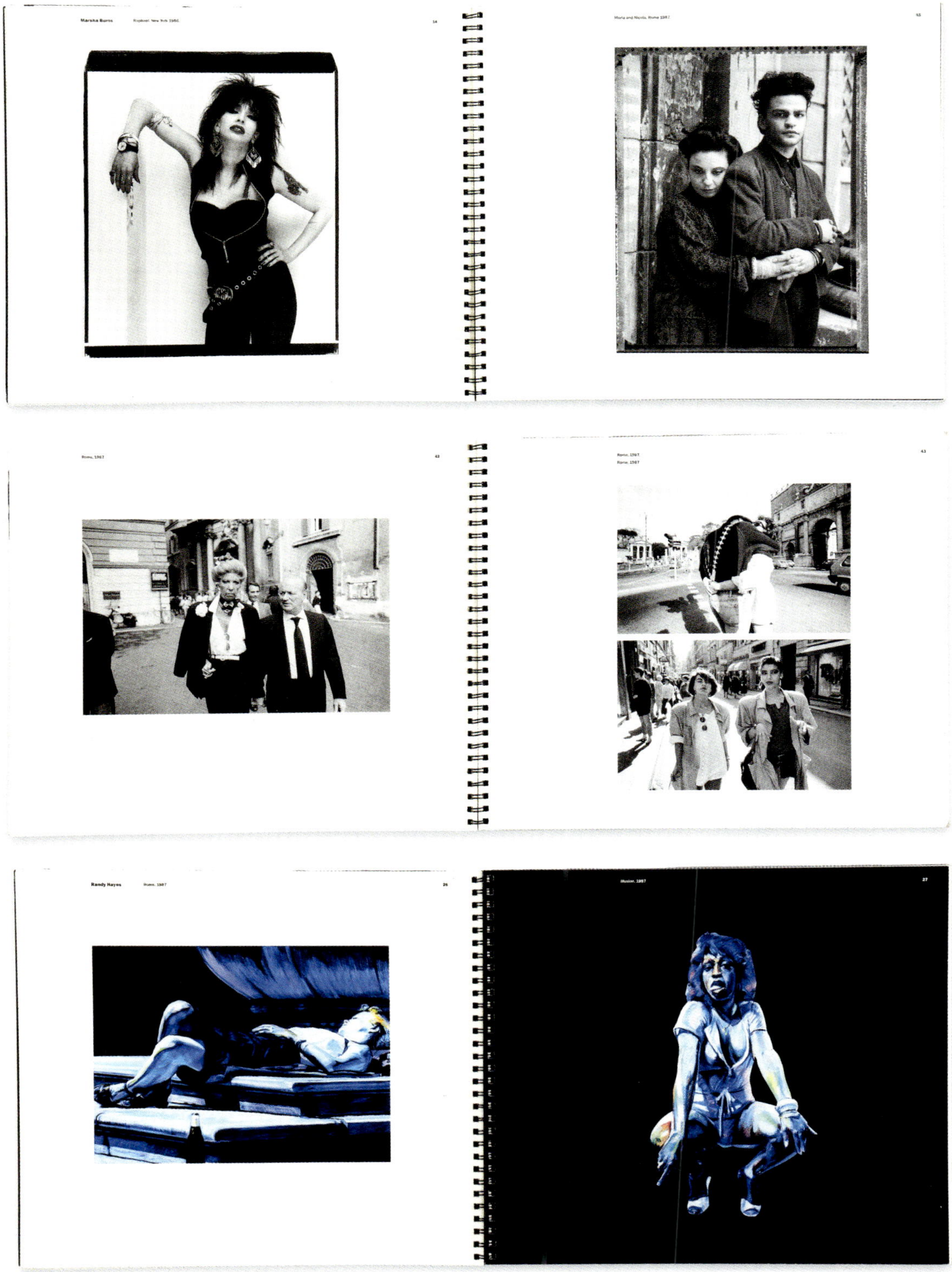

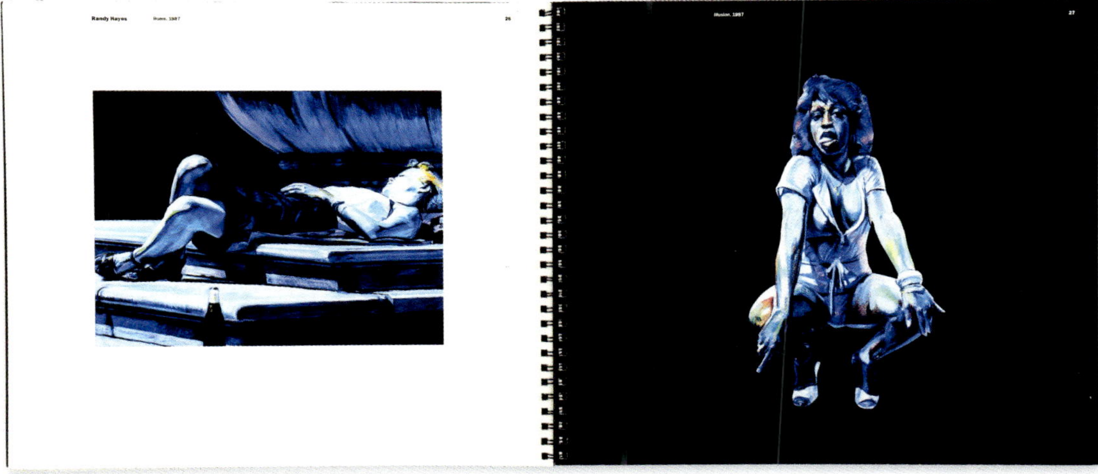

John Yau, Marsha Burns, Michael Burns, and Randy Hayes, *Cities*, 1987

SQUEAK CARNWATH

American, born 1947

In *One Hundred Poems*, the artist's book made with Squeak Carnwath, Yau offers just that quantity, with each poem consisting of the title and a single line (also known as a monostich). He composes matter-of-fact revelations about his most consistent subjects—isolation, difference, and mortality. Here are two examples[1]:

Old Man

My white hair touches the moon, but no one notices.

Familiar Complaint

My egg rolls look like dirty tube socks.

Yau's writing finds a sympathetic companion in Carnwath's portfolio of double-sided acrylic prints, with their nuanced renderings of cups, vases, plants, houses, clothes, charts, and body parts. She embeds these various figures in richly colored grounds that are the result of layering of gesso, pigment, marble dust, and modeling paste on the paper, giving each a surprising heft. The project is unabashed in its regard for the handmade and the potency of accessible imagery and language. Yau and Carnwath's collaboration might be summarized best by one of the poet's contributions to it[2]:

Universal

There is something in it for everyone.

[1] John Yau, "One Hundred Poems," in *Further Adventures in Monochrome* (Port Townsend, WA: Copper Canyon Press, 2012), 84-95. Originally published by Magnolia Editions in the artist's book *One Hundred Poems*, 2010.

[2] Yau, "One Hundred Poems," 84-95.

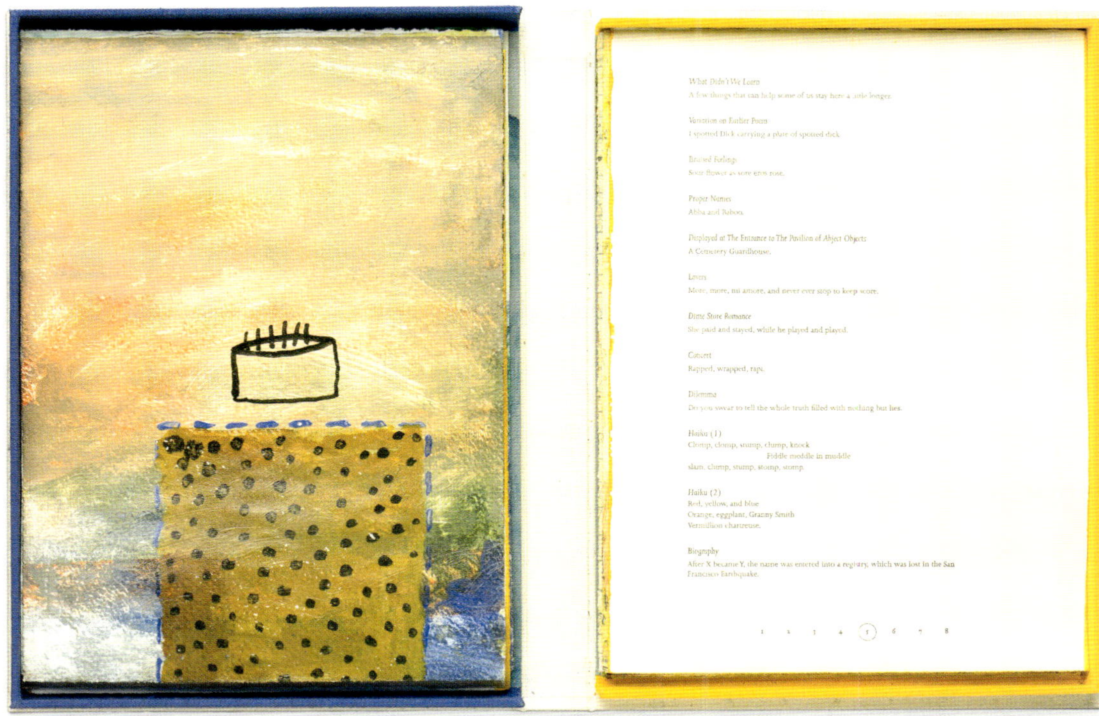

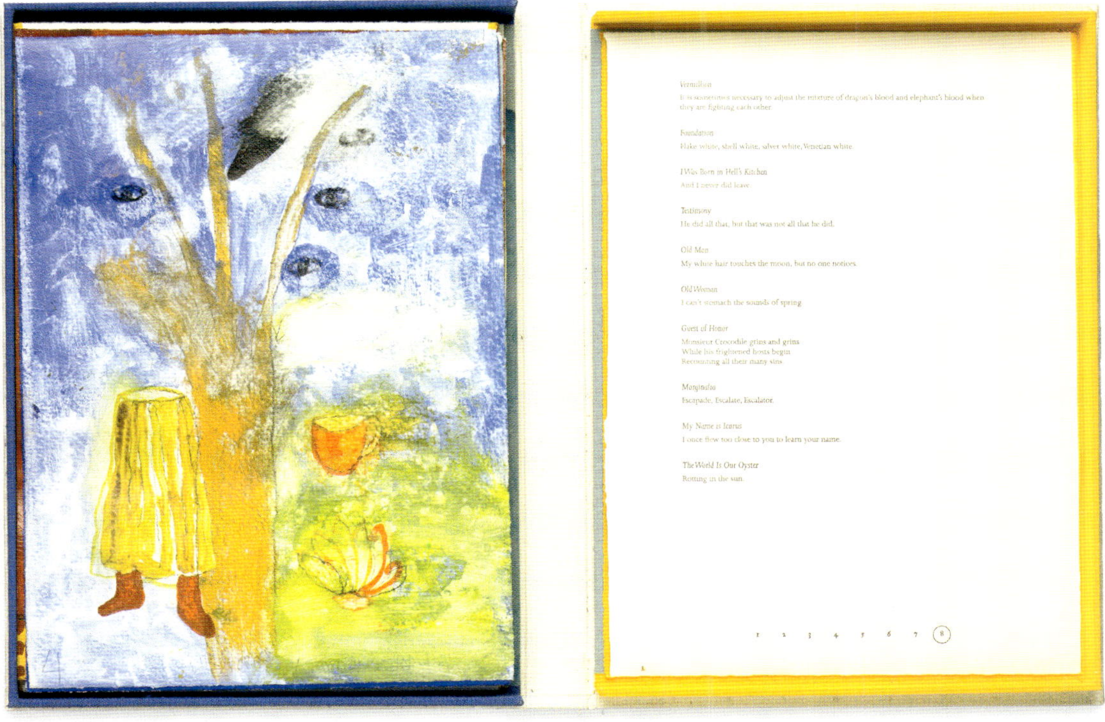

John Yau and Squeak Carnwath, *One Hundred Poems,* **2010**

AARON COHICK
American, born 1980

While working on his bachelor of fine arts degree at the Maryland Institute College of Art, Aaron Cohick took a double credit course in English and Printmaking, team-taught by Yau and artist Hilary Lorenz. He learned practical skills including how to silkscreen, set type, and bind books; and about the history of small press/DIY publishing.

English for You includes Yau's poem of the same name, accompanied by Cohick's artwork featuring figures situated within ornamental borders and printed in light pink. The project was printed by students at MICA's Dolphin Press, under the direction of Rebecca Childers.

The poem implies a beginning class for Asian students to help them learn the language. It includes declarative and interrogative sentences covering a variety of subjects. For example[1]:

> *You can consult the oracle to learn if separating*
> *is better than branching out, living separately*
> *is more advisable than living under separate*
> *covers or withdrawing into different paragraphs.*
> *You can disentangle, bid farewell, sell off, run out. . . .*

[1] John Yau, "English for You, 11," in *Ing Grish* (Philadelphia: Saturnalia Books, 2005), 53. Originally published by Dolphin Press in the artist's book *English for You*, 2002.

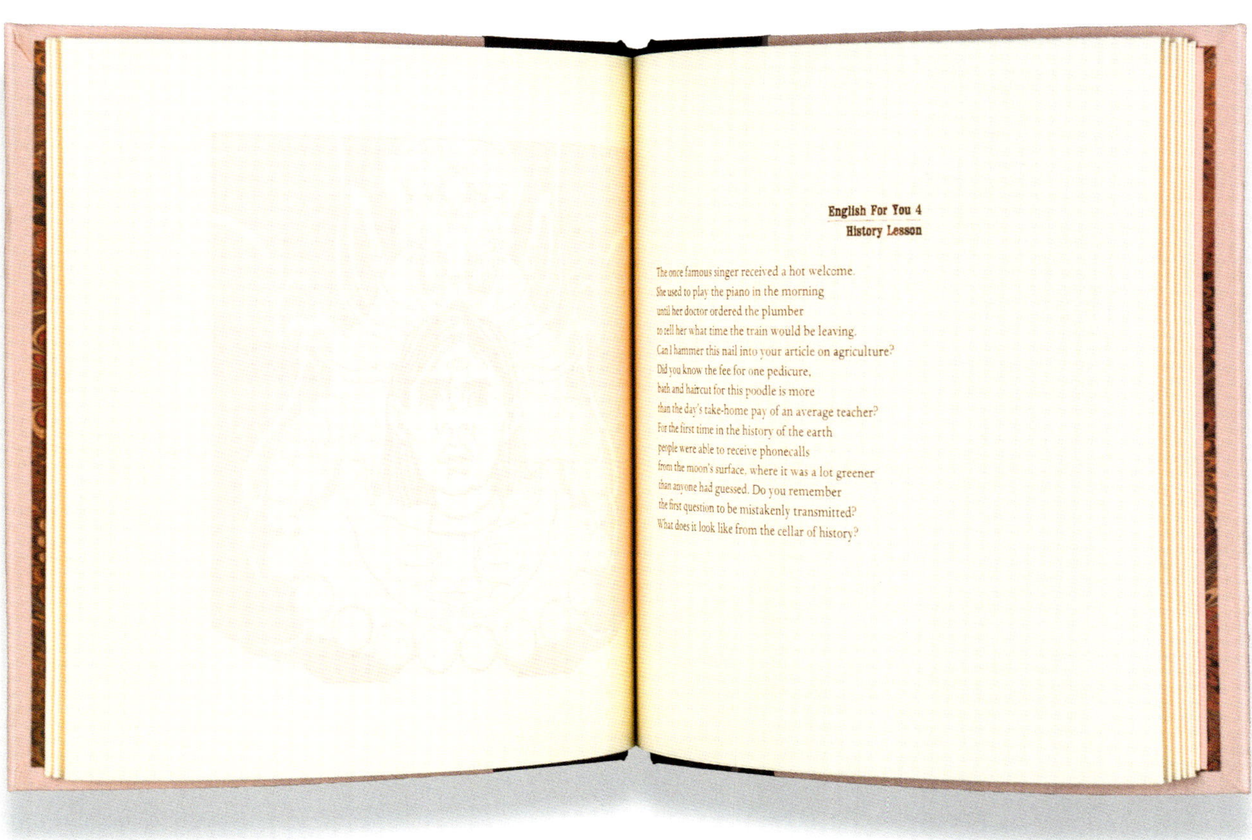

John Yau and Aaron Cohick, *English for You,* **2002**

EMERGENCY EYEWASH

BARRY SCHWABSKY
American, born 1957

SIV STØLDAL
Norwegian, born 1973

CAROL SZYMANSKI
American, born 1955

Emergency Eyewash is a conceptual brand and platform for developing collaborative endeavors with various writers, artists, and designers along specific topics and themes. It was founded by poet and editor Barry Schwabsky and artist Carol Szymanski in 2017.

For their first project, the couple invited Siv Støldal, a well-known menswear designer from Norway, to create garments around the notion of the hoodie, a familiar piece of clothing associated with youth culture. Schwabsky chose the poets and invited Yau (and Tyrone Williams and Judith Goldman) to each contribute works that would be used as part of the fashion element.

Yau offered four short poems, including "Genghis Chan: Private Eye XXXIII (First Ideogram)," with its playful punning and stereotypes about Asians speaking English[1]:

BEE WEAR

FLEE ADVICE

FOREST STRANGER

The beekeeper suit was Støldal's response to Yau's clever reworking of the phrase: *Beware free advice from a stranger.* She researched the history of clothing worn by forest rangers in the United States and writes, "I chose the hunter-green wool loden fabric and incorporated a particular pocket on the back of the uniforms. I found this pocket very interesting. Its function is to store big folded-up maps. Texts are very present in the Forest Ranger uniforms in the form of colorful embroidered patches."

Szymanski designed the patches with her and Schwabsky's daughter Willa. When the Emergency Eyewash project was shown at Tanja Grunert Gallery, a man wore the patch-covered garment and walked around the space for a month, as if he was a ranger serving as a security guard.

This collaboration is a superb example of how Yau cultivates mishearings and malapropisms in his poetry, but also how he seeks out equally experimental partners and new contexts for language.

---

[1] John Yau, "Genghis Chan: Private Eye XXXIII (First Ideogram)," in *Further Adventures in Monochrome* (Port Townsend, WA: Copper Canyon Press, 2012), 66.

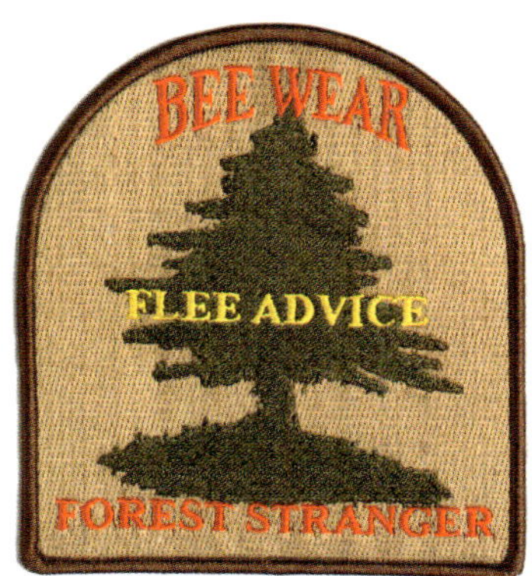

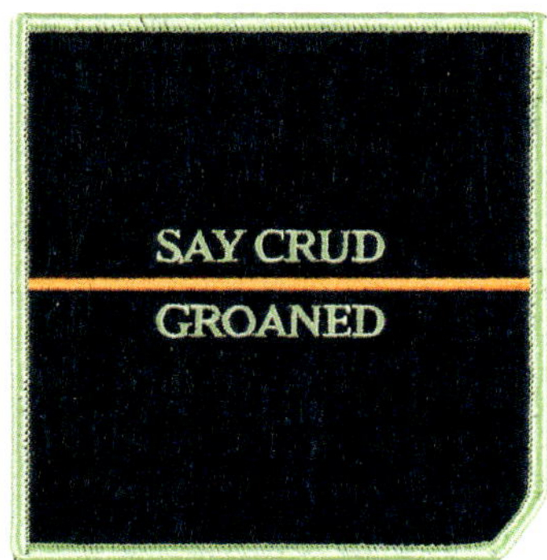

**Emergency Eyewash with
John Yau, Willa Schwabsky,
and Carol Szymanski,
Emergency Eyewash Patches, 2017**

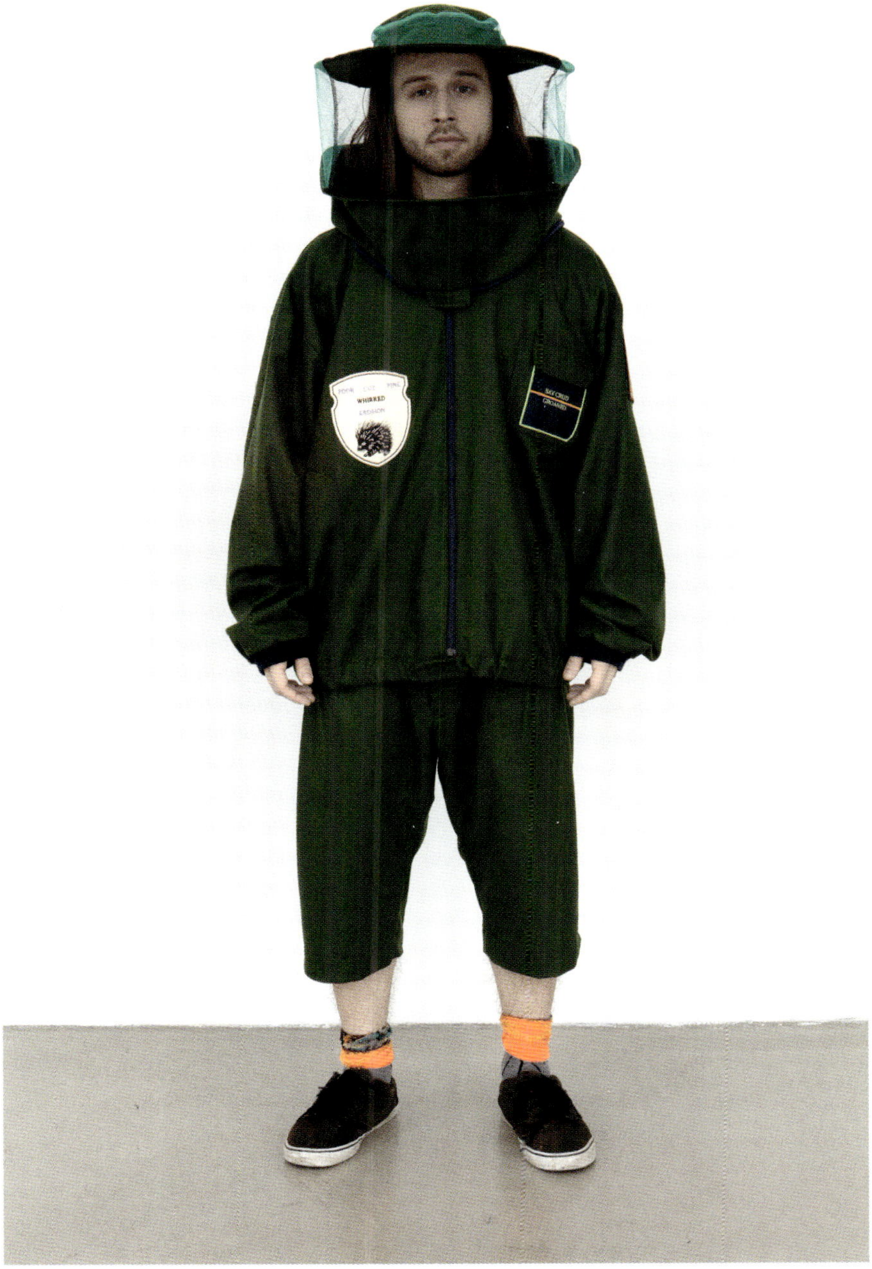

**Emergency Eyewash with John Yau, Siv Støldal, and
Carol Szymanski, *Bee Wear*, 2017/2023**

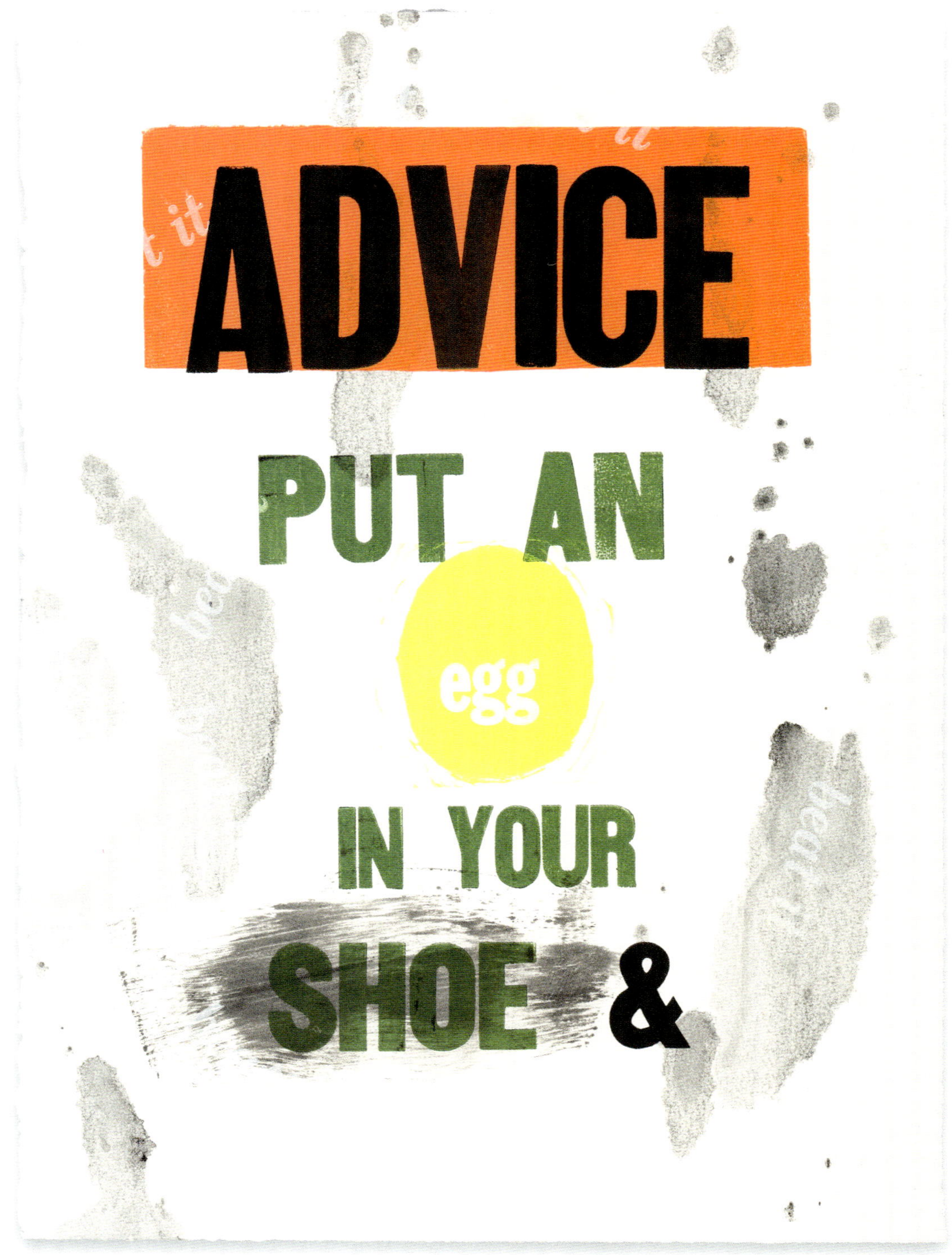

John Yau and Tracy Featherstone, *Advice: Put an Egg in Your Shoe & Beat It,* **2023**

TRACY FEATHERSTONE

American, born 1975

Yau met Tracy Featherstone when he was a visiting juror for the Young Painters competition at Miami University, where the artist is head of the printmaking department. Over the course of a few days, including visits with students and social events at night, they discussed collaborating together.

For practical reasons, working together in the print studio during Yau's stay wasn't possible, so instead they worked remotely.

Featherstone describes the process this way: "He sends the poems, actually a lot of them, and I think about the form they might take. I sketch ideas and then make some prints. He hasn't really protested any of the outcomes. I think he likes the surprise on his end as well . . . I like the idea of making multiples for what John has been sending me. We have been discussing different types of forms such as t-shirts and business cards, etc."[1]

---

[1] Tracy Featherstone, email message to author, June 5, 2023.

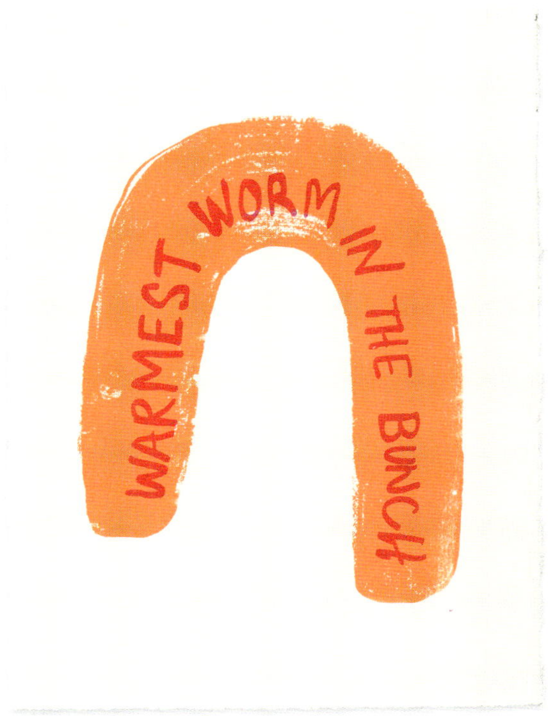

John Yau and Tracy Featherstone, *Warmest Worm in the Bunch*, 2023

ENRIQUE FIGUEREDO

Venezuelan, born 1980

In his collaboration with Enrique Figueredo, a then-graduate student at the Mason Gross School of the Arts at Rutgers University, Yau took a more directorial role. He had a definite idea about what the door to his detective's office should look like.

Figueredo writes that Yau "provided clear instructions on the structure of the print, for example:

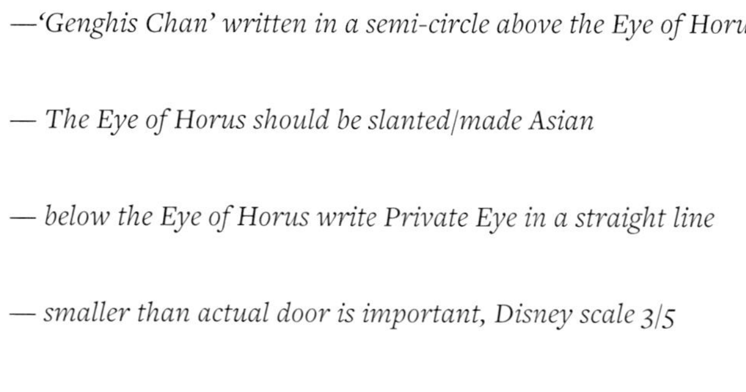

—'Genghis Chan' written in a semi-circle above the Eye of Horus

— The Eye of Horus should be slanted/made Asian

— below the Eye of Horus write Private Eye in a straight line

— smaller than actual door is important, Disney scale 3/5

— wooden door with glass window and gold and black lettering"[1]

Figueredo sourced the font and the style and era of the door, including the knob and mail slot. He sent Yau digital mock-ups of his compositions, and after agreeing on a color palette, the artist started to print the edition.

Yau writes about the project, "I told him what I wanted and then he came up with the design and made this print. I paid Enrique for the paper, etc., and told him I would always credit him for making this and I thought of it as a collaboration."[2]

This finely detailed work immediately conjures numerous films in which a prospective client walks down a hallway to reach the door of a detective's office. It is the gateway to Hollywood narratives of infidelity, embezzlement, betrayal, and murder; and in Yau's poems, Genghis Chan's interrogation of language and identity.

---

[1] Enrique Figueredo, email message to author, September 28, 2022.

[2] John Yau, email message to author, April 3, 2023.

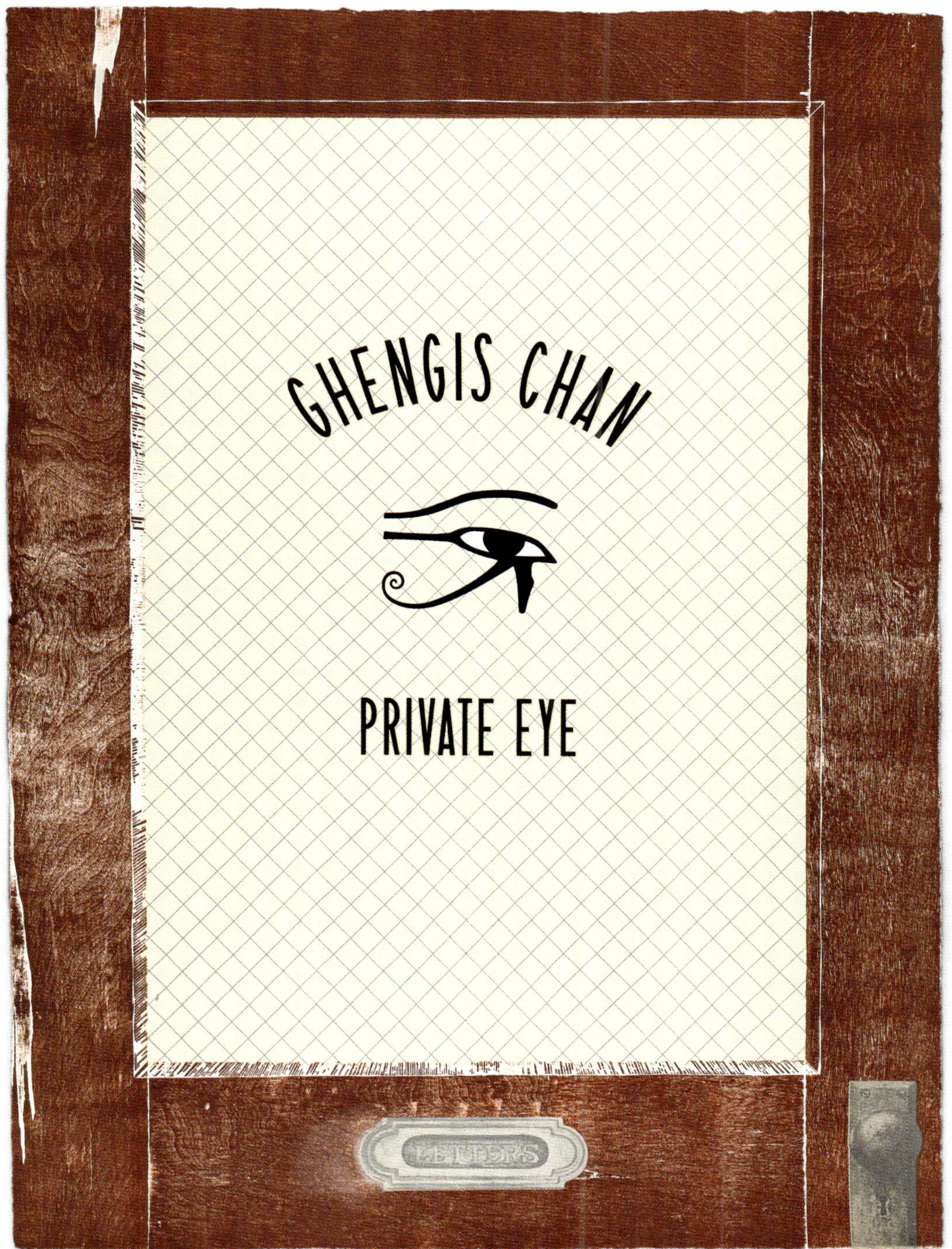

John Yau and Enrique Figueredo, *Genghis Chan: Private Eye*, 2018

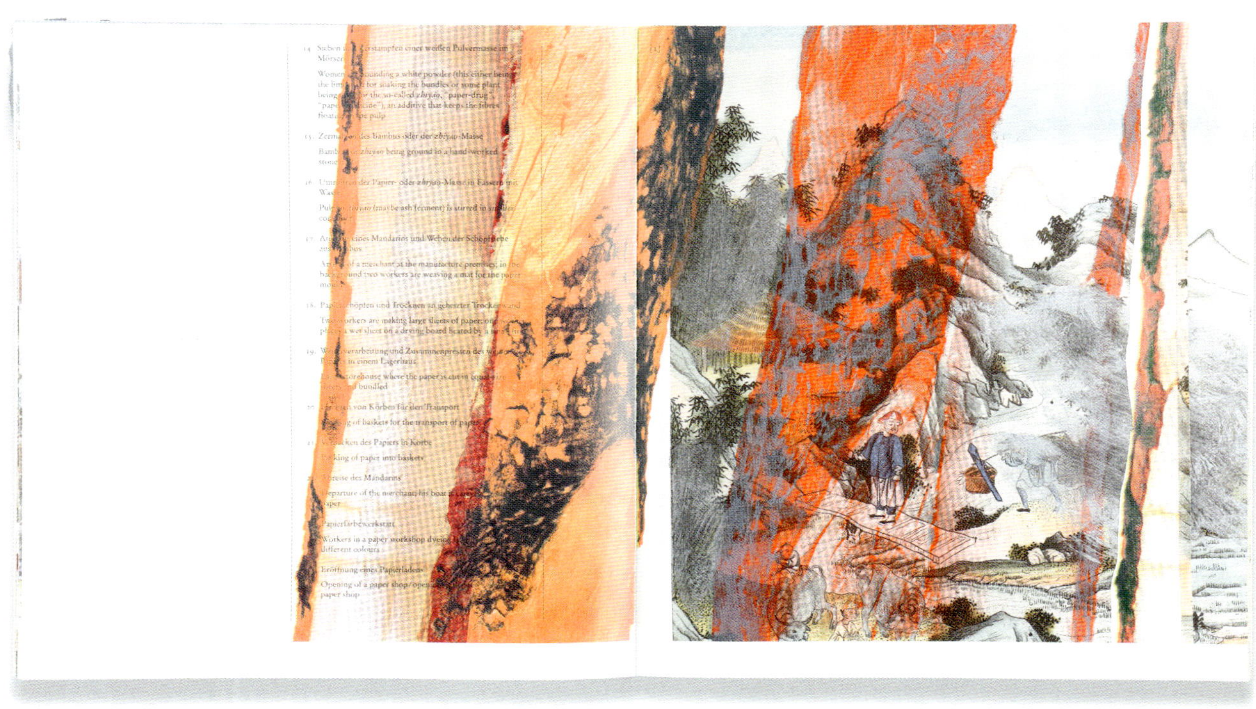

John Yau and Pia Fries, *tausend : einerlei*, 2022

PIA FRIES

Swiss, born 1955

Pia Fries often silkscreens recognizable images onto wood panels to serve as a starting point for her application of visceral strokes, puddles, and delicate washes of oil paint. She allows these layers of visual material to interact through her precise balancing of compositional control and serendipity.

In her collaboration with Yau, *tausend : einerlei* (a thousand : the same) she took apart three copies of *Chinesische Bambuspapierherstellung. Ein Bilderbuch aus dem 18. Jahrhundert*, a picture book on Chinese bamboo paper production from the eighteenth century, removed the text contributions, and reworked them using paint and printing. Behind dense passages of natural and synthetic color that flow like lava down and across the pages, glimpses of mountains, trees, pagodas, and figures are visible.

Yau's poem, "Too Far to Write Down," sits within the sequence of Fries's pages and seems to comment on the human actions taking place in the source material and the painter's abstract gestures. Here are the first four lines from Section 1[1]:

> *I, humble scribe of clouds, ask permission to make my case*
> *While you scatter ocher cumuli above black orchards and open huts*
> *Pull thick violet brushstrokes through cascading green mountains*
> *I watch my poems ferry fiery farewells downstream*

"Too Far to Write Down" has some of the sensitivity and surprise that defines the celebrated haiku of Matsuo Bashō with its focus on a heightened state of awareness as the poet wanders through the landscape. Here is an example[2]:

> *However close I look,*
> *not a speck on*
> *white chrysanthemum.*

---

1 John Yau, *"Too Far to Write Down,"* in *Tell it Slant* (Oakland, CA: Omnidawn Publishing, 2023), 13. Originally published by Snoek Verlag in the artist's book *tausend : einerlei*, 2022.

2 Matsuo Bashō, *On Love and Barley: Haiku of Basho*, trans. Lucien Stryk (London: Penguin Books, 1985), 66.

MAX GIMBLETT

American, born New Zealand, 1935

Max Gimblett is known for his adherence to the tenets of Abstract Expressionism and for utilizing symbols and sensibilities from both Western and Eastern religions in his work. He and Yau have collaborated on numerous projects including boxed sets of letterpress poems paired with calligraphic drawings; annotated family photographs collaged on round handmade paper and contained in a copper container; various mixed media paintings on paper; and several one-of-a-kind books.

All were created at the artist's former studio on the Bowery in lower Manhattan, utilizing an abundance of available materials, including black and colored inks, various acrylic paints, gold and silver gilding, paper sourced from around the world, and collage items. The extent of these options is evident in work including *I Wore Your Underwear Today* with its rich physical presence.

Writing about their process, Gimblett states, "Everything was made by hand, no machines, no press. Everything is about touch. Sessions would run 3–6 hours. There were no rules. It's called 'no rules study.'"[1]

Yau remembers, "I would go there and he would have set up things and then I'd start writing. He would say, 'You have to write twenty-six poems before you leave, you know, twenty-six haiku.' Or he'd send me a book of Zen koans and say, 'Read this and then come over and do something.' I'd go, 'I don't want to do this.' Then, I'd finally go, 'Why not? What am I fighting? What am I afraid of?' I'd go over and do something. We'd spend all day, you know, five or six hours. And he has all this fancy paper."[2]

Working together on *A Book of Broadway Koans* and *A Book of Millennium Koans*, the duo affirmed their commitment to being in the moment. Yau's poems (described as being "written in a trance" or "heard in the air") demonstrate his understanding of paradox in the search for enlightenment; and Gimblett believes that each splatter, drip, and stroke in the process of painting is imbued with presence and meaning.

"I would do a drawing in an instant, but John would write in a couple of minutes, too," Gimblett recalls. "So, we have speed in our thing, and speed keeps it fresh. Speed means it's not labored and you're acting out of your unconscious; and you're going to hear and see new things because when you're working with somebody else, it's all new . . . John's poetry has twists and surprises. Nothing's wasted, and the words loop on each other. They make curious connections. He's got these loops happening where two or three suggestions are in one little sentence."[3]

---

[1] Max Gimblett, email message to author, August 24, 2022.

[2] John Yau, interview with the author, September 27, 2022.

[3] Max Gimblett, interview with the author, September 28, 2022.

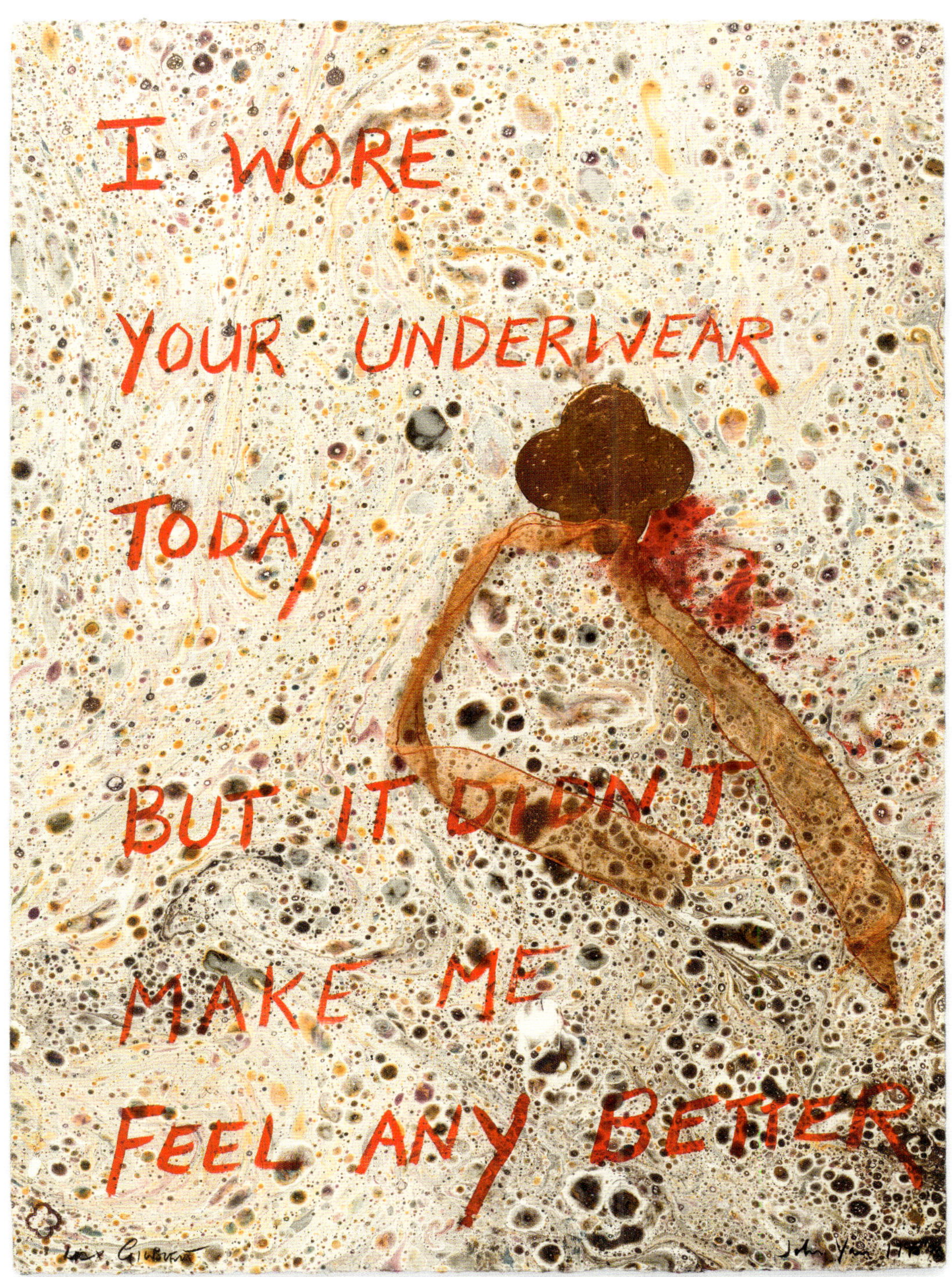

John Yau and Max Gimblett, *I Wore Your Underwear Today*, 1993/95

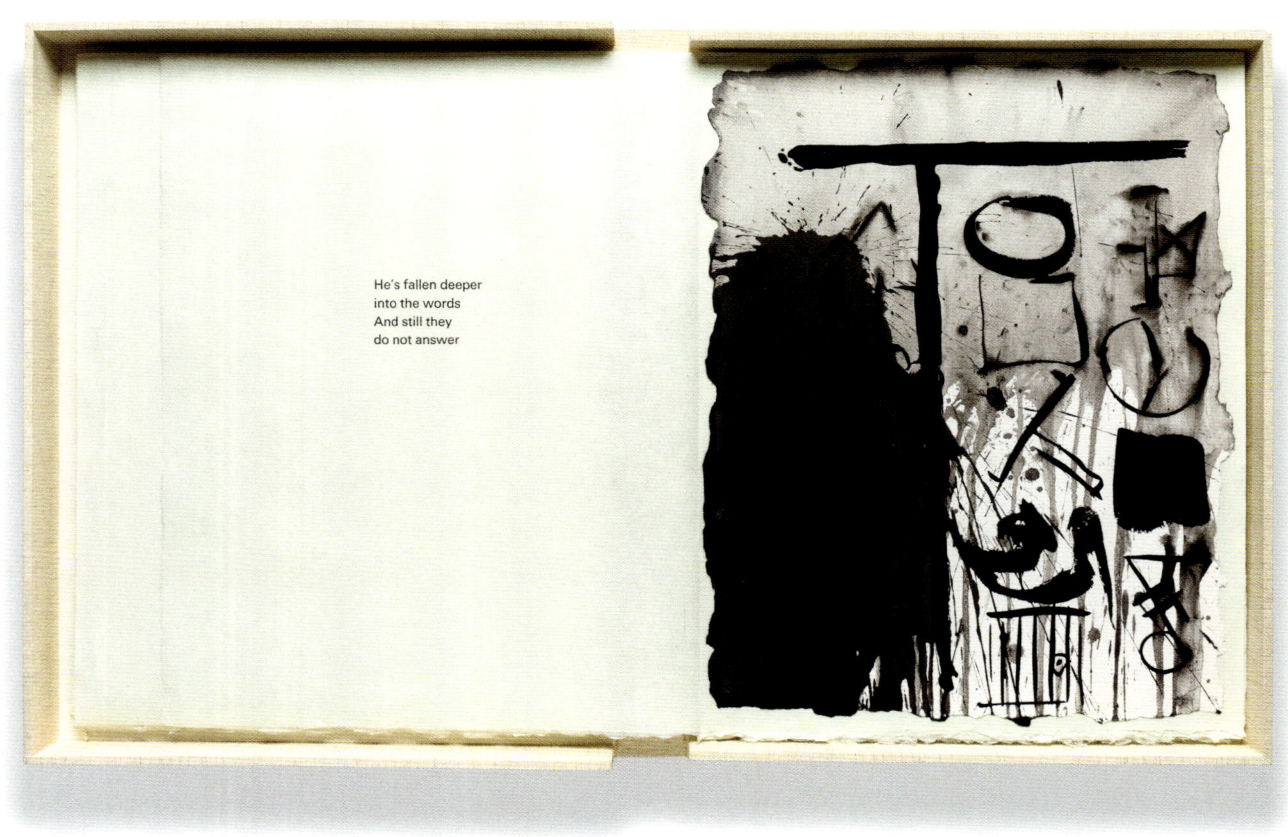

John Yau and Max Gimblett, *A Book of Broadway Koans,* **1988–2001**

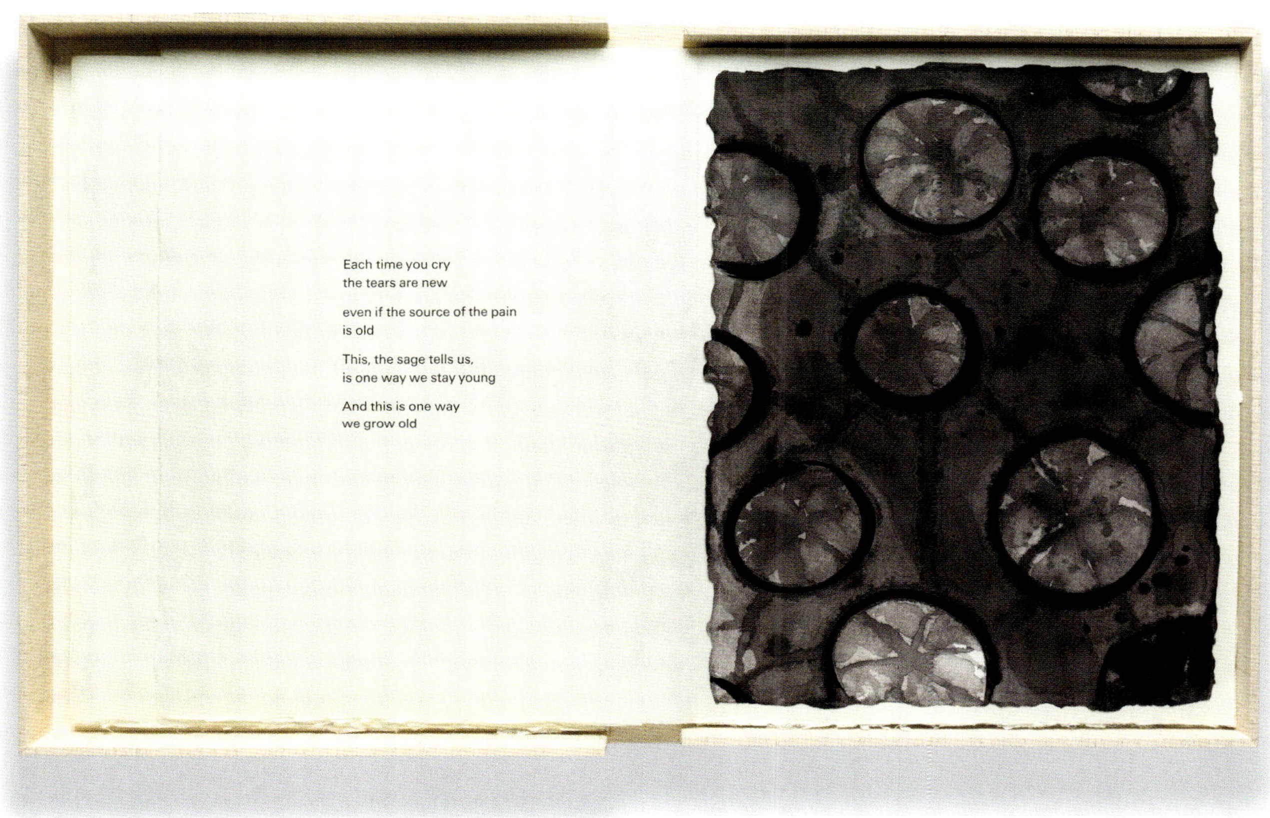

John Yau and Max Gimblett, *A Book of Millennium Koans*, 1988–2001

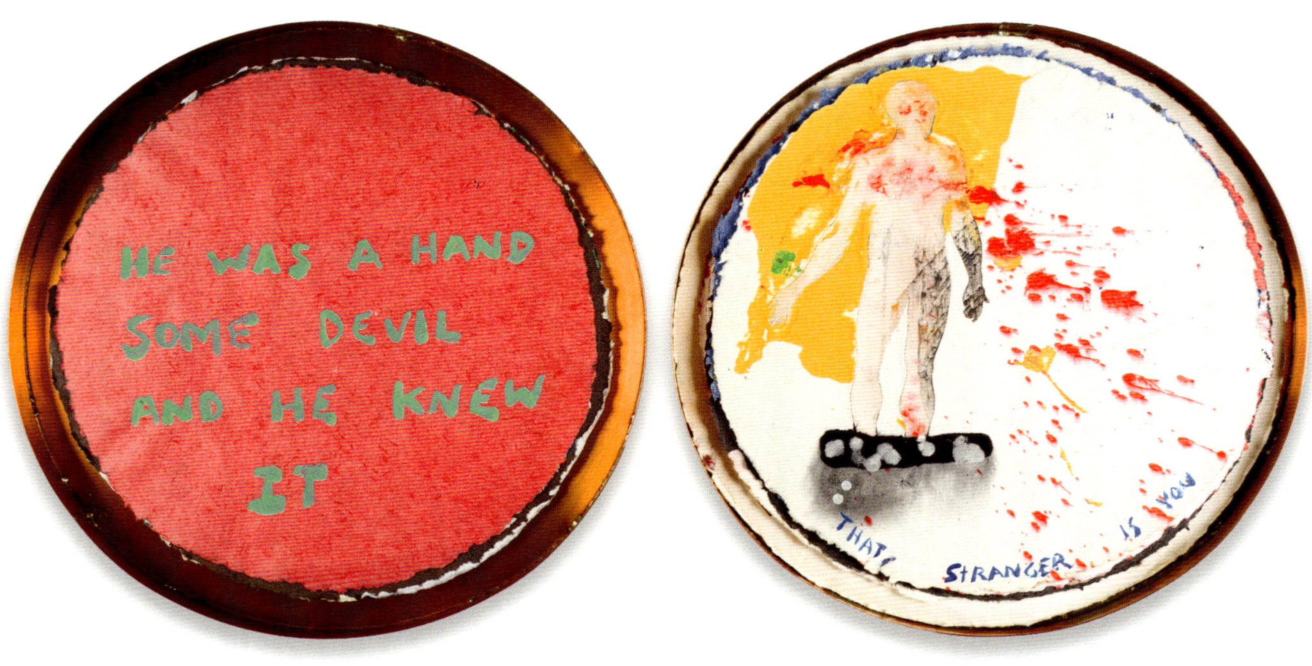

John Yau and Max Gimblett, *Leaves from a Chinese Album*, 2003

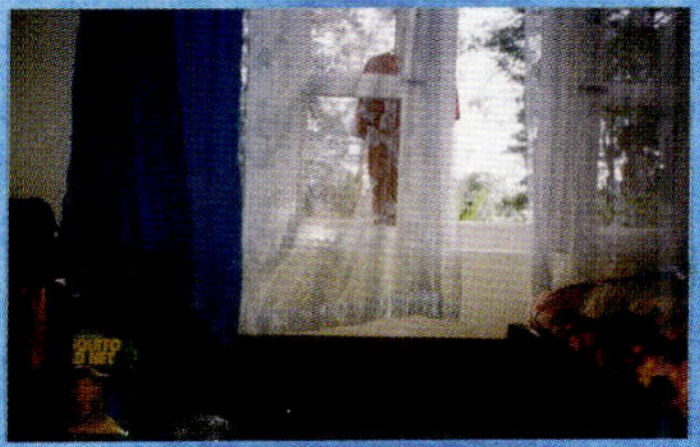

John Yau and Max Gimblett, *The sky has four sides but only one is visible*, 2001

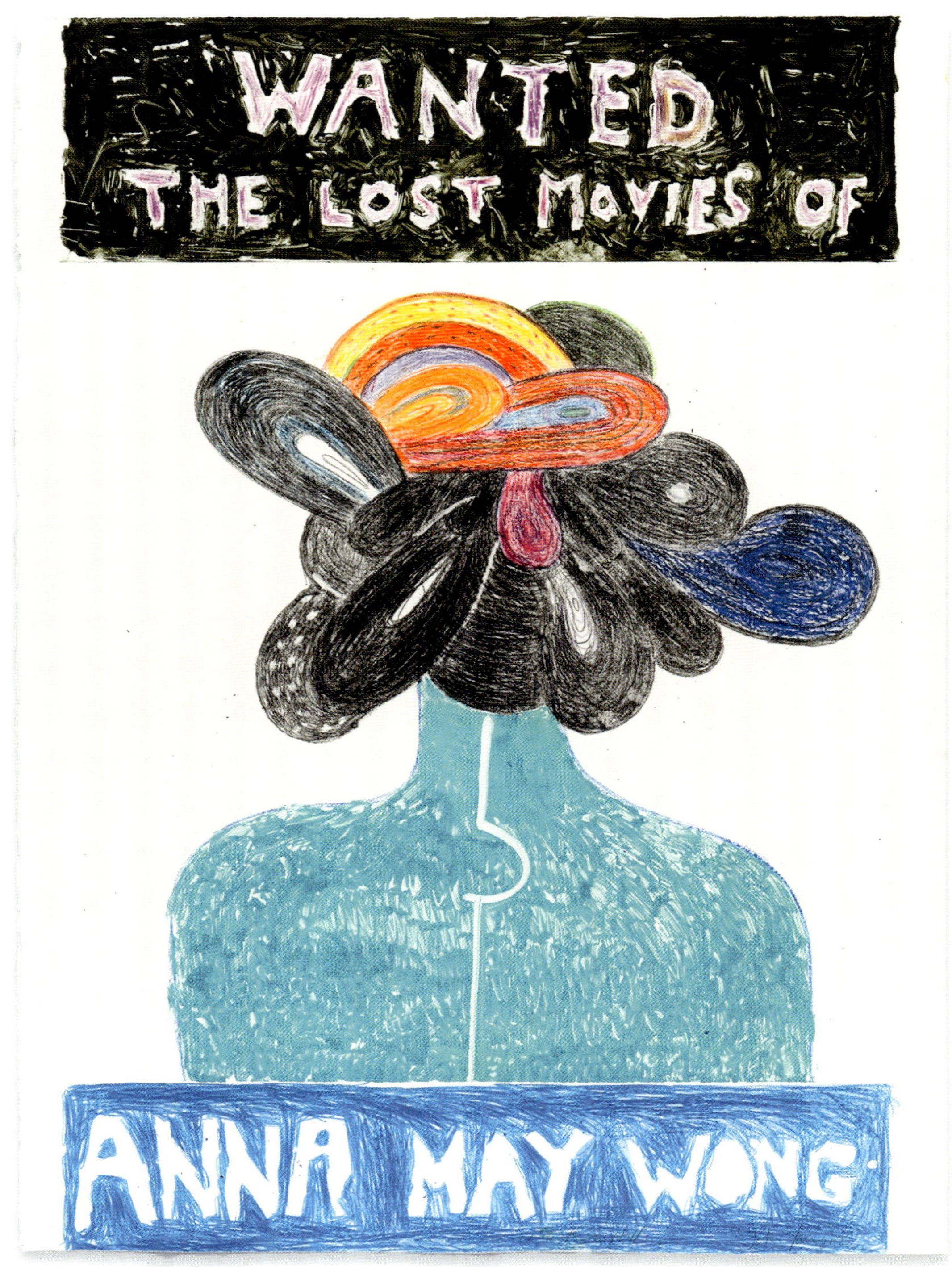

John Yau and Richard Hull, *Wanted: The Lost Movies of Anna May Wong*, 2023

RICHARD HULL

American, born 1955

Richard Hull is known for his figurative works in the Chicago Imagist tradition, creating abstract heads that are animated by riotously bulbous features and exuberant mark-making. His collaboration with Yau was made possible by Manneken Press, who published twenty-three monoprints that follow the format of "Wanted" posters from the old Wild West.

Each unique "being" (some appear to be a cross between a Philip Guston disembodied head and a balloon animal) is framed by a text panel on the top and bottom, where information is provided. Instead of seeking to catch criminals, some of these works are meant to address other wants, like putting "more eyes on" (gaining recognition for) under-recognized artists like the modernist John D. Graham and Miyoko Ito, who was sent to a Japanese internment camp a month before she graduated from the University of California, Berkeley. The prints celebrate Asian performers Anna May Wong and Sessue Hayakawa for their achievements while pining for the careers they might have had if the anti-miscegenation Hays Code laws were not in effect in Hollywood between 1934 and 1968. We can only screen the "lost movies" of Wong and "a lavish biopic" of Hayakawa in our mind.

Philip de Chirico/Giorgio Guston II is a mash-up that pays tribute to two of Yau's and Hull's favorite artists, whose late styles were the subject of fierce debate in their time and in subsequent decades.

Mortality enters the equation with the poster *Wanted: 50 More Years*, a reminder that Yau has interrogated getting on in years in several of his poems. "After I Turn Sixty-Nine" includes the following lines[1]:

> *I try to put aside obituaries but I am unable to do so for very long (maybe ten minutes)*
>
> . . . .
>
> *I dream that my ashes will be scattered in a remote spot in Ireland that no one visits*
> *I admit that shrinking into myself is not as unpleasant as I once thought*

---

[1] John Yau, "After I Turn Sixty-Nine," in *Genghis Chan on Drums* (Richmond, CA: Omnidawn Publishing, 2021), 103.

BILL JENSEN

American, born 1945

Bill Jensen's paintings use scale and materiality to maximum effect, bringing the viewer in close to confront his spiky, curved, and twisted forms in generalized landscapes. These particulars establish his connection to American Romanticism and artist predecessors including Arthur Dove, Marsden Hartley, and Albert Pinkham Ryder.

Yau and Jensen share an appreciation for the work of the Austrian poet Georg Trakl (1887 – 1914), who served as a medical officer on the Eastern Front during World War l, and whose experiences with injured and dying soldiers had a profound effect on his psyche and his writing. Trakl addressed conditions of doom, decay, and a sense of loss for the dead who cannot express themselves. The first lines of his poem "Grodek" (the name of a battle fought in 1914) are a good example of this[1]:

At evening the autumnal forests resound
With deadly weapons, the golden plains
And blue lakes, above them the sun
Rolls more darkly by; night enfolds
The dying warriors, the wild lament

In a 2007 interview with Yau, Jensen discussed his working method: "I seem to use the idea of seepage, where I will dredge something up physically in the painting, look at it, and then let it seep down again and then dredge it up again. Through this process, a hallucination of something might be in the painting."[2] This sense of bringing something into being (with the attendant anxiety about it) is palpable in their collaboration, *Postcards from Trakl*, with the combination of their individual efforts amplifying the elegiac mood of the project.

[1] "Grodek (1913)," Poetry by Heart, accessed December 6, 2023, https://www.poetrybyheart.org.uk/poems/grodek.

[2] John Yau, "Interview: Bill Jensen," *BOMB*, April 1, 2007, https://bombmagazine.org/articles/2007/04/01/bill-jensen/.

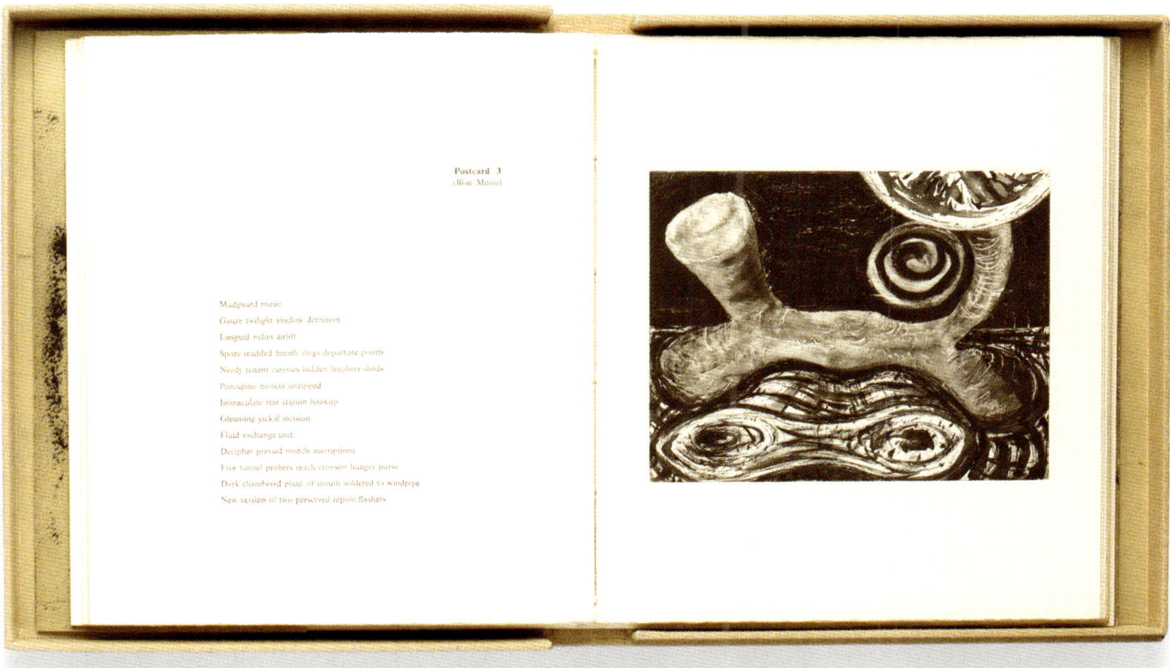

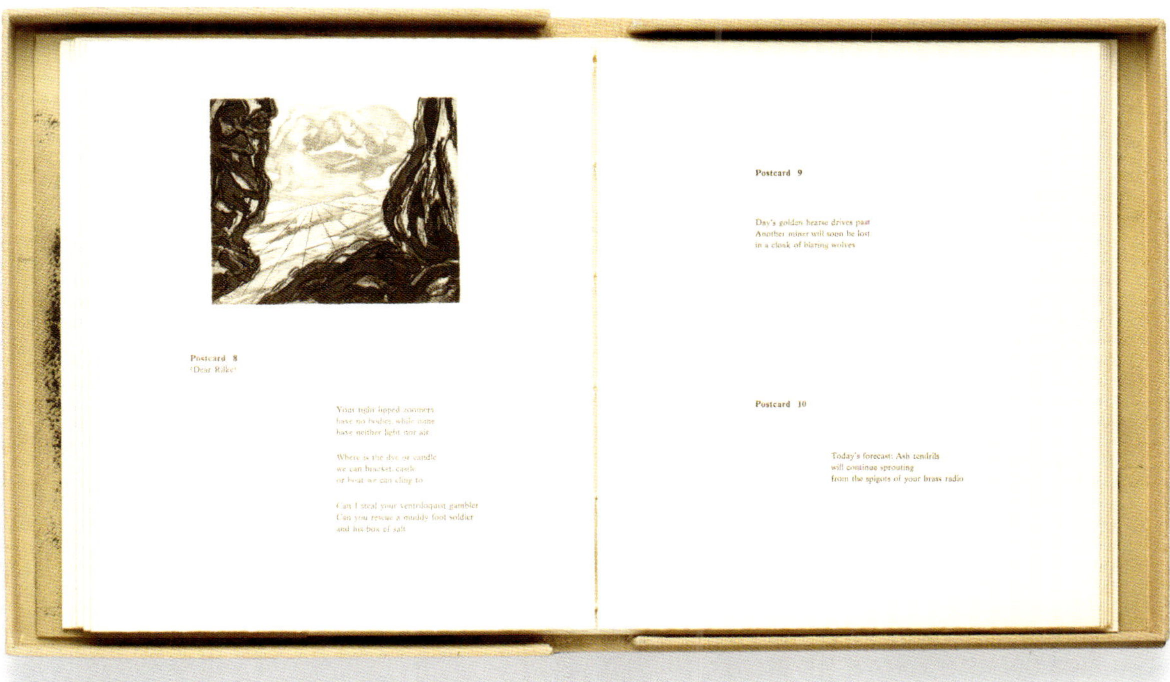

John Yau and Bill Jensen, *Postcards from Trakl*, 1989–94

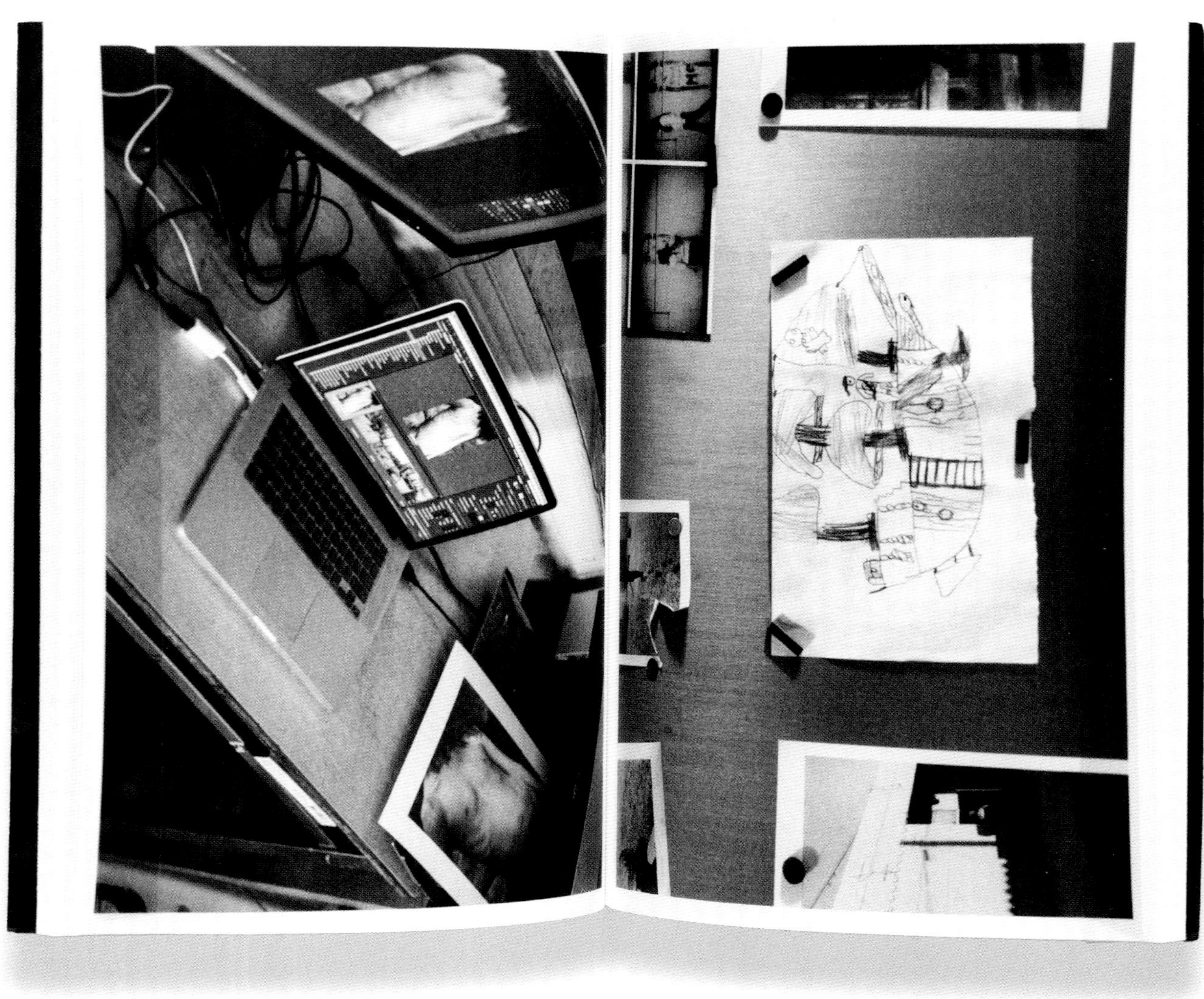

John Yau and Justine Kurland, *Black Threads from Meng Chiao*, 2015

JUSTINE KURLAND

American, born 1969

Known for her photographs featuring girls and young women in rural, wooded, and desert landscapes, Justine Kurland is familiar with collaboration. She has spent significant amounts of time scouting locations and recruiting models for her staged tableaus that imagine groups of runaways and utopian communities. She draws inspiration from English and German landscape painting traditions and the nineteenth-century photographs of Timothy O'Sullivan and Carleton Watkins.

When Kurland partnered with Yau, she was atypically housebound, describing the period this way: "I ended my road trips for a variety of reasons that spiraled from the death of my father and a fracturing of what I believed to be true. I knew I had to get off the road but had no idea how to continue working."[1] Yau had undergone surgery at this time and was recovering at home.

Their book, *Black Threads from Meng Chiao*, is titled after the Tang dynasty poet, known for his use of surrealist and symbolist techniques. It has an air of contemplation and claustrophobia to it, as Kurland documents the intimate realities of the East Village tenement apartment she's lived in for twenty years. This includes a photograph of her father hunting in the snow stuck to the refrigerator with magnets; a deadbolt lock and chain on the front door; images of her son Casper and some of the things he's made; and closely cropped views of her own nude body.

Kurland addresses the significance of their "call and response" project, stating: "John's poems influenced my work in their attention to details that could be allegorical, the abject romance of having any fantasy. He inspired me to imagine I could travel around my apartment. Ultimately, I think his poems are about death and a final measure of days, so I think that's in the photographs too . . . He is a brilliant poet. His poems have a simplicity and directness that gave me permission to do the same. I would have never made these pictures without him."[2]

---

[1] Justine Kurland, email message to author, April 7, 2023.

[2] Monica Uszerowicz, "On Shifting, Empathy, + Metaphorical Traveling, Justine Kurland in Conversation," *Ravelin*, March 2016, https://www.ravelinmagazine.com/posts/on-shifting-empathy-metaphorical-traveling/.

JUDY LEDGERWOOD

American, born 1959

In 2014, Judy Ledgerwood created *Chromatic Patterns for the Graham Foundation*, a site-specific installation in the historic Madlener House in Chicago, where the Foundation is housed. Throughout the first-floor galleries, she used vibrant florescent colors and metallic paint to cover the walls with an exuberantly rendered grid of flowers. Contained within the crown molding, baseboards, and door casings of the rooms, her painting effectively forced a discussion about pattern and decoration with the building's Prairie-style architecture.

Yau read his occasion poem, *26 Letters for Judy Ledgerwood*, at the opening reception. Ledgerwood describes the evening as "one of the finest moments of my professional life."[1]

Something Yau wrote about the painter almost ten years later for *Hyperallergic* could easily apply to the riotous architectural installation: "Ledgerwood has a current of impropriety, painterliness, waywardness, and humor in her work, upending the symmetry and repetition that are common to decorative and ornamental arts."[2]

The publication of *Chromatic Patterns After the Graham Foundation* was the result of dialogue between the artist and Jonathan Higgins at Manneken Press in Bloomington, Illinois, and Ledgerwood's desire to create a lasting reminder of the installation and Yau's honorific and playful writing. She writes, "I simply sent John an email and explained the project as a suite of three prints together in a portfolio along with his poem, and asked permission. The design of the portfolio in crisp florescent pink and the typesetting of the poem in silver metallic by Jason Pickleman brought it all together."[3]

---

[1] Judy Ledgerwood, email message to author, June 29, 2022.

[2] John Yau, "Judy Ledgerwood's Playfully Subversive Patterns," *Hyperallergic*, February 9, 2023, https://hyperallergic.com/799622/judy-ledgerwoods-playfully-subversive-patterns/.

[3] Ledgerwood, email to author, June 29, 2022.

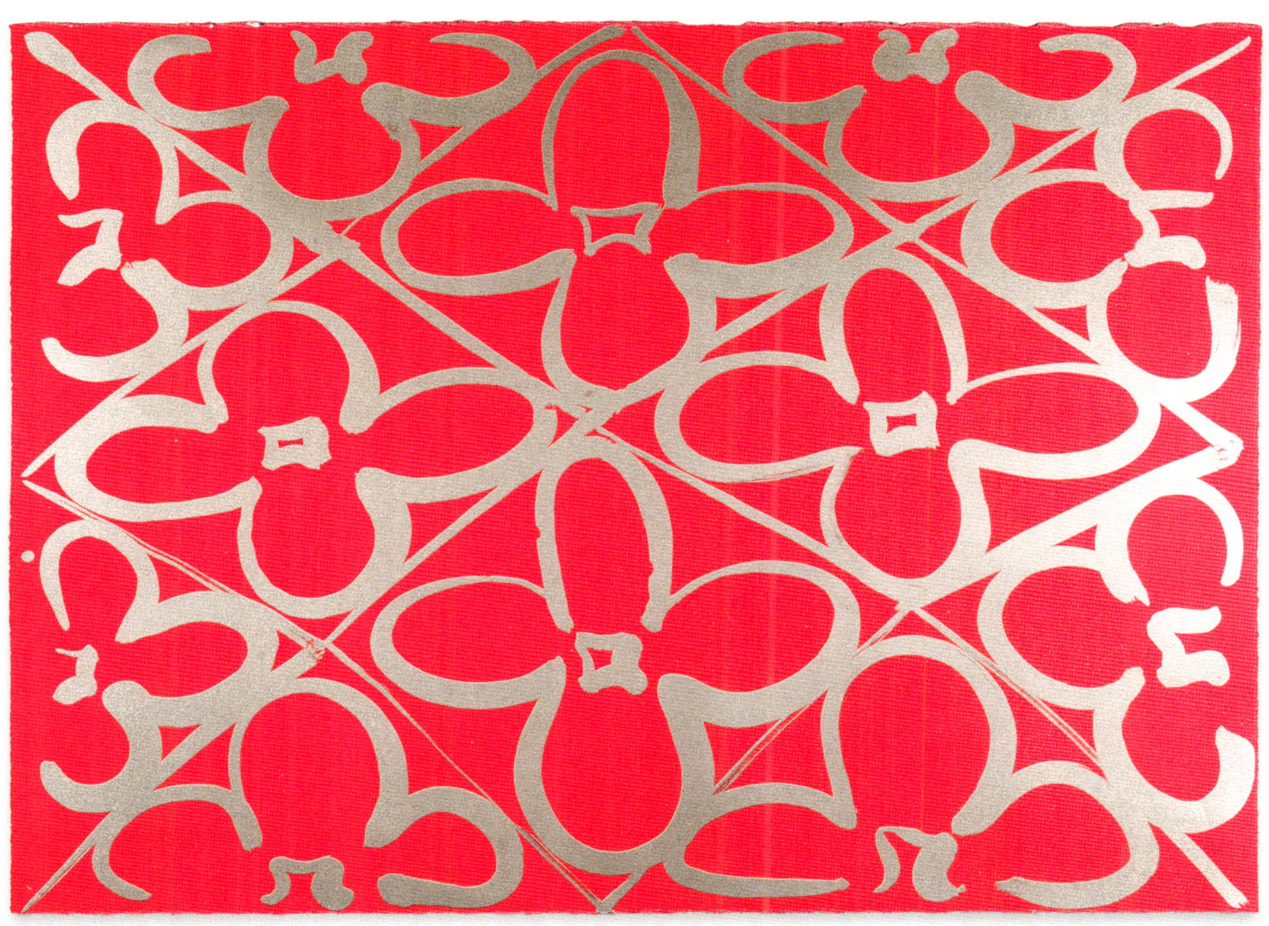

John Yau and Judy Ledgerwood, *Chromatic Patterns After the Graham Foundation*, 2014

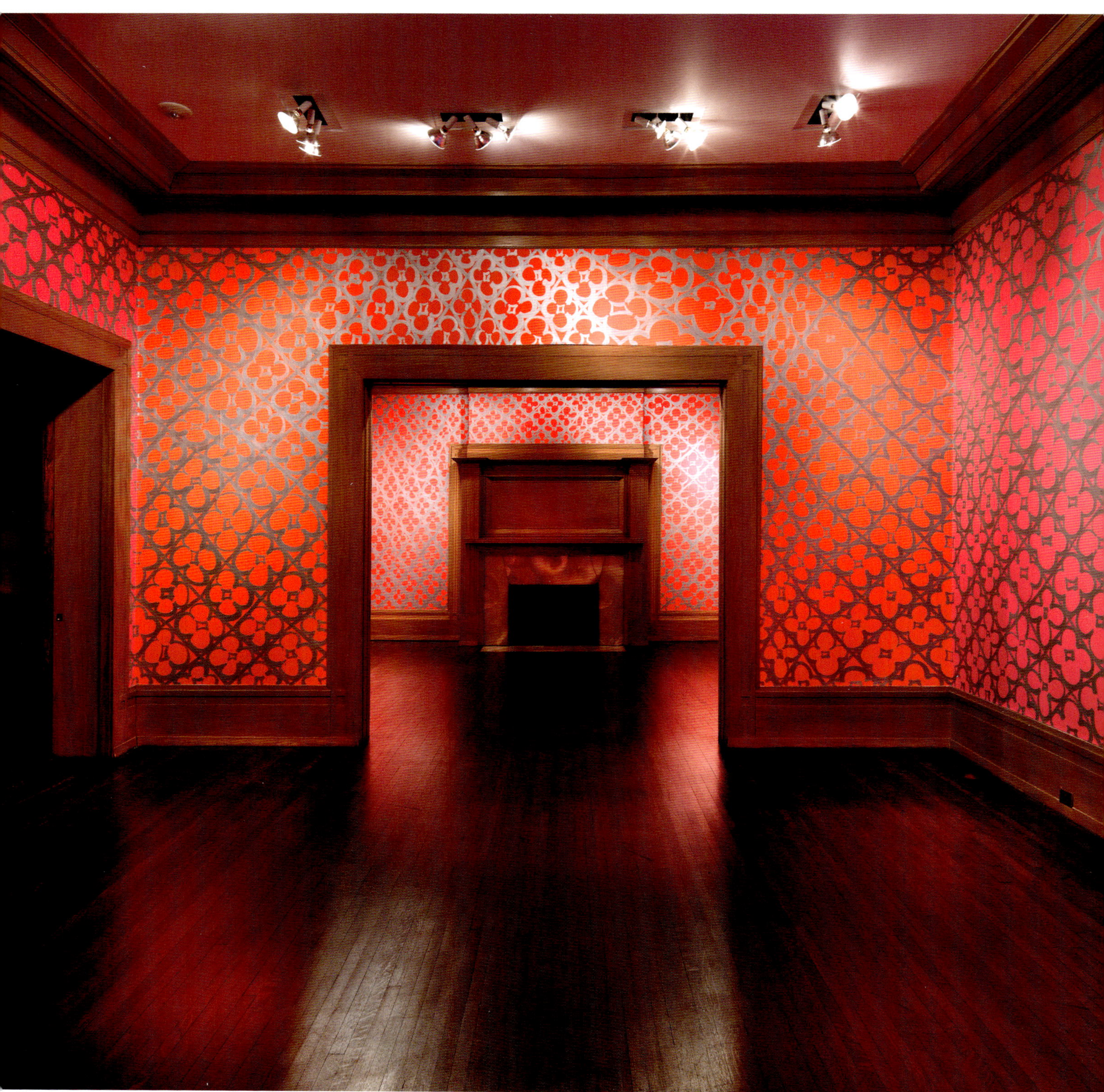

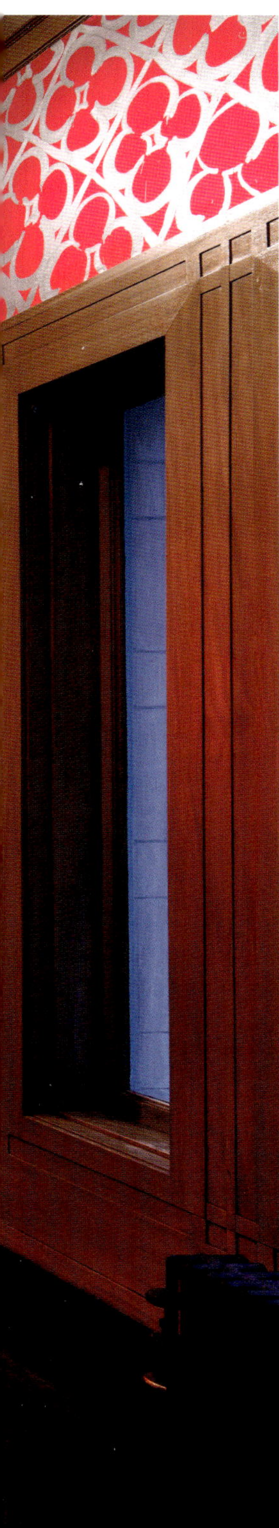

John Yau and Judy Ledgerwood, *Chromatic Patterns After the Graham Foundation*, 2014

View of *Judy Ledgerwood: Chromatic Patterns for the Graham Foundation*, January 23 – April 5, 2014

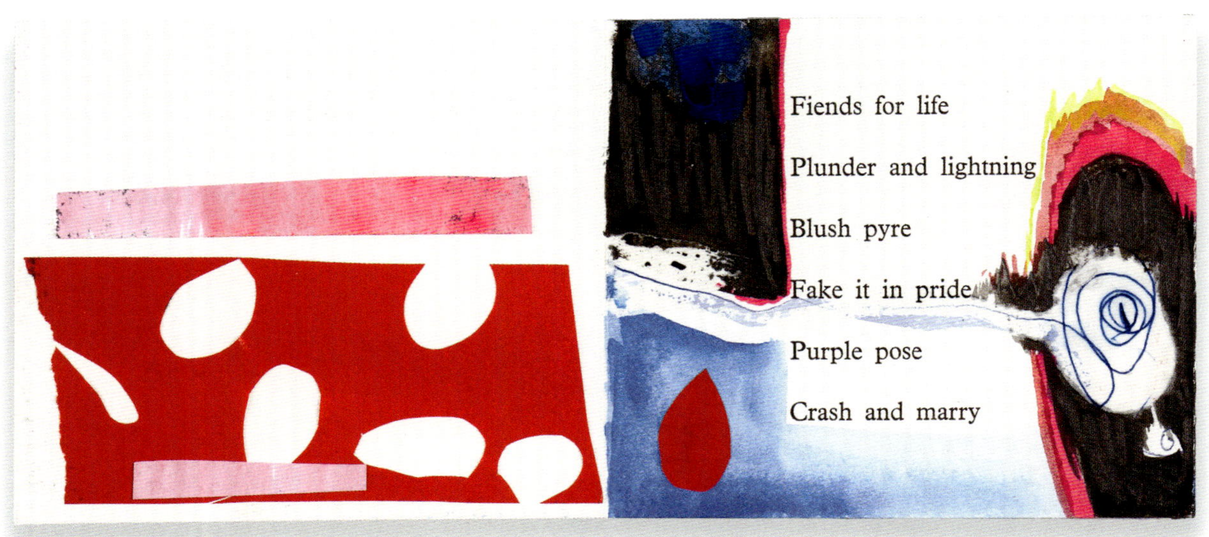

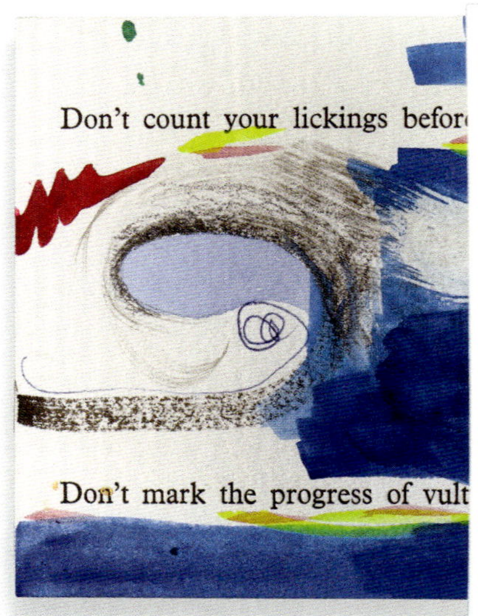

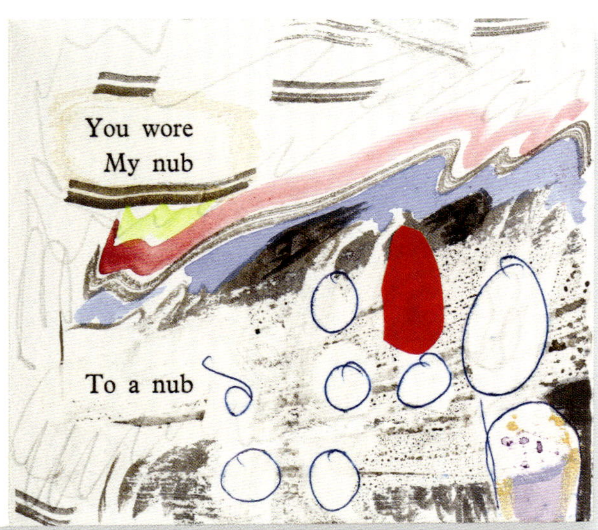

John Yau and Suzanne McClelland, *Flee Advice*, 1991

SUZANNE MCCLELLAND

American, born 1959

Yau was Suzanne McClelland's teacher in graduate school at the School of Visual Arts, and she served as researcher for his book *In the Realm of Appearances: The Art of Andy Warhol* and some of his poems. She recalled, "I had a great time looking up the history of prostitution in Manhattan and spent a lot of time in really odd libraries, like the one in the basement of City Hall."[1]

In his *Artforum* review of her 1992 exhibition at the Stephanie Theodore Gallery, Yau assessed her interests: "On a formal level, McClelland utilizes charcoal, acrylic, gels, clay, and rabbit-skin glue to investigate the conditional relationship between drawing and words, between painting and writing. Within these formal parameters, however, she pursues a more speculative and ultimately more engaging investigation of the zones between conventional and personal language usage."[2]

The artist's rich experiments in manipulating words and their component parts (stems, strokes, serifs, terminals, and bowls) make for an exciting partnership with Yau, who regularly mines the elasticity of language in his poetry.

In their accordion-style book, *Flee Advice*, Yau's language inspires McClelland to indulge in acts of dripping, coloring, outlining, stenciling, and collaging. She responds differently to each of the thirty copies in the edition.

McClelland recalls, "My approach was to pick a word and write a word in response to his language. *Flee Advice* includes the word "lick" a lot, so just taking fragments of the words that are already there and kind of finding the sound. I get a lot of my ideas for paintings through the sound of speech. The accordion felt like a potential stutter, and there's repetition but no page is the same. Some are more illustrative. I was using a lot of ballpoint pen then, so ballpoint pen and acrylic medium. I also just like looking at them page by page with that sort of anticipation of what might or might not happen."[3]

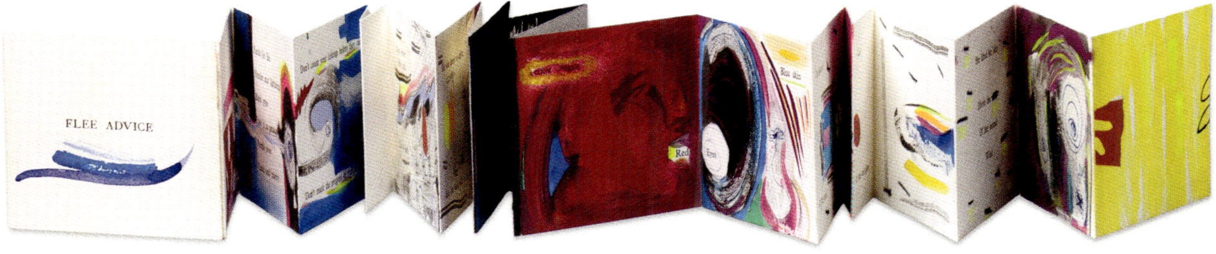

---

[1] Suzanne McClelland, interview with the author, September 28, 2022.

[2] John Yau, "Suzanne McClelland, Stephanie Theodore Gallery," *Artforum* 30, no. 6 (February 1992), https://www.artforum.com/events/suzanne-mcclelland-2-217286/.

[3] McClelland, interview with author, September 28, 2022.

MALCOLM MORLEY

British-American, 1931 – 2018

Over the course of Malcolm Morley's career, he explored several distinct painterly modes while repeatedly using images and models of cruise ships, planes, cars, and motorbikes. These subjects of travel and leisure have their own historical and cultural references but might also suggest a creative mandate to keep moving and not settle into a signature style, something that he and Yau both exemplify.

Travels to Greece inspired Morley's watercolors that explore mythology and the Classical world, with connections to archeology and the adventures of Ulysses in Homer's epic poem, *The Odyssey*. Add to this his interest in the American West and Native American objects and rituals, and one gets a sense of his desire to picture a melting pot of human history.

This is the case in the series of etchings and aquatints from *The Fallacies of Enoch*, published by Novak Graphics, which combine the Trojan horse, Minoan figures, French Legionnaires, and nude sunbathers.

Yau's poems were composed after the prints were made, and are fine examples of ekphrastic writing, with lively alliteration and startling imagery. These lines from *The Fallacies of Enoch* are an example[1]:

After his hand is severed in a hunting accident
he bought a dildo. It is a large finger, a substitute
teacher. Many years later the real one is found
pressed between the pages of a tree.

Departure dying doom delight
in the knowing and unknowing . . .

---

[1] John Yau, *Malcolm Morley: Fallacies of Enoch, with poems by John Yau* (Toronto: Novak Graphics, 1984), 1.

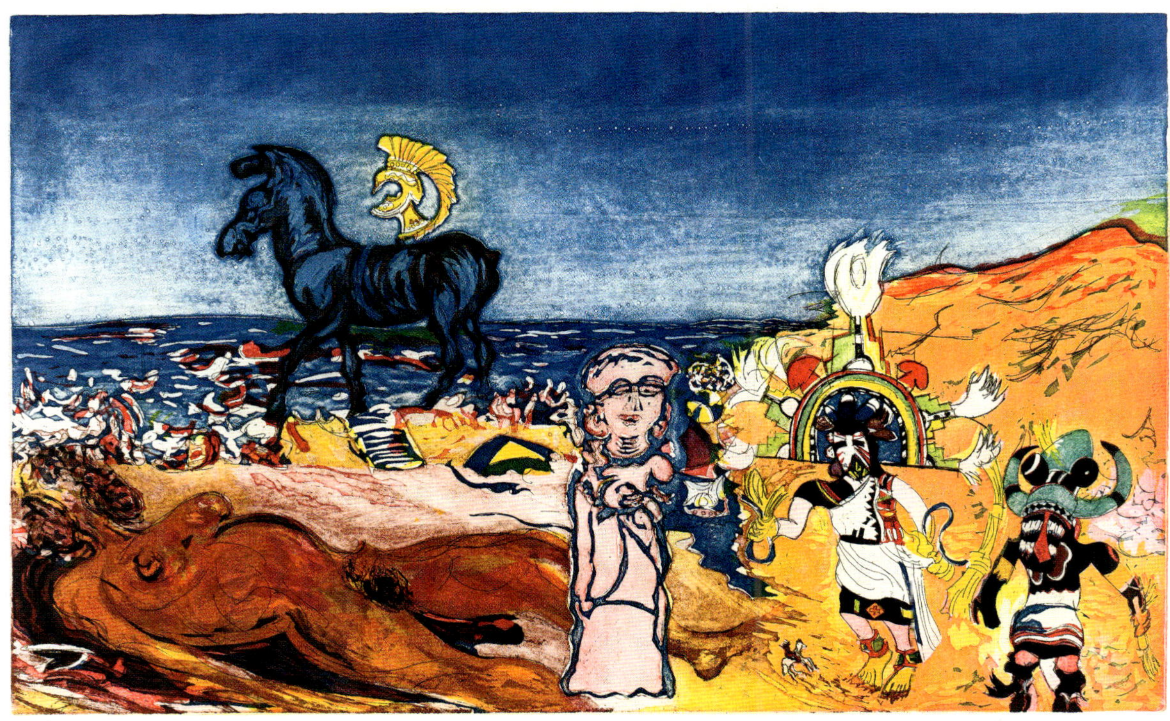

Malcolm Morley, *Cradles of Civilizations* from *The Fallacies of Enoch*, circa 1986

The Fallacies of Enoch

4

They don't believe they travelled to islands
that never existed. One morning they are sawed
in half. Dream after dream, like buckets of mud
dumped on our heads. I will tell a different story
each time I'm asked. On the inside of her thigh
is tattoed the dead actor's handprint. A horse
prances across the sky, its cloud a blue rectangle,
a window facing the sea. I will say nothing. Even
the knife flying around his head hums a familiar tune.
Her face, all the bones of anger singing at once.
I will point to the names erased from the blackboard,
instead. We were walking from one end of the island
to the other. He told me a story, showed me a mirror
or lie. Behind the wall of reason grazed the lunar
horse, he said, as he led me to the window facing
the courtyard. Thirty men shovelled sand onto the blue
cobblestones. Inside the stable actors dyed themselves
the same color as their uniforms. One practiced sticking
his head into the mouth of a lion. He was a penniless
duke with a penchant for chocolate. In the story
I am followed by a spear of lightning, a mirror or
lie. I escape to another island, where I meet an old
woman who described everything I have seen in detail.
One morning a torso emerges from the sea.

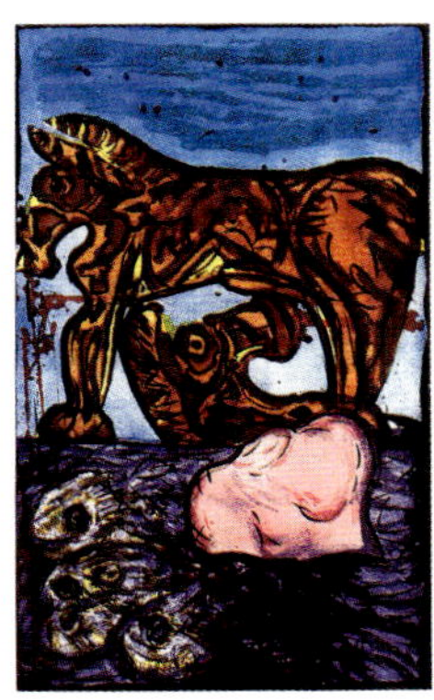

John Yau and Malcolm Morley, *The Fallacies of Enoch*, 1984

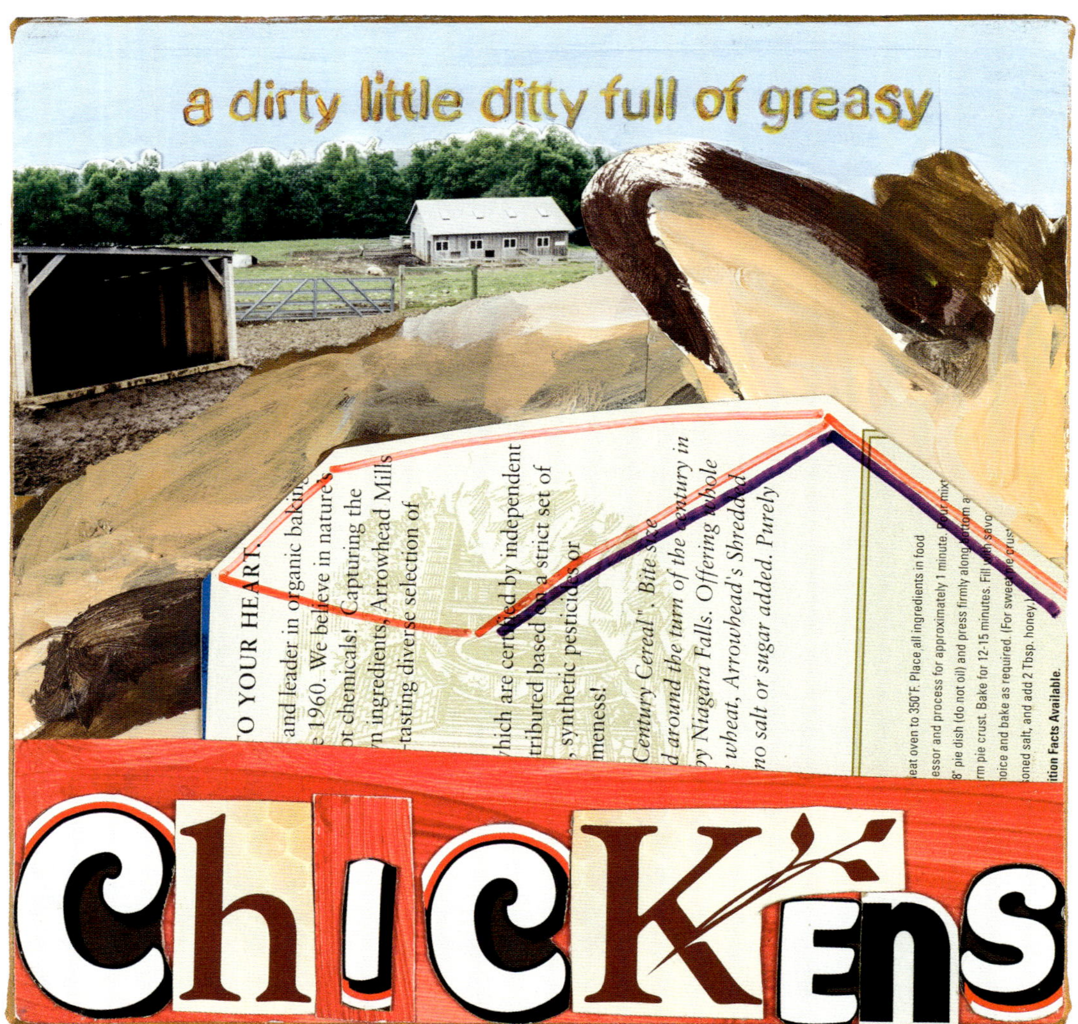

John Yau and Ilse Sørensen Murdock, *A Dirty Little Ditty Full of Greasy Chickens*, 2004

ILSE SØRENSEN MURDOCK

Danish/Scottish-American, born 1974

The idea for a collaboration between Yau and Ilse Sørensen Murdock was proposed in 2004 by Volume Gallery (now Freight & Volume Gallery). The artist was familiar with his writing and had been regularly incorporating words and letters into her various still-life paintings.

Murdock describes these as "post-binge scenes" with "piles of food remnants, wrappers and packages strewn across table settings."[1] A subsequent series of cereal box collages contain language and images from common food packaging, and views of landscape—a hint that the artist sees the glut of consumer waste as having a troubling effect on the environment.

After receiving images of Murdock's work, Yau responded with a list of phrases for her to use. Lines including "A dirty little ditty full of greasy chickens" and "Dross resurrection unit" are full of double consonant combinations and suggest advertising lingo gone awry.

Murdock's handling of paint has a confectionary quality, as swirls and bits of impasto become meringue-like clouds and chocolate chips. The works affirm a sense of joyfully devouring images with one's eyes.

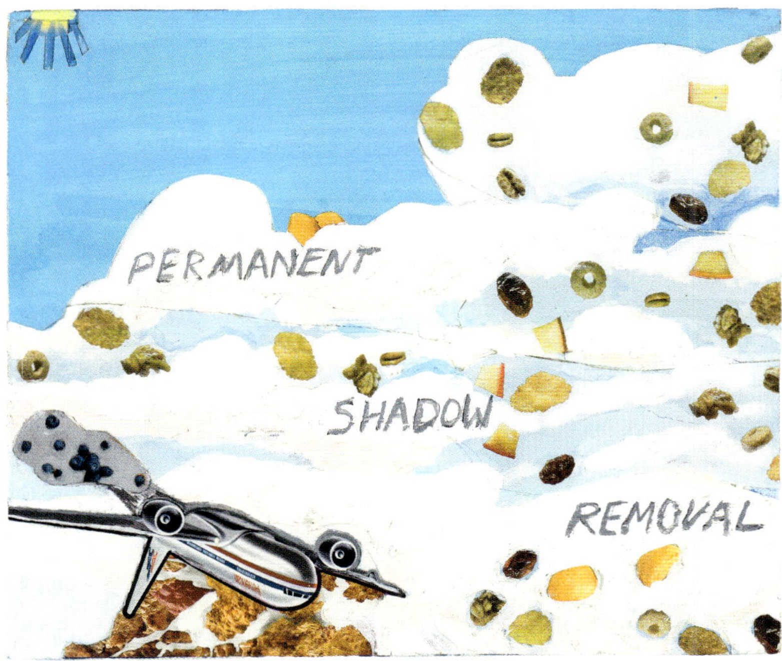

John Yau and Ilse Sørensen Murdock, *Permanent Shadow Removal*, 2004

1 Ilse Sørensen Murdock, email message to author, September 7, 2023.

MARTIN NOËL

German, 1956 – 2010

Martin Noël used experiences from everyday life, including noticing cracks in asphalt and the branching structure of trees, to generate imagery in his abstract paintings and prints. This extends to *New York Islands*, which includes his close-up photographs of walls or sections of pavement animated by the kind of bold gestures we associate with paintings by Willem de Kooning and Franz Kline (and the photographs by Aaron Siskind made in the same period). These images are combined with Yau's honorific texts that capture the specificity of various artists, writers, and musicians, who made New York their home. They include Max Beckmann, Eva Hesse, Billie Holiday, Jack Kerouac, Blinky Palermo, Jackson Pollock, Mark Rothko, and others.

Each section of the publication includes a glossy photograph; the street address of one of the subjects being celebrated; Yau's poems in English and German; and linear drawings and outlines that have a casual elegance in keeping with Noël's overall aesthetic.

It is worth remembering the idiom, "No man is an island," by the English poet John Donne[1] when considering Yau and Noël's collaboration. The phrase affirms that no matter how talented a person might be, their success is always the result of support and encouragement from others.

---

[1] John Donne, *Devotions upon emergent occasions* (London, 1638), 152.

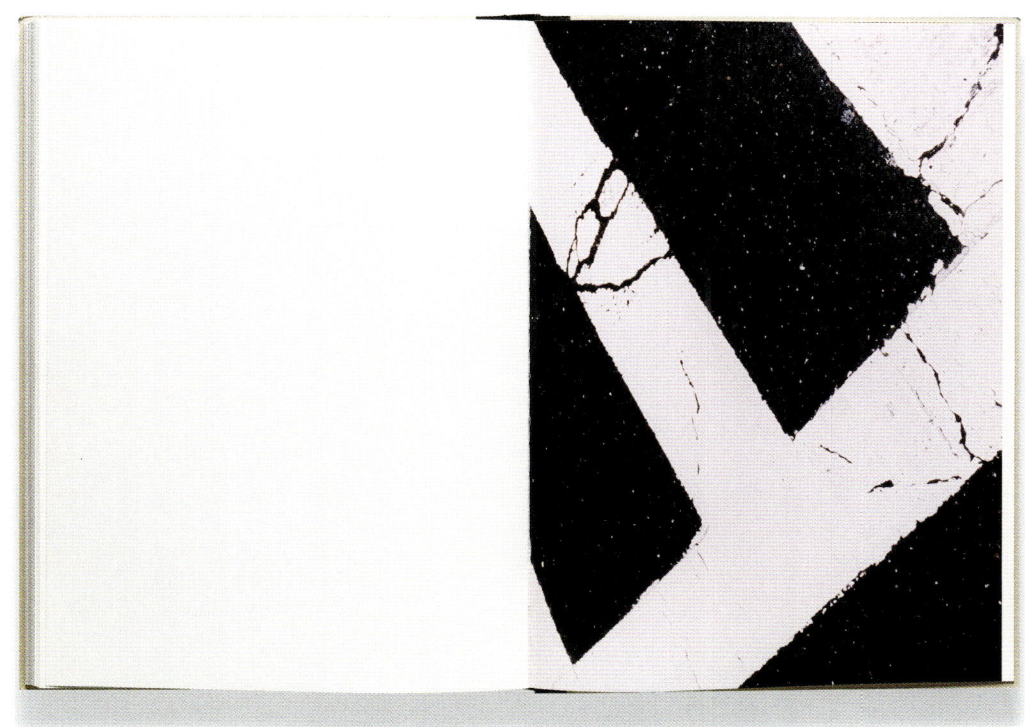

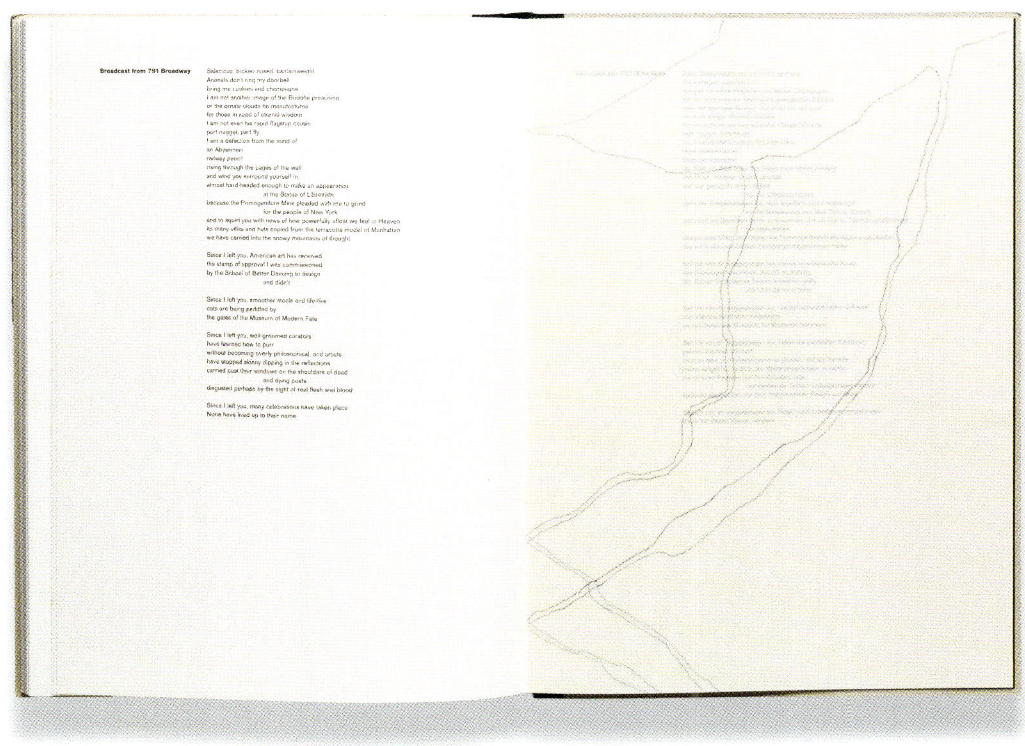

John Yau and Martin Noël, *New York Islands*, 1998

Unpromising Poem

I am writing to you from the bedroom of my ex-wife, where I have been stenciling diagrams on sheets and ceiling, intricate star charts of the paths modern soldier ants take to reach the lips waiting at the end of their long journey. There are no red messages in the balloons floating overhead, no tasty tidbits left from the first meeting. I have been told that the soft meat gets softer in the harsh helixes of the second sun.

I am writing to you from the bedroom of my ex-wife, the room in which flocks of birds have returned to the shelves of their one-syllable caves.
Dust settles on the eyelids of those who have yet to emerge from the shadows. Blue sparks etch the edges where the sky falls away, and black clouds fill the chalkboard with sleeping children.

I am writing to you from the bedroom my ex-wife keeps in her bedroom, the Library of Unusual Exceptions, Book of Gaudy Exemptions, Ledger of Lost Opportunities, wavelengths of archaeological soot drifting through the screen.

I am writing to you from the sleeping car temporarily disabled in the bedroom of my ex-wife. Dear Corraded Clouds, Dear Correspondence Principle, Dear Axle, Enzyme, and Ash, Dear Example of Excellence,
are you Frigg or Freya? Hoop Snake or Hoosegow?

O turtle in a kirtle, why must you chortle so?

Dear Hangman of Harbin, why did I wake in the bedroom of my ex-wife?

Dear ex-wife, I have learned to accept the small pleasures that come with being called The Hangman of Harbin.

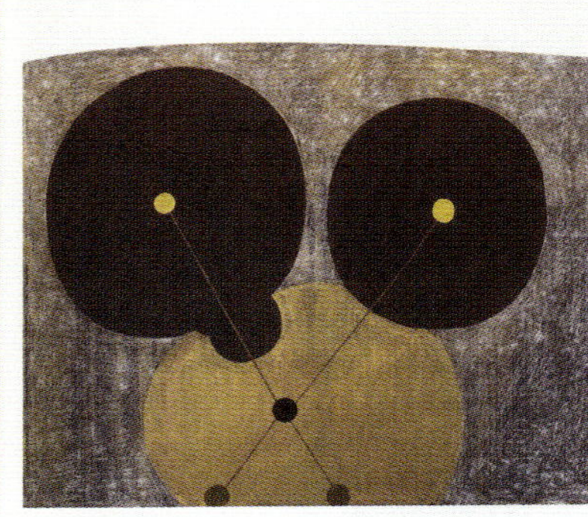

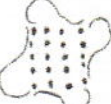

Alien Documentary

Tomorrow I will
say hello

unpredictable,
agitated

I will walk
upright and smile

hands, tongue,
eyelids quivering

In green air,
under purple sky

I will be elevated
and delirious

My involuntary parts
will not volunteer

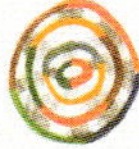

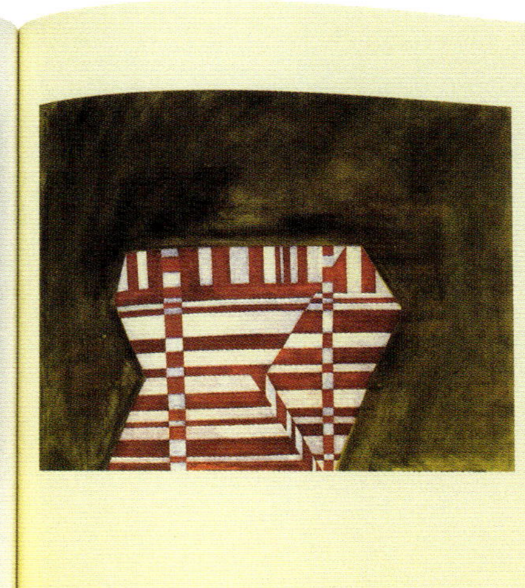

John Yau and Thomas Nozkowski, *Ing Grish*, 2005

THOMAS NOZKOWSKI

American, 1944 – 2019

Thomas Nozkowski was a consummate practitioner of the centuries-old tradition of oil painting, reveling in what the medium could do. Working on modest and "unserious" 16 x 20-inch canvas boards for much of his career, Nozkowski used his observations of nature, still life, and other art to generate his imagery. He situated biomorphic and geometric shapes in fields of unpredictable color, adjusting their relationship until a precise harmony was achieved.

In 2005, Yau and Nozkowski created *Ing Grish*, a book that includes the poet's meditations on racial stereotypes and gaps of understanding, paired with the artist's drawings of cellular forms and diagrams, and several completed paintings. Both men cultivated strategies of improvisation and refinement, and their collaboration is a testament to shared values.

In a 2010 interview with Yau in *The Brooklyn Rail*, Nozkowski stated: "Consciousness is complicated. What's interesting? What do you want to think about and how do you want to think about it? How hard do you want to think about it?"[1]

As if to answer these questions, Yau wrote the first monograph on the artist in 2017, affirming that he found Nozkowski's idiosyncratic works extremely rewarding to contemplate.

[1] John Yau, "Art in Conversation: Thomas Nozkowski," *The Brooklyn Rail*, November 2010, https://brooklynrail.org/2010/11/art/thomas-nozkowski-with-john-yau.

THOMAS OFFHAUS

German, born 1967

Thomas Offhaus worked on the publication *Russian Letter* from 2001 to 2003, responding to the second in a series of six Yau poems of the same name. Using a mix of etching and aquatint techniques, he created a hypnotic sequence of figures and botanical specimens that are seen against a ground of pulsing dot patterns.

There is a punk DIY quality to the book, and the imagery seems solarized, adding an air of harsh unpredictability to each spread. Couplets from Yau's poem are given ample room to stretch out on the page and seem to be the comments spoken by the depicted beings[1]:

Did you become a book I dreamed
or did I destroy

and contradict myself
like a moth

flying into language's
colorless flame

---

[1] John Yau, "Russian Letter [2]," in *Borrowed Love Poems* (New York: Penguin Books, 2002), 4-5.

Did you become a book I dreamed

or did I destroy

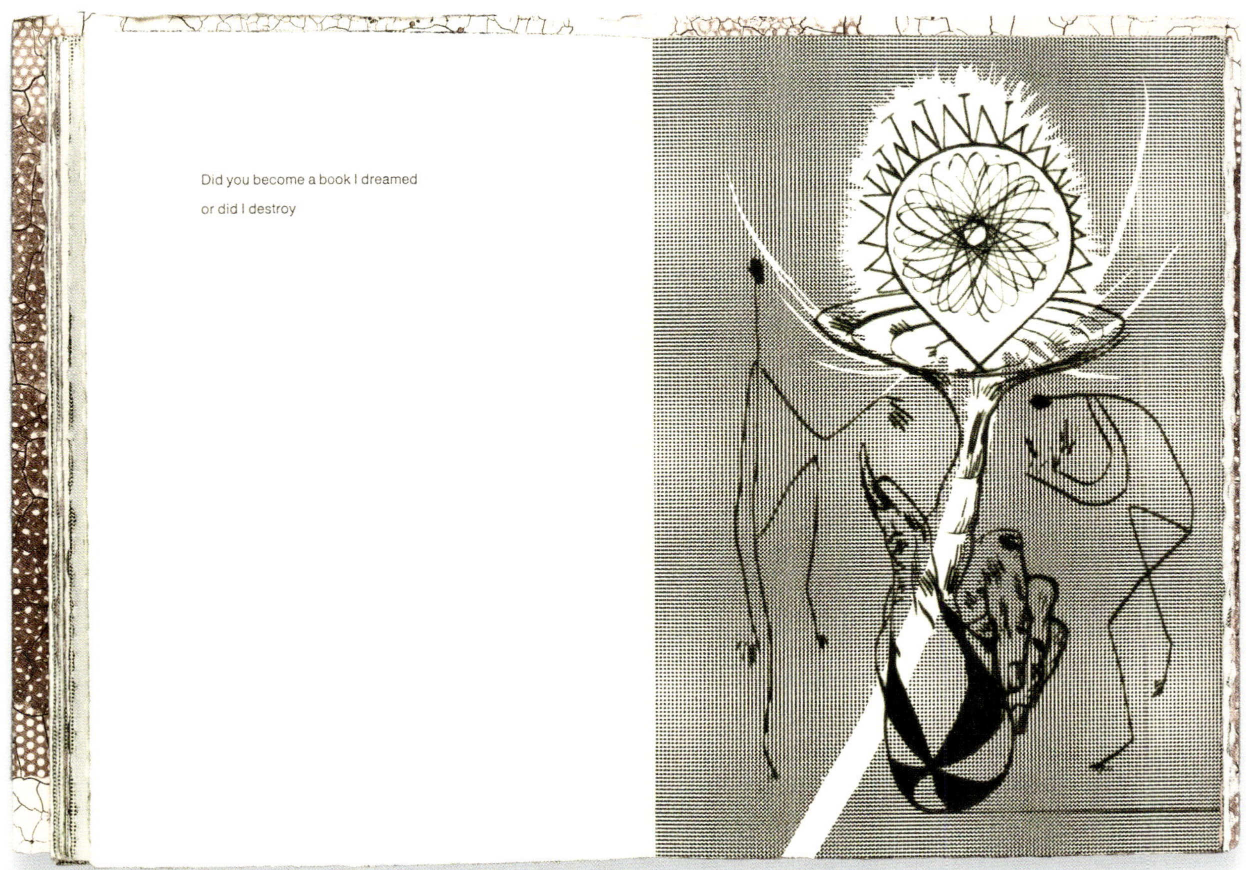

John Yau and Thomas Offhaus, *Russian Letter*, 2003

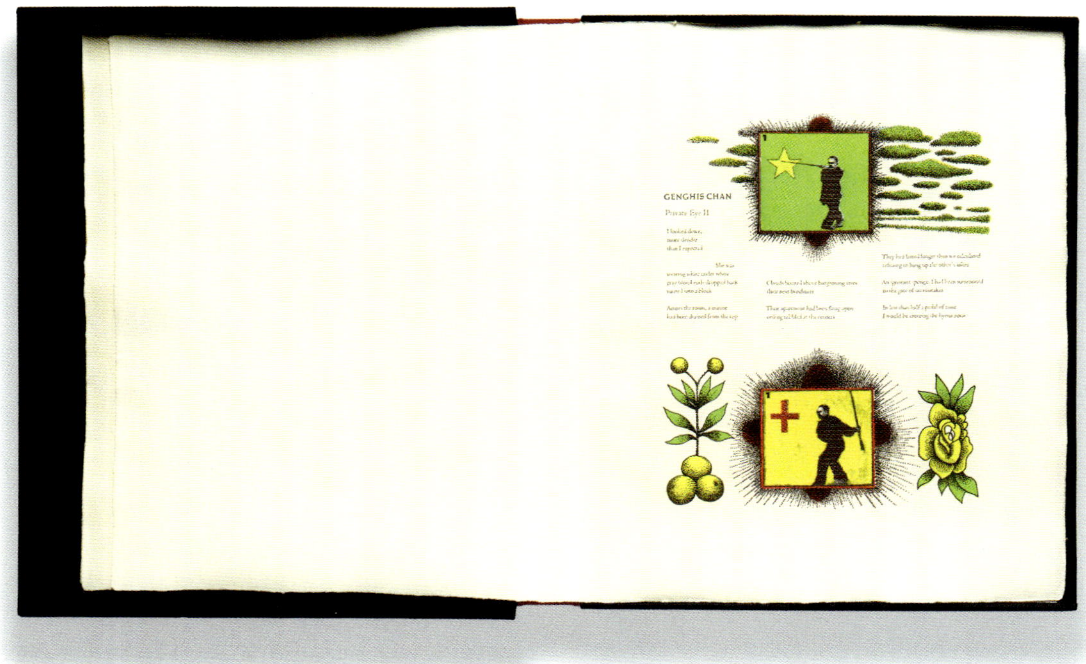

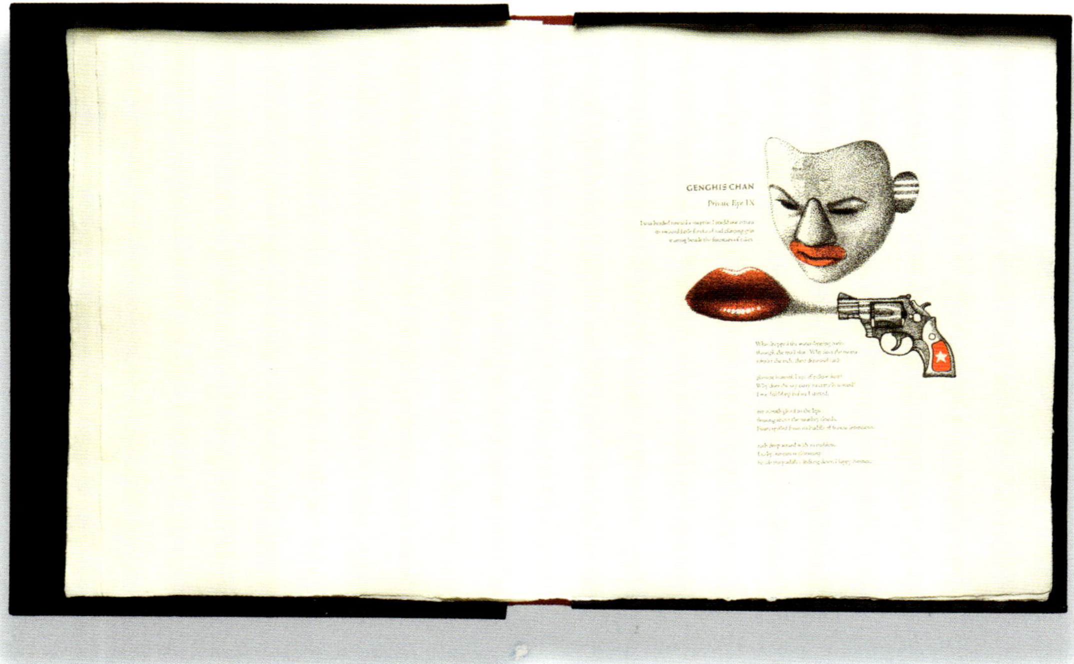

John Yau and Ed Paschke, *Genghis Chan: Private Eye*, 1997

ED PASCHKE

American, 1939 – 2004

Ed Paschke's body of work includes numerous depictions of burlesque queens, wrestlers, and others who could be considered outsiders. He combined a photo-based realism with garish coloration and static-like interruptions.

In his *Artforum* review of a 1987 Paschke exhibition, Yau writes that subjects the artist has explored since the mid-60s include "spectacle, glamour, fantasy, sexual and social identity, and the role played by the media in modern life."[1] While Yau was assessing the artist's pictorial concerns in terms of television, his paintings have a poignant kinship with our computer age and the digital capacities of Photoshop.

Paschke's illustrations that accompany Yau's "Genghis Chan: Private Eye" poems, effectively use a tattoo-informed drawing style with bold outlines, dot patterns, and numerous framing devices, heightening the sense of noir thrills and shifting perspectives in the texts.

"Genghis Chan: Private Eye VI," printed here in its entirety, could easily be the comments of a classic Paschke figure[2]:

I am just another particle cloud gliding across the screen

a swamp chanter doodling on the margins of the abyss

I prefer rat back flames to diplomatic curls

I am the owner of one pockmarked tongue

I park it on the hedge between sure bets and bad business

---

[1] John Yau, "Ed Paschke, Phillis King Gallery / Luhring Augustine & Hodes," *Artforum* 25, no. 9 (May 1987), https://www.artforum.com/events/ed-paschke-3-222057/.

[2] John Yau, "Genghis Chan: Private Eve VI," in *Radiant Silhouette: New & Selected Work, 1974 – 1988* (Santa Rosa, CA: Black Sparrow Press), 194.

NORBERT PRANGENBERG

German, 1949 – 2012

Known for his interest in process and the malleability of different materials, Norbert Prangenberg has made sculptures and paintings in both abstract and figurative modes. He and Yau met in the late 1990s, a decade after the poet-critic had first written about his work.

In a 2010 interview for *The Brooklyn Rail*, he told Yau: "I think when I make a painting, if it's really strong, then the painting has a power. And this power is the message. What can color do? What can structure do?"[1]

These questions can be felt in the artist's contribution to *A Child's Vi[r]gil*, his collaboration with Yau in the form of an elegant portfolio set within a red, yellow, and blue clamshell box. On translucent paper, Prangenberg made colorful ink paintings that have the feel of trails left by insects or tiny Rorschach tests. Yau's language, with a nod to Virgil's *Aeneid*, offers dreamlike images and the joy of manipulating words, like this stack of homophones[2]:

For the moment
the remaining idols

remain idle
in this idyll

set among stones

[1] John Yau, "Norbert Prangenberg with John Yau," *The Brooklyn Rail* (May 2010), https://brooklynrail.org/2010/05/art/ norbert-prangenberg-with-john-yau.

[2] John Yau, "A Child's Vi[r]gil" in *Radiant Silhouette: New & Selected Work, 1974 – 1988* (Santa Rosa, CA: Black Sparrow Press), 6. Originally published by Magnolia Editions in the artist's book *A Child's Vi[r]gil*, 2010.

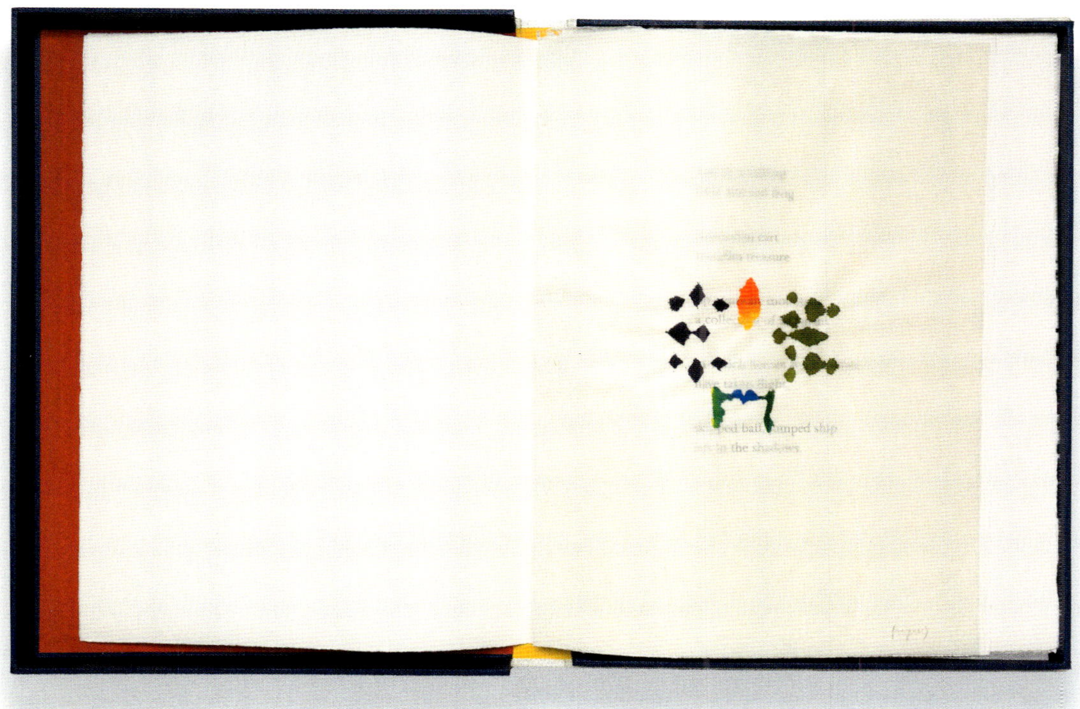

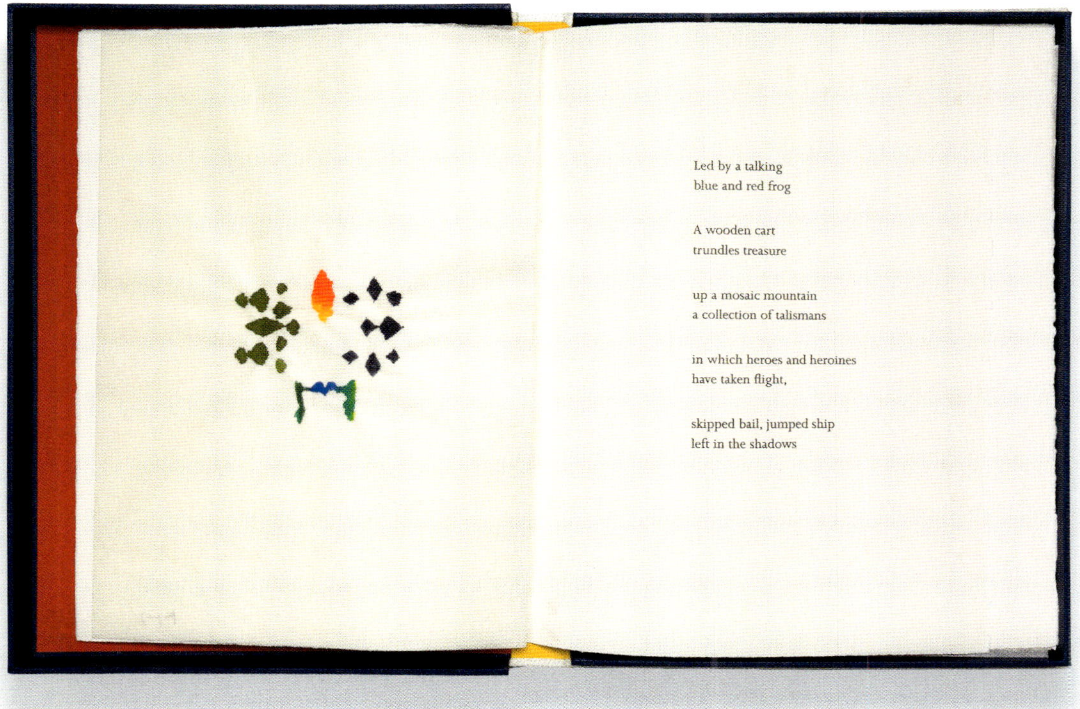

John Yau and Norbert Prangenberg, *A Child's Vi[r]gil,* **2010**

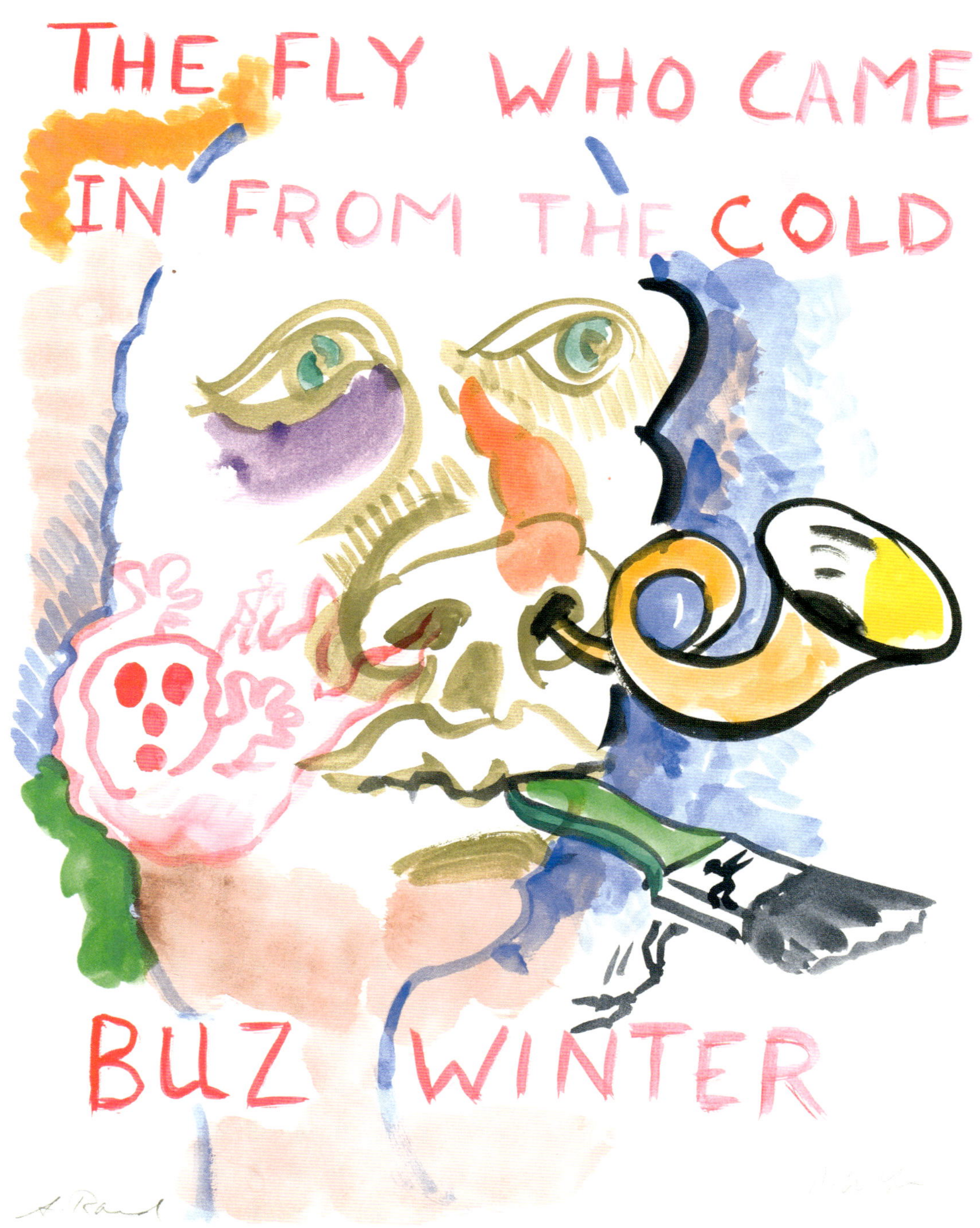

John Yau and Archie Rand, *The Fly Who Came In from the Cold*, 1987

ARCHIE RAND

American, born 1949

Bored during critiques at Bard College, Yau and Archie Rand would pass pieces of paper back and forth to each other, the poet penning smart-alecky phrases and the artist making outrageous images. This juvenile behavior and the laughter it produced was not appreciated. Rand recalls, "The rest of the faculty got really pissed . . . It got back to us that some people in the college community, I don't remember whether it was faculty or students, referred to us as either John Rand or Archie Yau. We became this inseparable couple."[1] Building on this experience, the men decided to start working on more formal collaborations.

Rand is known to have an eclectic set of interests and the ability to synthesize them effortlessly. Yau summarized this in a 1985 *Artforum* review: "Rand's passions include a cappella R & B groups from the 50s, early Florentine and Sienese art, stock magazine photographs, bebop jazz musicians, the New York School of painting, and obscure portraits by American regionalists."[2] Add to this: Jewish history and themes, religious and secular literature, and a love of poetry. This makes him an ideal collaborator for Yau, whose tastes are decidedly catholic, and who finds pleasure and inspiration in the deliverables of both high and low culture.

They have produced a bevy of painted and printed works, including *The Alphabet Paintings*, an A–Z collection of images (portraits, buildings, drapery, ships, food) and enigmatic language, rendered on gold canvas. Cultural references abound, including several nods to Asian actors and athletes (Anna May Wong, Bruce Lee, James Shigeta, Speedy Dado), art history (Max Jacob, Wifredo Lam, Pablo Picasso, the Cedar Bar), and tabloid sex scandals of the 1990s (John Wayne Bobbitt and Joey Buttafuoco). Some letters correspond to their associated phrases, as in D for *Donkey Maw Stew*; while others are more elusive, like Y for *Jail the Seven Fleas*. The language on all twenty-six canvases benefits from being sounded out for maximum effect, like the dubious advertisement for the letter I: *Need a facelift? Call 1800 IOU SHIT*.

Yau and Rand spared no effort in satirizing the ancient Egyptian *Book of the Dead*, the collection of texts and magic spells intended to assist a dead person in their journey through the underworld and into the afterlife. Their elaborate production, *100 More Jokes from the Book of The Dead* (a red clamshell box containing nine chapters of ten intaglio etchings each) features invented book covers, nimbly drawn figures and objects, and witty non sequiturs. Rand states, "It's probably closer to individual panels of a graphic novel. In fact, I think of it as graphic poetry, but not in a considered or didactic or declarative way; but in a way that had to evolve naturally into its own physicality. Art Spiegelman talks about this,

---

[1] Archie Rand, interview with the author, September 29, 2022.

[2] John Yau, "Archie Rand, The Contemporary Arts Center," *Artforum* 23, no. 8 (April 1985), https://www.artforum.com/events/archie-rand-3-224449/.

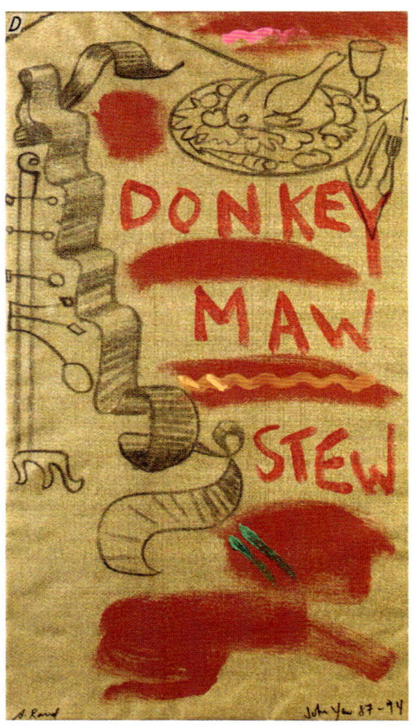

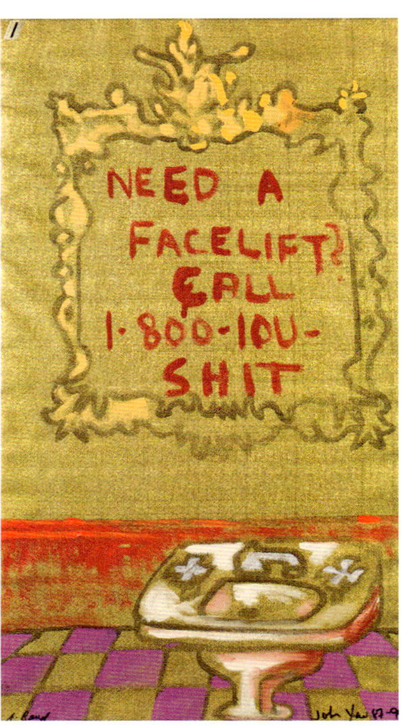

John Yau and Archie Rand, *The Alphabet Paintings*, 1987–94

about how potentially interchangeable the units of a cartoon are. If you just mixed them up, they make a different sense. But what he says, what he's implying, is that each frame has its own individual capacity."[3]

The title, *100 More Jokes from the Book of The Dead,* implies that a previous book was published, but this is sadly not the case. Who knows if jokes would help navigate what comes after this mortal coil, but as a Borscht Belt comedian might say, "They couldn't hurt."

It should not be lost on us that the underworld can refer to the realm of the dead and to participants in organized crime. In the drawings for *Mug City Moves*, Yau and Rand indulge their shared enthusiasm for the noir genre with its inclination towards cynicism. Quickly sketched detectives and denizens of the street make comments including "Did you say bamboo or bimbo," and "A modest man never stalks himself."

In a comment that can be applied to all of their collaborations, Yau says, "One of the first things I decided was that the writing had to be as fast as the image and it had to relate tangentially. Obliquely. You couldn't take them apart . . . It was like a sentence was too slow for anything Archie was doing. What does it mean to try and compress language or make a line change literally as it's going along, turn back on itself, undermine itself, crumble by the end?"[4]

---

[3] Rand, interview with author, September 29, 2022.

[4] John Yau, interview with the author, February 26, 2023.

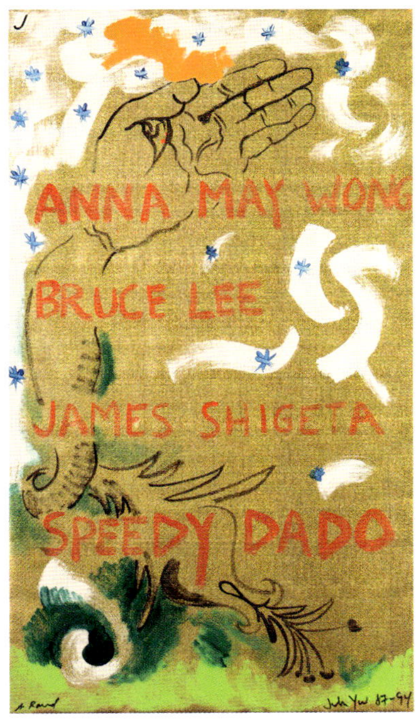

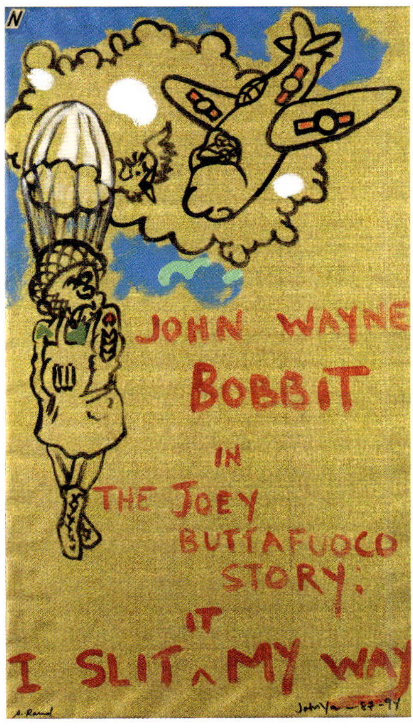

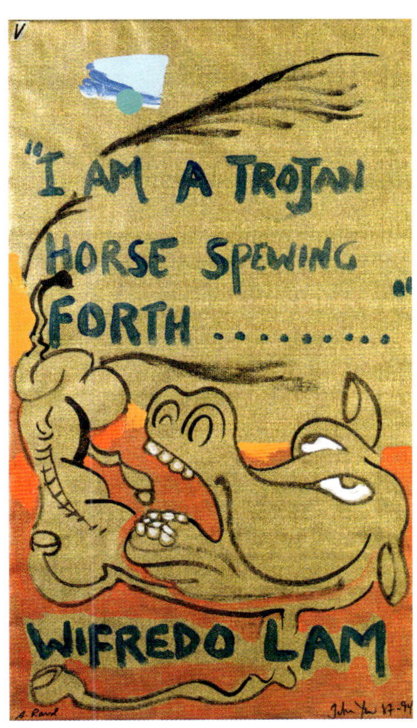

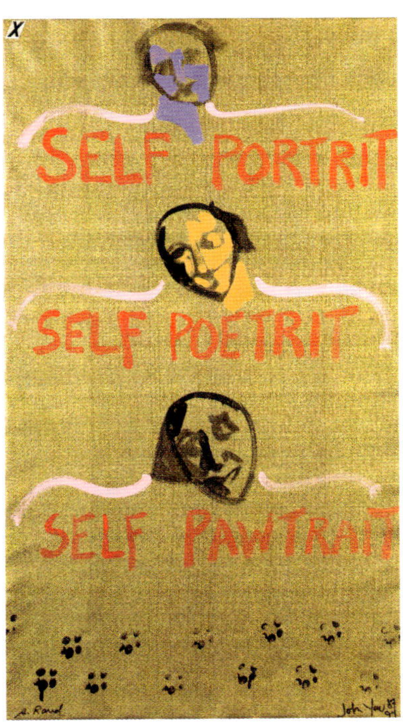

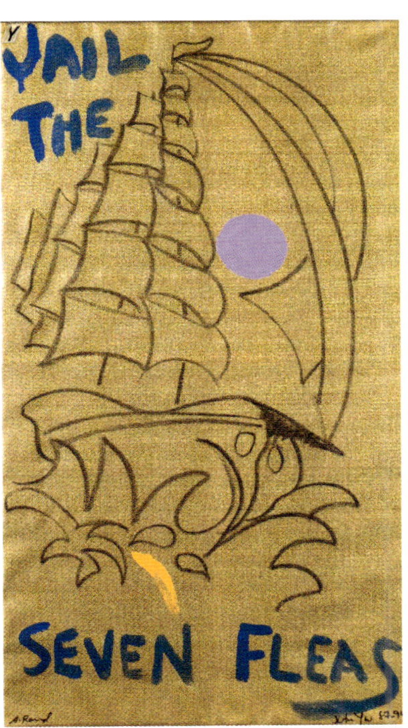

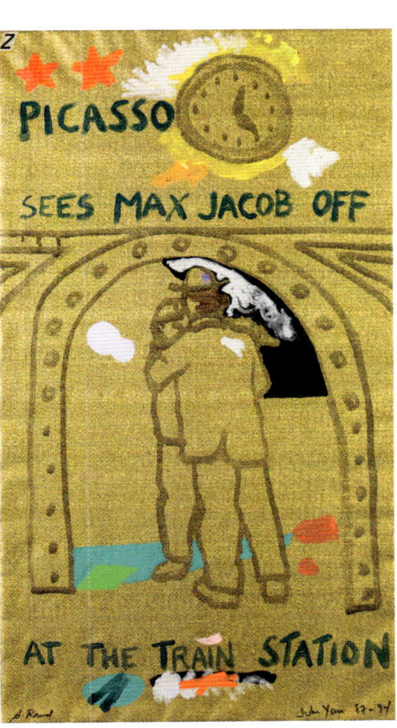

John Yau and Archie Rand, *The Alphabet Paintings*, 1987–94

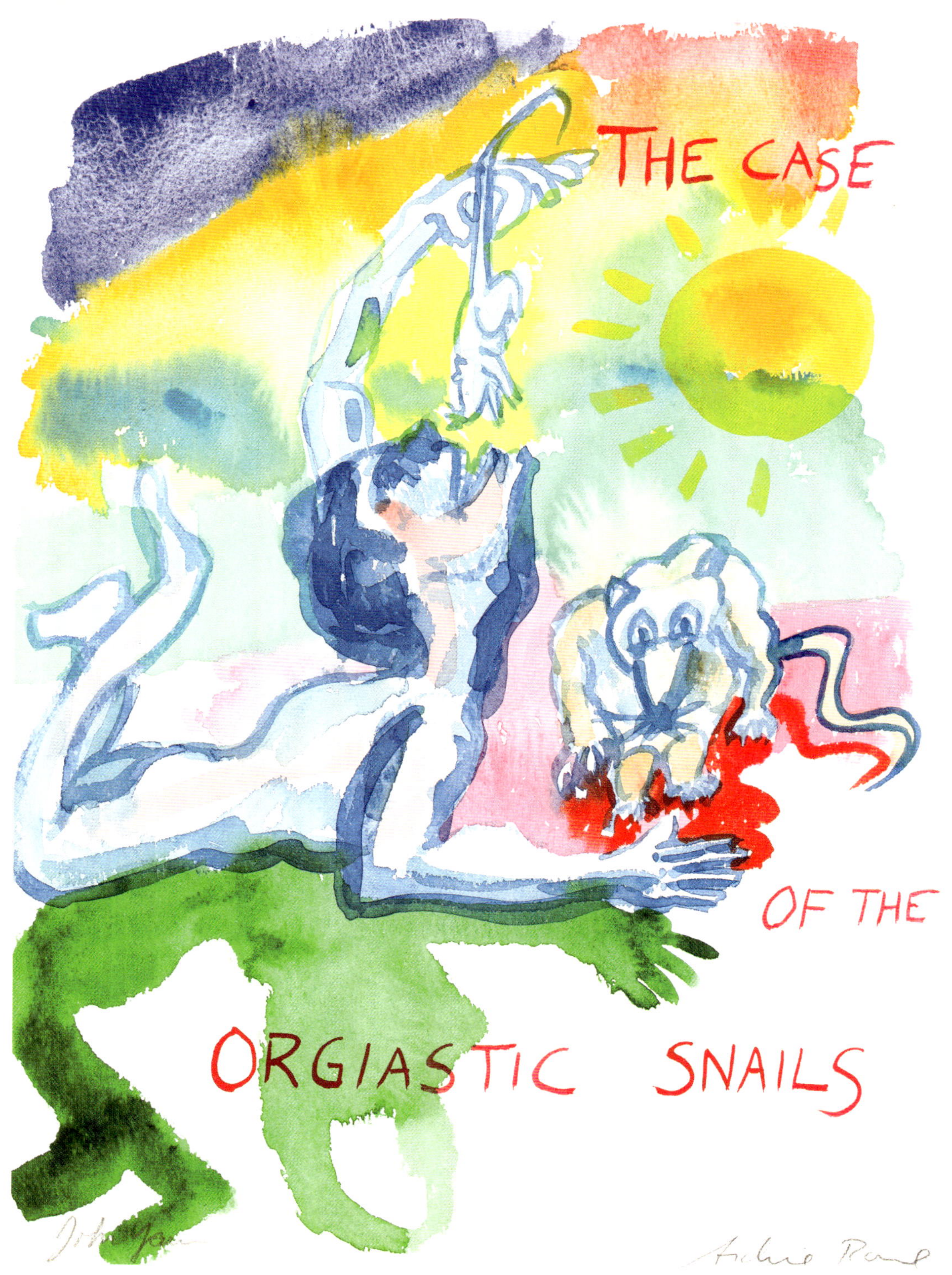

John Yau and Archie Rand, *The Case of the Orgiastic Snails*, 1987

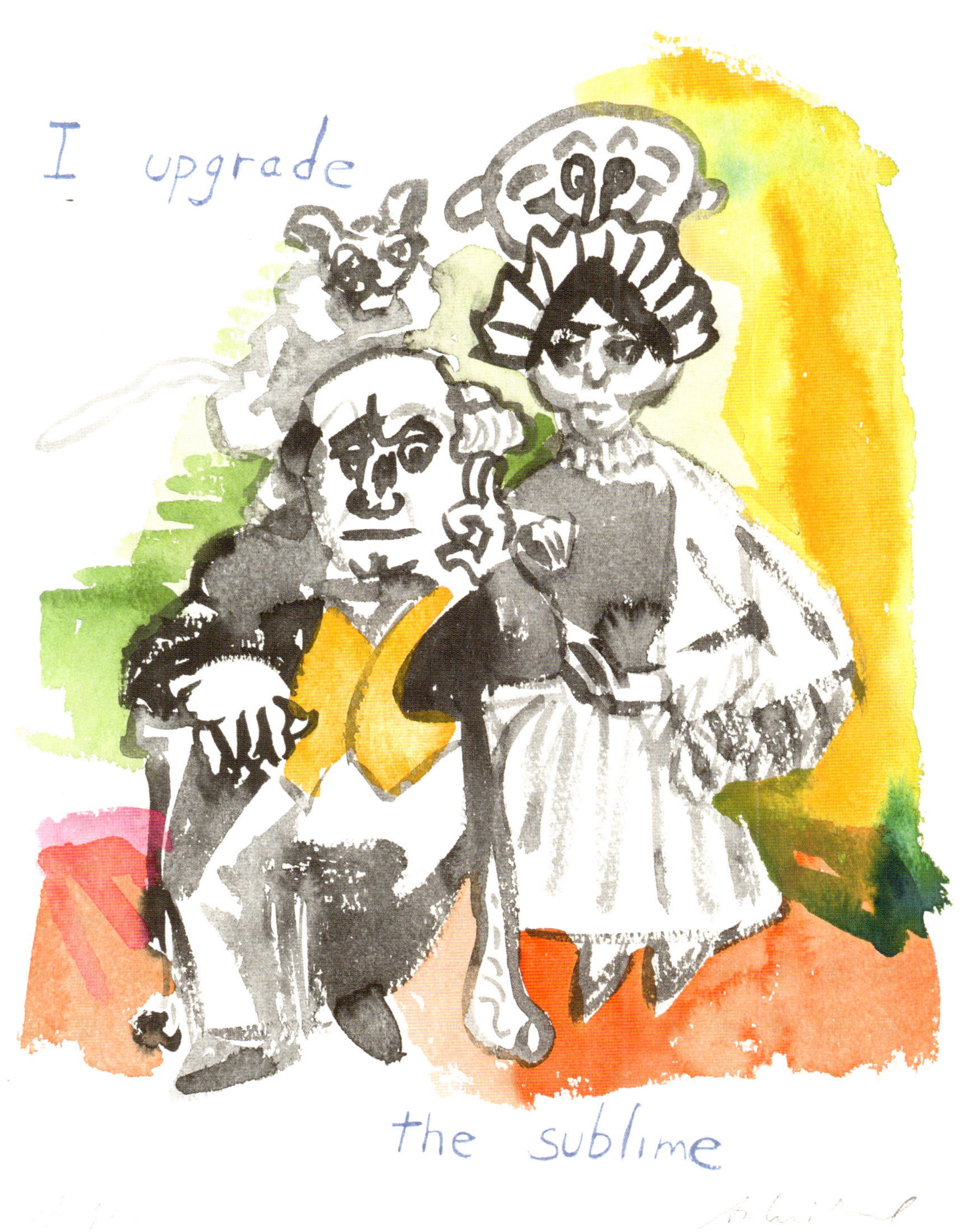

John Yau and Archie Rand, *I Upgrade the Sublime*, 1987

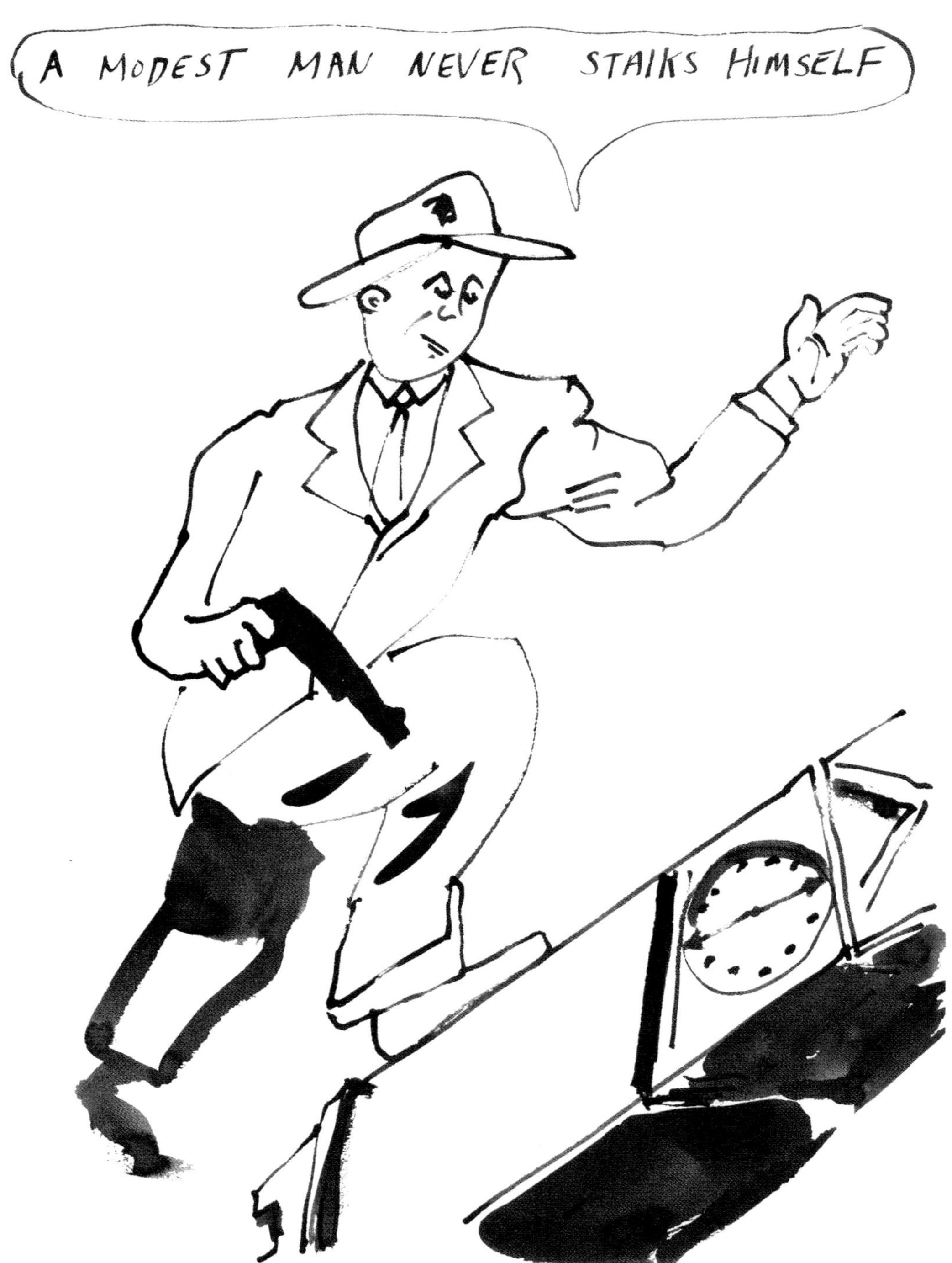

John Yau and Archie Rand, *A Modest Man* from *Mug City Moves*, 1991

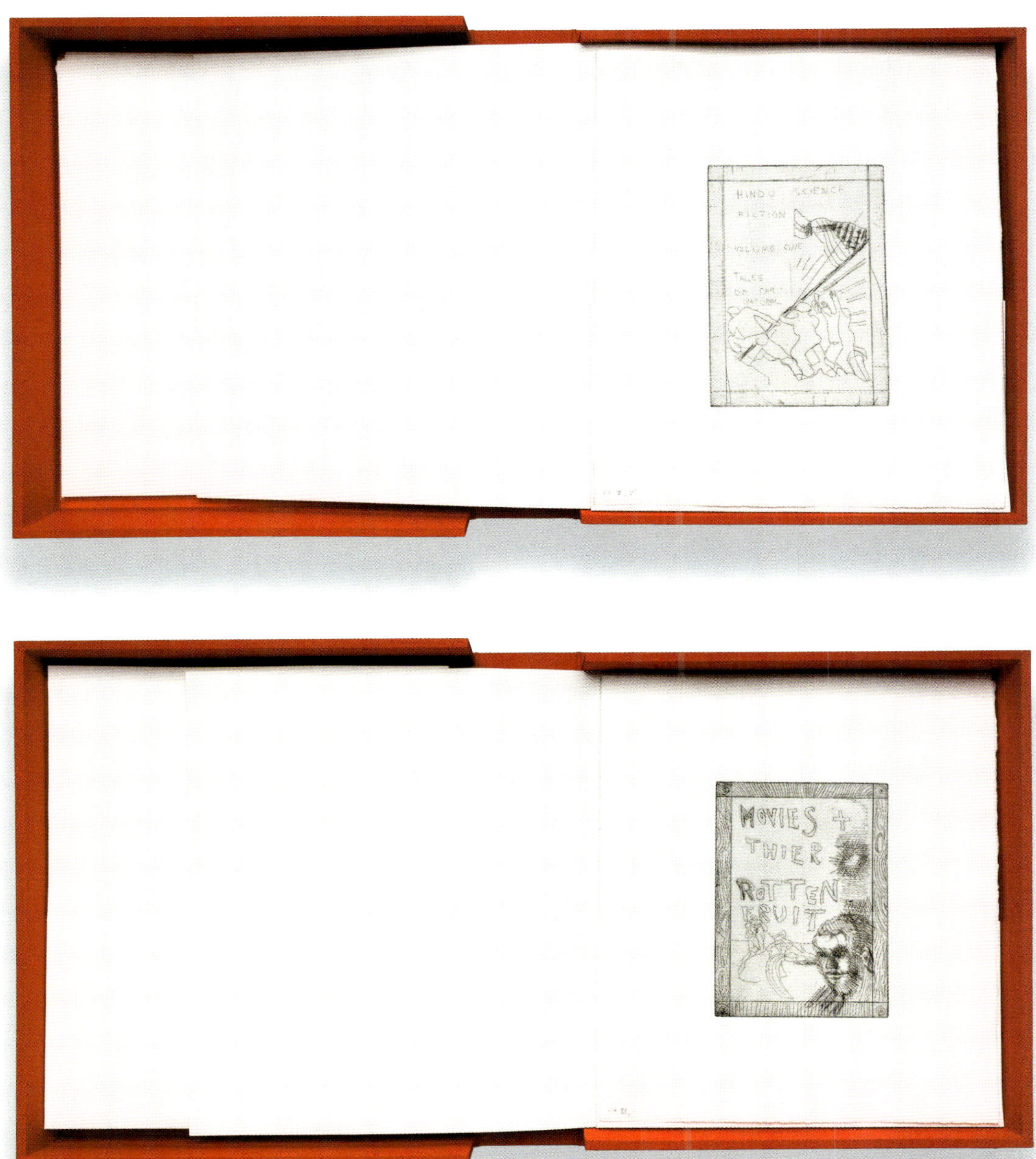

John Yau and Archie Rand, *100 More Jokes from the Book of the Dead,* **1997–2000**

SYDNEY JEAN REISEN

American, born 1981

Sydney Jean Reisen became friends with Yau after she sat in on one of his graduate school classes at the Mason Gross School of the Arts at Rutgers University, and they reconnected some years later. Reisen has finished converting her garage into a print shop and during a correspondence, she offered to print something for Yau. He sent her the poem "Catullus Sails to China."

Catullus was a popular poet in the Renaissance, and his work influenced many subsequent writers including Andrew Marvell, Ben Johnson, and Christopher Marlowe. Yau's writing imagines a trip that Catullus never made, and Reisen internalized his text in a way that informed her choices about the book's structure, materials, and the printing techniques to be used. She writes, "Because *Catullus Sails to China* is a voyage over water, I thought I would make a book that felt like water, or as much like water as a book can feel."[1]

Commenting on his own process, Yau recalls, "My kid was studying Catullus in high school, and they were talking about translations. So I thought, what if I took Catullus's poems? They're all online. And I cut them up and send them to Google Translate. I translate them to Russian. Then to German and to Swahili, and then I get it back. What do I do with the thing I get back?"[2]

---

[1] Sydney Jean Reisen, email message to author, July 4, 2022.

[2] John Yau, interview with the author, June 21, 2023.

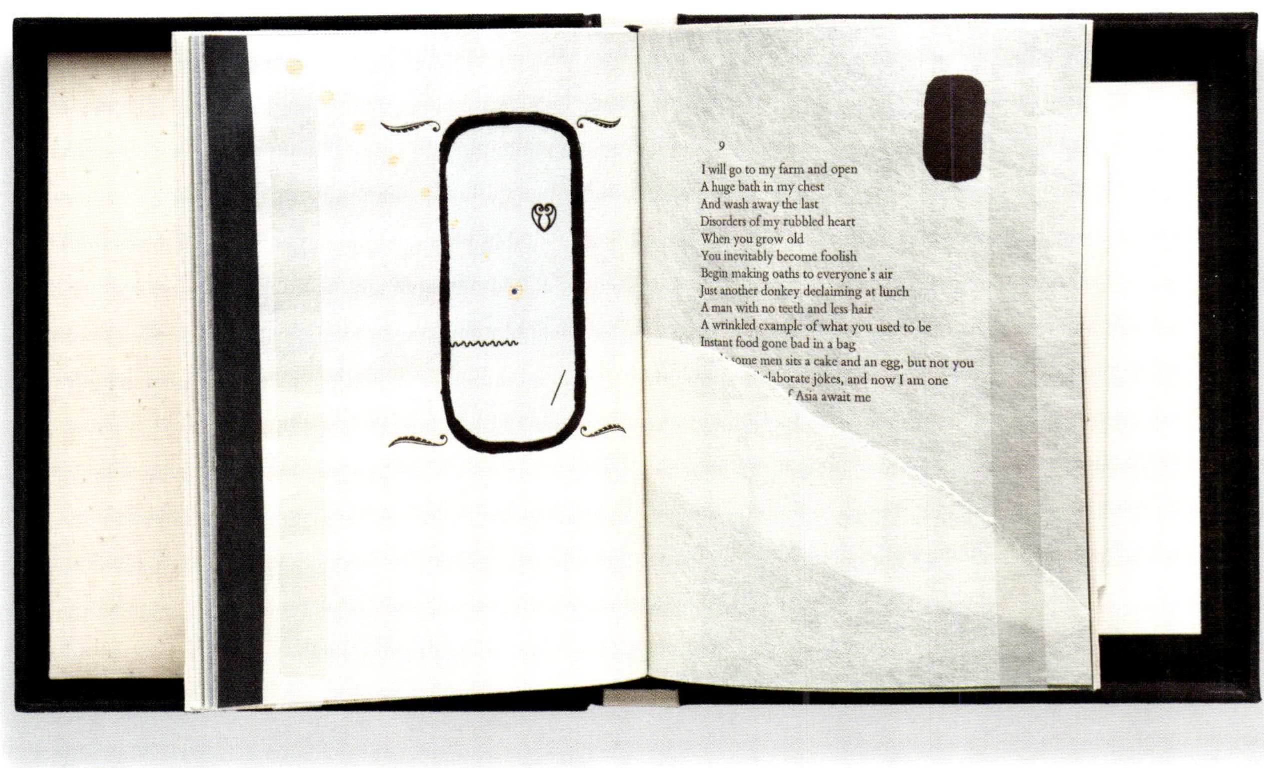

John Yau and Sydney Jean Reisen, *Catullus Sails to China*, 2020

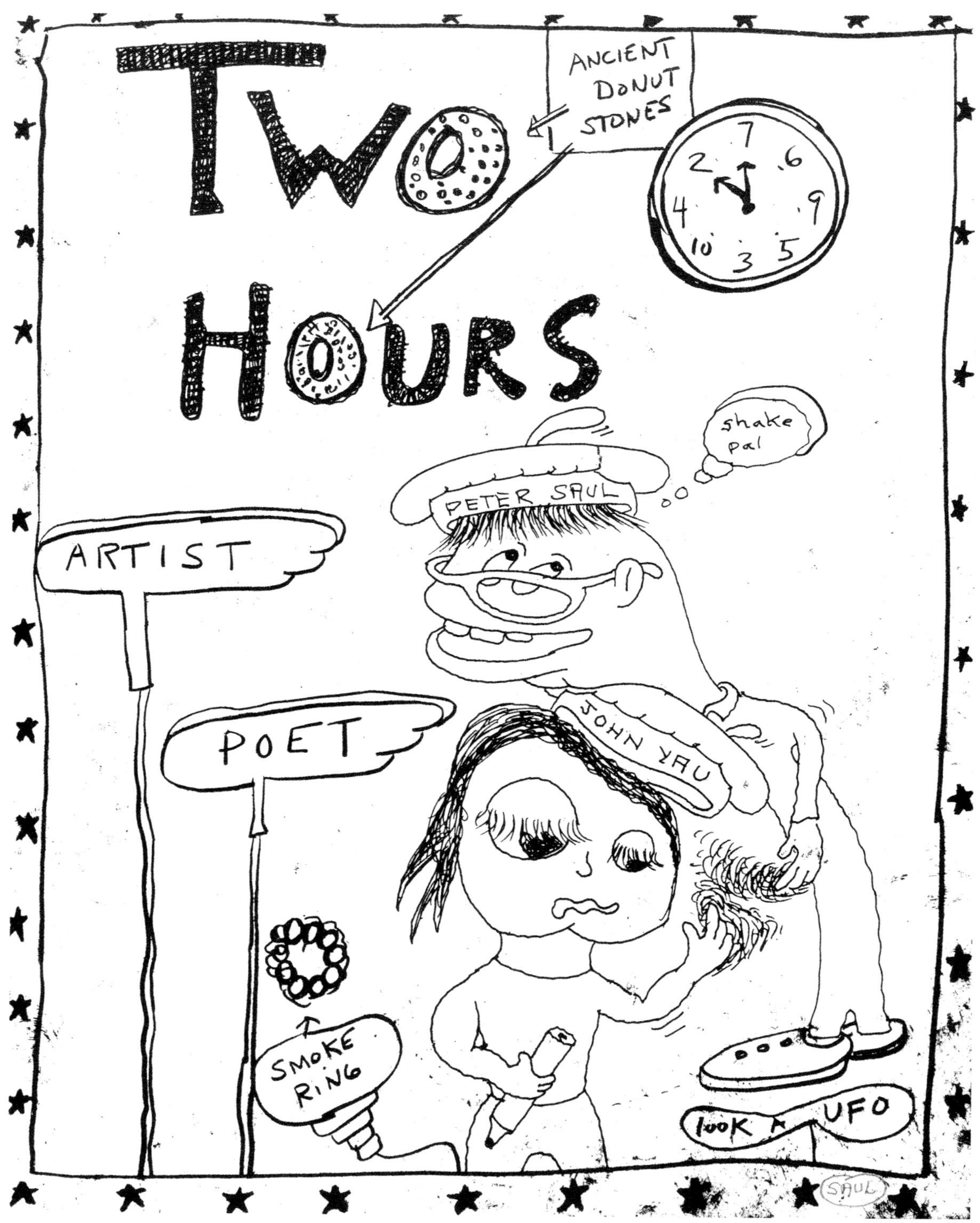

John Yau and Peter Saul, *Two Hours*, 1994

PETER SAUL

American, born 1934

What can be achieved in two hours? This was the amount of time Yau and Peter Saul had between student critiques at the University of Texas at Austin in 1994. The painter is known for his exuberant canvases featuring cartoon protagonists (Disney characters, superheroes, politicians, and various American misanthropes) engaging in bawdy and violent acts. He was a taxing partner for Yau, especially when he told the poet, "You have to do some drawing because I want to do some writing."[1]

Two Hours, their portfolio of nine lithographs, contains dense compositions of male and female figures who show their genitalia, cry, pass gas, unspool a roll of toilet paper, split their own heads apart with a hatchet, and variously express themselves. Speech bubbles and thought balloons contain their confessions and lamentations, and other language serves as titles for, or synopses of, each image.

Given the vitality of their collaboration, it is entertaining to think about what else Yau and Saul might have done together. Yau recalled, "Peter decided, more recently, that we should do another set of prints. No printmaker said they wanted to do it. This goes back to what happens to collaborations because they're unclassifiable. Seems to me the clearest example of 'they're not even going to let us have fun because they can't make money off of them.' It would be like opening up an ice cream stand in Death Valley."[2]

---

[1] John Yau, interview with the author, February 26, 2023.

[2] John Yau, interview with the author, September 27, 2022.

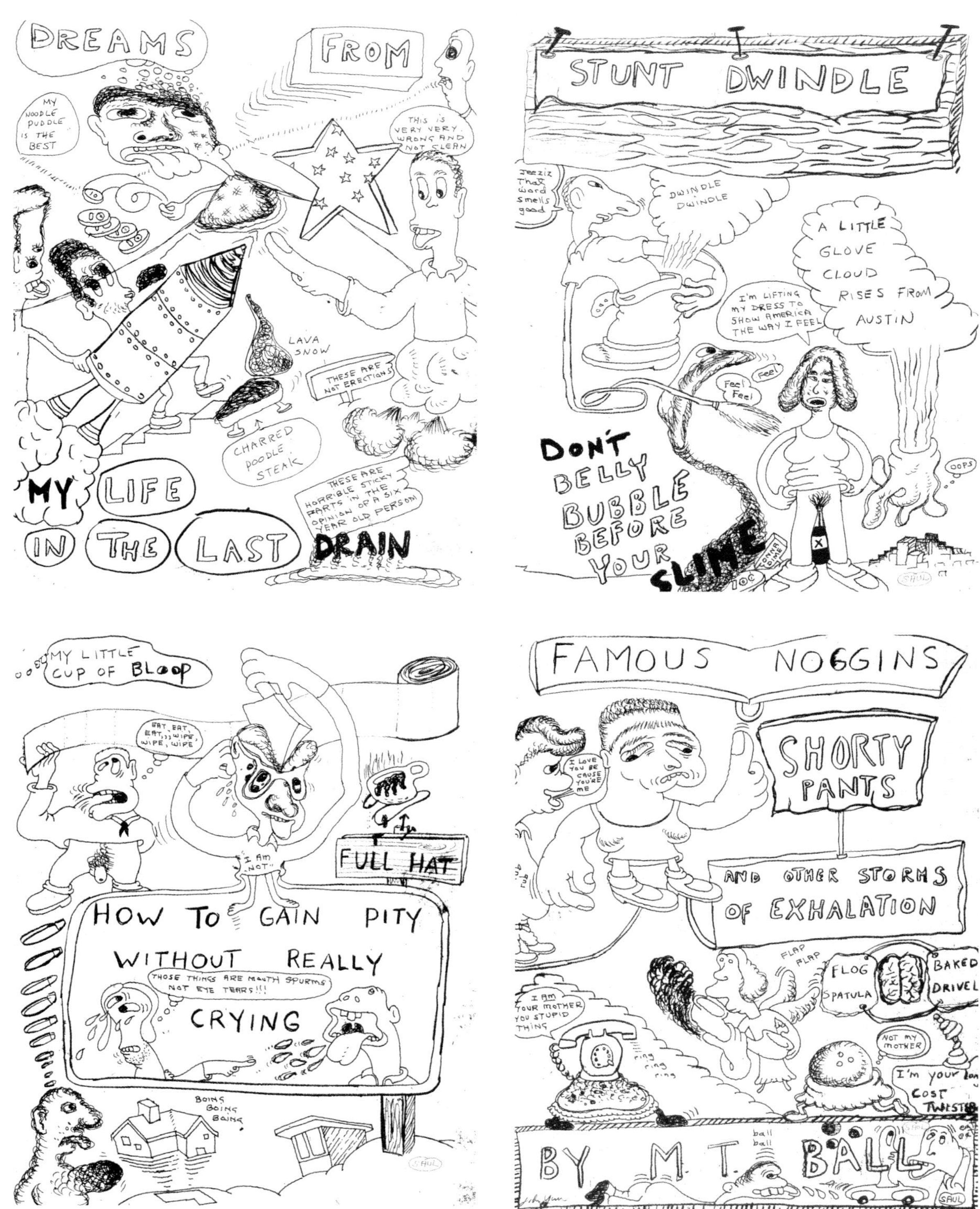

John Yau and Peter Saul, *Two Hours*, 1994

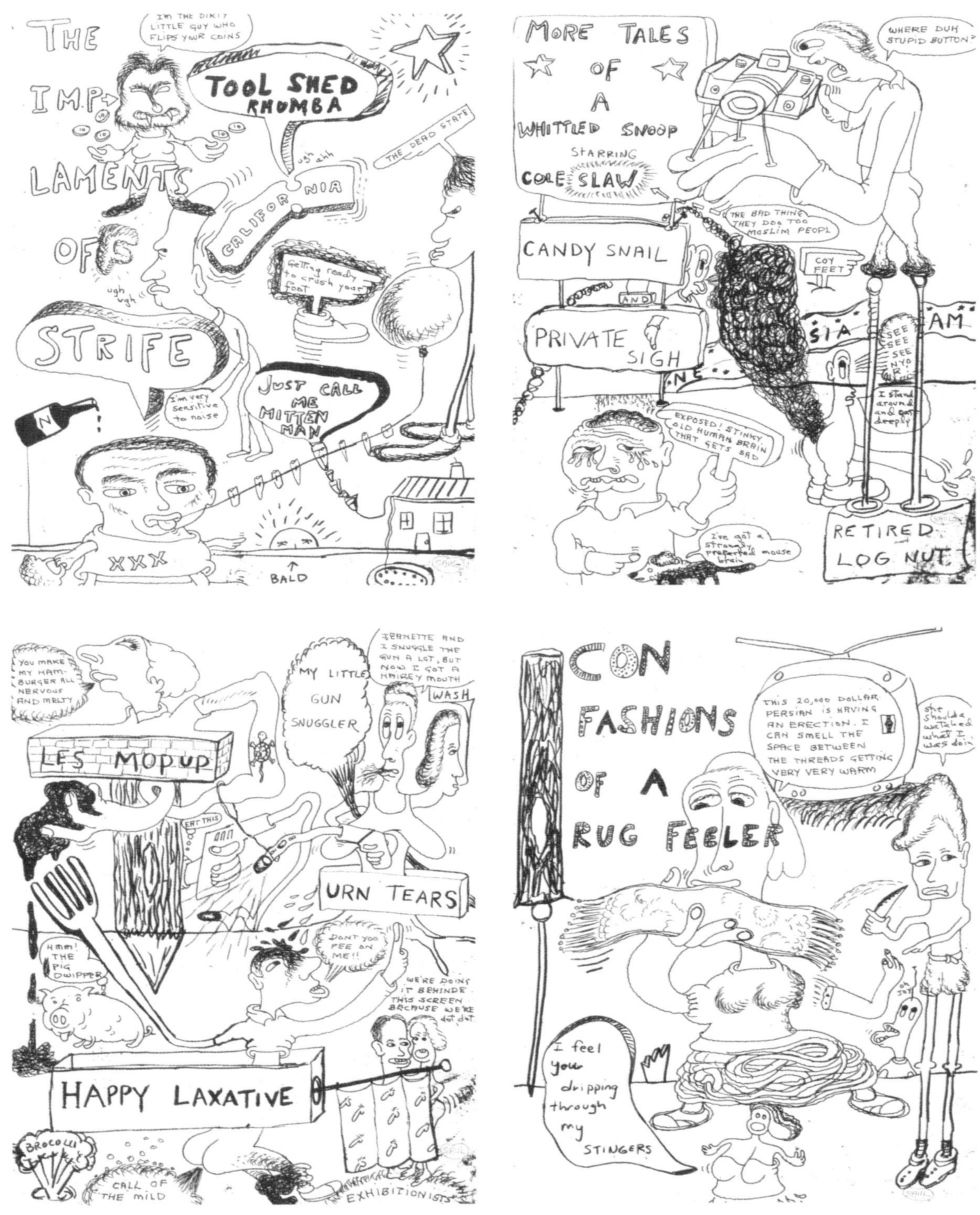

THE IMP LAMENTS OF STRIFE
I'M THE DIRTY LITTLE GUY WHO FLIPS YOUR COINS
TOOL SHED RHUMBA
THE DEAD STATE
ugh ahh
CALIFORNIA
ugh ugh
Getting ready to crush your foot
I'm very sensitive to noise
JUST CALL ME MITTEN MAN
N
XXX
BALD
MORE TALES OF A WHITTLED SNOOP STARRING COLE SLAW
WHERE DUH STUPID BUTTON?
THE BAD THING THEY DOO TOO MOSLIM PEOPL
CANDY SNAIL
COY FEET
PRIVATE SIGH
AND
NE SIA AM
SEE SEE SEE NYO AR
EXPOSED! STINKY OLD HUMAN BRAIN THAT GETS BAD
I stand around and act deeply
I've got a strongly preferred mouse brain
RETIRED LOG NUT
YOU MAKE MY HAMBURGER ALL NERVOUS AND MELTY
MY LITTLE GUN SNUGGLER
JEANETTE AND I SNUGGLE THE GUN A LOT, BUT NOW I GOT A HAIREY MOUTH
WASH
LES MOPUP
EAT THIS
URN TEARS
Hmm! THE PIG DWIPPER
DON'T YOO PEE ON ME!!
WE'RE DOING IT BEHINDE THIS SCREEN BECAUSE WE'RE dat dat
HAPPY LAXATIVE
BROCOLLI
CALL OF THE MILD
EXHIBITIONISTS
CON FASHIONS OF A RUG FEELER
THIS 20,000 DOLLAR PERSIAN IS HAVING AN ERECTION. I CAN SMELL THE SPACE BETWEEN THE THREADS GETTING VERY VERY WARM
She should a wetted what I was doin
I feel your dripping through my STINGERS

HANNS SCHIMANSKY

German, born 1949

Hanns Schimasky was trained as an agronomist engineer and is a largely self-taught artist. His principal medium is drawing, and he experiments with pencil, graphite, oil stick, chalk, and ink in precise ways.

In a 2012 essay for *Hyperallergic*, Yau describes his experiences with Schimansky and clarifies his process: "By establishing a particular, often awkward orientation between the medium and the surface, the artist goes a long way toward denying any kind of fluidity or mastery. By holding the instrument at an acute angle to the surface in order to make downward moving lines or rolling the drawing tool to make a twisting, rough-edged line, Schimansky undermines the movement of a pencil or paint stick across the paper. Within these and other processes, he often stops and starts, with each stop signaling a transition from one kind of line or shape to another. In some drawings, it's as if different abstract hieroglyphs have invaded each other's territory, forming a new hybrid language."[1]

Their collaboration, *Inside Machine*, features eleven intaglio prints by the artist which have the qualities described above; Yau's poem, "Storied fibs piled high," hand-written by Schimansky over seven pages; and a CD featuring eleven solo improvisations on double bass by Peter Kowald.

---

[1] John Yau, "What Happens When There is No Center and It Cannot Hold?, *Hyperallergic*, October 7, 2012, https:// hyperallergic.com/58075/what-happens-when-there-is-no-center-and-it-cannot-hold/.

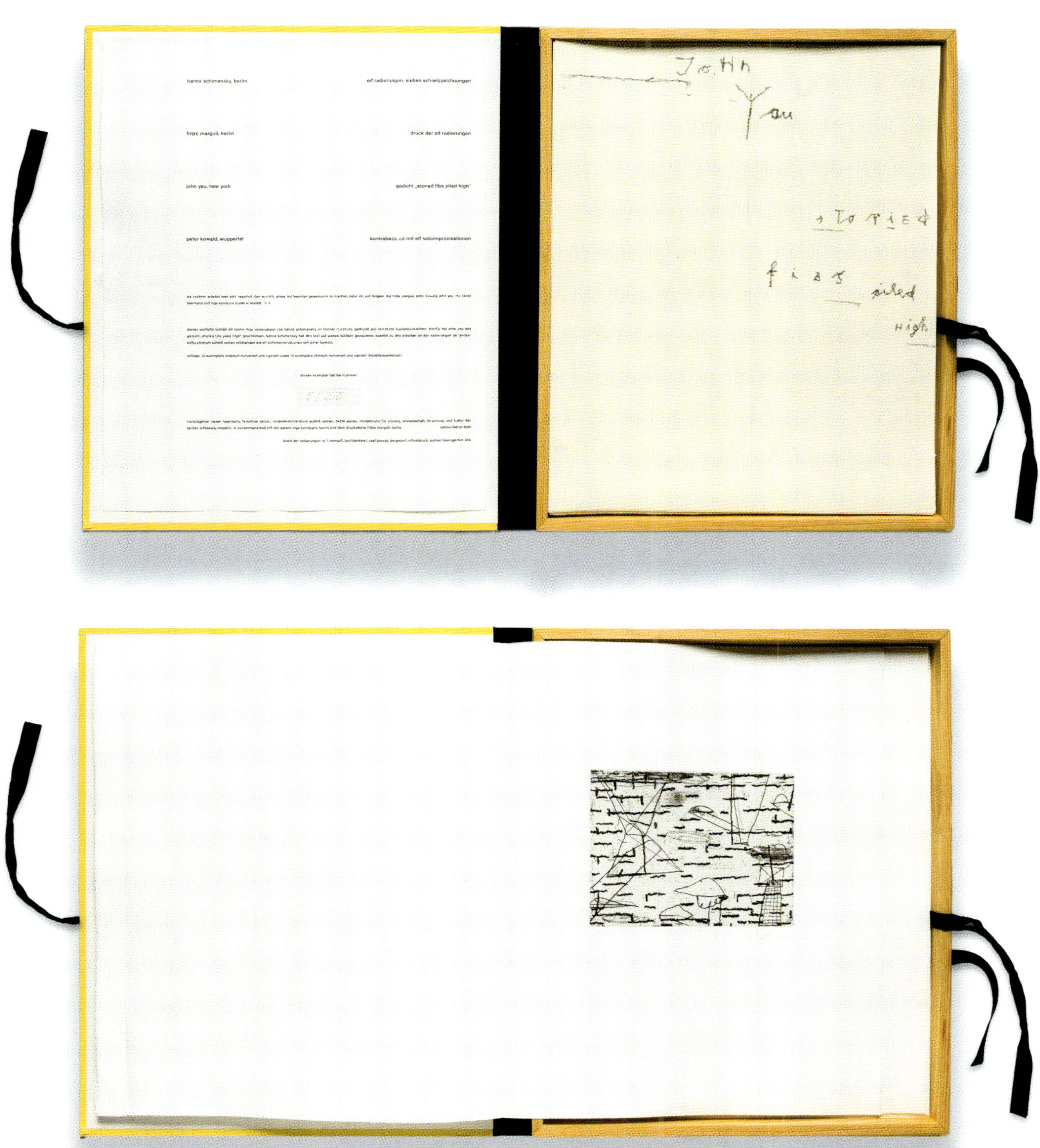

John Yau and Hanns Schimansky, *Inside Machine*, 2000

JENNY SCOBEL

American, born 1955

In 1992, Yau and Jenny Scobel made work together for the exhibition, *10 Steps*, organized by Horodner Romley Gallery, Muranushi Lederman Productions, and independent curator Saul Ostrow. Installed at the respective venues in the SoHo gallery district, it included a wide range of art and ephemera selected to parody a guide to connoisseurship produced by Sotheby's auction house. The publication offered advice for potential collectors and addressed considerations such as authenticity, provenance, rarity, subject matter, condition, and aesthetic quality.

Yau and Scobel utilized a popular toy known as the Magic Slate. It features a clipboard-like construction, with a sheet of translucent plastic film covering a rectangle of black wax paper mounted to cardboard; and it comes with a blunt stylus for writing or drawing. Making marks on the plastic film causes it to stick to the underlying wax to reveal the lines. To erase, one simply lifts the plastic which detaches it from the wax, and like magic, the lines disappear!

Neigh/Cud renders the toy's function obsolete, with the collaborators painting over the moveable parts and adding a faux woodgrain frame to create a playful barnyard lesson in phonics. One might use their altered object to explain that a neigh is the communicative sound a horse makes, and cud is the partially digested food a cow chews after it has been regurgitated from their stomach. Spoken aloud, the two words form a third: naked.

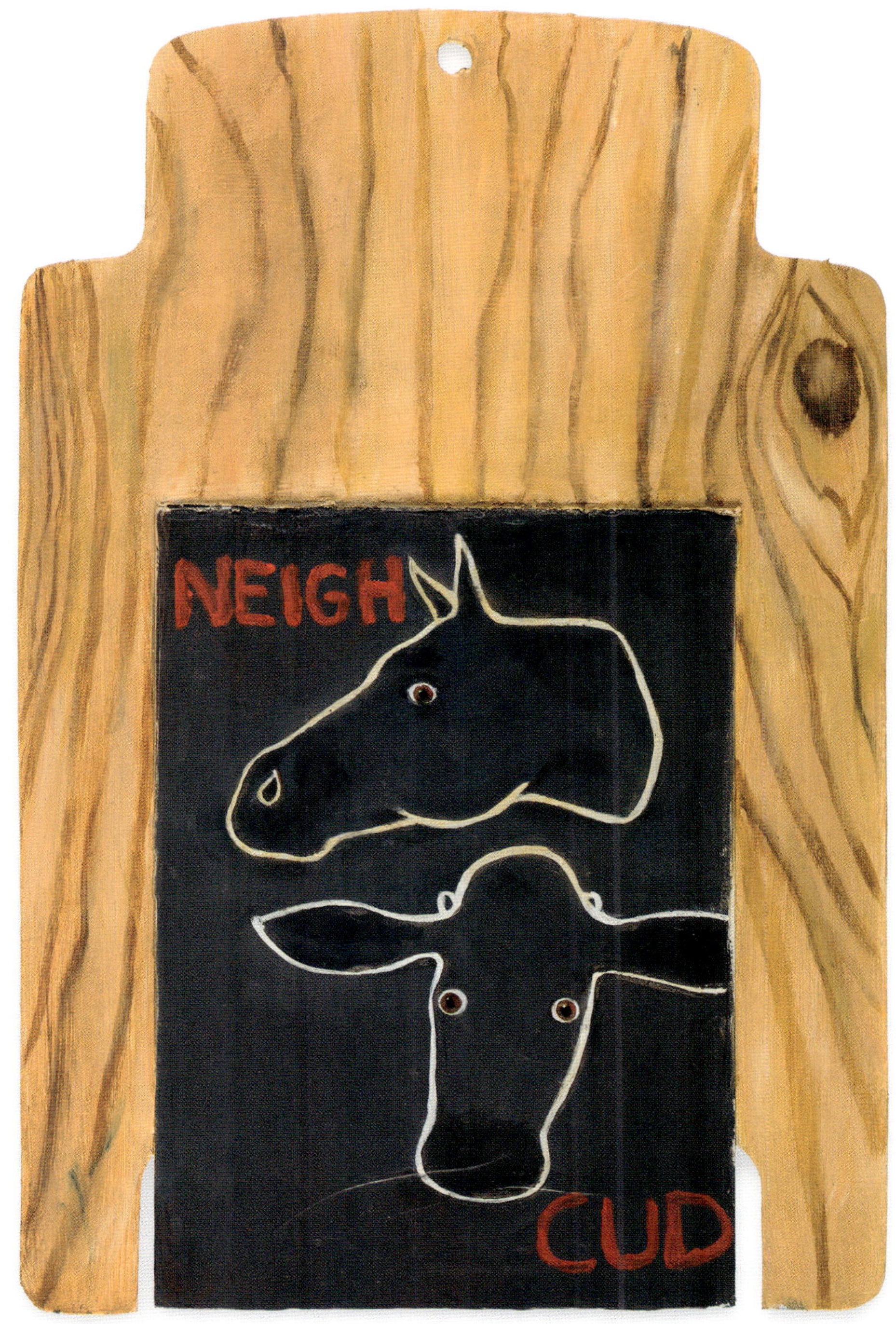

John Yau and Jenny Scobel, *Neigh/Cud*, 1992

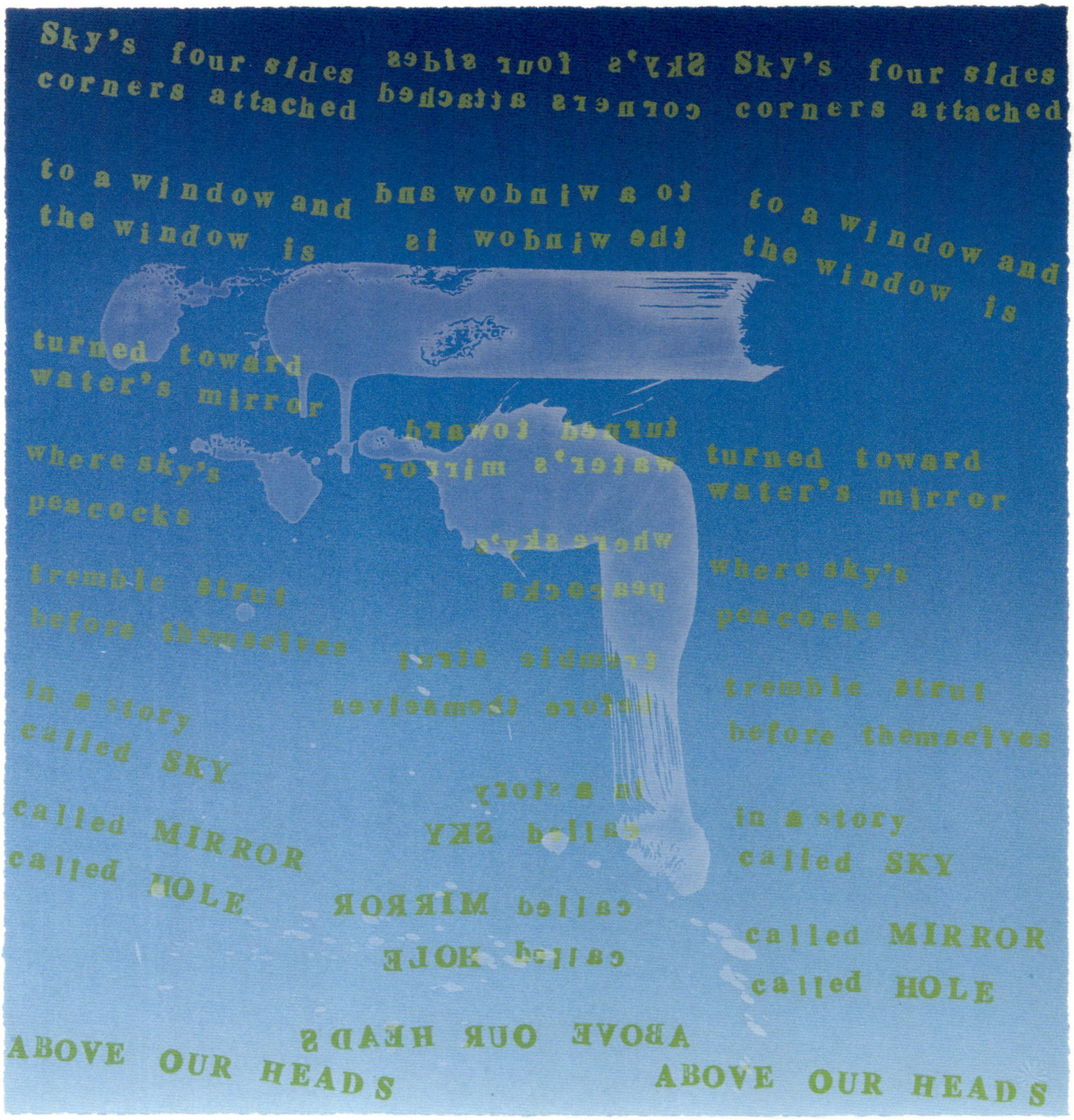

John Yau and Pat Steir, *Sky's Four Sides*, 2000

PAT STEIR

American, born 1940

In the early 1970s, Pat Steir became known for canvases filled with iconographic symbols, most prominently roses (with their literary associations to Shakespeare and Gertrude Stein, and as representations of love and passion) which she would routinely cancel out with purposeful X marks.

Representation and refinement would continue to be key issues for the artist into the 1980s when she developed her signature practice of pouring and flinging thin layers of paint onto canvas to create cascading physical events. Inspired by her study of Japanese and Chinese painting, and philosophies of Taoism and Buddhism, these dramatic "waterfalls" are not so much paintings of nature, but a synthesis of action and image.

For her collaboration with Yau, published by Graphicstudio at the University of South Florida, Steir continued her painterly pursuits, making distinct brushstroke gestures on the different colored grounds.

Yau recalls, "I know she's going to make waterfalls. The words go down the page, the waterfall goes down the page. Let's not be redundant. Let's see what else could happen. It was a little mischievous on my part. [The printers] said, 'We'll make the letters any way you want.' I decided I wanted to print some of the words backwards because the image seemed to me very quick. I was in a way, thinking, I'm gonna slow down how you see a waterfall by making the words backwards."[1]

Yau's plan for the treatment of letters and words does in fact make the viewing of the four images, and the reading of his integrated poems, into a more languid and satisfying act.

---

[1] John Yau, interview with the author, February 26, 2023.

John Yau and Pat Steir, *Sky's First Poem*, 2000

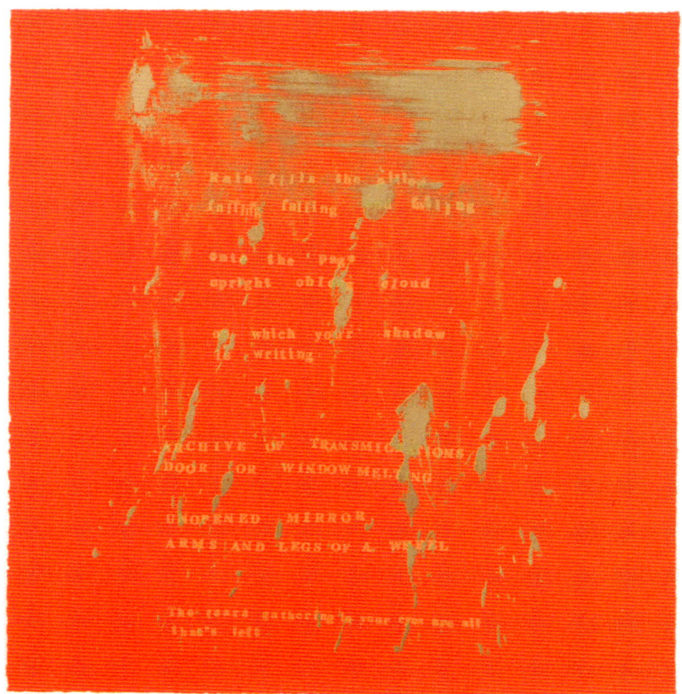

John Yau and Pat Steir, *Rain Pillow*, 2000

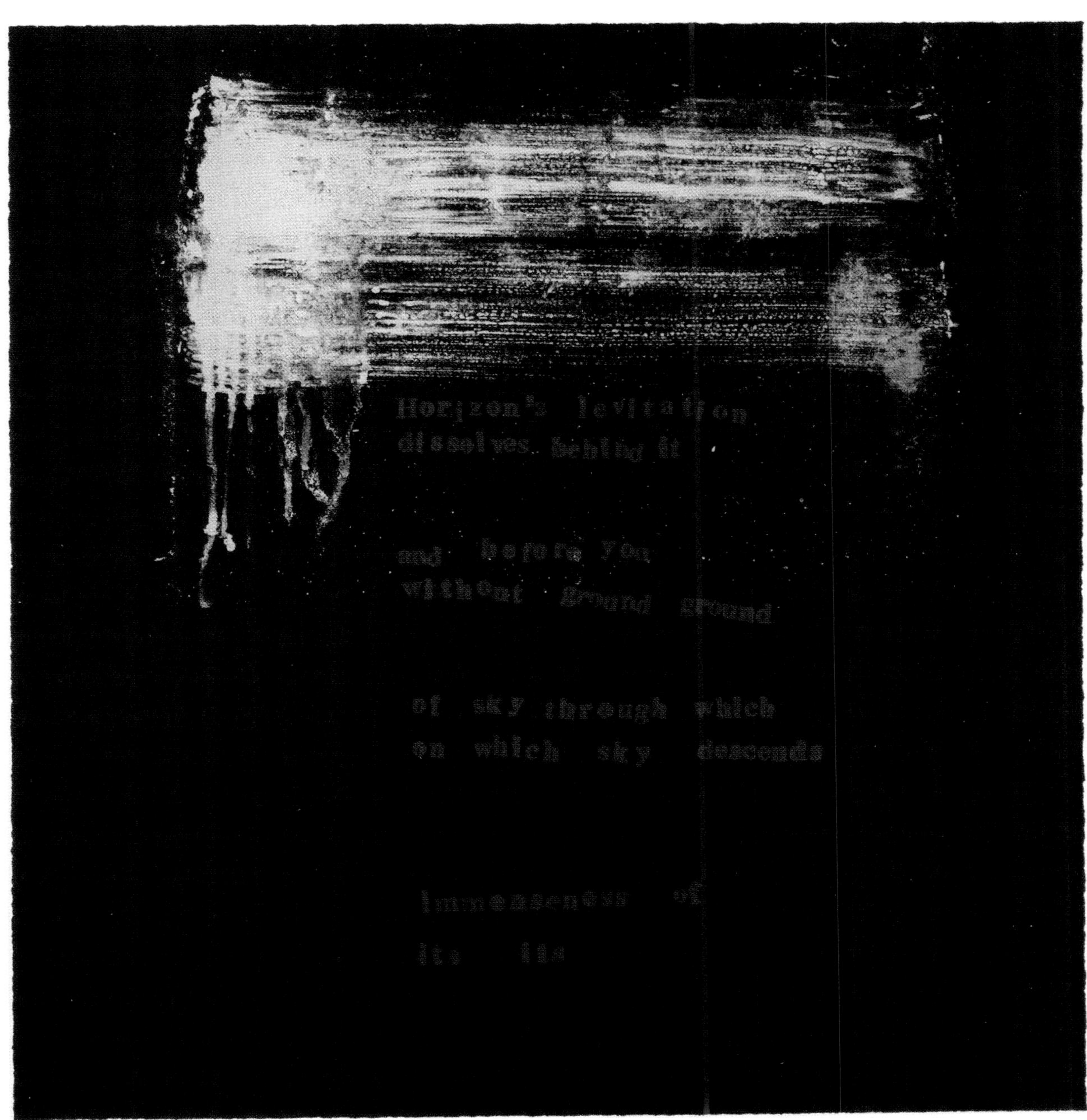

John Yau and Pat Steir, *Horizon's Levitation*, 2000

ALISON ELIZABETH TAYLOR

American, born 1973

Alison Elizabeth Taylor's collaborations with Yau take the form of her illustrations of his lines of text in reverie-like pencil drawings with an occasional collage element.

In *He got tired of being force fed unidentifiable lumps*, Taylor uses inexpensive wood grain contact paper for the bark of two trees; a harbinger of the fact that she would become known for using the centuries-old practice of marquetry, or wood inlay, with which she currently renders scenes of American life.

Taylor writes, "I would read lines of his writing and start to see images that I would then draw. I liked including his written line as a tether back to the original text so that the images could wander but the origin point of their meaning would remain intact"[1]

Asked to compare her collaborations with Yau to any others she has done, she replied, "I'm a hermit. This was the only time I've collaborated in the making of artworks. It was a wonderful experience to meet John and talk with him about writing and art. It was good to do this project with him at that time. I had just moved to New York and didn't know a lot of people. The fact that he thought deeply about both types of creative expression made for great conversations."[2]

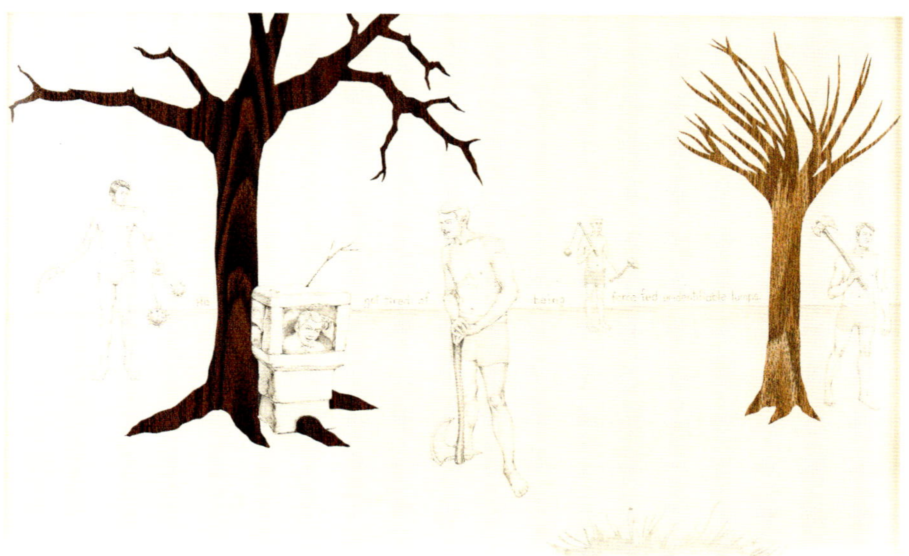

John Yau and Alison Elizabeth Taylor, *He got tired of being force fed unidentifiable lumps*, 2004

[1] Alison Elizabeth Taylor, email message to author, November 13, 2023.

[2] Taylor, email to author, November 13, 2023.

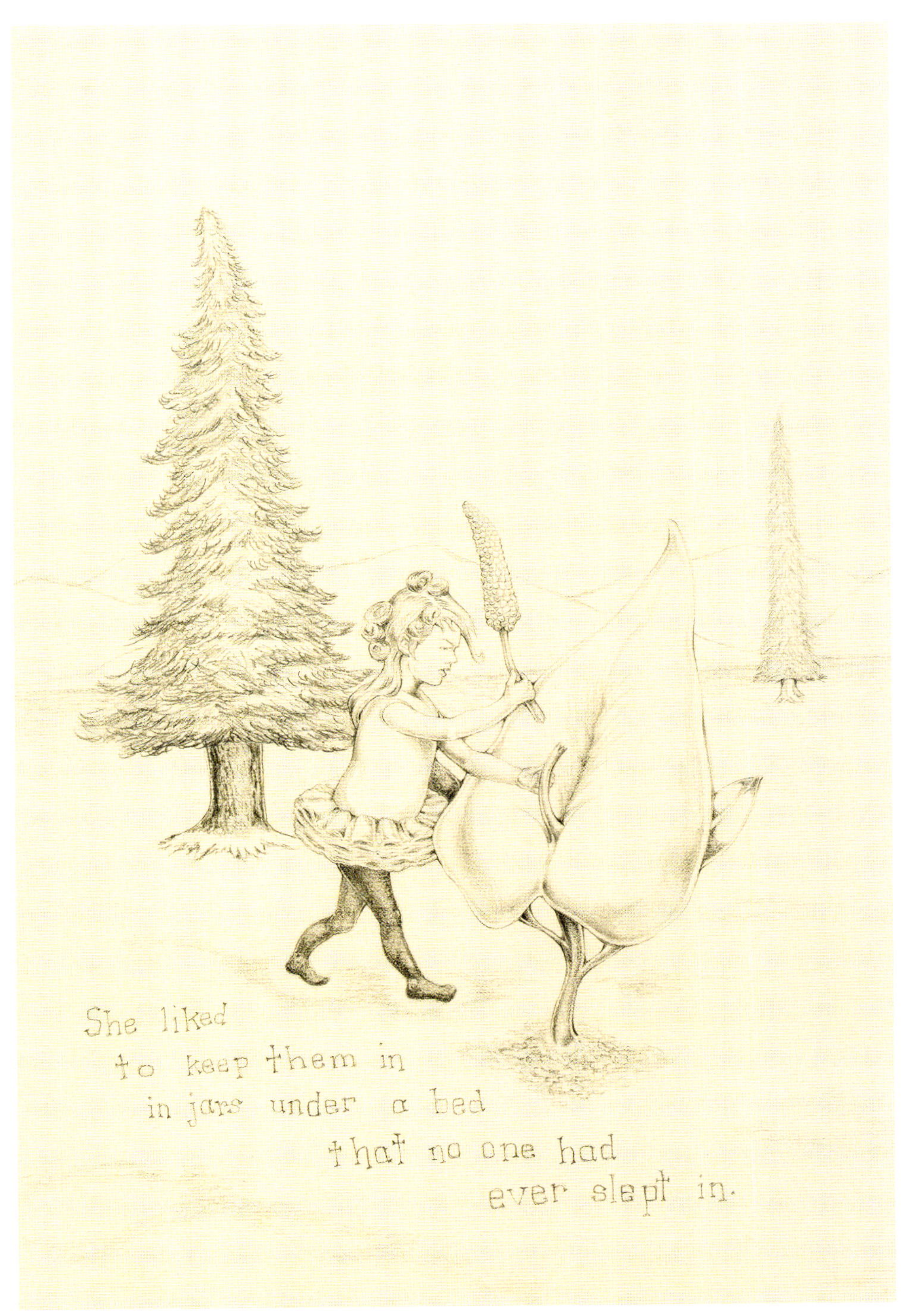

John Yau and Alison Elizabeth Taylor, *She liked to keep them in jars under a bed that no one had ever slept in*, 2004

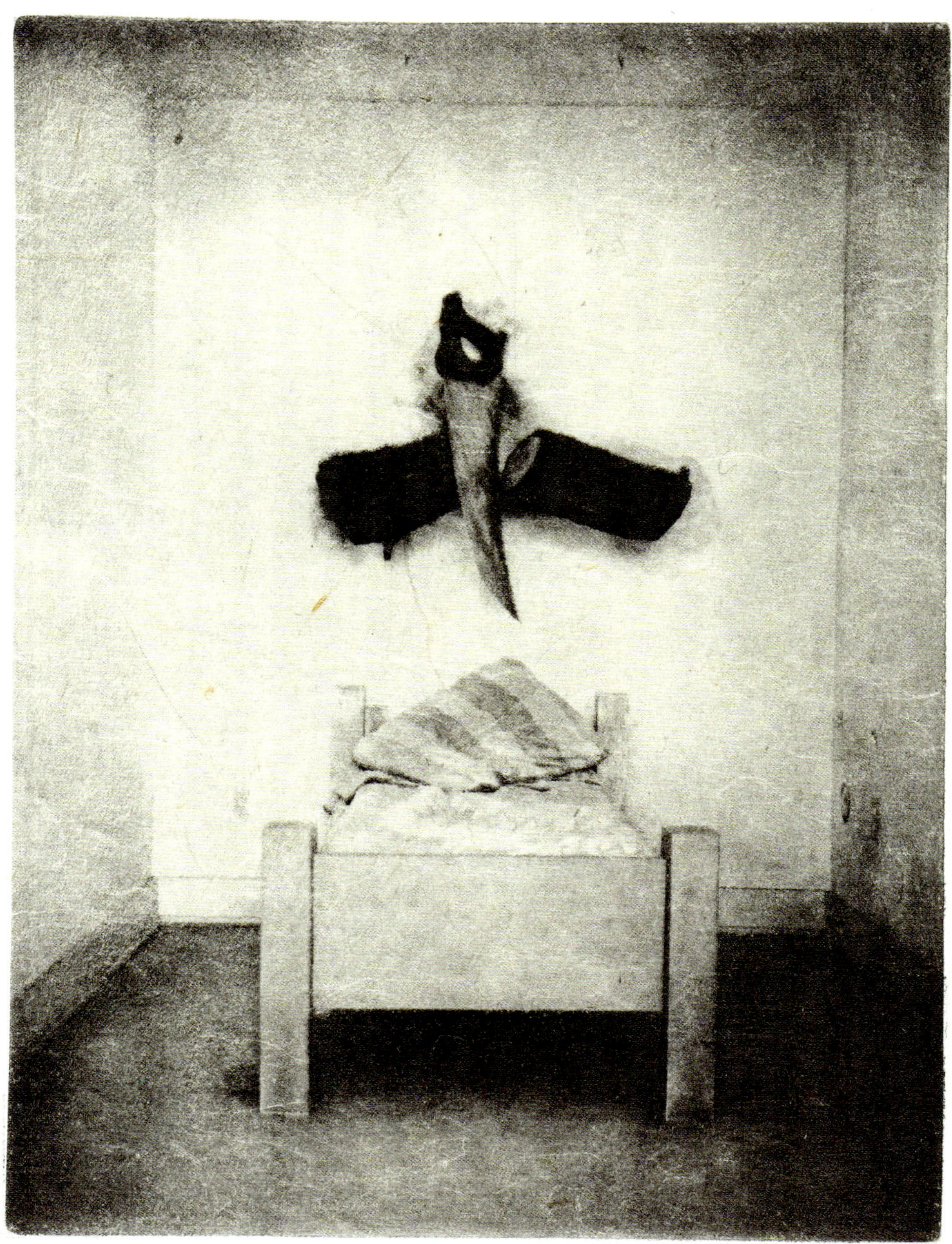

John Yau and Robert Therrien, *Dream Hospital*, 1995

ROBERT THERRIEN

American, 1947 – 2019

Robert Therrien is known for his images and objects that draw on vernacular forms (snowmen, oilcans, tables and chairs) but because of his precise use of materials and dramatic changes of scale, they shift between the ordinary and the uncanny.

In his use of repetition in the stacking of objects, Therrien shares an affinity with Yau, who often writes pantoums, a format in which lines of the poem repeat from beginning to end in a specific order.

Their collaboration, *Dream Hospital*, includes Therrien's photographs of staged domestic tableaux (stacks of pots and pans, mops and buckets, and different kinds of beds) made to illustrate Yau's poems which have the descriptive quality of fables. Therrien states that the poet's "[verbal] imagery pushed the work into the domestic realm a little, with beds and plates"[1] and inspired his monumental sculptures.

In several of Yau's collaborations with artists, skillful printers, designers, typesetters, and bookbinders are involved. Their expertise is essential in the physical presence of the finished work. In the case of *Dream Hospital*, the portfolio of photogravures with chine collé and letterpress text was designed and printed by Jacob Samuel.

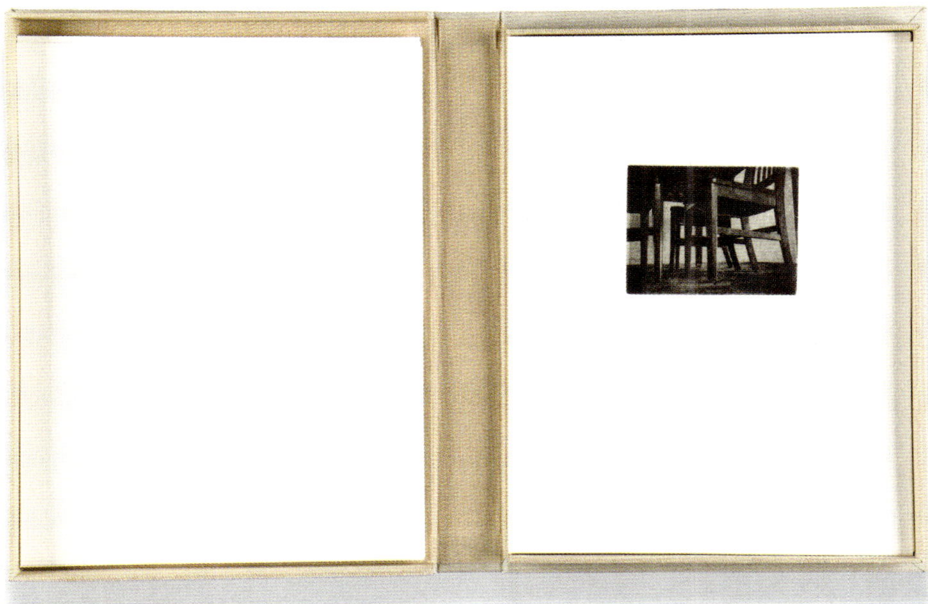

John Yau and Robert Therrien, *Dream Hospital*, 1995

---

[1] Hunter Drohojowska-Philp, "Call Him an Alchemist of the Everyday," *Los Angeles Times*, February 27, 2000, https://www.latimes.com/archives/la-xpm-2000-feb-27-ca-2960-story.html.

RICHARD TUTTLE

American, born 1941

Throughout his career, Richard Tuttle has probed the possibilities of painting, sculpture, drawing, and printmaking, and has often blurred the lines between them. Tuttle has made extremely spare works as well as bountiful ones, and he is particularly alert to where and how his pieces are installed and experienced.

Artist, curator, and writer Judith Brodsky invited Yau and Tuttle to collaborate as part of her projects at the Rutgers Center for Innovative Print and Paper (which was renamed the Brodsky Center in her honor and later became part of the Philadelphia Academy of Fine Arts). The result is *The Missing Portrait*, a wondrous book-as-sculpture, which demands slow and careful engagement.

Yau sent his poem to Tuttle and asked to see the work in progress at the print studio. He recalls, "I said to the printmaker, 'I'd like to see it.' And he said, 'Richard doesn't want you to see it 'til it's done because you might not like what he's doing to your poem.' I said, 'The poem exists anyway. I don't care what he does as long as he doesn't rewrite it.' And the guy said, 'No, no, he's not doing that.' In a way, I feel like the poem has its own existence. If I give it to somebody, whatever they do with it is fine. The poem will survive."[1]

While *The Missing Portrait* is obviously meant to be looked at and read, it could be satisfyingly experienced with one's eyes closed. Propped open on two pillows, the individual pages and spreads offer to the touch variously sculpted areas of paper pulp, stretched fabric, taut strands of thread, feathers, and other items. Tuttle did indeed manipulate Yau's poem with lines and words presented in different colors, sizes, and typefaces, each choice contributing to a sense of wonder and surprise.

---

[1] John Yau, interview with the author, September 27, 2022.

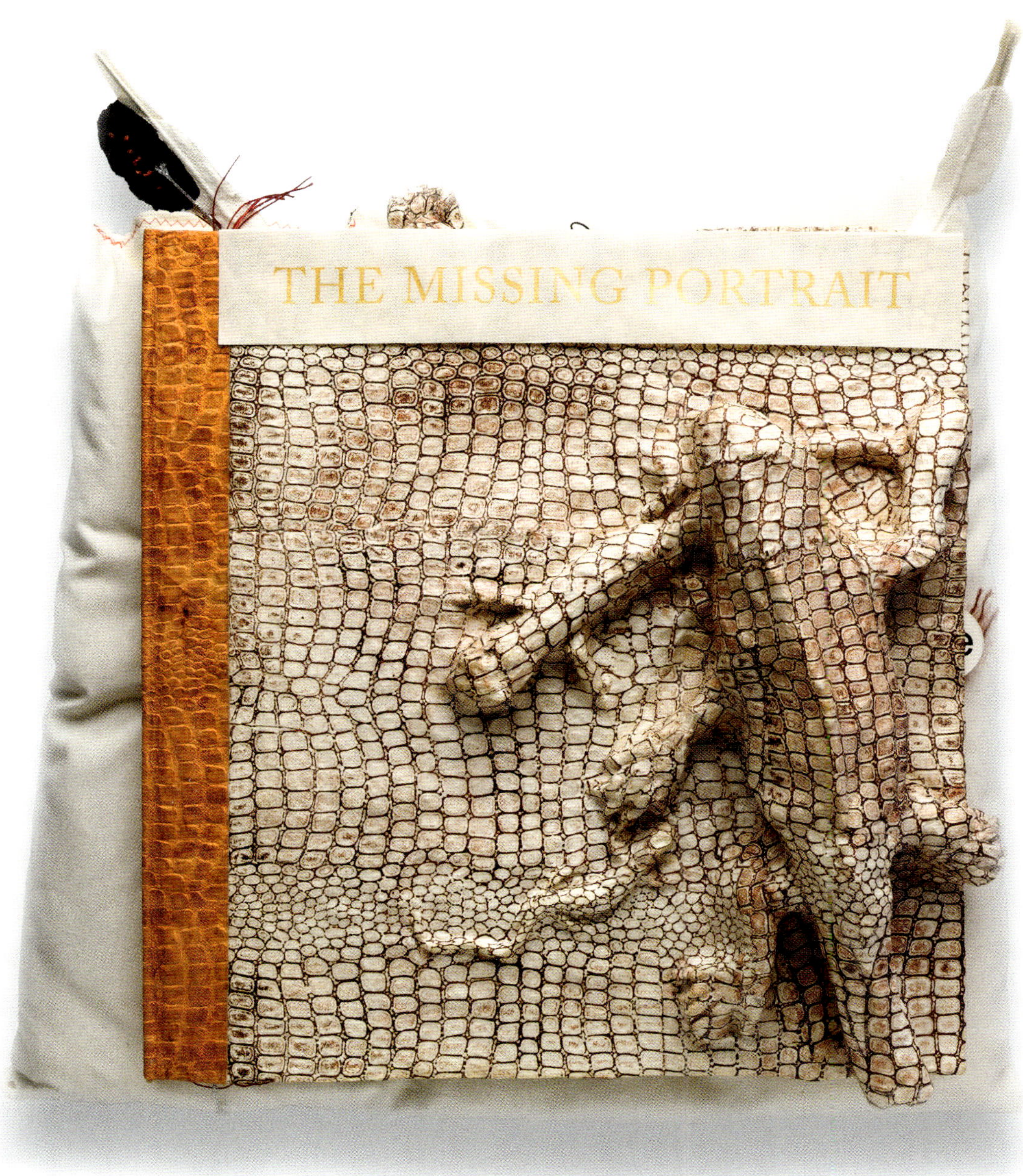

John Yau and Richard Tuttle, *The Missing Portrait*, 2008

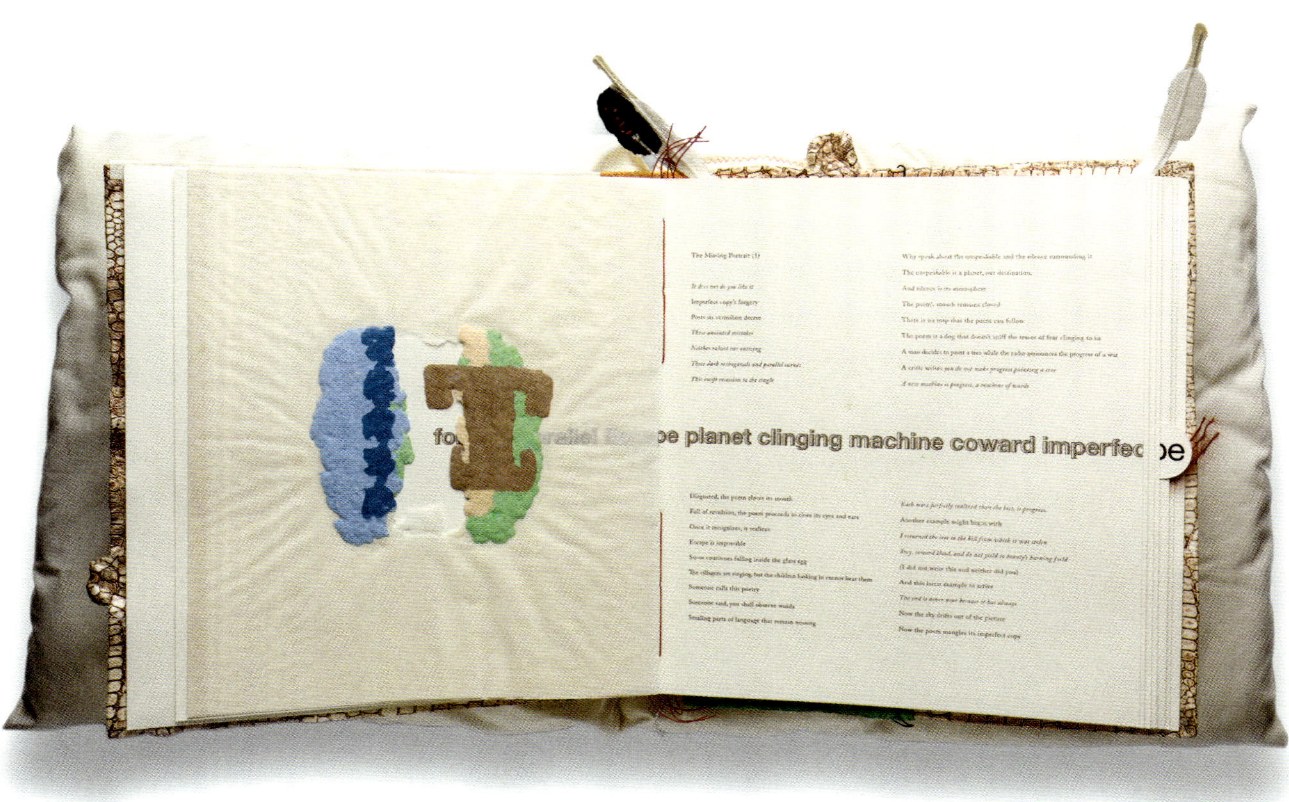

John Yau and Richard Tuttle, *The Missing Portrait*, 2008

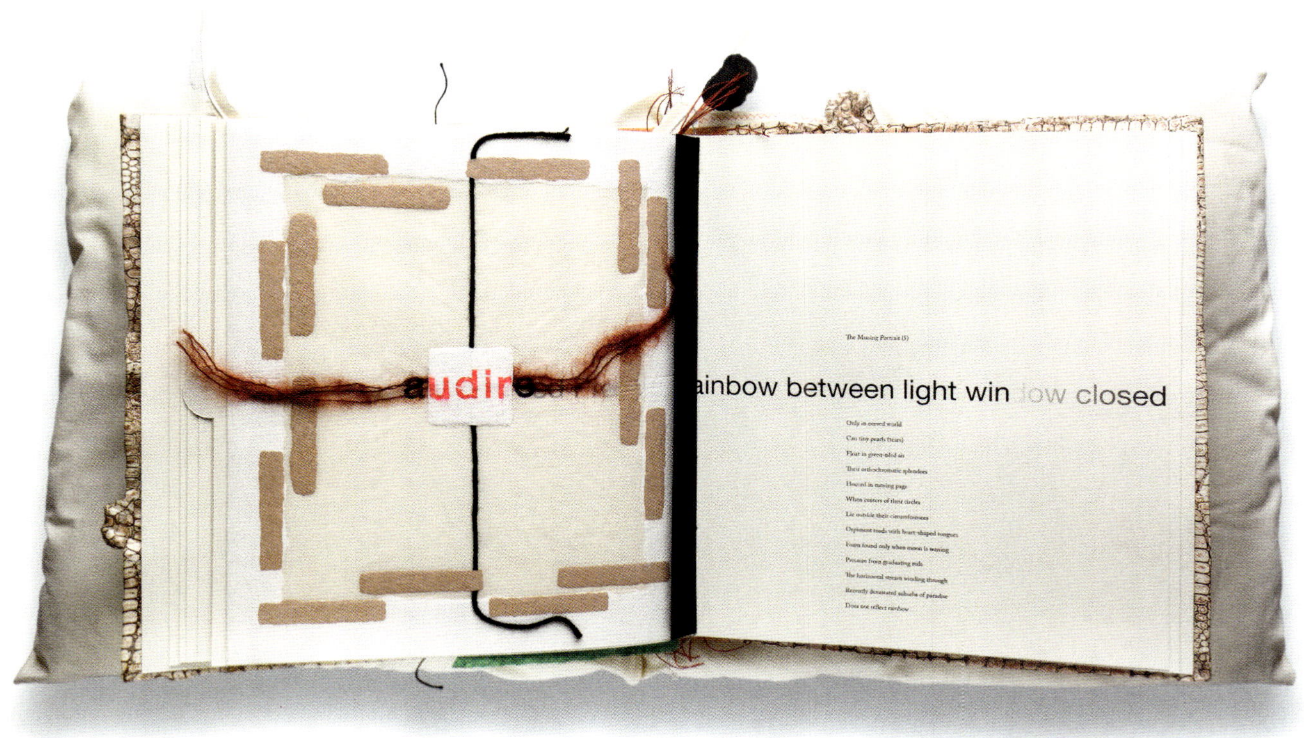

John Yau and Richard Tuttle, *The Missing Portrait*, 2008

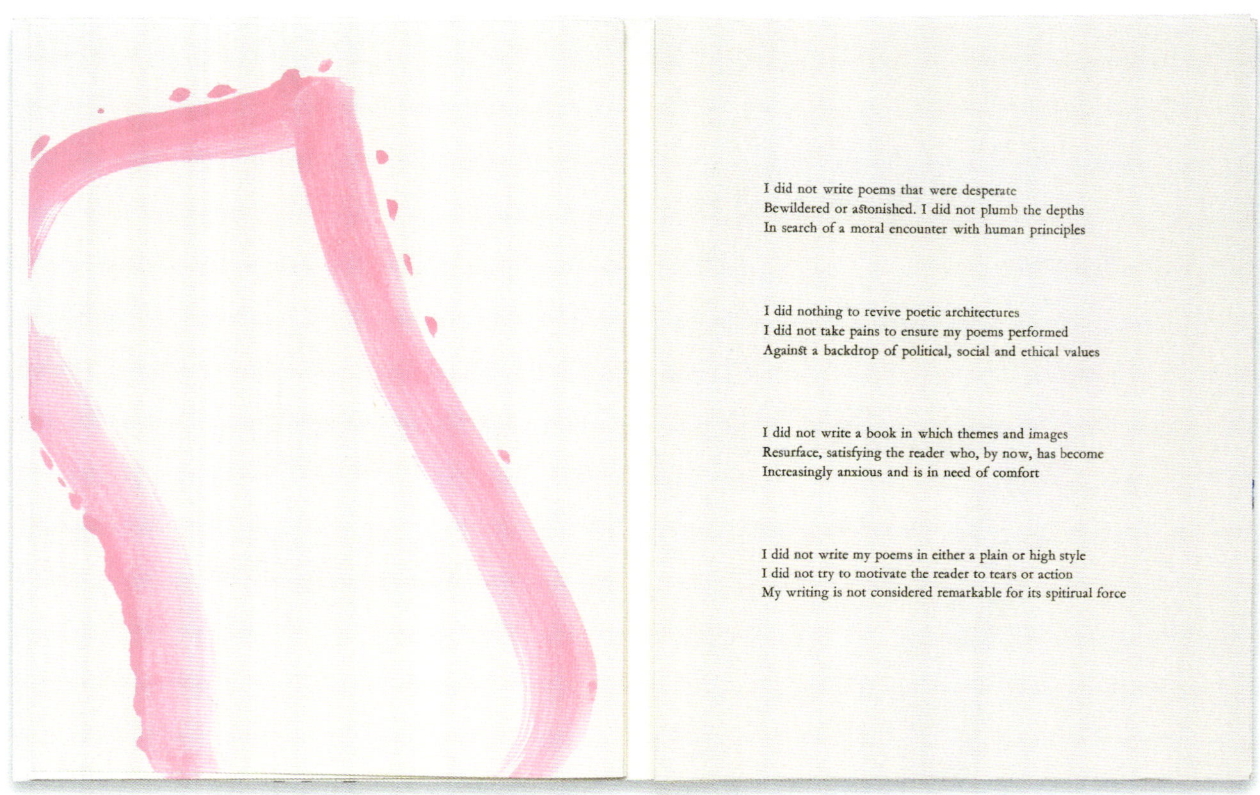

John Yau and Claude Viallat, *Midway*, **2017**

CLAUDE VIALLAT

French, born 1936

Claude Viallat is one of the founding participants in the radical French movement Supports/Surfaces, known for the exhaustive investigation of painting's component parts—the stretcher bars, canvas, and paint. Works made by artists associated with the group utilize acts of cutting, folding, and stacking materials including wood and wire; applying pigment and dyes to various commercial fabrics; and exploring different modes of presentation.

Primarily using unstretched canvas, Viallat would repeat his signature form—a wobbly rectangle or amoeba-like shape—painted with slight variations on rugs, tents, curtains, etc. This gives his compositions the feel of handmade wallpaper that could be produced ad infinitum.

Viallat and Yau collaborated on *Midway*, published by Gervais Jassaud under his Collectif Génération imprint. The artist's sure-handed pink and blue gestures animate the white space around Yau's self-effacing words. Other artists who worked on separate editions of *Midway* include Kathy Barry, Astrid Sylwan, and Chuck Webster. Regarding' Jassaud's publications, Yau has said, "With Gervais and the artist's books, he decides who the artist is. I often don't know who they are. Some of them I've never met, but I trust him implicitly."[1]

---

[1] John Yau, interview with the author, September 27, 2022.

CHUCK WEBSTER
American, born 1970

Chuck Webster's visual vocabulary combines forms from the real world and his imagination, and he utilizes elements of figuration, landscape, diagrams, and language in his paintings and drawings. His collage sensibility and inclusive attitude make for a sympathetic partnership with Yau, allowing for image and text combinations that can be beautifully blunt or disarmingly understated. This shared mindset yields works that imagine a fictional battle between Jolly Old Saint Nick and a prehistoric reptilian monster (*Santa Claus vs. Godzilla*); commemorate artists (*Braque's Last Breath* and *Jake Berthot's Last Words*); and playfully introduce one private investigator to another (*Mike Mallet Meets Mike Hammer*).

They explore the meanings and ambiguities of words and forms, as when poems from the *Genghis Chan: Private Eye* series are hand-lettered in different ways, using colored pencil, ink, and watercolor on various vintage papers. For example[1]:

SACK of RICE

SACK HER VICE

SACK · RIFF · ICE

The sounding out of the word *sacrifice* lets Yau make connections to some of his ongoing interests—identity, detective novels, theme, and variation. Rice is a staple in the Chinese diet; vice is criminal or immoral behavior (often leading to the hiring of a private eye); sack is slang for being dismissed from a job, and another way of saying, bed; and a riff is a short, repeated phrase in music or a humorous improvisation.

A comment Webster made about his own practice could summarize the collaborative synergy with Yau: "I draw completely aware and free. I don't think about anything and I think about everything."[2] They enjoy making language physical, using words compositionally, and examining how phrases operate when deployed in dry or wet media. Yau confesses, "With poetry, you don't think about waste because it's on a computer or in a notebook. Then you send it to a magazine, it goes digitally. You don't know when it'll exist materially. Working with artists, you get over certain apprehensions because you're writing on paper that's like $5 a sheet or whatever. So that was a fun material challenge for me. And look what I get back. How can I complain?"[3]

Their collaboration *Sea Quench* (a boxed portfolio that unfolds "in sequence") includes Yau's poems that contemplate the natural world and man's place in it and Webster's woodcuts of fanciful aquatic creatures that seem to swim on the page.

---

1 John Yau, "Genghis Chan: Private Eye XXXV (Third Ideogram)" in *Further Adventures in Monochrome* (Port Townsend, WA: Copper Canyon Press, 2012), 68.

2 Chuck Webster, in discussion with the author, September 27, 2022.

3 John Yau, interview with the author, September 27, 2022.

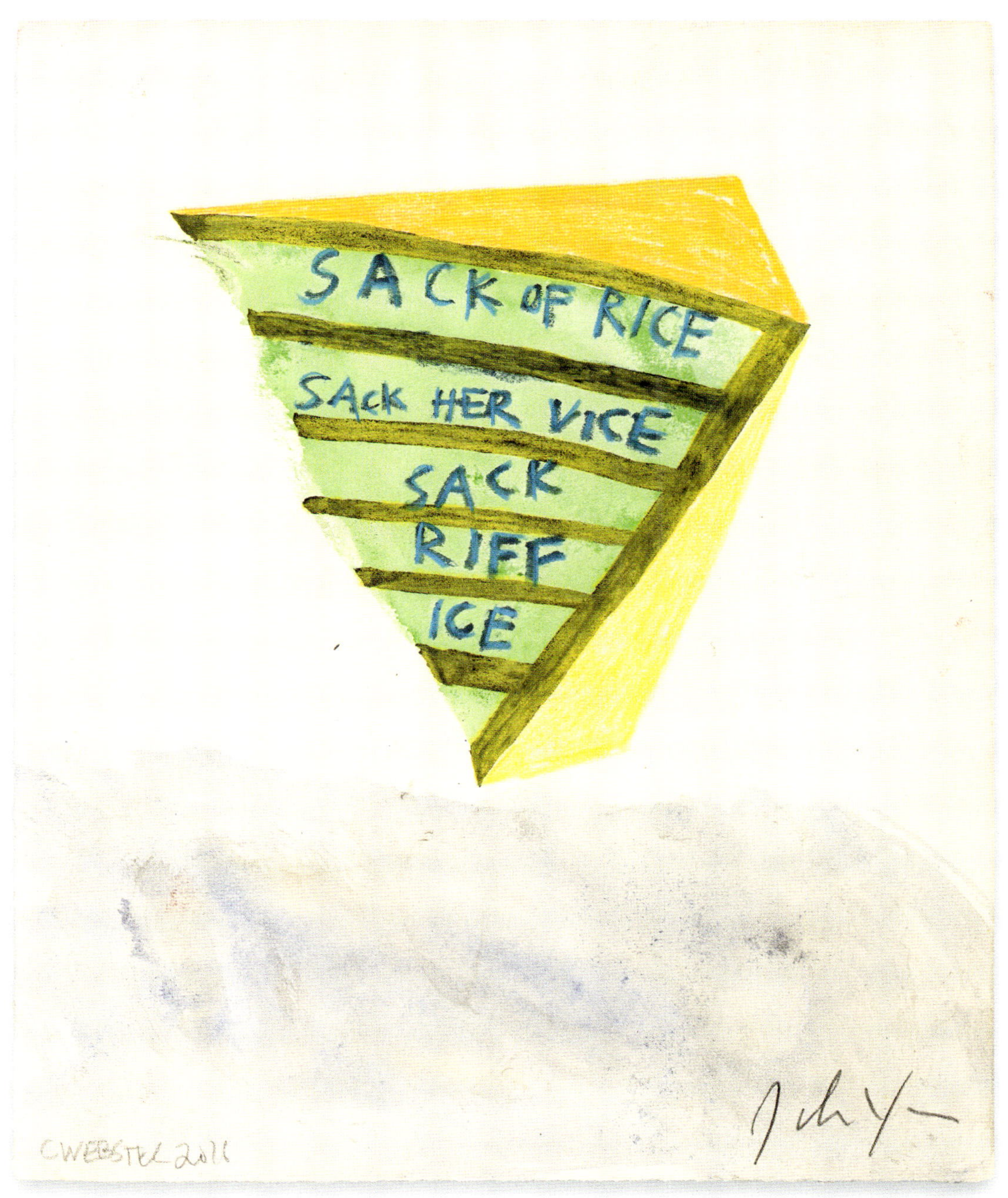

John Yau and Chuck Webster, *Sack of Rice / Sack Her Vice / Sack Riff Ice*, 2016

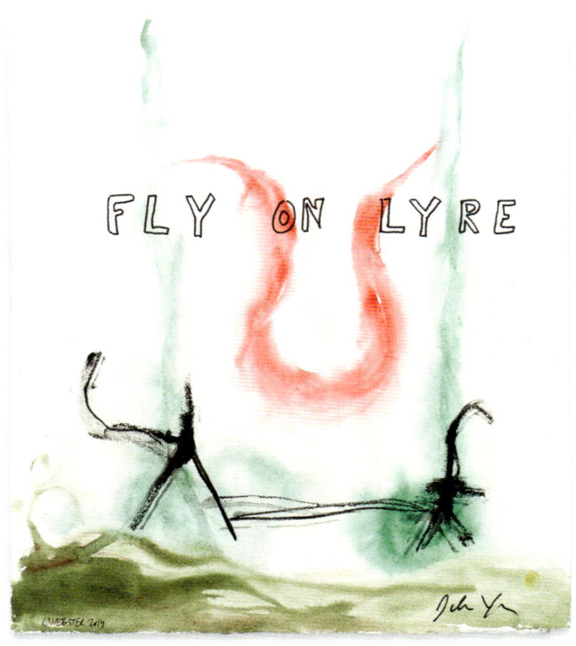

John Yau and Chuck Webster, *Fly on Lyre*, 2014

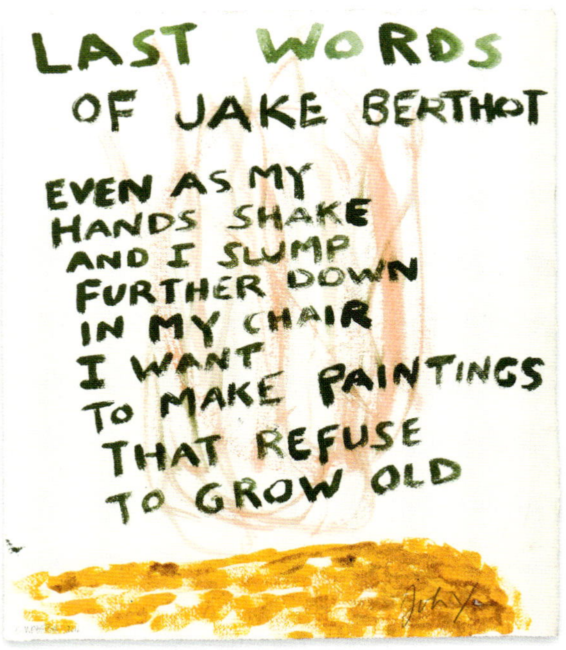

John Yau and Chuck Webster, *Last Words of Jake Berthot*, 2016

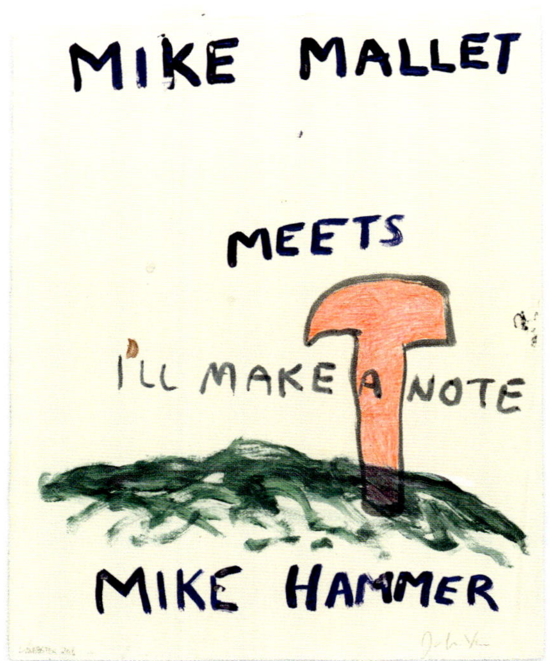

John Yau and Chuck Webster,
Mike Mallet Meets Mike Hammer, 2014

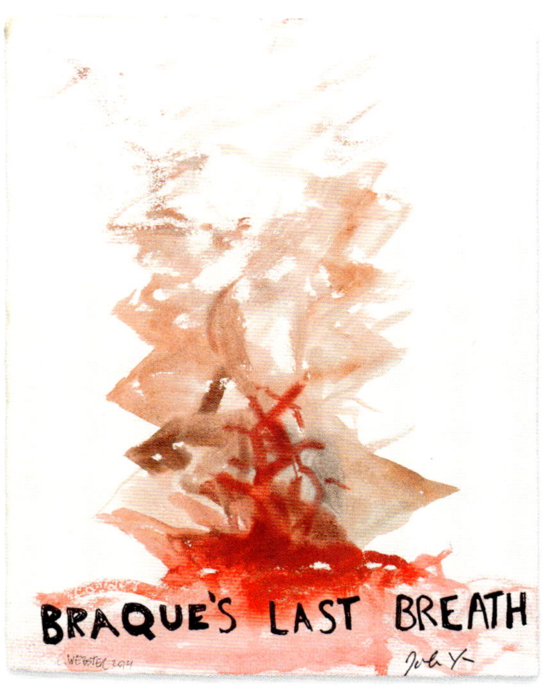

John Yau and Chuck Webster,
Braque's Last Breath, 2014

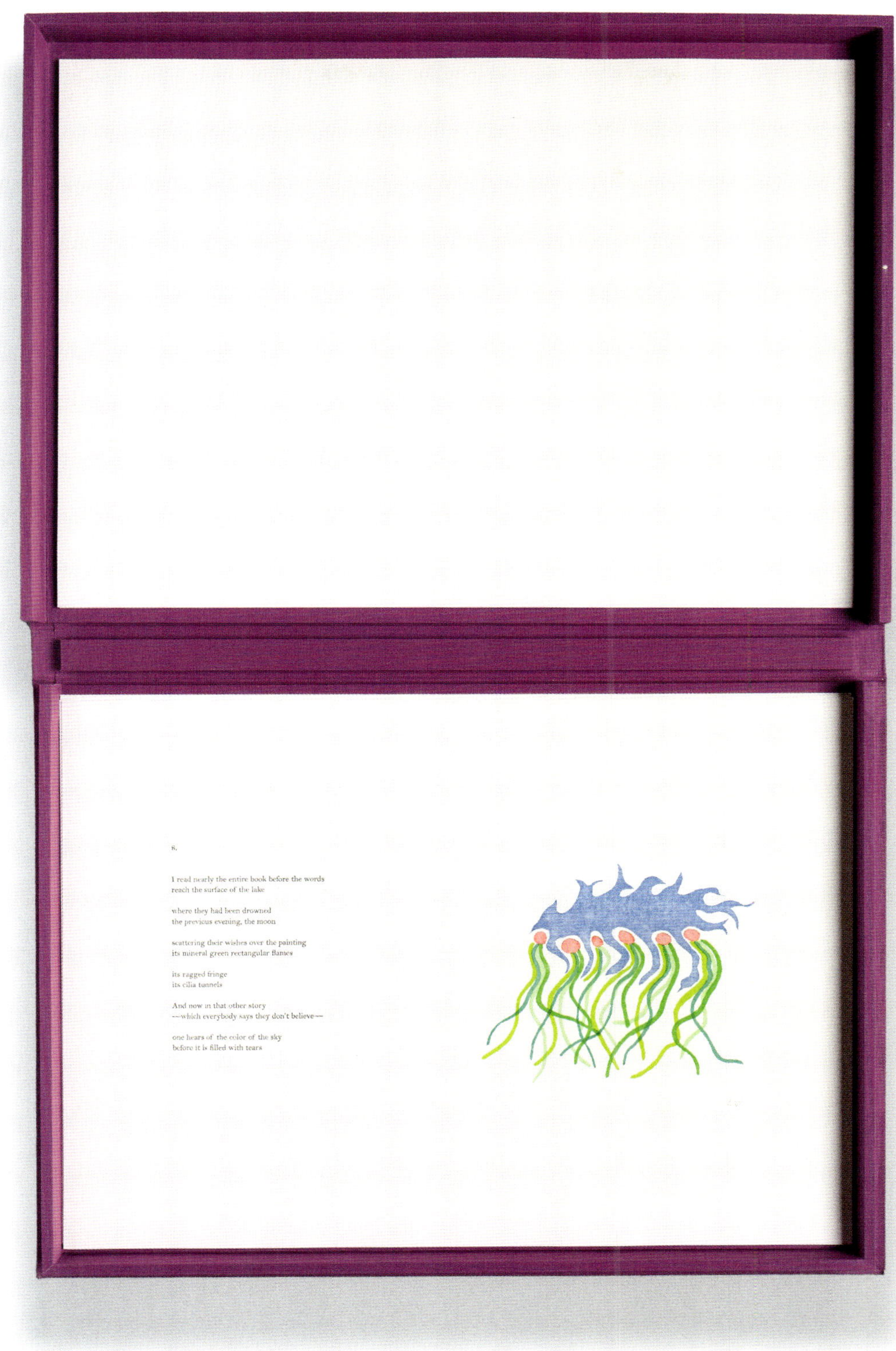

John Yau and Chuck Webster, *Sea Quench*, 2007

TREVOR WINKFIELD

British, born 1944

Artist and writer Trevor Winkfield is known for works that synthesize his interests in modernist art and literature movements, medieval architecture, and graphic symbols. They often feature stage-like settings that frame renderings of flowers, birds, lamps, and other familiar items, but in a crisp and detached style.

Yau has described Winkfield's work as "graphically precise, kaleidoscopic pictures" that are "visual rebuses with no apparent solutions."[1] The artist is also an inveterate collaborator, having worked with many writers including John Ashbery, Kenward Elmslie, Harry Matthews, and Ron Padgett, among others. He and Yau share affinities for previous eras and a sense that the job of the poet and artist involves engaging historical traditions and extending them into the present in unexpected ways.

The two men have made two publications together, *Annals of a Gumshoe* and *Piccadilly or Paradise*, both of which combine playful and inventive poems with elegant back-and-white illustrations. In *Annals of a Gumshoe*, Yau continues his investigation of the detective genre and feelings of loss. Here is an indicative section:

> *The gumshoe likes to wake up in the middle of the night and look out*
> *the window, but often wonders whatever happened to air shafts and*
> *movie theaters with painted ceilings and velvet curtains.*[2]

---

[1] John Yau, "My Travels in the Land of Winkfield," *Hyperallergic*, February 23, 2023, https://hyperallergic.com/802869/my-travels-in-the-land-of-trevor-winkfield/.

[2] John Yau, "Annals of a Gumshoe" in *Genghis Chan on Drums* (Richmond, CA: Omnidawn Publishing, 2012), 87-88. Originally published by Smoke Specs in the artist's book *Annals of a Gumshoe*, 2018.

Darts, Paddles and Brooms

1.
When I was a child, every story you told began with the same line: One
wants to become a squirrel capable of surviving winter. No one could ever
guess what you would say next, which is why we huddled around you each
evening and waited for the shadows to walk deeper into the crowded room.

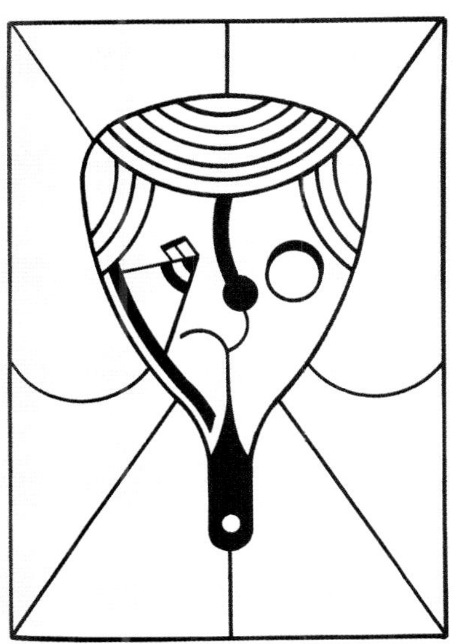

Other Ways of Describing A Vampire's Tongue

Vaguely discursive
Valid objection
Valuable acquisition
Vanished centuries
Vacillating disobedience
Vehement panting
Venomous compassion
Versatile triumph
Vindictive grace
Virulent embarrassment

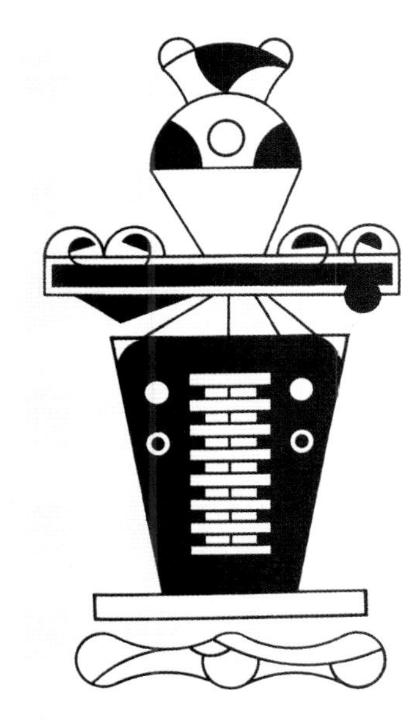

John Yau and Trevor Winkfield, *Annals of a Gumshoe*, 2018

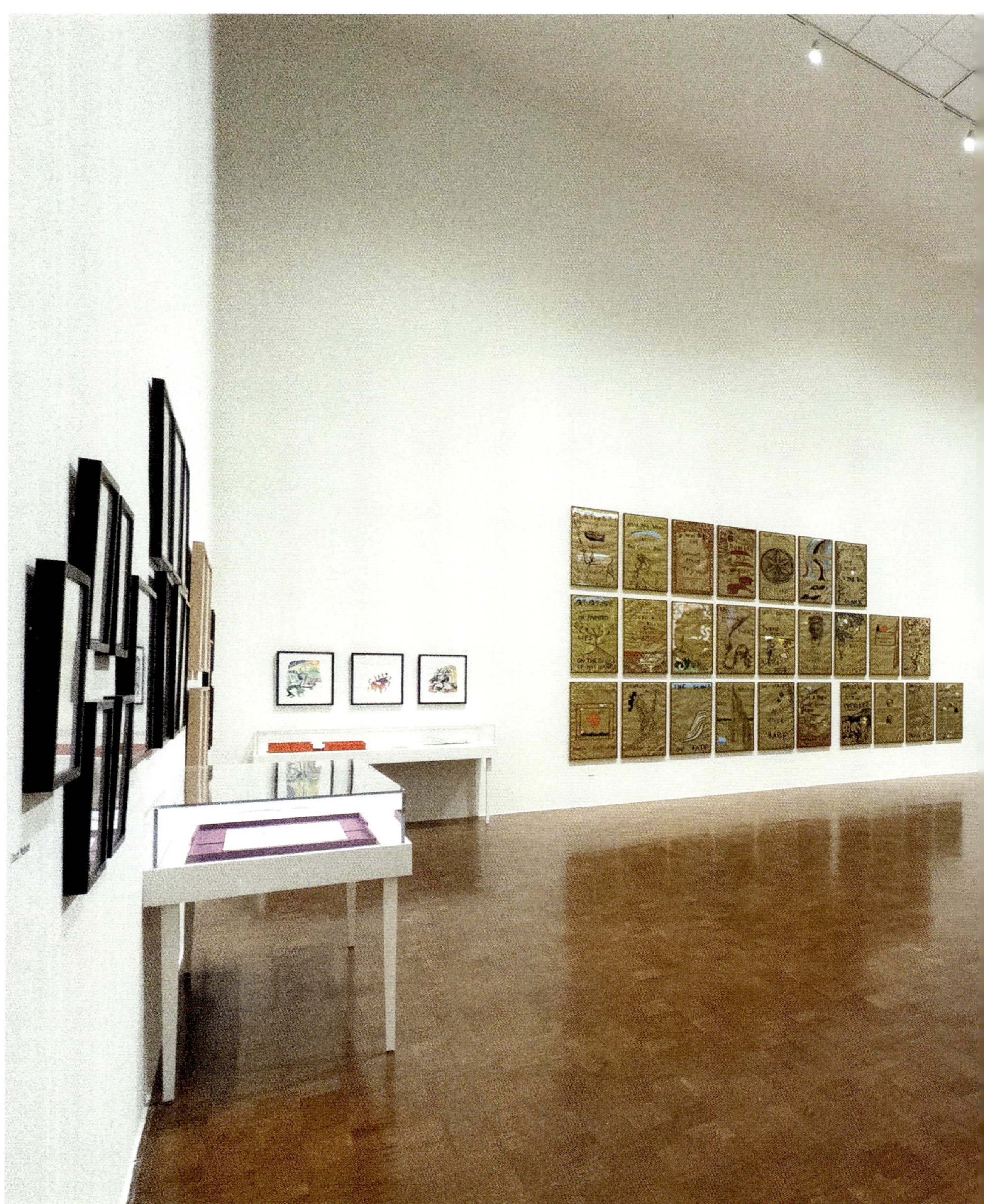

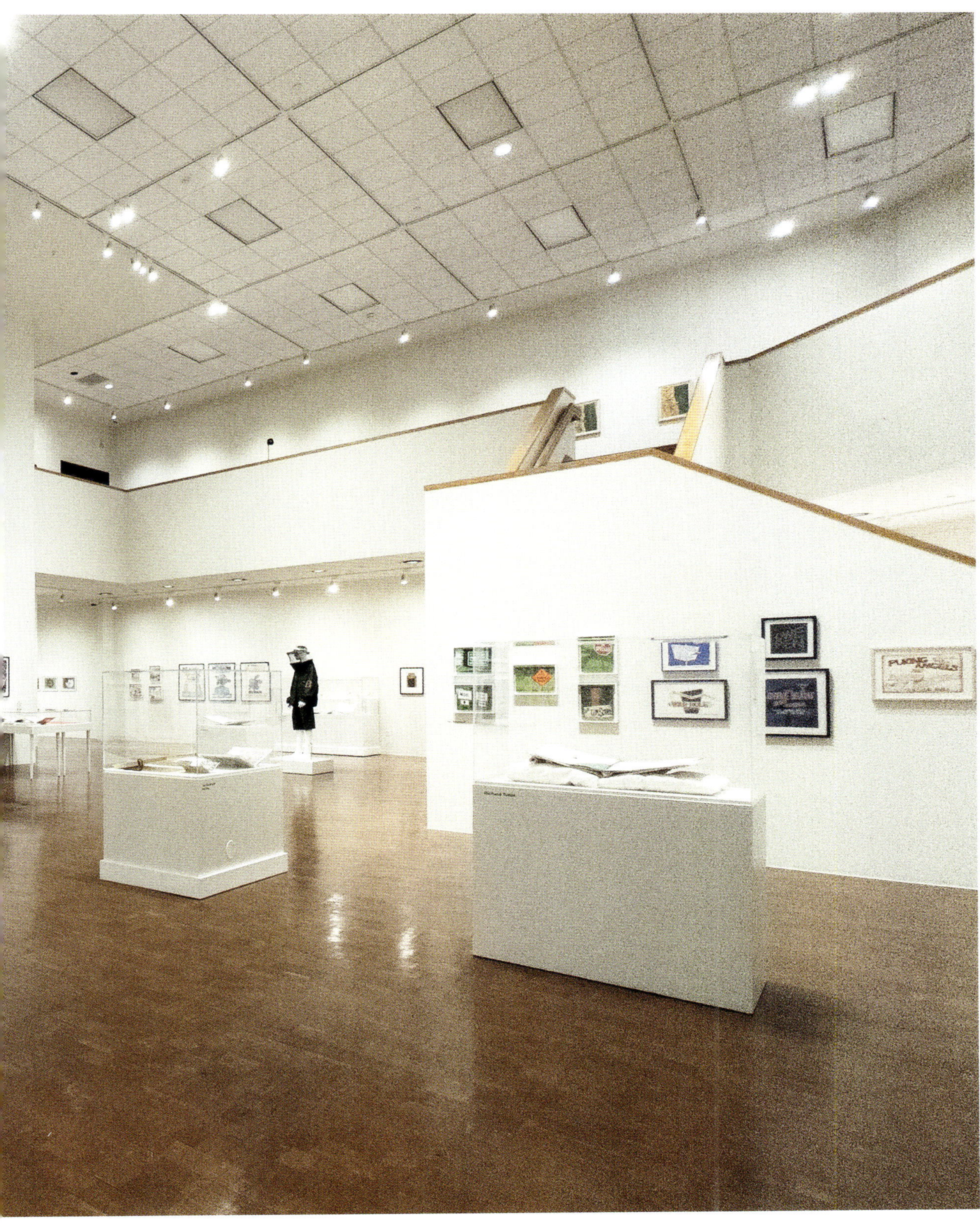

View of *Disguise the Limit: John Yau's Collaborations*, University of Kentucky Art Museum, January 9 – June 1, 2024

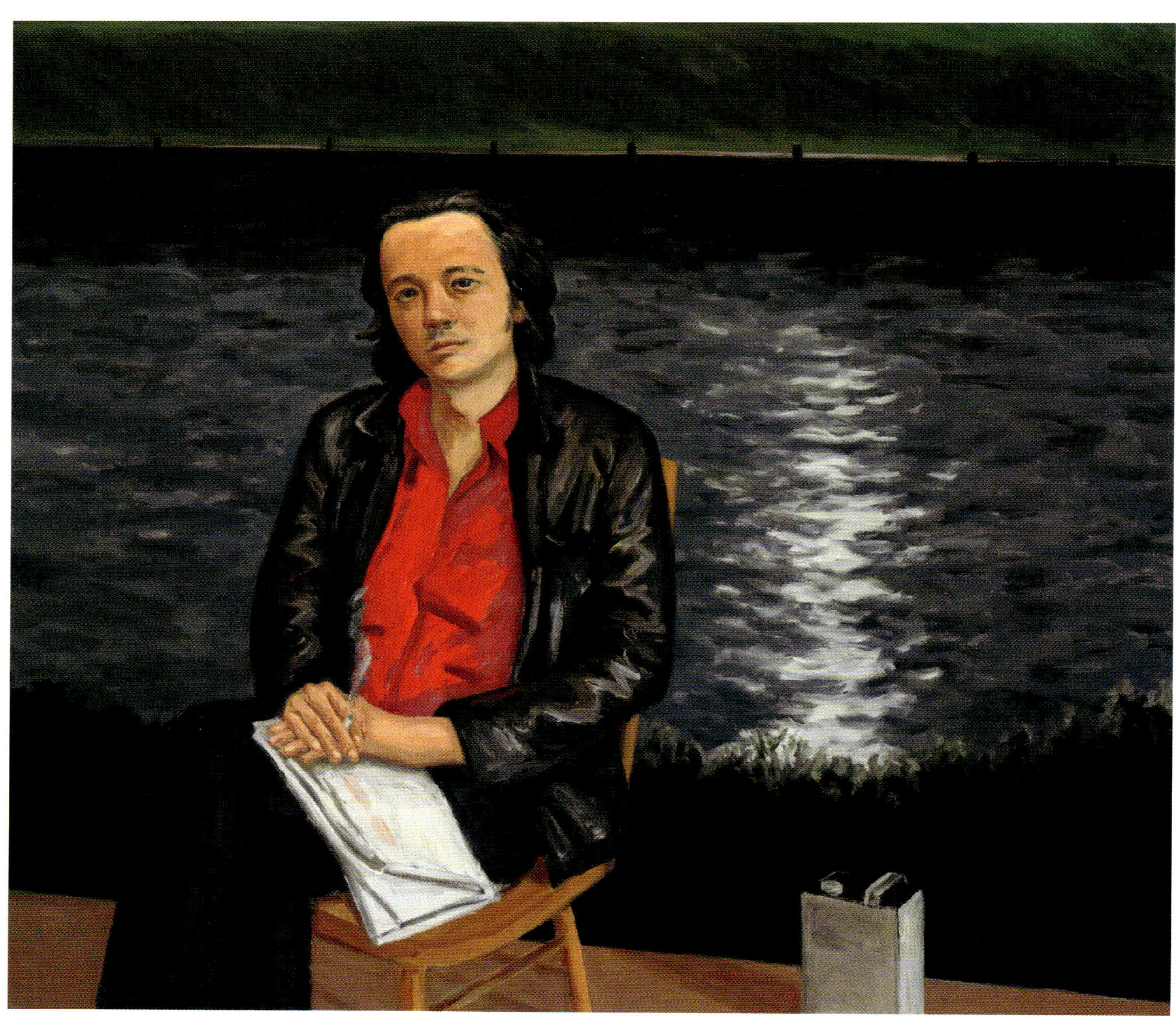

Robert Berlind, *John Yau*, 1983, oil on canvas.
National Portrait Gallery, Smithsonian Institution.
© Estate of Robert Berlind, Mary Lucier Executor

TIMELINE

—John Yau

1950

Born in Lynn, Massachusetts, to parents who arrived in America on separate ships leaving China in 1948 and '49. My mother often said that she was on the last passenger ship to leave Shanghai and her fellow passengers included a group of nuns and wartime correspondent, Pierre Trudeau, who became prime minister of Canada (1968–79; 1980–84). Later learn this was true, as was much else she told me about being the daughter of a wealthy diplomat in the government of Sun Yat-sen. Told I spent infancy living with parents in rooming house in Lynn, MA. No memory of this experience, which I am sure left an impression on me.

1950s

Grow up in Boston on Beacon Hill, where the poets Robert Lowell, John Weiners, and Stephen Jonas also live. Weiners and I live on Joy Street, but at different times.

The school decides to transfer me from fourth grade to fifth grade in the middle of the school year (one of many reminders of difference).

1956

Meet Douglas Way, son of the artist John Way (1921 – 2012) shortly after John and most of his small family move to Boston from Hong Kong. Our parents meet soon after and become friends; they play Mahjong on weekends and cook together because they all speak Shanghaiese, a dialect almost no other Chinese living in America speak. John Way, who is taking design courses at MIT, repeatedly tells my parents and me that Robert Motherwell and Franz Kline took their ideas from Chinese calligraphy but that no one will ever say so. This is the beginning of my alternative art education.

1958

Father—who was biracial (Chinese and English)—gives me the biography *Crazy Horse: The Strange Man of the Oglalas* (Knopf, 1942) by Mari Sandoz for Christmas. Father's mantra: "All Americans are foreigners."

Mother—who works the night shift in a drugstore across the street from the Charles Street Jail and attends Boston University during the day—brings me to the Museum of Fine

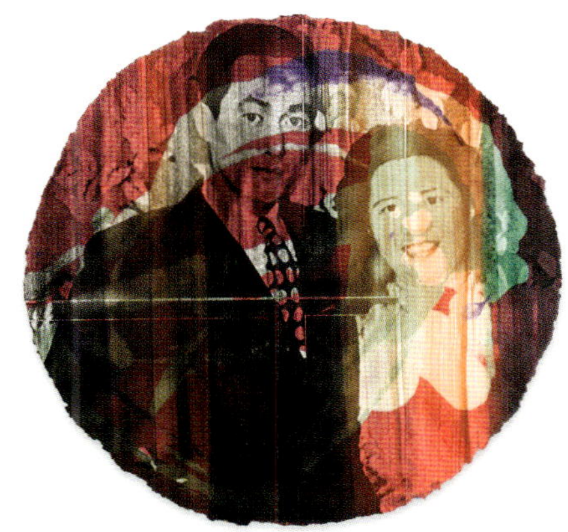

John Yau's parents, *Leaves from a Chinese Album*, 2003

Arts on weekends, where I see *Japonaise* (*Camille Monet in Japanese Costume*), 1876, by Claude Monet.

When parents decide they are too busy to take care of me, they leave me at movie theaters, after paying the usher to make sure no adults sit next to me. This starts when I am six.

1960–1967

Family moves to Brookline, Massachusetts in 1960. Attend Brookline High School (1963–67).

Begin going to Grolier Poetry Book Shop and Brattle Theater in Harvard Square. As I know nothing about poetry, I read indiscriminately.

Beginning around 1966, I see the following films:
Shanghai Express (1932) starring Marlene Dietrich and Anna May Wong, directed by Josef von Sternberg: I go to see the movie because of the title and mistakenly believe the opening scenes were shot in Shanghai, where my parents lived before coming to America. I have a "crush" on Anna May Wong;
The Big Sleep (1946) starring Humphrey Bogart and Lauren Bacall, directed by Howard Hawks: I learn that Raymond Chandler wrote the book and began reading him and Dashiell Hammett;
Yojimbo (1961) starring Toshiro Mifune and Tatsuya Nakadai, directed by Akira Kurosawa;

Woman in the Dunes (1964) starring Eiji Okada and Kyôko Kishida, directed by Hiroshi Teshigahara: I learn that the film was based on a novel by Kobo Abe and begin reading him, Yasunari Kawabata, and Yukio Mishima.

Read Lawrence Ferlinghetti, Jack Kerouac, Gregory Corso, and Allen Ginsberg.

I see *USA: Poetry; 11: Frank O'Hara and Ed Sanders* (1966) and *USA: Poetry; 4; Gary Snyder and Philip Whalen* (1966) on television in my parents' house.

Told by my high school counselor that I have graduated in the bottom tenth of my class and that I should enlist in the Air Force and learn discipline.

Begin writing poetry and try marijuana at thirteen. Friends tell me about meeting Timothy Leary and Richard Alpert at Harvard and learning about Harvard Psilocybin Project. Friends and I had already tried to obtain peyote from a shadowy antique dealer we befriended in Cambridge, but nothing came of it. By this time, I'm spending more and more time alone, reading. Later learn from Bruce Conner that he and Leary lived together in a commune in Newton, which is the town next to Brookline.

Summer jobs: dishwasher, newspaper boy, delivery boy.

1967–1969
Attend Boston University (1967–69, College of Basic Studies, a two-year program for "underachievers") and do not get good grades.

Hear Bill Baird (considered "father" of the birth control and abortion rights movement).

Go to meetings of Students for a Democratic Society (SDS) and attend anti-war demonstrations.

Listen to Junior Wells, Buddy Guy, and other blues musicians in small clubs.

Go to performance of The Living Theater at MIT but did not strip down to my underwear.

Read copies of the magazine *Tiger's Eye* in the house of the parents of Eve Melnechuk.

Meet Burt Held, who tells me that Jim Dine (who was friends with Burt's older brother) used to come to his parents' house

in Ohio for Sunday lunch. Burt is happy to learn that I have heard of Dine and I am happy to learn someone in my class has looked at contemporary art.

Read four anthologies: *A Controversy of Poets: An Anthology of Contemporary Poetry*, edited by Robert Kelly and Paris Leary (Doubleday Anchor, 1965); *The Imagist Poem*, edited by William Pratt (University of New Orleans Press, 1963); *The New American Poetry 1945–1960*, edited by Donald Allen (University of California Press, 1960); *The Modern Poets: An American-British Anthology*, edited by John Malcolm Brinnin and Bill Read, with photographs by Rollie McKenna (McGraw-Hill, 1963). Look at photographs almost as much as I read poems. The books seem to be proof of life on another planet. Unsure of how to get there.

Begin reading books by poets published in all four anthologies. Focus on books by Robert Creeley, Robert Duncan, Robert Kelly, Gerrit Lansing, Denise Levertov, and Frank O'Hara.

Go to anti-war readings and hear Robert Bly, Galway Kinnell, and Denise Levertov (learned years later that Arthur Sze and I were at same Levertov reading). Hear Kinnell read "The Bear" and Gary Snyder read "Smokey the Bear Sutra" the same year. Begin reading Snyder.

After reading Kelly, begin buying books published by Black Sparrow Press (except Charles Bukowski).

Regularly go to Fogg Art Museum and remember seeing silkscreen *For Love (Robert Creeley)*, 1966, by R.B. Kitaj, and discovering another connection between poets and artists.

In 1969, about to leave the College of Basic Studies, ask college guidance counselor about going to Black Mountain College and learn that it has been closed for many years. Decide to apply to transfer to Bard College (where Robert Kelly teaches) and—to my surprise and relief—am accepted. Discover I am the only Asian American at Bard.

1969–1972 (Bard College)
Take literature classes with Fred Grab, Robert Kelly, Ben LaFarge, Clark Rodewald, Elizabeth Stambler, Andrews Wanning, and William Wilson. Continue to read indiscriminately and take classes on poets in the Ezra Pound tradition and T. S. Eliot tradition. When told I should decide on one or the other, I decide to postpone my decision.

Meet sculptor Jake Grossberg, who asks what I am reading (a book of poems by Pablo Neruda), beginning our friendship. Learn from Jake that artists (Donald Judd) and poets (Frank O'Hara) write reviews of art and am told that I could do this (first inkling!!).

Begin going to New York City on weekends with Jake (leave Bard in the morning, return at night). Go to exhibitions in Soho and have no idea what I am looking at. Introduced to David Diao by Jake.

Meet other artists on Bard faculty: Alan Cote, Murray Reich, Jim Sullivan.

Read *Fragment* (Black Sparrow, 1969) by John Ashbery, *When the Sun Tries to Go On* (Black Sparrow, 1969) by Kenneth Koch, and *Relation* by Ken Irby (Black Sparrow, 1970).

Meet the composer Elie Yarden, who teaches at Bard, and learn about serial music.

Go to St. Mark's Church for the first time on February 4, 1970, to attend memorial reading for Charles Olson, after seeing the film *Fando and Lis* (1968) written by Fernando Arrabal and directed by Alejandro Jodorowsky. Remember two poets from memorial reading, Ray Bremser and Diane Wakoski, who points out that she is the only woman participating in the reading.

In 1971, after learning I have a very low lottery number for the draft (28), I am in a serious car accident and spend seven-plus months in double traction at Northern Dutchess Hospital in Rhinebeck, New York.

1972 (summer)
Attend a few of the classes that Robert Creeley teaches at Harvard, but am not officially enrolled. Meet Alan Davies, who was editing the mimeograph magazine *Oculist Witnesses* and published John Weiners's "The Lanterns Along the Wall," which John wrote for Creeley's class. John wore a suit to class and addressed Bob as Mister Creeley.

1973–74
Briefly work in mail room of publishing house Houghton Mifflin and meet the poet Joel Sloman, who was working as an editor.

Attend informal poetry workshop at Grolier run by Paul Hannigan. Other poets include Bill Corbett and Jay Boggis.

Meet Eileen Myles at poetry reading.

Corbett and Hannigan introduce me to artists Gregory Amenoff, John Imber, Ray Kass, and Michael Mazur, writers and poets Russell Banks, Arthur Freeman, Tom Lux, James Tate, and publisher Jim Randall, who runs Pym-Randall Press.

Work one weekend for Freeman wrapping first editions to be mailed to clients, and see a handful of amusing collages made by F. Scott Fitzgerald (a writer who makes art).

1974–1980
Move to New York City and live with artist Rae Berolzheimer, who I met at Bard.

Move from Manhattan (Upper West Side) to Brooklyn (Clinton Hill) to Manhattan (Chinatown), where I am told by shopkeeper I am "not Chinese."

Begin going to galleries and museums every weekend.

Work at South Street Seaport during Bicentennial. Live in Brooklyn and begin reading fiction I find in Brooklyn Public Library: Jonathan Baumbach, Steve Katz, Ronald Sukenick, and others.

1975
Meet Larry Zirlin and Alan Ziegler who run Release Press. Introduced by Zirlin to Bob Hershon who is one of the founders of Hanging Loose.

Meet Bill Zavatsky, whose magazine and press, *SUN*, publishes books by Phillip Lopate, Ron Padgett, Marjorie Welish, Raymond Roussel, Serge Gavronsky, George Economou, Michael O'Brien, Malcolm de Chazal, Max Jacob, and others, all of which I buy. Attend Zavatsky's writing workshop at Poetry Project.

Go to readings and performances. Hear Jackson Mac Low read different "Gathas" with other performers in a bar on Bowery (again, feel like I do not know what I am hearing and decide not to leave the room until I hear the entire performance).

I go to Joe Brainard's legendary exhibition at Fischbach, which had over 1000 works and would be the last time he showed in New York while he was alive. I was astounded and delighted by Brainard's ability to make art out of anything, from postcards to match books to pieces of colored paper.

1976

Move to Manhattan and begin going to New York Public Library Reading Room: read reviews by Ashbery published in *New York Herald Tribune* and other poets' reviews.

Hear Ashbery read at Columbia and learn that he has started teaching creative writing at Brooklyn College and decide to apply.

I am accepted to Brooklyn College MFA program where I take workshops with Ashbery and art history classes with Jack Flam.

After asking Ashbery if he could teach me how to write an art review, he suggests that I send something to *Art in America*, which I do (reluctantly). After more than a year passes, the editor Betsy Baker invites me to come into the magazine office, most likely because Ashbery kept recommending me, and I begin writing reviews for *Art in America*. My first review is of Alan Cote's paintings. After reading it, Ashbery tells me not to try and "solve the world's problems" in a single review.

Ashbery takes me to art openings. I meet David Hockney, Alex Katz, Rackstraw Downes, Pamela Berkeley, and Jane Freilicher. David Kermani (Director of Tibor de Nagy), who lives with Ashbery and later becomes his husband, invites me to write my first catalogue essay and introduces me to Archie and Maria Rand.

First chapbook, *Crossing Canal Street* (Bellevue Press, 1976), is published with "Foreword" by Robert Kelly.

1977

Receive poetry grant from the National Endowment for the Arts.

Meet Joe Donahue on train going to Boston during Christmas holidays. Only person who sits next to me on crowded train.

1979

Sheep Meadow Press publishes first full-length book of poems, *Sometimes*, with blurb by Ashbery (who suggested they publish me). Asked by the publisher and poet Stanley Moss to write an "Introduction." Ashbery says he won't do it because he feels whatever he writes will become my "albatross." Reluctantly writes blurb for back cover.

1980

I see collaborations of Philip Guston and Corbett at Corbett house when I teach a poetry workshop at Emerson College for a year, invited by Jim Randall. I have short correspondence with Guston before his death.

Release Press publishes book of short prose, *Sleepless Nights of Eugene Delacroix*, with cover by Rae Berolzheimer. This is first collaboration.

1980–1990 (New York and Catskill)

I work at Books & Co., where I meet the art dealer and writer John Bernard Myers who was director of the Tibor de Nagy Gallery, and I am invited to his garden apartment near the bookstore.

The only painting in Myers's apartment I don't immediately recognize is by Norman Bluhm, who I tell John I want to meet. Soon after, Paul Auster introduces me to him at a party at Books & Co, and after a short conversation I am invited to his house and studio.

For my job at *Art in America*, I begin going to more galleries than I had before. Realizing that I was not going to be allowed to write about a well-known artist, I looked at as many shows as I could find that no one was writing about, and discover the Chicago Imagists.

1981

Notarikon, illustrated with drawings by Jake Berthot, is published by Jordan Davies—my first artist book collaboration.

Introduced to Albert Mobilio by the poet Tim Dlugos, who would die of AIDS.

I spend a long weekend in the guest house of Norman and Cary Bluhm, who live in East Hampton. Norman shows me

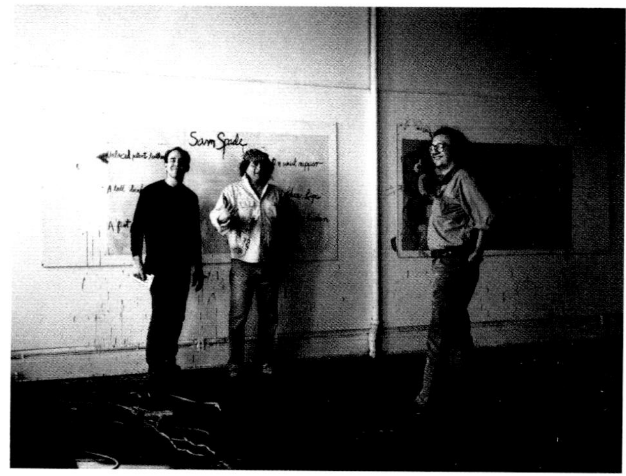

John Cone, Norman Bluhm, and John Yau, circa 1987. Photo credit: Eric Great-Rex.

work from "every decade," as he puts it. He also shows me
the only example of his collaboration with Frank O'Hara still
in his possession. Bluhm suggests we collaborate. Instead of
working on brown butcher block paper with black and white
ink, he chooses large sheets of white paper and different colors
in acrylic. Norman and I are invited by Jon Cone to do prints.
8 Poem Prints are shown in 1987 by Cone Editions Gallery, 560
Broadway, New York.

Teach as adjunct at Pratt Institute. Students include curator
Sergio Bessa and artist Jenny Scobel (an *Exquisite Corpse*
drawing with Scobel and Bill Barrette was made for a benefit
show at the Drawing Center in the 1990s and sold to Sharon
Stone. No record of it exists).

Teach as adjunct at School of Visual Arts. Students include
Suzanne McClelland and Julia Haywood.

1984–1986
Move with Rachel Stella from Manhattan to a farmhouse in
Catskill, New York. Her younger brother Michael, who lived
with us in New York, joins us.

Teach in MFA summer program at Bard, where I do first
collaborations with Archie Rand. Archie says "the goal is
[to] do 1000, so we will get beyond what we know." We
work in watercolor and acrylic on sheets of white paper at
dining room table—the first of many collaborations we do in
different media. Places we work: motel in Detroit; Columbia
University print shop (Tomas Vu); Archie's studio in Brooklyn;
somewhere in Connecticut.

Invited by Joseph Newland at Henry Art Gallery in Seattle to
collaborate with Marsha Burns, Michael Burns, and Randy
Hayes. *Cities* (Henry Art Gallery, University of Washington,
Seattle, 1987).

1990–2000 (New York)
Marry and divorce Jane Hammond.

Parents die within one year of each other.

Meet publisher Gervais Jassaud. This leads to artist books with
many artists from around the world, including Kathy Barry
(New Zealand); Kazuki Nakahara (Japan); Robert Zandvliet
(Netherlands); Suzanne McClelland (USA); Enrico Baj (Italy);
Toni Grand (France); Rob Wynne (USA); Astrid Sylwan
(Sweden); Claude Viallat (France).

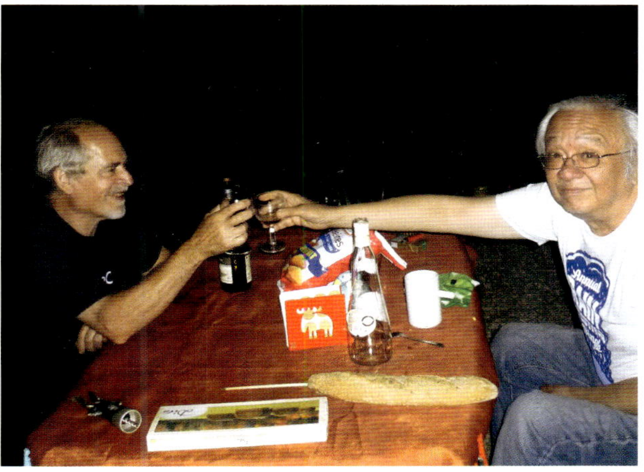

Gervais Jassaud and John Yau, Fréjus, France, 2013

Meet Max Gimblett and work on many collaborations in his
Bowery studio.

Meet artist Bill Barrette. Invited to collaborate with him on two
books—one about New York City, *Big City Primer: Reading New
York at the End of the Twentieth Century* (Timken Publishers,
1991)), and the other about Berlin and the reunification of
the city after the wall was jointly brought down on November
9, 1989. *Berlin Diptychon* is published in American (Timken
Publisher, 1995) and German editions (Weidle Verlag, 1995).

1995–97
Invited to be Visiting Professor at University of California,
Berkeley, and Visiting Critic at University
of Texas, Austin, where I meet Peter Saul and Christopher
Middleton.

Meet Les Ferriss (who teaches letterpress printing at UC
Berkeley) and Jacob Samuel (who works at Litho Shop and
The Lapis Press, run by Sam Francis).

Dream Hospital (Jacob Samuel, 1995) with Robert Therrien.

Piccadilly or Paradise (Ferris Editions, 1995), with Trevor
Winkfield.

Collaborate with Peter Saul on *Two Hours*, a portfolio of eight
lithographs with title page in "guest artist in printmaking
program" at University of Texas, Austin. Peter tells me that
I should draw on the prints as he intends to write on them.
This is the first time I do both. Printed by Ken Hale and
Warren Craghead.

Meet the artist Eve Aschheim for second time (first time was when she was MFA student at UC Davis in the 1980s). Marry in 1997.

Teach at Maryland Institute of the Arts. Hilary Lorenz and I team-teach a class called "Zines" and start Dolphin Press, which is run by students under our direction. Aaron Cohick is one of my students.

Collaborate with a number of students, including Aaron Cohick, who goes on to direct book-making at Colorado College and start NewLights Press. This is the first time I collaborate with students, which I continue to do when I start teaching at Mason Gross School of the Arts (Rutgers University) in 2002.

1999
Start Black Square Editions to publish translations of little-known books by well-known poets and fiction writers, as well as the work of emerging and established writers.

2000–2023 (New York)
2000
Hank Hine at USF Graphicstudio invites Pat Steir and me to do lithographs combining image and text. We do four "waterfalls."

2001
Cerise Tzara Aschheim Yau is born.

2002
Hired as Assistant Professor (tenure track) at Mason Gross School of the Arts (Rutgers University).

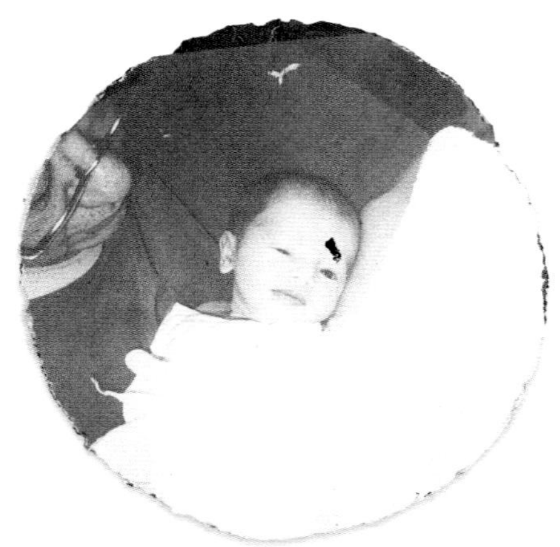

John Yau and his daughter, *Leaves from a Chinese Album*, **2003**

2007
Meet Phong Bui while going to galleries in Brooklyn. He is persuasive and convinces me to write for his free monthly magazine, *The Brooklyn Rail*. It has been some years since I wrote regularly for an art journal, as I felt they were tied to the art market and advertising, and there was little room to write about unknown and neglected artists. I become friends with the artist Tom Micchelli, editor and writer for *The Rail*. Tom and I develop a protocol by which writers pitch reviews, reviews are selected, and edited. We also ask that all writers be paid the same fee. Phong overrides us by inviting people with whom he wants to become friends to write. We edit and publish pieces we do not want to. I begin doing a series of interviews with artists such as Bruce Conner, Helmut Federle, Suzan Frecon, Sylvia Plimack Mangold, Catherine Murphy, Thomas Nozkowski, Norbert Prangenberg, Stanley Whitney, and others. I become increasingly disenchanted when Phong suggests I solicit artworks to be sold at auctions benefitting *The Rail*, and that I refrain from writing critical reviews (such as that of Julian Schnabel). The relationship further disintegrates when I write a satirical piece mocking Jerry Saltz's claim that Jeff Koons's *Puppy* is the greatest sculpture of the 1990s. It is clear when Phong stops talking to me that we have not agreed to disagree. Tom and I, who have been talking about starting an online magazine, leave *The Rail* in the winter of 2012. Phong and I never talk again.

2008
Judith Brodsky of the Brodsky Center (at Rutgers and now at PAFA, Philadelphia) invites me to collaborate with Richard Tuttle.

Collaborate with Ilse Sørensen Murdock before she is MFA student at Rutgers, and Alison Elizabeth Taylor while she is MFA student at Yale.

Begin collaborating on different projects with Chuck Webster after we are invited by Sienese Shredder Editions to do a book: *Sea Quench* (Grenfell Press, 2007).

Tom Burckhardt and I begin collaborating on collages, works on paper, and paintings. Either one of us will suggest a project, which the other one decides to do or not.

Inside Machine (Edition Salzau, 2000), with lithographs and handwritten transcription of a poem in which every word has to have the letter "I" in it by Hanns Schimansky and CD by bassist Peter Kowald.

One Hundred Poems (Magnolia Editions, 2010) with Squeak Carnwath.

A Child's Vi[r]gil (Magnolia Editions, Oakland, CA, 2010), with Norbert Prangenberg, who I first wrote about when he had an exhibition at Hirschl & Adler (1986).

2012–2018

Tom Micchelli and I meet with Hrag Vartanian, who is the publisher of the online magazine Hyperallergic to discuss what we would need to do to run an online art review. After realizing how much is involved, Tom and I agree that this requires more than we can handle. Later, Hrag calls Tom and proposes that he and I run a separate entity, *Hyperallergic Weekend*, over which we would have complete editorial control. When I ask Hrag if I can write about artists who don't have galleries or are not having a show, he says I can do whatever I want. Hrag and I routinely meet for coffee to talk about everyday life, politics, and art and the art world (they are not necessarily the same). These meetings help me think about what I am doing. I never look back.

Four fabric patches (*Emergency Eyewash Patches*, 2017) and beekeeper outfit with Carol Szymanski and Barry Schwabsky.

Genghis Chan: Private Eye (2018), silkscreen of a private detective's office door with Enrique Figueredo, who is MFA student at Rutgers.

2022

Joe Brainard: The Art of the Personal, published by Rizzoli Electa.

2023

I meet Tracy Featherstone who teaches printmaking at Miami University, Oxford, Ohio, where I have been invited to juror an exhibition of young artists, and we discuss ways of collaborating, settling on me sending her phrases and lines.

Partner with Richard Hull and Manneken Press on monoprints based on "Wanted' posters.

Collaborate with Phil Allen on works on paper. I send him phrases and lines.

Please Wait by the Coatroom: Reconsidering Race and Identity in American Art, published by Black Sparrow Press.

CHECKLIST OF COLLABORATIONS

Phil Allen and John Yau
Carnage Hall
2023
Collage on paper
24 x 18 inches
Courtesy of Phil Allen

Bill Barrette and John Yau
Berlin Diptychon
Published by Timken Publishers,
New York
Designed by David Bullen
Copyedited by Anna Jardine
Printed in Germany
1995
Offset-printed, bound
9 ¼ x 9 ¼ inches
Courtesy of John Yau

*Big City Primer: Reading New York at the
End of the Twentieth Century*
Published by Timken Publishers,
New York
Text set by Wilsted & Taylor, Oakland
Designed by David Bullen
Copyedited by Anna Jardine
Printed by Toppan Printing Co., Japan
1991
Offset-printed, bound, with
hardboard portfolio
10 ½ x 10 ½ inches
Courtesy of John Yau

Jake Berthot and John Yau
Notarikon
Published by Jordan Davies, New York
1981
Offset lithographs and letterpress on tissue
and paper, bound in cloth-clad boards
9 ¾ x 6 ½ inches
Courtesy of Stuart Horodner

Norman Bluhm and John Yau
Sam Spade Haiku #1
circa 1988
Acrylic, ink, and pastel on paper
26 ¼ x 58 inches
Courtesy of the estate of Norman Bluhm

Tom Burckhardt and John Yau
A Void Going Back
2022
Oil on panel
9 ½ x 12 inches
Courtesy of Tom Burckhardt

Music to My Ears
2022
Oil on panel
9 ½ x 12 inches
Courtesy of Tom Burckhardt

X Spelled
2022
Oil on panel
12 x 9 ½ inches
Courtesy of Tom Burckhardt

The George Seurat Bar and Grill
2018
Colored pencil on paper
15 x 11 ⅞ inches
Courtesy of Tom Burckhardt

The Yves Klein Dive
2017
Ink and oil on paper
8 ⅜ x 11 inches
Courtesy of John Yau

What I Got Don't Talk
2016
Collage on paper
20 x 26 inches
Courtesy of Tom Burckhardt

The Autumn Fields of a Young Art Handler
Published by EFA Robert Blackburn
Printmaking Workshop Program, New York
2019
Risographs on paper, staple-bound
8 x 5 ⅜ inches
Courtesy of Tom Burckhardt

**Marsha Burns, Michael Burns,
Randy Hayes, and John Yau**
Cities
Published by Henry Art Gallery,
University of Washington, Seattle
Edited by Joseph N. Newland
Designed by Douglas Wadden
Type set by Thomas & Kennedy, Seattle
Lithography by Atomic Press, Seattle
1987
Offset-printed, spiral-bound
10 ¾ x 12 inches
Courtesy of John Yau

Squeak Carnwath and John Yau
One Hundred Poems
Published by Magnolia Editions, Oakland
Designed by Squeak Carnwath and
Donald Farnsworth
Printed by Tallulah Terryll at
Magnolia Editions
Poetry printed by Les Ferriss,
Healdsburg, CA
Custom book box designed by Donald
Farnsworth and Andrew Rottner, created
by Andrew Rottner at Magnolia Editions
2010, ed. 1/20
Double-sided acrylic prints and poems on
letterpress pages in a clamshell box
Sheet: 13 ¾ x 10 inches
Box: 14 ⅜ x 10 ½ x 1 ⅛ inches
Courtesy of Magnolia Editions

Aaron Cohick and John Yau
English for You
Published by Dolphin Press, Baltimore
Handset, letterpress printed, and bound
by Aaron Cohick, Nathan Danilowicz,
Sarah Hromack, Kevin McCabe, Samantha
Hiroko Azuse, Kristen Tierri, Jesse
Lebwohl-Steiner, and Corina Albert (the
students of Dolphin Press), under the
direction of Rebecca Childers; with
special thanks to Laura Gencarella
2002, ed. 19/45
Color prints and letterpress on paper,
with hardboard cover
10 ⅜ x 11 ⅛ inches
Courtesy of John Yau

**Emergency Eyewash (Barry Schwabsky,
Carol Szymanski, and collaborators)**
Siv Støldal, Carol Szymanski, and John Yau
Bee Wear
2017/2023
Wool, mesh, and cotton thread
Dimensions variable
Courtesy of Siv Støldal
Photo credit: JSP Art Photography

Willa Schwabsky, Carol Szymanski,
and John Yau
Emergency Eyewash Patches
2017
Cotton thread
Dimensions variable
Courtesy of John Yau

Tracy Featherstone and John Yau
Advice: Put an Egg in Your Shoe & Beat It
2023, ed. 1/6
Monotype, letterpress, and relief print
on paper
15 ¼ x 11 ⅛ inches
Courtesy of Tracy Featherstone

Warmest Worm in the Bunch
2023, ed. 1/4
Screenprint on paper
15 ¼ x 11 ¼ inches
Courtesy of Tracy Featherstone

Enrique Figueredo and John Yau
Genghis Chan: Private Eye
2018, ed. 10
Silkscreen on German etching paper
42 ½ x 31 inches
Courtesy of John Yau

Pia Fries and John Yau
tausend : einerlei
Published by Snoeck Verlagsgesellschaft
mbH, Germany, Kienbaum Artists' Books
Edited by Jochen and Laura Kienbaum
Photography by Hans Brändli
Translation by Stefan and Barbara Weidle
Lithography by Gundula Seraphin,
Bad Münstereifel
Designed by Silke Fahnert, Uwe Koch,
Cologne
2022
Color lithographs, bound with hardcover
13 ¼ x 12 inches
Courtesy of John Yau

Max Gimblett and John Yau
I Wore Your Underwear Today
1993/95, ed. 87/91
Acrylic, polymer, and copper on
hand-marbled paper
26 ¼ x 19 inches
Courtesy of Max Gimblett

The sky has four sides but only one is visible
2001
Ink and collage on paper pulp
20 ¼ x 20 ¼ inches
Courtesy of Max Gimblett

Leaves from a Chinese Album
Prints by Doug Zucco
Assisted by James Carroll, Helene Zucco,
and Anthony Fodero
Published by Live on Paper, New Arts
Program, Inc., Kutztown, PA
Handmade paper produced at White Crow
Paper Mill, Fleetwood, PA
Text layout by Anne Dutlinger
Photos printed at Hawk Mountain
Editions, Leesport, PA
Copper cans designed and built by
Earl Smith, Kutztown, PA
2003
Ink, oil, and collage on handmade paper
in round copper can
Sheet, each: 20 inches diameter
Copper can: 22 inches diameter x
1 ⅛ inches
Courtesy of John Yau

A Book of Broadway Koans
Published by Jade Studio, New York
Text handset and printed by Carol Sturn,
Nadja
Box designed by Barbara Mauriello;
produced by Portfoliobox, Inc.,
Rhode Island
Edited by Barbara Kirshenblatt-Gimblett,
Wystan Curnow, and Carol Sturm
Curatorial assistance by Anthony Fodero
and David Aldera
1988–2001
Ink drawings and letterpress on paper in
clamshell portfolio
Sheet, open: 22 ¼ x 34 ½ inches
Portfolio: 23 x 17 ½ x 1 ⅞ inches
Courtesy of Max Gimblett

A Book of Millennium Koans
Published by Jade Studio, New York
Text handset and printed by Carol Sturn,
Nadja
Box designed by Barbara Mauriello;
produced by Portfoliobox, Inc.,
Rhode Island
Edited by Barbara Kirshenblatt-Gimblett,
Wystan Curnow, and Carol Sturm
Curatorial assistance by Anthony Fodero
and David Aldera
1988–2001
Ink drawings and letterpress on paper
in clamshell portfolio
Sheet, open: 22 ¼ x 34 ½ inches
Portfolio: 23 x 17 ½ x 1 ⅞ inches
Courtesy of Max Gimblett

Richard Hull and John Yau
Wanted: Another 50 Years I
Published by Manneken Press,
Bloomington, IL
2023
Monotype in oil and water-based media
on Arches Cover paper
30 ¼ x 22 inches
Courtesy of Manneken Press

Wanted: The Lost Movies of Anna May Wong
Published by Manneken Press,
Bloomington, IL
2023
Monotype in oil and water-based media
on paper
30 ¼ x 22 inches
Courtesy of John Yau

Bill Jensen and John Yau
Postcards from Trakl
Published by Universal Limited
Art Editions
Intaglio and woodcut printed by Hitoshi
Kido, John Lund, Ji-hong Shi,
Bruce Wankel, and Craig Zammiello
Letterpress printings by Bruce Wankel
Box and binding by Claudia Cohen
1989–94, ed. 25
Portfolio of 12 intaglios and 1 woodcut with
poems by John Yau on Lana Gravure and
T.H. Saunders paper
14 ⅜ x 12 inches
Courtesy of Universal Limited Art Editions

Justine Kurland and John Yau
Black Threads from Meng Chiao
Published by TIS books, New York
2015
Offset-printed with tritone plates on paper,
bound, with silkscreen dust jacket
8 x 5 ½ inches
Courtesy of Stuart Horodner

Judy Ledgerwood and John Yau
Chromatic Patterns After the Graham Foundation
Published by Manneken Press, Bloomington, IL
Printed by Jonathan Higgins, Manneken Press
Portfolio designed by Jason Pickleman
2014, ed. 3/8
Portfolio of three lithographs with aluminum dust by Judy Ledgerwood and a poem by John Yau printed in silkscreen
Sheet, each: 22 x 30 inches
Portfolio: 23 ½ x 32 ½ x ¼ inches
Courtesy of Manneken Press

View of *Judy Ledgerwood: Chromatic Patterns for the Graham Foundation*, January 23 – April 5, 2014, Graham Foundation, Chicago. Photo credit: Tom Van Eynde.

Suzanne McClelland and John Yau
Flee Advice
Published by Collectif Génération, Paris
Composed and printed by Francis Mérat
1991
Watercolor, ink, and letterpress on accordion-folded paper
5 ⅛ x 6 x ½ inches
Courtesy of Suzanne McClelland

Malcolm Morley
Cradles of Civilizations from *The Fallacies of Enoch*
Printed by Novak Graphics, Toronto
circa 1986
Etching and aquatint on paper
Image: 20 ½ x 33 inches
Sheet: 27 ⅝ x 39 ¼ inches
Courtesy of Gordan Novak

Malcolm Morley and John Yau
The Fallacies of Enoch
Published by Novak Graphics, Toronto
1984
Offset-printed, staple-bound
6 x 9 inches
Courtesy of Gordan Novak

Ilse Sørensen Murdock and John Yau
A Dirty Little Ditty Full of Greasy Chickens
2004
Acrylic paint and cardboard packaging on canvas
9 x 9 inches
Courtesy of Ilse Sørensen Murdock

Permanent Shadow Removal
2004
Acrylic paint and cardboard packaging on canvas
12 x 14 inches
Courtesy of Ilse Sørensen Murdock

Martin Noël and John Yau
New York Islands
Published by Weidle Verlag, Bonn, Germany
Typography by Friedrich Forssman
Printed by Robert Wilk
Binding by Schaumann, Darmstadt
Photographic prints by Frank Trier
1998, A.P.
Acrylic, ink, and watercolor, color photographs, and offset lithographs, bound
16 ½ x 12 inches
Courtesy of John Yau

Thomas Nozkowski and John Yau
Ing Grish
Published by Saturnalia Books, Philadelphia
2005
Offset-printed, bound
8 ⅞ x 6 ¾ inches
Courtesy of Stuart Horodner

Thomas Offhaus and John Yau
Russian Letter
Published by Bookart Studios, Gotha, Germany
Book design, etchings, and text printed by Thomas Offhaus
Binding by Henry Günther
Translation into German by Stefan Weidle
2003
Etching, aquatint, and letterpress on paper, stitch-bound
9 ½ x 6 inches
Courtesy of John Yau

Ed Paschke and John Yau
Genghis Chan: Private Eye
Published by the Friends of the Ryerson and Burnham Libraries, Art Institute of Chicago, and Landfall Press, Inc., Chicago
Etchings printed by Darryl Jensen and Diana Scudd under the supervision of Steven Campbell and Jack Lemon on paper made by John Koller, Woodstock, CT
Text layouts and title vignettes designed and printed by Pamela Barrie, Green Window Printers, Chicago
Box and chemise by the Campbell-Logan Bindery, Minneapolis
1997, ed. 86/150
Color etchings and letterpress on paper, in portfolio
Sheet, unfolded: 9 x 25 inches
Portfolio: 15 ¼ x 19 ¼ x 1 ¼ inches
Courtesy of John Yau

Norbert Prangenberg and John Yau
A Child's Vi[r]gil
Published by Magnolia Editions, Oakland
Design of the housing and folios digitally composed and supervised by Donald Farnsworth and proofed by Tallulah Terryll, Magnolia Editions
Folio pages letterpress printed by Jonathan Gerken; poem text printed at Peter Koch Printers, Berkeley
Portfolio designed by Donald Farnsworth and Andrew Rottner, Magnolia Editions
Clamshell cover printed by Tallulah Terryll at Magnolia Editions
2010, AP 4/4
Watercolor and letterpress on tissue and paper in clamshell portfolio
Sheet, open: 15 x 20 inches
Portfolio: 16 ¼ x 12 x 1 ⅛ inches
Courtesy of John Yau

Archie Rand and John Yau
The Alphabet Paintings
1987–94
Acrylic on gold lame fabric
Canvas, each: 36 x 19 ⅞ in.
Courtesy of Archie Rand and John Yau

The Case of the Orgiastic Snails
1987
Watercolor on paper
15 x 11 inches
Courtesy of John Yau

The Fly Who Came In from the Cold
1987
Watercolor on paper
16 ³⁄₁₆ x 12 ³⁄₁₆ inches
Courtesy of John Yau

I Upgrade the Sublime
1987
Watercolor on paper
15 x 11 inches
Courtesy of John Yau

My Favorite Recipes
1987
Watercolor on paper
15 x 12 inches
Courtesy of John Yau

Ode to the Dead Dancers of Denver
1987
Watercolor on paper
15 x 11 inches
Courtesy of John Yau

100 More Jokes from the Book of the Dead
Published by the Leroy Neiman Center
for Print Studies at Columbia University,
New York
Printed by Tomas Vu Daniel
Assisted by Gregory Mahoney, Nicola
Lopez, Ryan Graham, Kim Loewe, Pattie
Lee Becker, Laura Mahoney, Megan Foster,
Eric Oldmixon, and Beth-Ann Bovino
1997–2000
Intaglio and silkscreen on paper, in
clamshell box bound in fabric
Sheet: 12 ⅞ x 11 ¼ inches
13 x 15 x 3 inches
Courtesy of Archie Rand and John Yau

A Modest Man
1991
Ink on paper
Reproduced in *Mug City Moves*
Published by Monkey Choir Maestros,
New York
Photocopies, staple-bound
11 x 8 ½ inches
Courtesy of Archie Rand

Sydney Jean Reisen and John Yau
Catullus Sails to China
Published by Olchef Press, Maplewood, NJ
Bound and boxed by Sydney Jean Reisen,
with thanks to VFG and Z Partovi
2020, ed. 15/55
Letterpress, wood and resingrave block
prints, and pochoir on paper, bound in
muslin bookcloth and housed in a black
archival box
Book: 7 x 6 inches
Box: 8 x 7 x 1 inches
Courtesy of Sydney Jean Reisen

Peter Saul and John Yau
Two Hours
Published by The Guest Artist in
Printmaking Program, UT Austin
Printed by Ken Hale and Warren Craghead
1994
Nine lithographs on paper in portfolio
Sheet, each: 12 ½ x 10 inches
Courtesy of John Yau

Hanns Schimansky and John Yau
Inside Machine
Musical accompaniment by Peter Kowald
Published by Edition Salzau, Berlin
Printed by Fritze Margull
Edited by Rainer Haarmann
Bookbinding by Saal-Presse, Bergsdorf
Offset printing by Jochen Baumgarten,
KHB
2000, ed. 5/20
Intaglio and letterpress on paper,
with CD, in portfolio
Sheet: 17 ¾ x 14 ¼ inches
Portfolio: 19 x 15 ½ x 1 inches
Courtesy of John Yau

Jenny Scobel and John Yau
Neigh/Cud
1992
Mixed media on board
11 ½ x 7 ½ inches
Collection of the University of Kentucky
Art Museum, gift of Stuart Horodner

Pat Steir and John Yau
Horizon's Levitation
Published by Graphicstudio, University
of South Florida Collection
2000
Color lithograph on paper
21 x 20 inches
Courtesy of University of South
Florida Collection
Photo courtesy of USF Graphicstudio;
Photo credit: Will Lytch

Rain Pillow
Published by Graphicstudio, University
of South Florida Collection
2000
Color lithograph on paper
21 x 20 inches
Courtesy of University of South
Florida Collection
Photo courtesy of USF Graphicstudio;
Photo credit: Will Lytch

Sky's First Poem
Published by Graphicstudio, University
of South Florida Collection
2000
Color lithograph on paper
21 x 20 inches
Courtesy of University of South
Florida Collection
Photo courtesy of USF Graphicstudio;
Photo credit: Will Lytch

Sky's Four Sides
Published by Graphicstudio, University
of South Florida Collection
2000
Color lithograph and encaustic on paper
21 x 20 inches
Courtesy of University of South
Florida Collection
Photo courtesy of USF Graphicstudio;
Photo credit: Will Lytch

Alison Elizabeth Taylor and John Yau
*He got tired of being force fed
unidentifiable lumps*
2004
Graphite and contact cover on paper
19 ¼ x 31 ⅛ inches
Courtesy of Hillary Frileck

*She liked to keep them in jars under a bed
that no one had ever slept in*
2004
Graphite on paper
11 ¼ x 7 ½ inches
Courtesy of Alison Elizabeth Taylor

Robert Therrien and John Yau
Dream Hospital
Printed and published by Edition Jacob
Samuel, Santa Monica
Gravure plates by Anthony Zepeda and
Ken Farley
Digital text composition and letterpress
by Les Ferriss
Binding and boxes by Klaus-Ullrich S.
Rötzscher
1995
Photogravure and letterpress on paper, in
clamshell portfolio
Sheet: 12 x 9 inches
Portfolio: 12 ¾ x 9 ½ x 1 ⅜ inches
Courtesy of John Yau

Richard Tuttle and John Yau
The Missing Portrait
Published by the Brodsky Center for
Innovative Editions, Brunswick, NJ
Handmade paper by Master Papermaker
Anne Q. McKeown and assistant
papermaker Lisa Switalski
Silkscreen and letterpress printing
in collaboration with Master Printer
Randy Hemminghaus
Book structure and binding designed and
fabricated by Lisa Switalski
Book production done with help from
interns at the Brodsky Center for
Innovative Editions at Rutgers, The State
University of New Jersey, Brunswick, NJ
2008
Hand-cast cotton fiber, tissue collé,
silkscreen, and letterpress printing
18 x 16 ½ x 8 inches
Courtesy of John Yau

Claude Viallat and John Yau
Midway
Published by Gervais Jassaud, Collectif
Génération, Fréjus, France
Printed at the Vincent Auger Workshop,
Paris
2017
Watercolor and letterpress on paper
13 x 10 ⅛ inches
Courtesy of John Yau

Chuck Webster and John Yau
Blotto, Indiana
2016
Shellac ink and India ink on vintage
handmade paper
20 x 15 inches
Courtesy of John Yau

Braque's Last Breath
2014
Watercolor and ink on vintage
handmade paper
19 ¾ x 15 ½ inches
Courtesy of John Yau

Disguise the Limit
2016
Colored pencil, ink, and watercolor
on antique paper
9 ¾ x 7 ⅜ inches
Courtesy of John Yau

Fly on Lyre
2014
Watercolor and ink on vintage
handmade paper
17 ½ x 15 inches
Courtesy of John Yau

Last Words of Jake Berthot
2016
Shellac ink and India ink on vintage
handmade paper
17 ½ x 15 inches
Courtesy of John Yau

Mike Mallet Meets Mike Hammer
2016
Shellac ink and colored pencil on vintage
handmade paper
19 x 15 inches
Courtesy of John Yau

Sack of Rice / Sack Her Vice / Sack Riff Ice
2016
Watercolor, crayon, and shellac ink on
antique paper
8 ⅜ x 6 ⅞ inches
Courtesy of John Yau

Santa Claus vs Godzilla
2016
Shellac ink on vintage handmade paper
19 ½ x 15 ¼ inches
Courtesy of John Yau

Sea Quench
Published by The Grenfell Press,
New York City
Printed by Brad Ewing
2007, ed. 20/20
Woodcut and letterpress in cloth portfolio
Sheet: 14 ½ x 20 ⅜ inches
Portfolio: 15 ⅞ x 22 x 1 ⅛ inches
Courtesy of Chuck Webster

Trevor Winkfield and John Yau
Annals of a Gumshoe
Published by Smoke Specs, Seattle
Special thanks to Tetra Balestri and
Kreg Hasegawa
2018
Offset-printed, saddle-stitch bound
10 ½ x 8 inches
Courtesy of Stuart Horodner

ACKNOWLEDGMENTS

Disguise the Limit: John Yau's Collaborations is made possible because of the support and assistance of many individuals, and they are deserving of recognition and thanks.

Without a generous grant from the Terra Foundation for American Art, our project would not have been as comprehensive. Their recognition of the value of the exhibition and publication in telling more complex stories about American art is deeply appreciated. Our sincere thanks to Sharon Corwin and Amy Gunderson at the Foundation.

In making our application to the Terra Foundation, I was aided by University of Kentucky grant officers Michael Gabbard, Hannah O'Leary, and Jason Schubert. I am grateful for their help in shaping our proposal.

Special thanks to Professor Emeritus Jim Albisetti who has been a significant patron of the UK Art Museum for decades. His endowed exhibition fund helped support this ambitious endeavor.

I value my colleagues in the College of Fine Arts for their collaborative spirit and ongoing encouragement. Thanks to Dean Mark Shanda, Chief Financial Officer/Assistant Dean Paula Sandford, and Director of Philanthropy Lisa Blackadar.

Elisa Nadel brought our publication to the attention of Thomas Evans at Distributed Art Publishers, Inc. who enthusiastically committed to be our distributor. I thank them both.

We are indebted to the participating artists who loaned us works for the exhibition and offered their recollections of collaborating with John. We appreciate your creativity and generosity.

Other lenders of artworks, photographs, and information include Nina Bluhm; Hillary Frileck; Gordan Novak; Gervais Jassaud of Collectif Génération; Nicholas Price, Magnolia Editions; Jonathan Higgins, Manneken Press; Jill Czarnowski and Larissa Goldston, ULAE; and Shannon Annis, Curator of the Collection/Exhibitions Manager, USF Contemporary Art Museum. Assistants to artists and publishers include Matt Jones for Max Gimblett Studio, LLC; and Zoran Laka for Gordan Novak. Thank you all for your assistance.

Sharon Mesmer and Barry Schwabsky contributed insightful essays that illuminate aspects of Yau's poetry, criticism, and collaborations. Their voices make this a richer publication and I sincerely thank them.

A huge debt of gratitude goes to the UK Art Museum staff, especially our indefatigable registrar, Maggie Bond, and preparator Alan Rideout who contributed their extreme skills and dedication to each aspect of this project—photographing, editing, proofing, framing, mounting, shipping, and much else. You know how much I value working with you. To Michaela Miles, Joe Nipp, Dan Solberg, and Lyndi Van Deursen, my thanks for everything.

I'm thankful to Scott Malbaurn, Director of the Schneider Museum of Art in Ashland, Oregon, for agreeing to present the exhibition after its dates in Lexington. I can't wait to see it again.

Susan Bowman has my appreciation for her sensitive design of this publication. It is always a joy to work with her.

To Bill Zats at Shapco Printing, Inc., and Randy Bailey at Southland Printing, I offer my thanks for the quality and attention to all aspects of this production.

Leah Kolb supported me throughout the development of this project, especially reading drafts of my essay and providing valuable feedback. My heartfelt thanks to her.

Other friends and colleagues who have helped support our efforts include Chelsea Brislin, Margaret Galey, Julia Johnson, Linda and George Kurz, Shauna Morgan, Erik Reece, Julien Robson, Katerina Stoykova, Dianne Vanderlip, Frank X. Walker, and Natalie Weis. I appreciate you all.

And finally, I offer my deep gratitude to John Yau for being such a superb collaborator— with our Museum staff and me, and the many artists represented in our project.

—*Stuart Horodner*

This book is published on the occasion of the exhibition *Disguise the Limit: John Yau's Collaborations*.

University of Kentucky Art Museum, January 9 – June 1, 2024
Schneider Museum of Art, October 17 – December 14, 2024

First published in 2024 by
University of Kentucky Art Museum
405 Rose Street
Lexington, KY 40506
(859) 257-5716
https://finearts.uky.edu/art-museum

Distributed by
D.A.P. / Distributed Art Publishers, Inc.
75 Broad Street, Suite 630
New York, New York, 10004
t: (212) 627–1999
www.artbook.com

Library of Congress Control Number: 2024932204
ISBN 978-1-882007-01-1

Front cover: John Yau and Chuck Webster, *Disguise the Limit*, 2016

Design by SBowman Design
Printed by Shapco Printing, Inc., Minneapolis, in association with Southland Printing, Lexington.

Generous support is provided by the Terra Foundation for American Art.

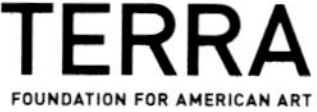